Topics in World History—Edited by Patricia W. Romero

# African History in Documents

# EASTERN AFRICAN HISTORY

## Vol. II of African History: Text and Readings

by

# Robert O. Collins
University of California, Santa Barbara

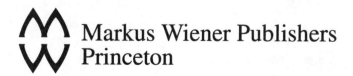 Markus Wiener Publishers
Princeton

Third Printing 1997

For information write to:
Markus Wiener Publishers
114 Jefferson Road, Princeton, NJ  08540

Library of Congress Cataloging-in-Publication Data

Collins, Robert O.
    Eastern African history/by Robert O. Collins.
        (African history; v. 2) (Topics of world history)
    Includes bibliographical references.
    ISBN 1-55876-016-4
    1. Africa, Eastern—History—Sources.   I. Title.   II. Series
    III. Series: Collins, Robert O.;   African history: v. 2.
DT1.C55   1990 vol. 2                                            89-70615
[DT470.2]                                                        CIP
967.6—dc20

Cover design by Cheryl Mirkin

Printed in The United States of America.

# PREFACE

# PREFACE

African history has come into its own. As we enter the 1990s, the old myths about the African past—that Africa had no history, or that no written records of that history existed—have been dispelled. The valuable discoveries about the continent that arose out of the study of archaeological remains and of the invaluable oral traditions have been extended and enriched through the analysis of documentary materials. The twenty years since I published the first edition of *African History*, have seen a burgeoning of scholarly material on Africa, not only in monographs and journals, but also in textbooks. Research in African history has been established as a respected scholarly discipline. Surprisingly, however, there are relatively few anthologies that provide primary historical sources for the historian or student of Africa. This was the case twenty years ago, and it is still true. The present edition represents an updating of the 1970 volume, including text of documents dealing with the past thirty years in independent Africa. Its three-volume format reflects the fact that Africa is no longer regarded as an undifferentiated unity, and makes the materials for regional study more acceptable and affordable for teachers and students.

The original purpose of the volume prepared nearly twenty years ago was to demonstrate to the student the extent of the valuable documentary materials available for analysis and interpretation, while in no way minimizing the enormous importance of oral traditions. The aim of the present volume on the history of Eastern Africa has been to republish, revise, and add text and documents. In this volume, I also introduce the reader to the long and rich history of Eastern Africa from the beginnings of recorded time to the present with a brief essay, and some of the principal documents that serve as landmarks in the history of the region.

If my purpose has been to expose the student to source materials in African history, my objectives have been guided by two principles—the same principles which inspired the original volume. First, I have sought to embrace the full time span of documentary records pertaining to Eastern Africa. Second, I have sought to cover the vast geographical sweep of Eastern Africa, from the countries of the Horn of Africa to those states—Kenya, Uganda, and Tanzania—which make up East Africa proper. To achieve these two very ambitious objectives in a single and modest volume has required an eclectic, if not random, selection that betrays my own personal inclinations and interests. I am sure that anyone with a knowledge of the Eastern African past might quarrel with the documents I have chosen, but I have endeavored to select those that describe Africans, and not just individuals who came to look or to rule. I have attempted to select passages from less well-known accounts and descriptions, as well as from the more standard authorities. I have also tried, where possible, to obtain passages of sufficient length to make them meaningful to the inquiring student.

Finally, I have prepared a brief introduction to guide the beginner and to refresh the memory of the more experienced student. I have also made addi-tions to the introduction in a feeble attempt to overcome the twenty years that have passed since the publication of the original text, and I have added documents more pertinent to the age of African independence and nationalism. In order to make the selections more understandable to the beginner, explanatory material has frequently been inserted directly into the text, either in brackets or as a footnote followed by "ed." (editor). All of the footnotes and bracketed material found in the various selections are the work of editors who have preceded me but whose efforts need not be duplicated or deleted.

I wish to express my appreciation to Professor Patricia Romero, who has been instrumental in reviving the text, and to the publisher, Markus Wiener, who has accepted the challenge of providing a volume for an increasing number of students interested in the Eastern African past.

I am also grateful for the suggestions of Ralph Herring, Russell Chace, Nell Elizabeth Painter, and Martin Legassick, whose assistance on the original volume provided many improvements. I am equally grateful to my colleagues and students at the University of California, Santa Barbara—Professor David Brokensha, Damazo Dut Majak, Kenneth Okeny, and Ruth Iyob—for their suggestions regarding the revisions. And, of course, there has always been Dorothy Johnson, who for so many years has seen my manuscripts to conclusion.

*Robert O. Collins*
*Santa Barbara*
*December, 1989*

# CONTENTS

## EASTERN AFRICA

# EASTERN AFRICA

# EASTERN AFRICA
## BY ROBERT O. COLLINS

## THE LAND OF PUNT

Although traders from Arabia, Persia, and India probably visited the coast of eastern Africa during the millennia before Christ, the ancient Egyptians were the first to record their voyages. They made frequent and regular journeys down the Red Sea to the land of Punt, which is usually identified with the modern coast of Somalia north and south of Cape Guardafui. Here they traded Egyptian products for incense, myrrh, spices, and gold. Perhaps even in periods of great mercantile activity, such as during the reign of Queen Hatshepsut (c. 1520–1480 B.C.), Egyptian merchant captains were carried by the northeast monsoon farther south to the coast of Tanzania or beyond to northern Mozambique.

## THE ZANJ

The next surviving description of the East African coast is the *Periplus of the Erythraean Sea*, a commercial handbook compiled by a supercargo in the first or second century in which he describes the commerce and important trading ports of the Indian Ocean. From India ships reached East Africa with cotton cloth, grain, oil, and ghee, while from the Mediterranean world Graeco-Roman ships brought copper, tin, iron, and wine. In exchange for these goods the traders obtained cinnamon, frankincense, ivory, and tortoise shell. With the exception of Ptolemy's *Geography*, the East African section of which appears to be a description of the fourth century, little is known of the coast until the narratives of Arab travelers after the tenth century A.D. By this time the inhabitants were unmistakably Bantu migrants who had pressed northward up the coast during the preceding centuries and settled in the commercial ports. The Arabs called them the *Zanj* (the Blacks). A non-Muslim people, they soon controlled the trading cities and provided the goods, whereas the carrying trade itself remained in non-African hands. Throughout this period trade appears to have increased. Slaves were now an important commodity along with the more traditional African products. The scope of the trade appears to have expanded with the volume as merchants from China and Indonesia joined those from India, Persia, and Arabia (Tuan Ch'ēng-shih, *China's Discovery of Africa*).

The East African coast slowly became Islamized, principally by the example set by Muslim merchants who traded with the Zanj cities. On the one hand, the spread of Islam to East Africa may be regarded as part of the larger process of Islamization that was taking place in the Indian Ocean region. On the other, conversion to Islam coincided with a period of prosperity founded on the expansion of trade, which had derived its stimulus from the growing Sofala gold trade. For centuries gold mined by African peoples in the interior of Central Africa (the Republic of Zimbabwe) had been taken to Sofala on the coast and then carried to Asia and the Middle East. By the fourteenth century, this trade had reached its height and with it the commercial prosperity of the coast. Kilwa was able to monopolize much of the gold trade and

consequently flourished, but the other city-states—Mombasa, Mogadishu, Pemba, and others north of Kilwa—all benefited from the general expansion of trade (João de Barros, *The Founding of Kilwa*).

The development of town life among the Zanj population was encouraged by the economic growth of the coastal trade and stimulated by frequent and regular contacts with foreign traders. As the Zanj adopted Islam, they applied the organization of Islamic states to suit their own circumstances. This acculturation, which included intermarriage, did not, however, result in the suppression of African culture but rather in a synthesis of the Muslim, Arabic ways of the traders and the ritualistic, Bantu-speaking customs of the Zanj to form the Swahili culture that dominates the East African coast today (Ibn Battuta, *The East African Coast in 1331*).

The prosperity of the coast did not last. By the end of the fifteenth century many of the city-states, particularly Kilwa, were in decline. No single reason can account for the waning of Kilwa, and the scholar must rely on intelligent speculation from the meager evidence. Clearly, Kilwa suffered from the problem of succession, as did most Muslim states. Intrigue and struggle for the sultanate undermined the power of the state as a succession of weak and debauched sultans undid the work of more competent predecessors. Moreover, the gold trade itself slipped into decline during the fifteenth century as the interior of Central Africa was convulsed by a new wave of

3

Bantu migrants that later swept up the coast from Mozambique and Malawi, upsetting the trade routes to the interior, attacking the city-states, and diverting commerce. Finally, the "Zanj Empire" about which nineteenth-century writers wrote was in fact a myth, for each of the city-states jealously guarded its independence and frequently made war on rival towns. This inability to weld the competing cities into a unified empire left them easy prey for the Portuguese who suddenly arrived on the East African coast.

## THE PORTUGUESE

In April 1498 Vasco de Gama cast anchor in Mombasa harbor. Forty years after the death of Prince Henry, Portuguese explorers had achieved his dream of discovering a seaway to India and the Orient. The aim of Portugal and her explorers was to monopolize the trade of the Indian Ocean and the East Indies, and in this grand Portuguese design Eastern Africa was regarded principally as a way station to the Orient. Although the Portuguese were astounded to find a culture in East Africa as sophisticated as their own, they were able to establish their control by their technological superiority in the possession of firearms. Portuguese control was thus established by force and violence and assisted by the rivalries among the Zanj states. Some city-states, like Malindi, cooperated with the Portuguese and flourished as a result. Others, like Mombasa, opposed the invaders and suffered from Portuguese efforts to suppress their rebellious subjects. The Portuguese viewed their occupation of East Africa as only part of the larger crusade against the Muslims, and resistance was crushed in the name of Christ and the extension of His heavenly dominion. The result was a rule that was more bloody, tyrannical, and oppressive than it was peaceful, prosperous, and tolerant. But if the Portuguese were able to dominate, they made little attempt to

establish systematic government on the coast and no attempt to administer the interior. Even Christian missionaries had few successes, and Portuguese endeavors to Christianize the coast left no lasting impression in East Africa. To the Portuguese, East Africa remained a revictualing station en route to the Orient. Portuguese settlers did not come to East Africa and the numbers of Portuguese on the coast never numbered more than a few hundred at any time (Duarte Barbosa, *The East Coast of Africa at the Beginning of the Sixteenth Century*).

## OMAN AND EAST AFRICA

The Portuguese monopoly could not long remain unchallenged. At the end of the sixteenth century, Turkish expeditions appeared on the coast as part of the Ottoman holy war against the Christians. More formidable were the *Wazimba*, a militant Bantu people who swept up the coast at the end of the sixteenth century, destroying many of the cities before their defeat at Malindi (João dos Santos, *The Wazimba*). Although both the Turks and the Wazimba were successfully driven off, the Portuguese failed to repulse the assaults of rival Europeans and Arabs from Oman in southeast Arabia. Throughout the seventeenth century, the Portuguese steadily lost their Far Eastern trading posts to the Dutch, the English, and the French. While Europeans struck at the heart of the Portuguese Empire in the Orient, the Omani Arabs assaulted Portuguese posts on the East African coast. In the mid-seventeenth century, the energetic Imam of Oman, Nasir ibn Murshid, drove the Portuguese from the Persian Gulf. His subsequent campaign in East Africa and that of his successor, Saif ibn Sultan, must be regarded as an extension of that holy war. By the end of the seventeenth century, the Qmani sultans had broken Portuguese power in East Africa. Under the leadership of Saif ibn Sultan, the Omani Arabs had taken Mombasa in

1698 and Pemba and Kilwa the following year.

Triumphant, Saif ibn Sultan did not remain in East Africa; instead, he appointed Arabian governors to rule over the East African city-states. Many of these rulers were soon united under the Governor of Mombasa, Muhammad ibn Uthman al-Mazrui, the head of the powerful Mazrui family, who gradually placed his relatives in key positions in numerous city-states. Soon members of the family controlled much of the East African coast, and although they nominally acknowledged the suzerainty of the Imam of Oman, they ruled in fact as independent sultans until the nineteenth century.

Throughout the seventeenth and eighteenth centuries, the Zanj city-states had steadily declined in power and prosperity. Destruction by the Portuguese, rebellions against them, and devastation by Turks, Wazimba, and Omani Arabs clearly precipitated the decay of the city-states. Moreover, the sixteenth and seventeenth centuries saw a general decline throughout the Muslim world. The rise of the Ottoman state had shifted the center of Islam from Mesopotamia to Asia Minor, and shortly afterward the eastern Muslim states were overrun by Mongol invaders. In these dismal centuries, Islam lost much of its earlier driving force at a time when European powers appeared to monopolize the commerce of the Indian Ocean. The absence of commerce meant that fewer emigrants arrived from Asia; East Africa became a cultural backwater of decrepit towns controlled by members of the Mazrui family who devoted their energies to squabbling among themselves. Even the 200 years of Portuguese occupation left little mark, and one must certainly agree with the judgment of the German historian Justus Strandes: Portuguese rule in East Africa was the rule of alien conquerors, based on force and destined to yield to greater strength when it appeared. It

[the Portuguese period] had no lasting influence whatsoever on the country, and East Africa today would appear the same even if there had been no Portuguese period in her past.*

## SAYYID SAID

In 1806 Said ibn Sultan succeeded to the Imanate of Oman. Known as Sayyid Said, he set about to regenerate the power of Oman, which had steadily declined during the undistinguished reigns of his father and grandfather in the eighteenth century. For twenty years Sayyid Said consolidated his rule in Oman, reorganizing the disorderly taxes, encouraging commerce, and enforcing order. While Sayyid Said was bringing peace and stability to southeast Arabia, equally important events were taking place in East Africa and the Indian Ocean. In 1810 the French Mascarene Islands—Île de France and Bourbon, now called Mauritius and Réunion, respectively— were captured by the British as part of their campaigns against Napoleonic France. Throughout the latter half of the eighteenth century, the French developed large sugar plantations on these islands, utilizing slaves taken from the East African coast. Like all commerce in East Africa, the slave trade had been in decline until it was revived by the demands of the French for slave labor to work their plantations on the Mascarenes. Once the British had occupied the islands, however, they set about to end the slave trade as part of Britain's larger campaign against the trans-Atlantic trade. Having learned from its experiences in attempting to curtail the American slave trade that slaving was best terminated at its source, the British government urged Sayyid Said, the titular ruler of East Africa, to prohibit the carrying of slaves. Unfortunately, Sayyid Said could hardly enforce his own claims to the East African towns against the

*The Portuguese Period in East Africa. East African Literature Bureau, Nairobi, 1961, p. 320.

virtually independent Mazfui sultans, let alone restrict a trade from which his subjects derived considerable profit. But in 1833 Sayyid Said did agree to forbid the trade between his Muslim subjects and any Christian power and subsequently signed a treaty with Captain Moresby of the Royal Navy. Not only did the Moresby Treaty solve the problem of the slave trade to the Mascarenes, but in return Sayyid Said received British friendship and support, which permitted him to reassert his claims to East Africa. Putting Oman in order, the Sayyid sailed to Mombasa in 1828 to enforce his suzerainty. This was no easy task, for despite their fraternal squabbles and harsh rule, the Mazrui successfully defied Sayyid Said, who in the end and after four military expeditions was forced to resort to diplomacy before breaking their power. By 1836, however, Omani troops had garrisoned the great stronghold at Mombasa, Fort Jesus, and Sayyid Said had firmly established his authority over the city. Within a year the whole coast acknowledged his suzerainty, and Sayyid Said became the first ruler to control the East African coast from Mogadishu to the Rouvuma River. Sayyid Said ruled East Africa and Oman for another twenty years, and at the time of his death in 1856, he had not only restored the authority of the Imam of Oman in East Africa but had also refashioned and welded together the city-states into an absolute monarchy that owed allegiance to no one but himself. In addition to the peace and stability he created on the coast, Sayyid Said founded Zanzibar as his capital, to which he moved from Oman. He developed the island as a religious and political center and introduced clove plantations, which soon provided Zanzibar with its principal export. Finally, to expand trade and commerce he encouraged political and commercial dealings with Europe and America. In 1833 Sayyid Said made a commercial treaty with the United States, and until the outbreak of the

Civil War the Americans continued to dominate Zanzibar's legitimate trade.

Sayyid Said was a strong and able ruler who sought to expand and develop commerce and trade, including the slave trade when that was possible. In doing so, however, he excited the interests of the European powers, not only by the profits to be made from trade with the West but even more because of the European humanitarian desire to suppress the slave trade. From such humanitarian beginnings the European presence in East Africa was soon to grow into an imperial adventure.

## KUSH

The land stretching southward from the second cataract of the Nile at 22 degrees north latitude to Lake Albert near the equator is known as the Sudan. In its full sense the term embraces the *Bilad as Sudan* ("Land of the Blacks") of the medieval Muslim geographers, which extended across Africa from the Red Sea to the Atlantic. This was the land where Arab and African cultures met and mingled. From that name the modern "Sudan" is derived. In the following pages the name "Sudan" is used in the restricted sense of the Sudanese territories acquired by Egypt in the nineteenth century that now constitute the Republic of the Sudan.

Our earliest knowledge of the Sudan takes us back some 5,000 years beyond the beginnings of the first dynasty in Egypt. The Sudan, or at least the northern Sudan, called Nubia, was inhabited by a homogeneous Kushitic culture to which were added in the subsequent millennia groups of Negroid peoples from the south and Kushitic peoples migrating from Libya. From the invasions of the Pharaohs of the twelfth dynasty (2000–1788 B.C.), Egypt set out to colonize Nubia; in the New Kingdom (1580–1050 B.C.), Nubia was divided into two vice-royalties—Wawat in the north with headquarters at Aswan, and Kush in the south with headquarters at Napata (Merowe).

Clearly, the Egyptian occupation of Nubia left an indelible imprint on Kush and the towns became centers of Egyptian culture where Egyptian law, medicine, art, and religion flourished; but Kush was not completely Egyptianized and the Nubians continued to practice their own customs and to make their own arts and crafts, which differed from the Egyptian-made products. By the eighth century B.C. Kush had grown in power, and as Egypt to the north became disrupted by civil war, the governors of Kush became independent kings. Under Kashta and his son Pianki (751–716 B.C.), Kush conquered Egypt and united the whole of the Nile Valley under the hegemony of its kings. The great days of Kush, however, were short-lived, for while Kush was establishing its control of the Nile Valley, the Assyrians were making themselves masters of the Middle East. Armed with iron weapons and under the leadership of Esar-haddon, the Assyrians invaded Egypt in 671 B.C. and defeated Taharqa, the King of Kush. In subsequent campaigns the Kushite armies were pushed back up the Nile to the safety of Nubia. The great days of Kush were over.

The story of Kush after the retreat from Egypt is one of gradual political and economic retrenchment in the face of growing competition from its neighbors and of social and cultural transformation. For as Egypt increasingly came under the influence of alien invaders, the cultural center of Kush shifted southward. In the seventh century B.C. the capital was moved from Napata to Mero near Shendi, although the center of religious life continued to be the temple of Jabal Barkal at Napata. This move inspired a Meroitic renaissance as Meroitic gods replaced those of Egypt, Meroitic writing became distinct from Egyptian, and Meroe became a civilization in its own right. For several centuries Meroe flourished as a trade center with ties to states as far distant as China and India, but at present there is little

conclusive evidence to prove that Meroe was an industrial state with an iron-based economy or that it was the center for the transmission of iron technology to other parts of sub-Saharan Africa. Nevertheless, there is little doubt that Meroe remained a viable and at times creative civilization well into the Christian era, with periods of prosperity that were marked by intense building activity and widespread trade with Egypt and the East. Despite this prosperity, however, Meroe's power was gradually being undermined by the increasing desiccation of the northern Sudan and the arrival of new groups of people from the southwest that hastened the decline of Kushitic culture. Then about 350 A.D., the King of Aksum marched into the Nile Valley from Ethiopia, sacked Meroe, and demolished Kush (Ezana, *The Destruction of Kush*). The royal family is believed to have followed the trade routes to the west, where they were swallowed up by the vastness of the savanna that stretches to the Atlantic. Although it was destroyed, Kush had made its contribution to history by preserving Nubian-Egyptian culture long after the culture of Egypt had vanished and by using this culture as the foundation of its own more distinctly African civilization.

## THE CHRISTIAN KINGDOMS

Little is known of the history of the Upper Nile prior to the introduction of Christianity in the sixth century. The country was inhabited by a people called Nubas or Nobatae, who grouped themselves into the kingdoms of Maqurra in Nubia and Alwa with its capital at Soba on the Blue Nile upstream from the modern city of Khartoum. Christianity was introduced in the Sudan as a definite missionary effort on the part of the Church of Egypt. In 543 A.D. the Byzantine empress Theodora sent off a missionary, Julian, to convert the Nubians. He worked with success in Maqurra and on his return to Constantinople was succeeded by Theodore, Bishop of Thebais, who continued the work until 551. In 569 a third missionary, Longinus, arrived to guide the spread of Christianity, converting the King of Alwa. Christianity was received with great enthusiasm in the Nile Valley and was accompanied by a spate of church building whose ruins today dot the banks of the Nile from Dunqula to Sennar. Following the departure of Longinus, little is known of Maqurra and Alwa until the coming of the Arabs in 639.

Exploding from the desert of the Arabian peninsula in the seventh century, the Arab armies swept westward along the North African littoral and up the Nile. Between 651 and 652, a well-equipped expedition marched on Dunqula, the capital of Maqurra, and laid siege to the town. The King of Maqurra sued for an armistice, and a peace was established according to which the king paid an annual tribute in slaves while the Arabs gave presents of grain and other goods. Both Arabs and Nubians agreed not to settle in the territory of the other. This arrangement, sometimes called the Treaty of Dunqula, appears to have set the pattern of Arab-Sudanese relations until the thirteenth century. During these centuries relations between Arab Egypt and Christian Sudan remained peaceful. The Arabs restricted themselves to limited trade and the Nubians were determined to prevent the permanent settlement of Arabs in Nubia.

## THE COMING OF THE ARABS

While Egypt remained under Arab control there was peace between Egypt and Maqurra, but when Egypt came under Mamluk rulers, conflict erupted. To rid themselves of troublesome subjects, the Mamluks encouraged the Arab Bedouins in Egypt to move southward and indulge their propensity to pillage the frontiers of Maqurra. The Bedouins were followed by regular Mamluk military expeditions, and although Maqurra fought back, the

corrosive effect of Bedouin raids and Mamluk invasions weakened the authority of the king so that by the mid-fourteenth century, internal security had dissolved into anarchy. The country was now open to Arab immigration, and once the Bedouins learned that the lands beyond the Aswan Reach were capable of supporting their flocks and herds, they poured into the Sudan, intermarrying with the Nubians and settling down beyond the authority of the Mamluk government in Egypt. The Arabs did not overwhelm Maqurra, but rather infiltrated, dissolving Nubian culture and Christianity, and then wandered off to the east and to the west with their herds. South of Maqurra the Kingdom of Alwa continued to resist the Arab encroachment, principally because the Arab tribes could never combine to overcome Alwa, which, unlike Maqurra, had not been subjected to generations of corrosive raids. Steadily, however, Arab infiltration weakened Alwa until suddenly in 1504 an alliance of the Rufaa Arabs with a mysterious people, the Funj, forever put an end to the Kingdom of Alwa.

## THE FUNJ

The Funj are one of the greatest mysteries of the African continent. They first appeared in 1504 when, in alliance with the Arabs, they defeated the forces of Alwa and established their own capital at Sennar. Although there are numerous conflicting theories that the Funj were from the Upper Nile, were Bulala from Bornu, or were exiles from Eritrea or even the Yemen, they were most likely a Negroid people of Hamaj descent from the Blue Nile. Under a dynasty of kings they controlled the Middle Nile in a loosely knit confederation with few common institutions and little centralization. The Arab tribes preserved much of their autonomy by paying tribute, although the Abdallab Arabs, whose chiefs resided at Qarri on the main Nile north of Khartoum, retained a unique position as the

principal vassals of the Funj. Founded on the famous Black Horse cavalry, Funj power reached its heights in the seventeenth century (James Bruce, *Shaykh Adlan and the Black Horse Cavalry of Sennar*). The court itself was a melting pot of pagan African with Arab, Muslim elements. Arabic was spoken by the upper class and Islam was practiced by many members of the Funj aristocracy, but the acceptance of Arab culture and religion remained at best only a veneer. In the latter half of the seventeenth century, the Funj kings relied increasingly on slave troops, who took the place of the Funj aristocracy. At first the rulers could depend on the loyalty of their slave army, but by the eighteenth century their authority had been gradually undermined by *wazirs*, who reduced the kings to puppets. Without a powerful ruler, the Funj kingdom declined as aristocrats and slave commanders indulged themselves in petty wars and court intrigue in a kaleidoscopic competition for control of the hapless king. Upon the approach of Muhammad Ali's troops from Egypt in 1821, the last wazir was murdered, his supporters fled, and the titular king, Badi IV, submitted and was pensioned off into the limbo of history.

## THE SOUTHERN SUDAN

Beyond the Funj kingdom in the remote regions of the southern Sudan live a large group of peoples that speak Nilotic languages. The origins of the Nilotes are unknown, but Abyssinia has been suggested as their homeland from which they migrated into the Southern Sudan with their beloved cattle. Once equipped with a cattle complex, the Nilotes began to migrate from their cradleland in the Bahr al-Ghazal during the fifteenth century. The Dinka and the Nuer did not move far, wandering off to the northeast to the swamplands around Lake No and the Bahr al-Jabal. A second group, the Luo-speaking Nilotes, pressed south up the Nile to northern Uganda. Before reaching their destination the Luo split, with one group reversing its movement and marching northward through the Bahr al-Ghazal. During their travels several smaller groups splintered off to remain in the Bahr al-Ghazal or, as in the case of the Anuak, to cross the Nile and settle in the upper reaches of the Sobat. The Luo remnant, under the leadership of Nyikang, pressed on to occupy the northern bank of the White Nile from Fashoda to Lake No, where their successors founded the Shilluk kingdom in the sixteenth century. Meanwhile, further south the Luo invaders of Uganda pressed on into Bunyoro-Kitara, where their *Bito* clans replaced the *Chwezi* aristocracy as rulers of the interlacustrine Bantu.

The Nilotes were not the only African inhabitants of the southern Sudan. At the beginning of the nineteenth century, groups of *Azande* were moving up the valley of the Mbomu and by midcentury had consolidated themselves along the Congo-Nile watershed. During their expansion from their homeland far to the west the Azande, under their aristocratic chiefs the Avungara, had developed an efficient military ogranization, as had the neighboring Mangbettu people, which either assimilated non-Azande or drove them before the advancing Azande armies (Georg Schweinfurth, *King Munza*). Ever expansionist, the Azande continued to press northeastward, where they would have inevitably collided with the equally militant Nilotes if alien powers had not intervened in the southern Sudan.

### The *Turkiya*[1]

In 1820 Muhammad Ali, the Turkish

---

[1] The period of Egyptian-Turkish rule in the Sudan. The alien invaders of the Sudan in the nineteenth century were the Turkish-speaking rulers of Egypt. Ethnically, they were a composite of the peoples of the Near East. Few would have identified themselves with the inhabitants of Egypt today.

Viceroy of Egypt, decided to conquer the Sudan. He was lured southward by tales of gold and the need to recruit slaves for his army. Commanded by his son Ismail, Muhammad Ali's troops defeated the *Shayqiya*, who sought to oppose the advance near Kurti, and marched triumphantly on up the Nile to Shendi (John Lewis Burckhardt, *Shendi*). By May 1821, Ismail reached the juncture of the White and the Blue Niles, crossed the river, and proceeded to Sennar where Badi IV surrendered, ending the long drawn-out death agony of the Funj Kingdom. While Ismail was marching unopposed up the Nile, Muhammad Ali sent a second expedition to conquer the regions of Kordofan and Darfur, west of the Nile. Under the command of Muhammad Ali's son-in-law, Muhammad Bey Khusraw, the *daftardar* (treasurer), the army assembled at ad-Dabba, marched southwest across the Bayuda, and routed the army of the Fur sultan at Bara to add Kordofan to Muhammad Ali's growing empire.

The new administration of the Sudan began very favorably. The conquest had been carried out with very little bloodshed, at least in the Nile Valley, and Ismail could begin his government with no past obstacles or former obligations. Unfortunately, however, Muhammad Ali had conquered the Sudan to exploit it, and the subsequent actions of his officials confirmed this policy. Taxes were instituted at a crushing rate, and the demand for slaves threatened to strip the petty chiefs of their retinues, upsetting the social structure in the Sudan. The result was a rebellion that began with sporadic attacks on Egyptian troops and culminated in the assassination of Ismail and his guard at Shendi in November 1822. Upon the death of Ismail, the daftardar was hastily ordered from Kordofan to the Nile to lay waste to the Nile Valley with fire and sword and brutally to stamp out the ill-coordinated and poorly armed Sudanese rebels. By 1824 the revolt was over. The daftardar returned to Egypt and Uthman Bey took over the administration of the Sudan with two objects in mind—to repress rebellion and to collect the taxes. Although Uthman Bey founded Khartoum at the juncture of the Blue and the White Niles, his policies did nothing to restore the Sudan. Soon an epidemic accompanied the economic depression, and even the army was drifting into anarchy when Uthman died in 1825.

Ali Khurshid Agha succeeded Uthman Bey in 1826, and his administration marks the turning point in Egyptian relations with the Sudanese. Ali Khurshid Agha first enticed the cultivators back to their lands with letters of amnesty and promises not to repeat the oppressive practices of the past. He then convened a council of notables to devise an equitable system of taxation and confirmed the appointment of Abd al-Qadir wad az-Zayn to act as liaison officer between the administration and the Sudanese and to attempt to associate the Sudanese more closely with the administration. Trade was encouraged and the caravans were protected. Khartoum was developed and settlers were given tracts of land and privileges. Khurshid returned to Cairo in May 1838. He had successfully rescued the Sudan from anarchy and transformed it into a peaceful and prosperous country and fully deserved the honors that were heaped upon him by a grateful Muhammad Ali.

Ahmad Pasha Abu Widan was appointed Khurshid's succesor. He carried on the policies and schemes of development of his predecessor, but upon his death in 1843 the Sudan relapsed into twenty years of stagnation precipitated by the vacillating policies of the viceroys in Cairo. Concerned about the power that Abu Widan had concentrated in his own hands, both Muhammad Ali and his successor, Muhammad Said, sought to decentralize administration in the Sudan, weakening the authority of the governors–general by means of short tenures. Between 1843 and 1862 eleven governors–general sat at Khartoum, many of whom did not exercise authority over the governors of the outlying provinces.

In 1863 Ismail Pasha succeeded his uncle as Viceroy of Egypt and set out to transform Egypt from a petty, oriental state into a modern, westernized empire. He constructed schools, hospitals, and palaces. He expanded and modernized the army. His greatest achievement was the Suez Canal, and clearly the Sudan would not be left out of his grandiose projects. Three themes dominate Ismail's reign in the Sudan: the expansion of Egyptian territory, the fight against the slave trade (if for no other reason than to attract European and American capital), and the use of European, Christian administrators to carry out these objectives. The first drive to the south was led by Samuel White Baker, in whose person all three of Ismail's objectives were combined (Sir Samuel Baker, *Khartoum and the Nilotic Slave Trade*). Baker left Khartoum in February 1870 at the head of a mammoth expedition. He pushed through the swamp regions of the Nile, known as the *sudd*, and by 1873 he had occupied Equatoria, broken the power of the slave raiders along the Nile, and forced the inhabitants to acknowledge the rule of the khedive. In the same year the Egyptian flag flew as far south as Fatiko, near the Albert Nile. On Baker's return, Ismail appointed Charles George Gordon to continue the task of consolidating and expanding Egyptian rule in equatorial Africa. Gordon served in Equatoria from 1874 to 1877, during which time he consolidated the work of Baker and established effective Egyptian administration in Equatoria.

Ismail did not, however, confine his plans for expansion to the Nile. In 1865 the Red Sea ports of Suakin and Massawa were ceded to Egypt, precipitating several abortive attempts by Egyp-

tian forces to penetrate into Abyssinia. Checked in the east, Ismail had greater success in the interior regions of the southern Sudan, the Bahr al-Ghazal. Ever since a passage through the Nile swamps had been found between 1839 and 1840, powerful commercial firms had established vast and complex trading networks in the Bahr al-Ghazal in order to carry on the ivory and slave trade. By the 1860s az-Zubayr Rahma Mansur, a northern Sudanese, had achieved a predominant position among the traders. He controlled most of the trading stations scattered throughout the Bahr al-Ghazal and was supported by a vast slave army that had been employed to round up the slaves and escort them to markets in the north. In 1871 Ismail sought to end the slave trade and annex the Bahr al-Ghazal to the Egyptian Sudan by sending a military expedition to crush the slavers. Under the leadership of az-Zubayr, however, the slavers rallied their private armies and defeated the Egyptian forces. In December 1873 the khedive, happy to make the best of an unfortunate setback, appointed az-Zubayr as the Egyptian Governor of the Bahr al-Ghazal. The recognition of az-Zubayr allowed the slavers to continue their nefarious trade, but in return Egypt had acquired nominal sovereignty over the Bahr al-Ghazal.

In February 1877 Gordon was appointed governor-general of the whole Sudan. One of his principal tasks was to implement the Anglo-Egyptian Slave Trade Convention, which provided for the termination of the sale and purchase of slaves in the Sudan by 1880, and he set out with his accustomed energy to break the slave trade. He lightened taxes, fired corrupt officials, issued a stream of reform legislation, and personally led the campaign against the slavers. But Gordon was illiterate in Arabic, impulsive, and a fanatical Christian in a fanatically Muslim land. He soon alienated not only the bureaucracy but all the very numerous and wealthy interests that derived their power from slaving. Suddenly, in 1879, the khedive's financial position collapsed. He could no longer pay the interest on the capital that he had borrowed from European bankers to modernize Egypt, and after cleaning out the spare cash in the treasury, Ismail sailed away to a gilded exile in a palace on the Bosporus. With the khedive gone, his own resources fast drying up, and many groups of Sudanese bitterly hostile, Gordon resigned. He was succeeded by Rauf Pasha, a more pliant and mediocre man. With a weak governor-general at Khartoum, the bureaucracy demoralized, and deep discontent running through the land, Muhammad Ahmad proclaimed himself the Mahdi on June 29, 1881.

## THE END OF THE TURKIYA

The Mahdist Revolution in the Sudan was the result of widespread Sudanese dissatisfaction with Egyptian rule and coincided with the collapse of the khediviate in Egypt and the subsequent British occupation. British officials in Egypt were too preoccupied to restore order and to protect the interests of the European bondholders. Nor were they concerned about the Sudan, which, with an ineffectual governor–general, drifted without direction or determination in the face of the rising dissatisfaction. The Sudanese found a spokesman for their discontent in the Mahdi, Muhammad Ahmad, a religious mystic and holy man living the life of a religious ascetic on Aba Island in the White Nile south of Khartoum. He regarded himself as a reformer, a *mujaddid*, a renewer of the Muslim faith, whose duty was to purge Islam of the corruption introduced during the Egyptian regime and to return it to the pure form practiced by the Prophet. The Mahdi was to guide the Muslim community as its Imam, or leader—the successor to Muhammad, the Prophet of God. The Mahdi appealed, of course, to the pious men, whose position in the Sudanese community was very influential. But the slave traders, who came mostly from settled riverain tribes, also rallied to the Mahdi's cause, not out of religious piety but in the hope of overthrowing the government and restoring the slave trade. His staunchest supporters, however, came from the Baggara Arabs, the cattle nomads of Kordofan and Darfur, who simply sought to rid themselves of the government and the burden of taxes.

The administration in Khartoum replied to the Mahdi's call to arms with a series of military expeditions that were annihilated, partly by the incompetence of their commanders but principally by the zeal of the Mahdi's followers. Victory followed victory for the Sudanese, culminating in the disastrous defeat at Shaykan of a large military expedition of 10,000 men under Colonel Hicks, formerly of the Indian Army. The Hicks expedition was the final effort of which the Egyptian Army was capable. Its destruction left the Mahdi master of the lands west of the Nile and convinced the British authorities in Cairo that the Sudan should be abandoned. To effect the Egyptian evacuation, or at least report on how to carry it out, Gordon returned to the Sudan for the third time. He arrived in Khartoum in February 1884 and quickly realized that both evacuation and negotiation with the Mahdi were out of the question. The city was soon besieged, and in spite of Gordon's heroic and skillful leadership and the appearance of a British relief expedition, Khartoum was taken by assault on January 26, 1885, and Gordon was killed. The Turkiya was over.

## ETHIOPIA

Several centuries before the birth of Christ, immigrants from the flourishing kingdoms of southern Arabia crossed the Red Sea to settle in the fertile highlands of the Ethiopian Plateau. The colonists brought with them not only the technical skills employed to terrace, dike, and irrigate the land but a sense of social and religious organization that evolved some time during the second century B.C. into the city and Kingdom of Aksum in northern Ethiopia. Aksum flourished, prospering in the trade with Arabia to the south and east and with Greece and Rome to the north and west, and gradually expanded along the Red Sea and Blue Nile by means of powerful armies, which the wealth of Aksum could afford. During the fourth century A.D., Aksum appears to have reached its golden age under Ezana, who unified Ethiopian Aksum, conquered the Yemen, and destroyed the decrepit Kingdom of Kush. Of more lasting importance than his expansion of empire, however, was Ezana's conversion to Christianity in approximately 333 A.D. Monophysite Christianity became the state religion and gradually spread among the pagan peoples, facilitating the integration of the diverse groups within the kingdom. Not only did the monasteries that sprang up in Aksum become the cultural repositories of the Kingdom, but the clergy interwove religious innovations into the traditional fabric of Ethiopian life.

Throughout the fifth and sixth centuries, Aksum continued her vigorous trading with Byzantium, Persia, India, and Ceylon. Emeralds, gold, incense, and spices were traded in her markets for the goods of the Orient and the merchandise of the Mediterranean (Cosmos Indicoplenstes, *Trade in Ethiopia*). However, trade and the political power it engendered were gradually disrupted by rivals on the periphery of the kingdom. In Arabia, Aksumite hegemony in the Yemen was destroyed by the Persians in the last decade of the sixth century, while depredations from the Beja of the Red Sea hills threatened Aksum from the north. The corrosive effects of these attacks could not, in themselves, have forced Aksum into decline had not the

rise of Islam and the Muslim depredations of the seventh and eighth centuries isolated the kingdom, which thereafter turned in upon itself.

Although the rulers of Aksum reasserted their control along the Red Sea coast in the ninth and tenth centuries, as a result of their attempts to include the Agau, a supposedly Jewish people of the interior, the forces of Queen Gudit of Agau defeated the Aksumites and drove their king to Shoa. Little is known of Queen Gudit's successors, but not until about 1270 did Yekuno Amlak regain the Aksumite throne for the Solomonid dynasty (which claimed its origins from Solomon), move the capital to Shoa, and introduce Amharic as the language of the court. Thereafter, his successors were preoccupied with the consolidation of the empire throughout the Ethiopian highlands, in which Christian evangelism played an important role, while waging war against the Muslims on the frontiers. By the fifteenth century Ethiopia had assumed its modern shape, but the political organization of the kingdom proved inadequate to control such a vast area or to weld its diverse peoples into a common whole. Consequently, the same problems—traditional internal conflicts and the Muslim threat—remained to challenge the empire into modern times.

To maintain its position in the face of hostile tribesmen from within and the threat of Muslim states from without, Ethiopia appealed to the Christian powers of the West, particularly the Kingdom of Portugal, for assistance in driving back the Muslim sultanate of Adal. Between 1520 and 1525 a Portuguese embassy visited Ethiopia but failed to conclude an alliance (Françisco Alvarez, *The Land of Prester John*). Despite the lack of Portuguese support, the emperor reopened the conflict with the sultanate of Adal during the second quarter of the sixteenth century. Assisted by the power of the Ottoman Turks and led by the Muslim reformer Ahmad ibn

Ibrahim al-Ghazi, who regarded himself as having been divinely appointed to conquer Christian Ethiopia, the Muslims swept all before them until Portuguese reinforcements arrived in 1541, checked the Muslim advance, and killed Ahmad in 1543. Thereafter Emperor Galawdewos successfully ended the Muslim occupation but failed to reassert the unity of old Ethiopia. In the south the Galla drove into Harrar, while within the empire the Falasha, Agau, and Sidama were in constant revolt.

Harried by Muslims from without and revolts from within, Emperor Susneyos (1607–1632) converted to the Church of Rome and permitted Roman Catholic missionaries to campaign against Monophysite Catholicism in the hope of receiving Christian military assistance from Europe (Father Lobo, *Portuguese Missionaries in Ethiopia*). Unhappily, religious strife soon degenerated into civil war between the emperor and the conservative leaders of the traditional religion. Unable to stem the tide of popular reaction, Susneyos abandoned his hope for a European alliance and returned to the Ethiopian Coptic Church just before his death in 1632. The reconversion of Susneyos, however, was but a momentary check in the long decline of the empire. Thereafter the spread of Islam, the growth of Galla power, and the endemic internal rebellions eroded the authority of the emperors. In the latter half of the seventeenth century, Emperor Fasiladas retired to Gondar in the heartland of the *Amhara*, where he established the first permanent capital. Although it was relatively secure, Gondar was too isolated for the emperors to control the far-flung territories beyond the Amhara area. During the eighteenth century the empire of Ethiopia disappeared. The Galla chiefs ousted the Christian Amhara chiefs and assumed control, although the Solomonid dynasty continued to provide petty kings for the principality of Gondar. Only the Monophysite Christian Church remained to provide a sense of unity throughout the fragmented empire.

In the mid-nineteenth century, Ethiopia consisted of numerous autonomous warlords ruling Christian peoples that spoke different languages and practiced divergent customs. In the 1840s one such warlord, Karsa, acquired control of Amhara, Gojjom, Tigre, and Shoa and persuaded the *abuna*, or head of the church, to install him as Theodorus II, King of Kings and Emperor of all the Ethiopians. Thereafter, Theodorus set out to consolidate his rule. Autonomous chiefs were defeated and rebellions were decisively crushed. The capital was moved from Gondar to Magdala, but there Theodorus acted with ever-greater capriciousness and his behavior became increasingly neurotic. Affronted by Queen Victoria's failure to answer his letters, he incarcerated British representatives, who were released only by a British military expedition that captured Magdala in 1868. Theodorus committed suicide. Although the British quickly withdrew, they had demonstrated the weakness of Ethiopia and aroused the interest and cupidity of the other European powers.

Upon the death of Theodorus, Johannes IV, the former Prince of Tigre, acquired the throne in 1872 after several years of struggle and ruled until his death in 1888 during the battle of Al-Gallabat against the Mahdists from the Sudan. His successor, Menelik, Prince of Shoa and one of the most remarkable rulers in African history, found himself beset from without by Italian efforts to establish a predominant influence in Ethiopia and from within by the centrifugal designs of princes, warlords, and chiefs that always appeared in Ethiopia upon the death of an emperor. The Italian threat proved the more serious, and in 1896 an Italian army marched into Ethiopia to the place where Menelik had gathered a great host to repel the invaders. The two armies met at the village of Adua in March 1896. The Italian Army was overwhelmingly defeated and the Italian sphere of influence was reduced to Eritrea and the coastal port of Massawa. Ethiopia remained triumphantly independent.

Having thrown back the foreign invaders, Menelik skillfully played one European power against another in order to acquire assistance to expand the empire within Ethiopia itself. Equipped with European arms, he annexed Wallamo Galla, the Beni Shangul, Kaffa, and carried the emperor's authority as far south as Lake Turkana. Nevertheless, Menelik's death in 1913 precipitated numerous intrigues against his successor, Lij Yasu, who openly espoused Islam, denounced his Solomonid ancestry, and claimed descent from the Prophet Muhammad. This flagrant advocacy of Christian Ethiopia's most ancient and traditional enemy deeply angered the Christian princes of Shoa, who marched on the capital, Addis Ababa, and in 1916 elevated Menelik's daughter Zanditu to the throne. Ras Tafari, the future Haile Selassie, became regent and the active ruler of the empire. As his influence grew he set out to bring Ethiopia into the modern world, and by 1930, when he assumed the title of emperor on the death of the Empress Zanditu, he had already set Ethiopia on a new and difficult course to break its traditional isolation from the world beyond the highlands.

## BANTU AND CUSHITE IN EAST AFRICA

Perhaps before and probably no later than the arrival of the Bantu on the East African coast from south-central Africa, a second body of Bantu cultivators reached the great lakes in the interior of eastern Africa. Here in the salubrious upland heart of Africa the Bantu settled, tilled the fertile soils surrounding the lakes, and came in contact with Cushitic peoples from southwest Ethiopia. The

nature of these first contacts between Bantu and Cushite is unknown, but in subsequent centuries Cushitic pastoralists appear to have moved into the lake region and superimposed their culture upon the sedentary Bantu. Oral traditions indicate several such groups of Cushitic peoples, the last being the famous *Hima* pastoralists under kings of the Chwezi clan. As Hima kings, the Chwezi established their authority over the Bantu agriculturalists and ruled a kingdom called Kitara, which embraced much of the area of modern Uganda. Their capital was at Bigo on the Katonga River. The Hima clearly formed a pastoral aristocracy that the Bantu treated with respect and deference.

## THE NILOTES

At the end of the fifteenth century a third group, the Nilotes, entered the lake region of eastern Africa from the north, the southern Sudan. The Nilotes are an African people who may have followed the dispersion of Sudanic crops from the Niger region of West Africa. To add to the confusion surrounding "origins," other transitions place the origins of the Nilotic peoples in western Abyssinia. Whatever their source the Nilotes flourished upon their settlement in the upper Nile Basin on the plains of the Bahr al-Ghazal. Here the Nilotes remained as a small group of cultivators devoted, however, to pastoralism. How the Nilotes acquired cattle remains unknown. Perhaps they borrowed the techniques necessary for a pastoral complex from the Cushites in Abyssinia. Perhaps they developed other techniques independently of other peoples. But once the Nilotes learned to subsist on pastoral nomadism, they began to expand and to move. One group, whose modern descendants are the Dinka and the Nuer, moved only a short distance, settling by the great swamps of the Nilotic Sudan. A second group pressed east and south from the region between Lake Turkana and the Nile into Kenya, where they met Cushitic peoples that were gradually assimilated but from whom the Nilotic nomads acquired numerous cultural traits. Today these Nilotes form an elongated funnel stretching from the Kenya-Sudan border west of Lake Turkana southward to the Tanzania frontier and are represented by such famous tribes as the *Masai*, the *Nandi*, and the *Karamojong*. A third group of Nilotes, the Lwo-speaking peoples, dispersed from their cradleland in the Bahr al-Ghazal province of the southern Sudan south up the Nile and into Kitara. Here they drove out the Hima pastoral aristocracy and their Chwezi kings, settled among the Bantu, adopted Bantu speech, and established dynasties of rulers over Kitara, now called Bunyoro-Kitara, from the Bito clans of the Lwo. Although the Lwo became Bantuized, their Bito clans formed new political nuclei around which grew kingdoms.

The impact of the Lwo, however, did not stop at the limits of Kitara. The Hima pastoralists, whom the Lwo had driven out, settled in northwest Tanzania, southwest Uganda, and Burundi, where they introduced the idea of chieftainship and even resurrected kingdoms. Thus the Lwo invasions into northern Uganda not only created new chieftainships but stimulated political evolution beyond the limits of Lwo expansion.

Buganda is the outstanding example of the evolution of chieftainship. In the sixteenth century Buganda was but a small tributary state of the great feudatory kingdom of Bunyoro-Kitara. At the end of the sixteenth century, Buganda broke away from Bunyoro-Kitara and not only managed to maintain its independence but, in its confined state, developed a more homogeneous and centralized society than the sprawling structure of Bunyoro ever achieved. When Buganda began to expand in the seventeenth century, the conquered clans were not simply confirmed in their

positions of authority; rather, new chieftainships were created for the conquered clans by the appointment of rulers who were *Baganda*, loyal to the Buganda king, the *kabaka*, and controlled from the central capital. Thus, in the seventeenth and eighteenth centuries Buganda developed a bureaucratic system under the absolute control of the kabaka, who monopolized the trade with the coast and exposed Buganda to external influences. Equipped with a centralized, efficient administration and alert to the outside world, by the nineteenth century Buganda had eclipsed Bunyoro as the predominate power in Uganda (Sir Apolo Kagwa, *Court Life in Buganda*).

The remaining area of eastern Africa never developed states like those of the coast or the lakes. In western Tanzania, Unyamwezi, a multiplicity of small units existed that never coalesced into a whole but tended to divide and proliferate. Even further south, between the Rufiji and Rouvuma rivers, the Bantu peoples remained hunters or fishermen or shifting cultivators—scattered, chiefless, anonymous. Even in eastern Kenya the presence of Nilotic peoples did not result in state building. In the lake regions the Lwo were the invaders; in Kenya the Bantu must be regarded as the incomers. As the Bantu reached the Kenya highlands, they came in contact with Cushitic peoples and adopted many Cushitic customs. The Bantu were followed many centuries later by the Nilotes. The *Nandi* settled near Mt. Elgon as early as the sixteenth century and were followed by other Nilotic peoples, culminating with the *Masai*. Later, Bantu migrants, like the *Kikuyu*, pressed into the area, settling around the fringe of the Nilotic core and in turn adopting many Cushitic-Nilotic customs. Although people like the Masai, Kikuyu, and Nandi were tribes or even nations, they never developed the centralized political structure that characterized the kingdoms further west.

Until the middle of the nineteenth

century, the interior of East Africa remained undisturbed by outside influence. There had, of course, long been contact between the Africans of the interior and the coast, but trade remained in the hands of the Africans, the greatest traders of whom were the *Nyamwezi*, the *Yao*, and the *Kamba*, who monopolized the hinterland trade throughout the first half of the nineteenth century. Moreover, trade among the peoples of the interior was carried on in peace and even in times of war by the women. During the second quarter of the nineteenth century, however, the interior beyond the East African coast was penetrated by an ever-increasing number of non-Africans. In 1825 two Khojas from Surat, India, arrived in the Unyamwezi country, and by 1842 caravans of coastal Arabs had reached Lake Tanganyika. Others followed, and in 1852 an Arab caravan traversed the African continent from the east coast to Benguela on the Atlantic Ocean.

The Arabs pressed into the interior principally in search of ivory. Slaves, of course, were of value to the traders, particularly as porters to carry the ivory out of Africa, but in these early years of the caravan trade, slaves were regarded as a secondary item. However, as the ivory regions became exhausted as Africans and Arabs sought to meet the growing world demand, the interests of the traders shifted to slaves. In this sense the slave trade grew out of the ivory trade. The main source of supply was near the lakes in western Tanzania, where the village was the largest political unit and the inhabitants possessed no strong, centralized political organization to oppose the Arabs. Occasionally the Arabs themselves would capture the Africans, but more frequently they would induce an African chief to raid his neighbors (who were probably his rivals) and hand over the captives in return for Arab possessions and trade goods. Slave raids produced yet more raids, resulting in the great increase of intertribal warfare, depopulated areas, and misery and desolation for those who were left behind in the smoking villages or pillaged fields. The march to the coast was the worst experience for a slave. It took generally three months, during which the slaves were roped or chained together. The recalcitrant Africans wore heavy yokes, and those who resisted were shot or left to starve. Once the slaves reached the coast they were placed in *barracoons*, or stockades, and then packed into the Arab dhows for the three-day crossing to Zanzibar. In Zanzibar the slaves were sold at the great market and shipped to Arabia, Persia, or beyond. Again they were packed in dhows that cruised north along the coast and then dashed to ports in the Red Sea, South Arabia, or the Persian Gulf. Those who survived the long and terrifying journey were sold to Muslim masters, and their lot improved considerably. For in contrast to the dehumanizing plantation slavery of the Americas, in the Middle East slaves were employed principally as domestic servants. Thus, many slaves were well-treated and respected members of the family whose relationship with their masters was regulated by the *Quran*. Many slaves in Zanzibar, for instance, were permitted to sell their own produce and to hold slaves in their own right.

The slave trade expanded because it was profitable and because Sayyid Said, the ruler of Zanzibar, provided a favorable climate for the growth of commerce, including slaves. He encouraged Banyans from India to settle in his domains, and they were soon the principal source of capital to finance the interior trade. Sayyid Said himself promoted expeditions to the mainland, and thus it was no coincidence that caravans began to penetrate into the interior during his reign. Despite the profits from his own commercial ventures, however, his chief sources of revenue remained the export and import duties on Zanzibar's main commodity—slaves.

As the slave trade expanded in East Africa, so too did Europe's and particularly Great Britain's interest in the region. Although some Victorian writers eloquently described East Africa's potential wealth, early British interest was fundamentally humanitarian and scientific. The development of the slave trade in East Africa therefore resulted in a European reaction against it led by Britain, which had championed the fight against the West African slavers. The great British missionary David Livingstone was also one of the foremost explorers of East Africa. Emotionally less powerful but intellectually more stimulating, however, was the scientific search for the source of the Nile. For whereas David Livingstone marched through East Africa as a great missionary general directing the attack on the slave trade, men like Richard Burton, John Hanning Speke, and Henry Morton Stanley were in Africa to solve the riddle of the Nile.

Burton and Speke set out in 1857 from Bagamoyo "for the purpose of ascertaining the limits of the sea of Ujiji" in the interior and to determine whether the lake was the source of the Nile. They had been attracted to East Africa by adventure and the Nile quest, which had been aroused by the preliminary explorations of German missionaries—Ludwig Krapf, J. Rebmann, and J. Erhardt—employed by the Church Missionary Society, the British Anglican missionary organization. The German missionaries had made numerous journeys into the interior from their coastal mission stations and had traced their explorations on a map published in Europe by Erhardt in 1856. Burton and Speke reached Lake Tanganyika in February 1858, traveled to the northern end of the lake, and found, to their disappointment, that the Ruzizi River flowed into the lake and thus could hardly be a headwater of the Nile. The two explorers returned to Tabora, from

where Speke marched northward alone to the shores of Lake Victoria. He jumped to the conclusion that Lake Victoria was the source of the Nile and upon his return to England organized a second expedition with Captain J. A. Grant. Speke and Grant set out for Lake Victoria in 1860. They skirted the western shore of the lake, sojourned in Buganda and Bunyoro, and continued on down the Nile to Cairo, returning to London in 1863 (John Hanning Speke, *Unyamwezi and Uganda*). Although Speke asserted that the Nile question was settled, others remained unconvinced. Speke and Grant had not circumnavigated Lake Victoria; it might, in fact, be many lakes. Moreover, they had not followed the Nile from Victoria, but rather went overland, meeting the Nile far to the north at Gondokoro. The skeptics maintained that the river that flowed out of Lake Victoria might be but a tributary of the main Nile stream. No, the Nile question was not settled, but the controversy and the explorers' accounts were widely followed in England and focused British attention on East Africa.

Speke died tragically in 1863. Two years later, after the explorations of Sir Samuel Baker near Lake Albert had only deepened the mystery of the Nile source, Sir Roderick Murchison announced that Britain's foremost explorer, David Livingstone, would return to Africa to ascertain Africa's watersheds and resolve the problem of the Nile source. In 1866 Livingstone set out for Africa a third time. Twice before he had spent long years in Africa on epic journeys: from 1853 to 1856 he had traversed the continent and from 1858 to 1863 he had sought to find a high road into central Africa by way of the Zambesi River. Now Livingstone returned to Africa, more famous than ever and more possessed of the spiritual quality that the Arabs call *baraka*, to find God, as well as the source of the Nile, through Africa. For five years Livingstone wandered alone in East Africa, while the world wondered. His letters about the conditions of the slave trade and the havoc caused to African society by the raiders were decisive in launching the great campaign against the slave trade. But such reports were punctuated by long silences, which soon elicited efforts to relieve if not rescue the good doctor. In 1871 the New York *Herald* sent its star reporter, Henry Morton Stanley, to Africa to find Livingstone. In November of the same year the two men met at Ujiji and Stanley provided Livingstone with the resources to continue his explorations. After two additional years of wandering in the interior, even Stanley's supplies were lost or exhausted, and, sick and failing, Livingstone died, as he wished, near the village of Chitambo on May 1, 1873.

Although Livingstone's last journey had ignited the antislave trade crusade in Britain, it had only confused the Nile question. For Livingstone had mistaken the upper Congo River, known as the Lualaba, for the Nile. Stanley resolved to piece together this geographical puzzle once and for all, and under his expert but ruthless leadership a large expedition plunged into Africa in 1874. In three years' hard marching he circumnavigated Lake Victoria, proving it to be one body of water, and then in like manner confirmed that Lake Tanganyika has no outlet. Then he and his men journeyed down the Lualaba-Congo to the Atlantic Ocean, establishing that it had no relation to the Nile. Stanley returned to Zanzibar in 1877. The Nile question was all but settled. Subsequently Europeans and an American explored lakes Albert and Albert Edward and the short stretch of the Victoria Nile, filling in the brief gaps that Stanley's continental explorations had neglected.

While Stanley was in the interior solving the geographical questions raised by previous explorers, on the coast the humanitarian forces of the antislave trade crusade, aroused by Livingstone, stood ready to halt that trade. For years the British government had sought to attack the slave trade by restricting it to the dominions of the Sultan of Zanzibar, but this policy was not completely successful. Although British squadrons patrolled East African waters, the commanders frequently could not determine whether a slave cargo was legally passing between Zanzibar and the sultan's domain in South Arabia or illegally bound for some other port. In 1873 the British government realized its failure, abandoned the policy of restriction, and sought to force the Sultan of Zanzibar, Barghash ibn Said, to abolish the trade. Sir Bartle Frere was sent to Zanzibar to negotiate with the sultan, and when negotiations failed, the British Navy enforced British policy by seizing the slavers and threatening war on Zanzibar. Barghash gave way and agreed to end the trade.

To his credit Barghash enforced the antislave trade treaty more rigidly than the British had ever expected. He was, of course, supported by British power, which probably prevented his overthrow by the powerful slaving interests on the coast, but his coercion was successful (Salim al-Mazrui, *The Sultan and Mombasa*). The seaborne trade was virtually halted, and when Arab traders tried to evade Barghash's decrees by marching slaves northward for sale in Somaliland, Barghash in 1876 forbade the conveyance of slaves on the mainland of Africa itself. For many years thereafter a surreptitious slave trade continued in East Africa and an occasional slave dhow slipped by British patrols bound for Arabia, but in fact as well as in theory, the British humanitarians had triumphed in East Africa as they had triumphed in West Africa. The Zanzibar slave trade was broken and European interest in East Africa was now aroused. Perhaps the legitimate commerce of Britain and Europe could replace that of human chattels.

## PARTITION OF EAST AFRICA

Although the efforts of the Sultan of Zanzibar to curtail the slave trade fulfilled the requirements of British policy, the extent of his rule in the interior remained ill-defined, and this breach in his authority enabled the international powers to divide up East Africa amongst themselves. Ironically, however, the partition of East Africa was begun not by a European but by an African power. In preparation for a thrust into the interior, the Khedive of Egypt attempted in 1875 to extend his empire by acquiring ports on the coast of Somaliland that were loyal to the Sultan of Zanzibar. Although Barghash was powerless to eject the Egyptian invaders, his British allies were not, and British pressure at Cairo forced the khedive to recall his forces. The first attempt to contest the sultan's authority on the African mainland had failed.

No sooner had the Egyptian expedition withdrawn, however, than a flock of European concessionaires swarmed like flies around the sultan, their appetites whetted by the rapid increase in East African trade in the 1870s and the weakness of the sultanate, which the Egyptian invasion had so glaringly exposed. Before his energies were turned to the Congo, King Leopold of the Belgians promoted several expeditions to East Africa, which ostensibly were in the cause of science but in reality were the probable forerunners of political claims. Not to be outdone, the French Chamber of Deputies supported an expedition that reached Lake Tanganyika in 1879, where its leader died. But the French and Belgian interest in East Africa never developed beyond these tentative probings, and the serious challenge to the sultan's authority was left to the Germans. Numerous German explorers had wandered under their own impetus in various and widely separated parts of East Africa, but not until the appearance of Carl Peters in Usagara, behind Bagamoyo, was German enterprise in Af-

rica given an imperial direction. Peters was one of Germany's more unsavory advocates of German colonial expansion. He had founded the Society for German Colonization in 1884 and went out to East Africa for the express purpose of acquiring territory for the German Empire. Although reluctant to embark on imperial adventures, Bismarck, the German Chancellor, was quite prepared to use the work of German explorers in Africa in order to strengthen his domestic position in Germany and his international policy in Europe. He therefore supported Peters' claims in East Africa and declared a German protectorate over Usagara, where the Sultan of Zanzibar had always exercised jurisdiction and through which passed his strategic caravan route to the west. Barghash protested but to no avail, and this time the British government did not rush to the sultan's rescue. It was one thing for the British to push around a petty Oriental potentate; it was quite another to attempt to tamper with the wishes of the new and vigorous German Empire. The partition of East Africa was now begun in earnest.

Ever since 1882, when the British had occupied Egypt, they had welcomed German diplomatic support on the International Debt Commission for the administrative and financial reforms in the lower Nile Valley. In 1885 the Gladstone government still required German support in Egypt and elsewhere. Moreover, Gladstone himself welcomed Germany's appearance in Africa as a partner in the task of civilizing the continent. Consequently, not only did the British refrain from defending the sultan, but they even used their influence at Zanzibar to convince him to give way to German demands. Barghash had little choice. In December 1885 he recognized the German protectorate and signed a treaty giving the Germans commercial privileges and easy access from the port of Dar es Salaam to their protectorate in the interior. But the loss of Usagara was only the beginning. In the following year a commission composed of representatives of Britain, France, and Germany ascertained the limits of the sultan's territory on the East African mainland. Britain and Germany agreed to recognize his authority along the coast but divided East Africa into spheres of influence. The German sphere stretched south of a line drawn from Tanga on the coast to 1 degree south latitude on the eastern shore of Lake Victoria and thence along that line to the west. The British sphere lay to the north.

Although the Anglo-German Agreement of 1886 had demarcated the respective spheres of Britain and Germany along the coast and beyond in the immediate hinterland, the agreement did not establish a western limit, so that the rear of each sphere was open to encroachment by the other; and as both British and German companies sought to exploit their spheres, the rivalry intensified for control of the interlacustrine Bantu kingdoms of the great lakes. British hopes to acquire predominant influence in Uganda rested with the Imperial British East Africa Company (IBEA), founded by Sir William Mackinnon in 1888 to carry on trade and commerce and even to administer the British zone. On the urging of the British government, the company decided in 1889 to push into the interior in order to secure the Bantu kingdoms of Uganda within the British sphere. The IBEA, however, was not alone in the field. Carl Peters set out ostensibly to rescue a fellow German, Emin Pasha, who was beleaguered on the Upper Nile, and at the same time to claim Uganda as a German protectorate. Peters arrived too late to relieve Emin Pasha, who was already on his way to the coast accompanied by a British relief expedition under Henry Morton Stanley. However, in February 1890, Peters arrived in Uganda before the representatives of the IBEA and signed a treaty

with Mwanga, the Kabaka of Buganda, placing Buganda under German protection. But Peters' victory was short-lived. Throughout the spring of 1890 negotiations between the governments of Great Britain and Germany continued and on July 1, 1890, culminated sucessfully in an agreement commonly called the Heligoland Agreement, whereby the British government, in return for Uganda and the vital sources of the Nile River, conceded the strategic island of Heligoland in the North Sea. The partition of East Africa was complete; the arduous task of pacification could now begin.

## RESISTANCE

The partition of East Africa was but the prelude to occupation, and the demarcation of the respective spheres of Britain and Germany did not automatically result in African acquiescence to the imposition of European rule. Neither consulted nor advised, the East African peoples generally opposed the invaders until they were overwhelmed by the technological superiority of the Europeans. The Africans did not want European overrule, even if it meant all the manifold and humane benefits that Western science and technology could provide. They resented Western interference in their traditional way of living and only submitted after a decade of forceful resistance.

The Germans were the first to experience African resistance. In 1888 the coastal Arabs and their African allies, led by Bushiri of Pangani, rebelled against the German East Africa Company. Although the revolt was crushed by German troops under Captain Hermann von Wissmann, the Imperial German Government was determined to intervene directly and took over the administration of the protectorate from the company. Gradually the German administration spread out from the coast into the interior, playing on the divisions among the African tribes and crushing resistance with their superior weapons. But having conquered the African peoples, the Germans had equal difficulties keeping them subservient. In July 1905 the Maji-Maji Revolt erupted in the Matumbe Hills northwest of Kilwa. (Records of Maji Maji: *The Maji Maji Rebellion, 1905–1907*) The Maji-Maji Revolt was the most serious challenge to German control. Once again the technological superiority of the German weapons was decisive, but only after heavy fighting that resulted in large numbers of casualties on both sides. By 1907 the revolt had been brought under control and the Germans turned their energies to the economic development of the protectorate. The Africans had been pacified—beaten into a reluctant acceptance of German rule (Ruhanantuka, *Flight of the Ekirimbi*).

To the north the British, like the Germans, also had to crush African resistance before their occupation was complete. Although Uganda had been reserved for Britain after the Helgoland Agreement of 1890, the task of occupation was left to the Imperial British East Africa Company. When the company representative, Captain F. D. Lugard, arrived in Uganda in 1890, the Kingdom of Buganda was divided among rival religious factions—Protestants, Catholics, pagans, and Muslims—each competing for control. The rival Christian parties were followers of the European Protestant and Catholic missionaries who had answered the invitation of the *Kabaka* Mutesa. (Ernest Linant de Bellefonds: *Kabaka Mutesa I*) In 1877 Mutesa had requested Christian missionaries for Buganda, not so much because he was concerned to learn the teachings of Jesus Christ, but to offset the growing influence of the Muslim powers, particularly Egypt to the north, which, under the Khedive Ismail, was relentlessly extending its control up the Nile Valley. Largely through the force of his personality, Lugard was able to convince Mutesa's

successor, Mwanga, to transfer suzerainty to the IBEA. He then rallied the Christian parties in Buganda and drove the Muslims into exile before setting out to the west, where he signed treaties with the chiefs of Toro and Ankole and recruited 500 Sudanese troops in Equatoria who were formerly in the employ of the Khedive of Egypt but had been abandoned when Emin Pasha evacuated the province. With his force considerably augmented by the Sudanese troops, Lugard returned to Kampala, where in 1892 he intervened between the feuding Catholic and Protestant parties to resolve the religious wars that had divided the Baganda. Although Lugard imposed a semblance of stability on Buganda, his military operations had been expensive and commercially unprofitable. Consequently, the Directors of the IBEA decided to withdraw from Uganda, precipitating a great outcry from missionary and imperial groups in England who sought to include Uganda within the empire. Lugard himself returned to England to lead the campaign for the retention of Uganda and aroused such interest within the country that in 1894 the British government agreed to take over Uganda from the IBEA and set about the task of pacifying the territory. During numerous arduous campaigns from 1893 until 1900, British forces occupied Bunyoro, stamped out revolt in Buganda, and crushed a mutiny by the overworked Sudanese troops whom Lugard had enlisted. Although the campaigns of pacification had placed a great drain on British resources, by 1900 Uganda was thoroughly pacified and the introduction of administration could begin. The British had next to turn their attention to Sayyid Muhammad Abdille Hasan, who opposed European encroachment into Somaliland until sufficient forces were massed after World War I to crush him (Muhammad Abdille Hasan, *The Sayyid's Reply*).

## ADMINISTRATION

The administration of German East Africa was characterized by concentration on economic development (which left few men and little money to provide services for the Africans) and exploitation by both government and private investors of the latent resources of the territory. In 1892 sisal was brought from Florida, flourished, and today remains Tanzania's principal export. Coffee and cotton plantations were established, and roads, rail lines, and the famous Amani Biological and Agricultural Institute were constructed to make the economic achievements possible. The administration itself was in the hands of a governor. The territory was divided into districts usually administered by officers seconded from the German Army, and their methods frequently reflected their military background. The Sultan of Zanzibar had administered his coastal regions through *walis* in the towns and *akidas* in the countryside who supervised *jumbes*, or headmen, in the villages, and the Germans simply adopted this system for the interior. Thus, when local authorities were unable to control the laborers induced to work on the plantations of the northern hinterland, akidas were appointed by the Germans. Similarly, they placed akidas in the more sparsely populated south. But throughout the vast region of the interior the traditional chiefs were either tacitly accepted or formally recognized by the Germans.

British East Africa was divided and administered as two separate territories: the East African protectorate, later known as Kenya, and the Uganda protectorate. From the first the Uganda protectorate was regarded as the more important; the East African protectorate was considered only as a passage to the rich and productive territories around the great lakes. Before Uganda could be developed, however, a cheap means of transport would have to link the interior with the coast, and throughout the 1890s the Uganda railway was pushed up from Mombasa until it reached Lake Victoria in 1903. Unhappily the railway proved a costly venture, and the economic exploitation of British East Africa was required to pay for such a heavy capital investment. The Governor of the East African protectorate, Sir Charles Eliot, consequently encouraged the immigration of European and South African settlers to East Africa. Not only would the technically knowledgeable Europeans transform the subsistence economy, but by example they would introduce the Africans to the "benefits" of Western civilization. Between 1903 and 1904, several hundred Europeans settled on large farms in the Kenya highlands on land that the Kikuyu regarded as their traditional territory. The colonists not only required land but needed labor to work it, and they at once demanded that the government institute means to recruit African labor for the European farms and plantations. Thus, while the economy expanded and the railway began to pay for itself, the seeds of racial tension were planted in the fertile soil of the highlands of Kenya (Lord Delamere, *White Man's Country*).

At first the 1914 war was not expected to spread to East Africa, but on the outbreak of hostilities the outnumbered Germans, under their great guerilla leader, General Paul von Lettow-Vorbeck, sought to wage a long drawn-out campaign that would drain allied resources from the western front in Europe. Von Lettow-Vorbeck succeeded brilliantly, occupying many thousands of British, Indian, and South African troops who, at the time of the armistice in 1918, had still failed to force von Lettow-Vorbeck and his African and German troops to surrender. Although the British were ultimately victorious and acquired German East Africa as the Tanganyika mandate of the League of Nations, the war had created great economic problems in all the territories. In Tanganyika itself the British Governor, Sir Donald Cameron, introduced a system of indirect rule—that is, administration through the traditional African leaders and hereditary authorities. Indirect rule was in striking contrast to the very direct control of the Germans, which had destroyed many indigenous institutions of authority, and although British officials not infrequently had to rediscover African leaders or their descendants and install them in positions of authority, in coastal areas where the Arabs and Germans had obliterated the tribal leaders, the people regarded the government-appointed chiefs much as they had regarded the akidas. In the interior, however, where German administration had been less thorough, indirect rule functioned more rationally, even though many of the new-found chiefs proved to be unsuited or adopted a bureaucratic mentality toward their people. The benefits of indirect rule are still hotly debated among scholars, but at least it did provide for African participation, no matter how minimal, in the process of governing.

If British rule in Tanganyika was characterized by attempts to include Africans in the administration, in Kenya it had to devote its energies to protecting the Africans from the designs, for good or evil, of non-Africans. Following World War I the Kenya settlers demanded increasing participation in the government in return for their loyal services during the war. Ironically, the greatest opposition to the settlers came not from the Africans but from the Indian community. Indian traders had long been active on the coast, and their numbers were increased by those Indian laborers brought over to construct the Uganda railway who had refused repatriation to India. As petty traders they ventured into areas of East Africa where Europeans, because of the diminutive returns, were unwilling to risk capital. Thus, not only were Indian merchants responsible for opening far-off places in East Africa to world commerce, but their low standard of living gave them an economic edge over the Europeans. The British settlers, of course, were determined to protect their economic advantage, but to justify their privileged position they argued that Europeans, and Europeans only, should be entrusted with the responsibility for protecting African interests. The settlers employed this argument to further their own political ambitions for participation in the government of Kenya, but the British Colonial Office turned the argument around to declare in 1923 that African interests were paramount and were to be protected—not, however, by the European settler community, but by British civil servants of the Colonial Office (The Devonshire White Paper, *The Indians in Kenya*). The decision had momentous results, for Kenya never acquired self-government by a European minority (as did Rhodesia), and until the Africans themselves won the right to govern their own affairs the officials of the British Colonial Office continued to carry out the role of imperial trustee.

Since Uganda possessed few Europeans and Indians, the administration was more concerned with the Africans and particularly the relations of Buganda to the other interlacustrine kingdoms. As in Tanganyika, colonial administration in Uganda sought to include African participation in government through the institution of a legislative council. When the council was established in 1921, however, the Baganda chose not to participate, preferring to deliberate matters pertaining to Buganda in their own parliament, the *Lukiko*, which they completely controlled, rather than in a legislative council for the whole of the Uganda protectorate, where they would be outvoted. Thus the legislative council remained remote from the most powerful and active kingdom in Uganda, creating the impression that the government cared little for the welfare of Buganda.

## NATIONALISM

World War II prepared the way for the rise of nationalism in East Africa and a greater emphasis on economic development. In all three territories plans were drafted during the war for development projects, and although all were not successful (such as the disastrous failure of the Tanganyika groundnut scheme), the progress in economic development in the postwar period was generally encouraging. Constitutional development, however, was complicated by the emergence of African nationalism which in Kenya erupted in the more violent form of Mau Mau.

The origins of Mau Mau are obscure, but the object of this secret society was clear—to drive the Europeans out of Kenya. Mau Mau was virtually a Kikuyu movement, and from 1952 until 1955 the society spread terror in Kenya by its acts of violence to African and European alike. Fundamentally, the movement was a reaction to British rule and the paternalism, no matter how benevolent, which dismissed a whole people as irresponsible (Jomo Kenyatta: *Meeting at Nyeri July 26, 1952*). For half a century relations between Kikuyu and the Europeans were a tragic tale of frustration on the one hand and misunderstanding on the other. Although the rebellion was crushed, the Mau Mau did accomplish their goal by driving home the realization that it would be Africans who would ultimately rule in Kenya. And to the credit and foresight of the British, their officials pushed forward constitutional advance in a series of complex constitutions and elections in which the Africans, through two political parties, the Kenya African National Union (KANU) and the Kenya African Democratic Union (KADU), emerged as the most powerful force. Led by Jomo Kenyatta, African demands soon proved irresistible. The Europeans and Asians accepted, with reluctant grace, their positions as minority groups and on December 12, 1963, Kenya at-

tained its independence. (Tom Mboya: *Kenya as a Nation July 23, 1962*)

Although constitutional development in Uganda was not opposed by the European community, the separate status of Buganda retarded political advance. When the British sought to bring Buganda into the process of constitutional development in Uganda as a whole, they were opposed by the kabaka, who was subsequently exiled in 1952. Without the kabaka, however, constitutional change could hardly go forward, and after long and difficult negotiations he returned to Uganda and agreed to revise Buganda's position to permit its political participation in the Uganda National Assembly. Under the leadership of A. M. Obote, the Uganda Peoples Congress won control of the Assembly in the elections of April 1962, resulting in independence the following October.

Of all the three East African territories, Tanganyika presented the fewer obstacles to independence. Under the leadership of Julius Nyerere, the Tanganyika African National Union (TANU) was organized in 1954, and following a program of gradual advancement toward self-government that was marked by cordial relations between TANU and British officials, Tanganyika achieved independence on December 9, 1961.

## THE MAHDIST STATE

After the fall of Khartoum the Mahdists quickly secured control of all the Sudan except for a few enclaves on the northern, eastern, and southern frontiers. The Mahdi regarded the fall of Khartoum as but the beginning of holy war throughout the Muslim world, but he never lived to carry out this larger design. On June 22, 1885, he died of the plague, six months after his greatest victory at Khartoum. The death of the Mahdi brought to a head all the underlying tensions of the revolutionary movement. The three groups—the pious men, the riverain tribes from which came the slave traders, and the Baggara—now became bitter rivals in the struggle for control of the Mahdist state. From the first the Baggara appeared the strongest of the three groups, and their support of their kinsman, Khalifa Abd Allahi, was decisive in his selection as the Mahdi's successor. The Khalifa set out at once to secure his position. He neutralized his riverain rivals as well as the Mahdi's relatives, the Ashraf, whose influences had steadily diminished after their kinsman's death. He then appointed his Baggara supporters to key positions in the Mahdist Army. Once the threat to his rule was overcome, the Khalifa sought to extend the holy war beyond the borders of the Sudan, but after several years of campaigning on the frontiers of Egypt, Ethiopia, and Equatoria, his forces had made few gains and many losses. In 1889 the Mahdist Army, while advancing into Egypt, was crushingly defeated at Tushki, ending the Khalifa's attempts to carry Mahdism to the Muslim lands of the Middle East. Moreover, conditions in the Sudan after 1889 precluded any attempt to renew the holy war. A sequence of poor harvests in 1889 and 1890 brought famine and epidemic, aggravated by the large and unproductive standing armies on the frontiers and exacerbated by the decision of the Khalifa to bring the Baggara nomads from their western grazing lands to settle in Omdurman, the capital of the Mahdist state, situated across the White Nile from the ruins of Khartoum. Ever since he had succeeded the Mahdi, the Khalifa had found himself surrounded by the riverain tribes that had never reconciled themselves to his rule. He now sought to bring the Baggara to Omdurman as a counterweight, or a tribal standing army, to secure his position. Although they were reluctant to leave their beloved plains, the Baggara obeyed and came to settle in the capital. Unhappily they failed from the very beginning to play

the role the Khalifa expected of them. Wild and unruly, they never proved an effective instrument of government. Moreover, they were unproductive in times of famine and flaunted their privileged position before the settled cultivators, who, with their literary and religious traditions, rightly regarded the Baggara as ignorant and uncouth interlopers. Once again the riverain tribes, joined by the Mahdi's kinsmen, sought to seize power, but the Khalifa was able to put down the revolt and break the political power of the rebels. By 1892 peace and prosperity had returned to the Sudan, and the position of the Khalifa was never more secure. Gradually the Khalifa sought to transform the state into an Islamic monarchy, intending that the succession should pass to his son. More and more he himself retired from public view, defended by a bodyguard (*mulazimiyya*) that was, in effect, a reliable and powerful standing army. To be sure, his rule was autocratic, but as the threat of an Anglo-Egyptian power loomed on the northern horizon there was a gradual consolidation of Sudanese support for the regime and a widespread feeling that any invasion from the north would be an attempt to interfere with Sudanese independence.

## EUROPEAN POWERS ON THE UPPER NILE

After the fall of Khartoum in 1885, the British government had neither reason nor desire to conquer the Sudan. Ten years later it had both. This great sea change in British policy was the result of Britain's determination to remain in Egypt. In 1882 the British occupation was regarded as temporary—until order throughout the country was restored and reforms were undertaken. Unfortunately, the task of regenerating Egypt required a British presence longer than any British government, whether Conservative or Liberal, had originally contemplated. By 1890 the British had decided to remain in Egypt, not only to complete their task of modernization but to defend the bondholders and the Suez Canal—the lifeline of the empire to the East. But once the decision to remain in Egypt had been made, British officials in both Cairo and London had to secure their position in Egypt, and since the life of Egypt depends on the Upper Nile, Britain's position had to be secured in the Sudan as well. At first there was no cause for alarm. The Mahdists, who controlled the Sudan, had neither the technological skills nor the interest to obstruct the flow of the Nile waters on which the life and stability of Egypt depended, but in 1889 European nations that possessed the capabilities to cut off the river flow sought to advance into the Nile Valley. Clearly, the British would have to ward off their European competitors by diplomacy, and failing that, by the outright military conquest of the Sudan.

The first threat came from the Italians, who in 1889 sought to slip into the Nile Valley from their sphere of influence in Abyssinia. The second threat came from the Germans in 1890, whose explorers were moving toward the headwaters of the Nile, the central African lakes. Lord Salisbury, the British Prime Minister, resolved both dangers by diplomacy, defining the German sphere in the Anglo-German (Heligoland) Agreement of 1890 and the Italian sphere in the Anglo-Italian Treaty of 1891, so that both nations were denied access to the Nile Valley. However, in keeping the Germans out, Salisbury had unwittingly let King Leopold in by providing him with a way to the Nile. But if Leopold was to become a long-standing irritation in Salisbury's Nile policy, the French soon became a very real and powerful threat.

France had always opposed the British occupation of Egypt and never lost an opportunity to try to force the British to leave. French interests in Egypt stretched back to Napoleon's abortive oc-cupation in 1799 and had been carried on throughout the nineteenth century by French traders and scholars who were foremost in the study of Pharaonic Egypt's great monuments and ruins. When France had been invited to join with Britain in the task of restoring order to Egypt in 1882 she had refused, only to find herself excluded from Egypt and resentful of the British occupation all the more because of her own indecisiveness. Thus in 1893, after the French were abruptly rebuffed for suggesting Anglo-French negotiations to effect a British withdrawal, French officials seriously began to consider forcing the British to evacuate Egypt. The instrument to ac-complish such a bold stroke in the face of British power was the French Fashoda expedition.

The Fashoda expedition was con-ceived in 1893 for the purpose of march-ing from French possessions on the coast of western Africa, across the continent, to the Shilluk village of Fashoda on the White Nile in territory that was at that time under Mahdist influence. Once as-tride the Nile the French, with their technical capabilities, could threaten to construct barrages and dams if the Brit-ish did not acquiesce in withdrawal from Egypt. Like many other French projects during the partition of Africa, the Fashoda expedition had a heroic, car-tographic sweep, but few seem to have considered the dangers of a head-on col-lision with Britain on the Upper Nile. Almost from the inception of the plan the British government knew of the Fashoda expedition. As with the Ger-mans and the Italians, the British sought to exclude the French by diplomacy, first by leasing the southern Sudan to Leopold of the Belgians, thereby block-ing a French advance to Fashoda, and second by offering territories in West Af-rica to keep the French out of the Nile Valley. The French forced Leopold to repudiate the first project, while haughtily rejecting the second. The race to Fashoda was on.

In the center of all this activity the Italian position in Ethiopia suddenly collapsed, enabling both the British and the French to make gains. On March 1, 1896, the Italian Army, advancing into Ethiopia, was destroyed by the Ethiopian Army under the Emperor Menelik. Not only was this battle a significant victory by a technologically backward people over a European invader, but the Italians, in their distress, appealed to the British for a demonstration in the Sudan to relieve Mahdist pressure on their position at Kassala. Clearly, an advance into the Sudan from the Anglo-Egyptian outpost of Wadi-Halfa could hardly have saved the Italians at Kassala some 700 miles away, but the British Cabinet saw the Italian pleas for support as an opportunity to acquire Sudanese real estate without objections from the other European powers. Thus in 1896 Anglo-Egyptian forces advanced to Dunqula and began to prepare for a final advance to Omdurman. But the French were as quick to profit from Italian misfortune as the British, thus replacing the Italians as the most influential Europeans at the court of Menelik. In 1897 France secured the emperor's dubious support for a French expedition to Fashoda from the east and by the beginning of 1898 was inexorably closing in on its goal. After several abortive attempts, a French expedition under Faivre reached the mouth of the Sobat in June and planted the French flag but was forced to retire by the heat, fever, and lack of supplies. In the west Marchand was more determined. Moving up the rivers and crossing over the Congo-Nile watershed, he and his men made their way through the swamps of the Nile and reached Fashoda in July, six weeks after Faivre's furtive visit to the east bank.

Although Marchand had beaten the British to Fashoda, the powerful and well-supplied Anglo-Egyptian forces were not far behind. Advancing up the Nile in 1898 under the command of General Kitchener, they swept all before them, defeating the Mahdist Army at the Atbara and moving to Omdurman, where, on September 2, 1898, the great army that the Khalifa had assembled was destroyed on the plains of Karari outside the city. Five days later Kitchener and a strong flotilla headed south up the White Nile toward Fashoda. Here, in a dramatic confrontation with Captain Marchand, Kitchener demanded that the French retire. Marchand refused. The great Fashoda crisis was on.

The immediate reaction in both Britain and France was to fight, and although today it appears absurd for the two great liberal powers to have plunged into war for possession of the desolate swamps of the Upper Nile, it must be remembered that Fashoda was a symbol of two imperial designs of sweeping proportions and that the fate of far-off lands from West Africa to the Far East would be determined by the outcome of the crisis. The British prepared for war, but unhappily for the French, France could not. Deserted by her allies, torn by the Dreyfus Affair, and with her navy in deplorable condition, France was in no position to make war. Marchand was recalled, and the French recognized British influence throughout the Upper Nile. This influence, however, did not go unchallenged. In their diplomatic maneuvering to check the French, the British had leased a large portion of the Bahr al-Ghazal to the Congo Free State in 1894. Leopold now revived these rights, and only after many years of frustrating negotiations and numerous near–clashes between British and Congolese forces did Leopold finally agree to withdraw upon his death. In 1909 he died. Six months later the last of his territory in the Nile Valley was handed over to the English authorities. The Upper Nile basin, from its source to its mouth, was at last securely British.

## THE ANGLO-EGYPTIAN CONDOMINIUM

The defeat of the Mahdist state created complex legal and diplomatic problems for the British. The reconquest of the Sudan had been undertaken on British initiative and with British financial and military support, yet the Sudan was the former territory of Egypt and had been retaken in her name. But no Englishman, in 1898 or later, was prepared to return the Sudan to the maladministration of the Egyptians against whom the Sudanese had first rebelled. Yet to attach the Sudan to the British Empire would be a gross injustice to Egypt's historical claims. The result was the condominium—an ingenious device whereby sovereignty was conferred jointly in the Khedive of Egypt and the British Crown. Within the Sudan, however, the supreme military and civil command was vested in a governor–general nominated by the British government and appointed by the Khedive. The result was not a true condominium (joint partnership) but an administration dominated by British officials and served by Egyptian officials. Nevertheless, so long as Britain controlled Egypt, the Anglo-Egyptian condominium in the Sudan worked smoothly, but after the independence of Egypt had been won, the British and Egyptians in the Sudan became bitter rivals.

Although the battle of Karari brought about the collapse of the Mahdist state, dangers to the new administration appeared on every side. For a decade local risings of Mahdists in the northern Sudan, as well as rebellions of those who claimed to be the Mahdi's successors, were crushed. Even more difficult was the establishment of British rule in the southern Sudan, where the Nilotes opposed the British as they had done all alien invaders. Over a generation passed before the southern Sudan accepted imperial rule and the transformation of traditional customs resulting therefrom.

The administration of the Sudan at first consisted of military personnel and later of civilians from Oxford and Cambridge Universities who joined the Sudan Political Service and, although it was always a relatively small group (no more than 150 administrative officers at any one time), the administration developed an *esprit de corps* that was the envy of both the Colonial Service and the Indian Civil Service. The primary task of the administration was to establish order and win over Sudanese acquiescence to alien, Christian rule. Taxes were light, education was practical, and the basic infrastructure—railroads, steamers, and communications—was constructed to provide the foundation (particularly in the Gezira region between the White and the Blue Niles) for large-scale economic development. Under the leadership of Kitchener and Sir Reginald Wingate, his successor as governor-general, the Sudan gradually cast off its dependence on Egypt and quietly developed ever-increasing independence.

The outbreak of the First World War provided an opportunity for the Sudan government to stabilize its western frontier by incorporating the Sultanate of Darfur into the Anglo-Egyptian Sudan. Upon the defeat of the Khalifa and the downfall of the Mahdist State in 1898, the Sultan of Darfur, Ali Dinar, who had been held in exile in Omdurman by the Khalifa, had fled to El Fasher, the capital, whence he established his authority over the sultanate. Lacking the resources to conquer this remote but historic state, despite its location in the Nile basin, the officials of the Sudan government tacitly recognized his rule in return for a minor tribute. The very autonomy of Darfur, however, prevented the delimitation of the frontier between French and British territories. Concern increased in Khartoum when French forces annexed Wadai in 1909 and seized much of Dar Masalit in 1911; both sultanates lay directly west of Darfur along the Nile watershed. Following the Anglo-French alliance at the declaration of war, Ali Dinar found himself increasingly isolated and susceptible to Ottoman propaganda and requests to join the *jihad*, or holy war, against the infidel British in the Sudan. As a result of Ottoman encouragement and promises of arms, Ali Dinar became more truculent, writing insulting letters to the governor-general of the Sudan, and reinforcing a border garrison. These hostile acts provided the Sudan government with the excuse to invade Darfur, defeat the Fur army, and occupy El Fasher on May 23, 1916. Five months later, Ali Dinar was surprised in his camp and shot to death, bringing a close to a thousand years of history. (Ali Dinar, *The Last Sultan of Darfur*)

The future course of events in the Sudan was conditioned by the assassination of Sir Lee Stack, commander of the Egyptian Army *(Sirdar)* and governor-general of the Sudan, in Cairo in 1924. His murder by Egyptian nationalists convinced the British officials in the Sudan of their own anti-Egyptian attitudes. In retaliation the British removed Egyptians from the Sudan, forcibly when necessary, and although British officials in London refused to terminate the condominium, for all practical purposes Egyptian participation in the Sudan ceased to exist. Moreover, Stack's assassination created a crisis between the rulers and the ruled. Rather than turn to the small number of Western-educated Sudanese, British officials fell back on their more conservative fathers, the traditional leaders and the hereditary chiefs. As previously mentioned, this technique of ruling through tribal leaders was known as indirect rule and was regarded as a preliminary stage in the political development of African peoples. In reality, indirect rule frequently resulted in the appointment of authorities who were regarded as servants of the government and not of the people, while the officials themselves adopted a pater-

nalism toward the chiefs that turned to scorn for their sons who were educated and oriented to the West (Sir John Maffey, *British Rule in the Sudan*).

In the late 1930s new forces appeared in the Sudan. The Anglo-Egyptian Treaty of 1936 permitted the return of Egyptians to the Sudan, and although they never regained the ground lost after their expulsion in 1924, their presence was increasingly felt in the rise of Sudanese nationalism. During the early 1920s embryonic Sudanese nationalists, such as Abd al-Latif and members of the White Flag League, had sought to rally support against the British. At best they were naïve and at worst confused, but their program collapsed in the face of British resistance and was not revived until the formation of the Graduates' General Congress, consisting of educated Sudanese who represented a national consciousness and not simply the more limited, tribal concerns of their fathers. Supported both morally and with money by the Egyptians, the Congress asserted in 1942 that it spoke for all Sudanese nationalists and raised difficult constitutional questions about the future of the Sudan. Preoccupied by the threat of German and Italian advances into the Middle East, the Sudan government brusquely refused to recognize the claims of the Congress. The result was a split between the extremists, known as the Ashiqqa, and the moderate elements who grouped themselves under the Umma. The Umma was supported by the Mahdists under the leadership of Sayyid Abd al-Rahman, al Mahdi. The Ashiqqa was supported by the patronage of Sayyid Ali al-Mirghani, the leader of the Khatmiyya *tariqa* (traditional religious rivals of the Mahdists). The alliances between the Umma and the Mahdists and the Ashiqqa and the Khatmiyya evoked all the bitter memories of the past and revived the feuds between the riverain peoples of the Nile and the wild Baggara nomads of the west. The hatreds and suspicions that were aroused soured Sudanese politics for years, bringing independent parliamentary government into disrepute.

However, the British officials of the Sudan government did not ignore the stirrings of the new Sudanese elite and in 1944 set up an Advisory Council to consult with the governor–general, which was followed in 1947 by a Legislative Council with even greater powers of legislative initiative. The Egyptians regarded such unilateral actions with great suspicion, but after the coup d'état in Egypt in 1952 the military government sought to come to an accommodation with all the Sudanese political parties, and with the essential support of the Sudanese was able to force favorable amendments to a draft self-government statute that was put forward by the Sudanese government. Without the confidence of the Sudanese the British gave way, and according to the amended self-government statute elections were held that resulted in the triumph of the pro-Egyptian former Ashiqqa leader, Ismail al-Azhari, and his Khatmiyya supporters, who formed the hard core of the National Unionist Party.

Ismail al-Azhari was elected Prime Minister in January 1954. His principal task was to determine the future of the self-governing Sudan, whether as an independent country or an autonomous part of Egypt. Although Azhari had campaigned in 1953 on the slogan of "the unity of the Nile Valley," the possibility of tying the Sudan to Egypt became increasingly remote. Anti-Egyptian riots by Umma supporters in 1954, followed by the revolt of the Equatorial Battalion in the southern Sudan, convinced Azhari that any declaration of the Sudan as part of Egypt would have resulted in civil war. Thus in 1955, as the full effect of responsible government was brought home to him, Azhari abandoned his earlier campaign promises and, on January 1, 1956, unilaterally declared the Sudan an independent republic.

## THE INDEPENDENT SUDAN

The parliamentary government bequeathed to the Sudanese by Great Britain was at first held in high esteem as a symbol of nationalism and independence, but it became clear that at best the parliament was a superficial instrument. Parties, the machinery by which parliamentary government functions, were, in the Sudan, not well-organized groups with distinct objectives, but loose alliances attached to personal interests and sectarian loyalties. Such groups were difficult to manage, almost impossible to direct. When the tactics of party management were exhausted, parliament became debased, benefiting only those politicians who reaped the rewards of power and patronage. Disillusioned with their experiment in liberal democracy, the Sudanese turned once again to the authoritarianism to which their traditions had accustomed them.

On November 16, 1958, General Ibrahim Abboud, with the blessing of the parliamentary Prime Minister, Abdallah Khalil, seized control of the government in a bloodless coup d'état. Few in the Sudan mourned the passing of parliament and, in fact, the greatest threat to the new regime came from within the army itself, as the colonels maneuvered for power until, by November 1959, Abboud was able to suppress their plots. Despite the internal struggles, military rule brought rapid improvement in the Sudan's deteriorating economic position and, in 1959, the resolution of a long-standing dispute with Egypt over the Nile waters. These were positive achievements marred only by the continuing conflict in the southern Sudan precipitated by the mutiny of the Equatorial Corps in August 1955. Determined to maintain a united Sudan, both the parliamentary regime and its military successor sought to crush the Southern Sudanese dissidents for whom the Arabization and Islamization of the Northern Sudan had little appeal. The politicians had been moderate in their efforts to impose new cultural values upon the indigenous African cultures of the Southern Sudanese, but the army officers of the military government operated under no such restraints, and numerous measures designed to facilitate the spread of Arabic and Islam were introduced by the Abboud regime. The Southern reaction was flight and rebellion. This was followed by increased repression that was in turn met with ever more vigorous reaction by the organized insurgents known as the Anya-Nya guerrilla movement.

The failure of General Abboud to resolve the "Southern Problem" led him to appoint a twenty-five man commission to seek a solution in the South. Meanwhile, the Northern intelligentsia, the trade unions, and the civil servants, as well as the powerful religious brotherhoods, were bored and disgusted with the incapacity of the military regime. In 1958, these groups had applauded the efforts of the patriotic and progressive army officers to clean the Aegean stables of Sudanese parliamentarianism, and to solve pressing economic and international problems. But within a few years after the military government had consolidated its power, the intelligentsia had come to resent its exclusion from the councils of government and the trade unions to chafe at the restrictions placed upon their activities, while the civil servants sulked at orders from their military ministers. Even the more conservative religious brotherhoods grew restless when they were unable to carry on their former political activities. Military reviews, parades, and heroic pronouncements proved no substitute for the enthusiasm of party politics and the passions stirred by political action. If they even considered the problem, the mili-

tary rulers never did provide an outlet for the political frustrations of the Sudanese. In the end, the regime was overwhelmed by boredom. It was overthrown in October 1964 by the reaction to its lassitude and its failure in the Southern Sudan. On November 14, 1964, General Abboud officially resigned as President of the Republic, and a Transitional Government was formed under the leadership of Sirr al-Khatim al-Khalifa, a civil servant with no political affiliation who was extremely popular among the Southern Sudanese.

The Transitional Government was not a stable institution but a misalliance of intellectuals of the "Professional Front," who favored a radical restructuring of the country's economic and political systems, and the conservative political parties, whose notables, secure in the knowledge that they could command the votes of their sectarian followers, sought to insure their own dominant position in Sudanese affairs. The demand for democracy was overwhelming, and the fragile and constantly changing coalition of Sirr al-Khatim al-Khalifa agreed to hold elections in April 1965.

While attempting to govern in Khartoum, the Transitional Government also sought to deal with the intransigent Southern Problem. The urgent need to end the Southern conflict was made all the clearer when hundreds were killed in clashes between Northern and Southern Sudanese in Khartoum on December 6, 1964, Bloody Sunday. This event led to the convening, on March 16, 1965, of the Round Table Conference, at which representatives of all the principal political parties, together with leading Southerners, sought to negotiate peace in the Sudan. They failed. Neither side appeared committed to peace, although they agreed on certain rhetorical principles to determine a policy for the South; the adamant positions adopted by Northerners and Southerners on the constitutional status of the South precluded any practical arrangement acceptable to both.

Meanwhile, preparations were undertaken for the long-awaited elections in April. The election returned a coalition government of the traditional sectarian parties, the Umma Party of the Mahdists, and the National Unionist Party of the Mirghani family (NUP—later renamed the Democratic Unionist Party, or DUP), with the veteran Umma politician Mohammed Ahmed Mahgoub as Premier. Though supposedly a "national" government, the coalition was no more successful in dealing with the problem of the Southern Sudan, or in maintaining internal cohesion, than its predecessors. In the Southern Sudan, Southerners were massacred in Juba and Wau in July 1965 by the Sudan Army. The army was faced, however, with ever-greater resistance from the Anya-Nya, who had acquired sophisticated weapons from the Congo and other foreign sources. Nor was political life in Khartoum improved by the Sudan's second experiment in democracy. Mahgoub was pompous and ineffective; Ismail al-Azhari, the leader of the NUP opposition, was obsessed with his own petty ambitions. Both were more concerned with sectarian and personal politics than with democracy. Expediency rather than principles characterized the administration of the war-torn Sudan. This did not end with the coming of age and accession to the Premiership of Sadiq al-Mahdi, the great-grandson of the nineteenth-century religious reformer, Muhammad Ahmad al-Mahdi.

The personal rivalries among Sadiq, Mahgoub, and Azhari brought no stability to the government in Khartoum, and gradually eroded Sudanese confidence in the parliamentary system. Political manipulation and personal maneuvers brought only discredit to the Sudan's leaders. When Colonel Jaafar Numayri, leader of the Free Officers' movement, seized control of the government in a bloodless coup d'état at the end of May 1969, few mourned the passing of the second parliamentary regime.

Numayri's government consisted of a Revolutionary Command Council (RCC) of ten members and a cabinet of twenty-three responsible to the RCC. Numayri himself was not motivated by any particular ideology, considering himself more the successor of the Professionals' Front than another General Abboud. He took a centrist position that challenged both the right and the left.

The right struck first, in March 1970, when the leader of the Ansar, the Imam al-Hadi, from his stronghold on Aba Island in the White Nile south of Khartoum, defied Numayri, precipitating rioting in Omdurman. This resulted in an invasion of Aba Island on March 27 in which over 12,000 Ansar were killed, including the Imam himself. The next challenge came from the left. Numayri's relations with the Sudan Communist Party had, from the beginning, been ambiguous at best, uncertain at worst. Following his victory over the Ansar, Numayri's relations with the Communists rapidly deteriorated. Although he extended the Sudan's relations with socialist states and employed much of the rhetoric of the Communist Party, he became increasingly suspicious of their objectives and aware of the latent hostility of the Sudanese toward communism. On July 19, 1971, an attempted coup was staged by Major Hashim al-Ata. Numayri was taken captive, and a new regime which would carry out an industrial and agrarian revolution was proclaimed. Major Hashim, however, had miscalculated the Sudanese response to a government openly committed to communism. Numayri himself made a daring escape from the palace, rallied his loyal troops, and, with timely assistance from Libya and Egypt, crushed the coup, destroyed the Communist Party and its leaders, and purged leftists from the army and the government.

Having eliminated any threat from right or left, Numayri had to deal with the single most intractable problem of the country, one which had been the downfall of all previous governments—the Problem of the Southern Sudan. He had other pressing problems, as well. His victories over the Ansar and the Communists had denied him the support of significant and influential groups within the Sudan, while his flirtations with the Soviet bloc had alienated the Sudan's traditional friends among the Arabs and in the West. He sought to resolve all three of these dilemmas by a drastic reorientation of his domestic and foreign politics to include peace with the South and the establishment of a single party, the Sudan Socialist Union (SSU). The party would buttress his administration within the Sudan, and reorient foreign policy to favor the West and the Arab states, particularly Egypt, rather than the Eastern bloc.

Numayri's greatest, although ultimately ephemeral, achievement, was the conclusion of peace with the Anya-Nya in the Addis Ababa Agreement of February 1972, in which the Southern Sudan emerged with a significant degree of autonomy, broadening Numayri's base of support. Immediately following the communist coup d'état, Numayri appointed Abel Alier, the respected Southern lawyer from Bor, as Minister for Southern Affairs with a mandate to seek peace with the Anya-Nya. On their part, the Anya-Nya had been growing year by year in strength by acquiring arms from abroad and distributing them under the supervision of Joseph Lagu. Lagu brought together the numerous but ineffective political groupings which had always been distrustful of each other because of personality conflicts and historic ethnic rivalries. Under Lagu, personalities and ethnic politics were submerged, as the Anya-Nya served as the military arm of the Southern Sudan Liberation Movement. Both sides to the conflict were weary of war, and after a series of secret meetings and the timely intervention of the Emperor Haile Se-

lassie, the Addis Ababa Agreement was concluded, and, on March 3, 1972, became the *Regional Self-Government Act for Southern Provinces*. (The Problem of the Southern Sudan: *The Addis Ababa Agreement* February 27, 1972)

The Addis Ababa Agreement created regional autonomy for the three southern provinces of the Sudan with its own legislature (the People's Regional Assembly), and its own executive (the High Executive Council) with authority over all local affairs. The central government retained control over defense, foreign affairs, currency, and other national concerns, such as economic and educational planning. The agreement was hailed as one of the few settlements of internecine strife to be achieved peacefully, by compromise and negotiation. President Numayri received international recognition as a statesman of stature for his common sense, if not his wisdom. He had indeed broadened his base of support, particularly in the South, and his position appeared unassailable.

He himself, however, did not appear to appreciate that lasting peace in the Sudan required more than a dramatic gesture at Addis Ababa. The Southern Sudan had been ravaged by seventeen years of civil war, but the Southern Regional Government, led by Abel Alier, never received from Khartoum the resources or support for social and economic development either promised or implied during the negotiations at Addis Ababa. On their part, the Southern politicians devoted much of their energy to fighting amongst themselves for the few spoils, rather than to the regeneration of their war-torn land. Their failure to put regional interests above their own brought them disrepute among their own people and the contempt of the Northern Sudanese. It also led to intervention by President Numayri in the governance of the South—in direct and unilateral contravention of the Addis Ababa Agreement. In October 1981, Numayri dissolved the Regional Assembly and dismissed Abel Alier. After a series of convoluted and cynical maneuvers, the Southern Sudan was redivided into the three old provinces of the Bahr al-Ghazal, Equatoria, and the Upper Nile. Regional autonomy and the Addis Ababa Agreement was dead, and, with its demise, Southern support for President Numayri dissolved.

This tragedy in the South was accompanied by deteriorating political and economic life in the Northern Sudan. Determined to replace the last vestiges of the traditional authorities *(Nazir, Shaykh, Omda)*, Numayri introduced a pyramidal structure of local government linked with the Sudan Socialist Union, the sole political organization in the Sudan. The administration of the Sudan was now no longer in the hands of rustic and "unprogressive" chiefs, but in those of a highly politicized bureaucracy—inefficient, top-heavy, corrupt, and alien to the customs and traditional laws of the rural peoples who comprised ninety-five percent of the Sudanese. This unwieldly structure could neither administer nor govern, so all decision-making, no matter how trivial, was soon concentrated in the hands of President Numayri. Numayri in turn increasingly used the administrative structure which he had created (the SSU) as an instrument to support his personal control and a vehicle for distributing personal patronage. The members of the former personal parties, the Umma of the Mahdists and the DUP of the Mirghanists, consoled themselves by profitable collaboration or sullen opposition.

The decline of Sudanese political life was matched by vacillation and mismanagement of the economy. During his early "leftist" years, Numayri had instituted widespread nationalization, but after the failure of the communist coup of 1971, and the Addis Ababa Agreement of 1972, the Sudan turned increasingly to the West and neighboring Arab states for economic assistance. Abandoning the policy of state intervention, the government created large schemes of economic development in which foreign investment was encouraged. Unfortunately, the new economic policies came at a time of world-wide depression in the markets that absorbed much of the Sudan's agricultural commodities. These global events, however, cannot account for the mismanagement of the economy throughout Numayri's regime. Mesmerized by the prospects of large-scale economic developments, the government neglected older projects like the Gezira and the railways. The result was a disastrous decline in productivity, while Numayri and his managers, the recipients in the 1970s of large sums of money from their oil-rich Arab neighbors, inaugurated huge, ambitious agricultural schemes. These projects were designed as the productive vindication of the regime, but, in fact, they required long-term investment before profitability could meet intermediate costs. By 1980, the Sudan Government had lost control of the economy. Numayri's unending search for popular support delayed until 1981 his introduction of austerity measures demanded by the World Bank. They proved too little and too late. Imports continued to rise as exports continued to decline. Corruption and the black market flourished, while the external debt soared out of all proportion. By 1984, the Sudan's economy had been further battered, seemingly beyond repair, by drought, by the renewal of the civil war, and by the imposition of the *Sharia*, the holy law of Islam.

In September 1983 President Numayri announced the imposition of the Sharia. It was to be vigorously enforced by, among other measures, the *huddud*, or physical punishment (loss of limbs, stoning, flogging), for the crimes of theft, adultery, and consumption of alcohol. In a country as ethnically and religiously diverse as the Sudan, where a third of the population are non-Muslim, the results were disastrous. With his popular support dwindling, Numayri sought to embrace religion, falling under the influence of holy men and the Muslim Brotherhood. Numayri sought to confirm his place in heaven, as well as on earth, by seeking their support through the establishment of the Sharia. He only succeeded in further disrupting the economy with the replacement of income and other taxes by Islamic taxation, the *zakat*, resulting in a collapse of government revenue. Nature intervened also, providing the most severe drought and famine in recorded history. Numayri refused to acknowledge the severity of the disaster or to alleviate the plight of its victims. International pressure and aid agencies finally came to the rescue, but not before half a million Sudanese had perished.

The greatest blow to the Numayri regime came, however, before the famine or the imposition of the Sharia when, in May 1983, Colonel John Garang led the 105th battalion of the Sudan Army stationed at Bor into the bush in rebellion against the government. Mismanagement, corruption, and above all Numayri's destruction of the Addis Ababa Agreement were the spurs to the revolt. The famine and declaration of Sharia only strengthened Garang's determination to revolt. A well-educated and respected officer in the army, Garang swiftly established the Sudan People's Liberation Movement (SPLM), a powerful and sophisticated political organization whose military representatives, the Sudan People's Liberation Army (SPLA), have since consistently defeated the poorly equipped, ill-led, and demoralized units of the Sudan Army stationed in the Southern Sudan. (John Garang de Mabior: *The Genesis of the Sudan People's Liberation Movement (SPLM)*, 1983). Supported by Ethiopia and its large armory of Soviet weapons, Garang and his men were fighting not only for the downfall of

Numayri, but for a democratically elected, federated Sudan. They were determined to avoid another government controlled by the notables of the Mahdists and Mirghani families in Khartoum, to the detriment of the rural peoples on the peripheries in the West (Darfur), the South, the North (Nubia), and the East (Beja).

By 1984, the collapse of the economy, the famine, the Sharia, and the civil war had brought an end to the legendary tolerance of the Sudanese. Even the army turned against Numayri, and, reluctantly succumbing to a populist revolt while Numayri was on a visit to Washington, the Commander-in-Chief, Abd al-Rahman Muhammad Siwar al-Dahab, announced the formation of a Transitional Military Council to rule in the Sudan. Although there was doubt about the intentions of the military, the army agreed to appoint a civilian cabinet, and conducted an election in April 1986 which produced no clear majority for any of the revived political parties. The largest single party, the Umma, under the leadership of Sadiq al-Mahdi, formed a coalition with the Mirghanists of the DUP, but the greatest gainers were the Muslim Brothers under Hasan al-Turabi. At first the Sudanese regarded this third experiment in democracy as the beginning of a new era. These hopes were soon dashed and their disillusionment confirmed, as three years passed without a solution to the problems of war or famine, only political manipulations and machinations by the notables in Khartoum. Sadiq al-Mahdi, despite his Oxford education, rhetoric, and historic position as the great grandson of the Mahdi, proved incapable of dealing with any of the problems facing the Sudan, let alone the civil war in the South. There John Garang and the SPLA continued, with embarrassing consistency, to defeat the Sudan Army and dominate the region. By the spring of 1989, Sadiq had lost all popularity and credence among even his followers in the Umma. His prevarications, mistakes, and conflicting charges marked by personal interest and vanity put him in a position where he was forced to accept, in March 1989, a Government of National Salvation in which all parties, except the Muslim Brothers (National Islamic Front, or NIF), but including the trade unions, the professions, and the army, signed the four-point Charter of Peace. The charter was based on the principles of the "Peace Initiative" negotiated by representatives of the DUP and the SPLM in Addis Ababa on November 16, 1988, which was designed to bring peace with honor to the Sudan.

These hopes for peace were, however, yet again frustrated by the coup d'etat of Colonel Umar Bashir on June 30, 1989, and which has since represented the ideology of the Muslim Brothers.

## THE RISE AND FALL OF HAILE SELASSIE

In November 1930 Ras Tafari ended his long quest to be the Conquering Lion of Judah, Elect of God, and King of Kings of Ethiopia with his coronation as Emperor Haile Selassie I. His goal was to modernize Ethiopia by breaking the authority of the traditional nobility through concentrating power at his capital of Addis Ababa. The legal basis for his policies of centralization was formally established in the constitution of July 1931. The emperor, and the emperor alone, was to wield power over the legislature, the judiciary, and the army. His objective was to replace the feudal barons with civil servants appointed by, and consequently loyal to, himself.

The centralizing policies of Haile Selassie did not go unchallenged. By 1934, however, he had suppressed provincial revolts and appointed reliable followers in the Amhara territories of Showa, Gojam, and Gondar, as well as in Kafa and Sidamo to the South and West. In order to modernize and bind together the empire, Haile Selassie increasingly recruited foreign advisors. The new military academy at Holeto was administered by Swedish officers; the Imperial Bodyguard was trained by the Belgians; an American construction company was employed to carry out the surveys for a dam at Lake Tana. Elementary and secondary schools were established at Addis Ababa; their purpose was to train a cadre of Ethiopians to participate in the process of modernization and centralization. Electricity, telegraph, and telephone services were introduced; the Bank of Ethiopia was established in 1931 to issue Ethiopian currency with Haile Selassie's portrait prominently featured on the notes of exchange. These internal developments were accompanied by an international effort to include Ethiopia in the family of nations. As early as 1919, Ras Tafari, as Regent to the Empress Zawditu, sought to join the League of Nations; he thought this would protect his vulnerable kingdom from the designs of imperial interlopers. The League of Nations granted Ethiopia full and legitimate membership in 1919 on condition that she end the slave trade.

The Regent-Emperor was primarily concerned about Italian designs in the Horn of Africa. The Italian invasion of Ethiopia in 1896 had not been forgotten. Despite their defeat at Adua, the Italians had retained control of Eritrea (Latin: *Maro Erythenan* or Red Sea). There they carried out numerous development projects under a succession of able Italian administrators, who were sensitive enough to include Eritreans in the civil service, and in their medical and agricultural projects. These progressive moves were frustrated by the advent of the government of Benito Mussolini, whose fascist ideology presupposed the racial superiority of the Italians to the Africans. The Eritreans became second-class citizens in their own land, which the Italian government regarded merely as a base for further expansion.

By 1935, the intentions of Mussolini's government had become clear. Italy was prepared to acquire Ethiopia for the "New Roman Empire" by force of arms. Despite the Treaty of Friendship which Italy had negotiated with Ethiopia in 1928, the Italian government pursued an aggressive policy in the Horn of Africa. Mussolini was undisturbed by the impotent foreign policies of Britain and France, and was encouraged by the belligerence of a resurgent Germany. In December 1934, at Wal Wal, the site of several dismal wells used by Somali nomads some sixty miles within acknowledged Ethiopian territory, Ethiopian and Italian forces clashed. The League of Nations, dominated by Great Britain and France, exonerated both parties—indicating to Mussolini that he was free to pursue a forward course in his imperial designs, unhindered by any objections from the Great Powers.

On October 3, 1935, Italy launched its offensive against Ethiopia from its base in Eritrea and Somaliland without a declaration of war. On October 7th, the League unanimously declared Italy the aggressor, but took no action. The war lasted seven months. To achieve victory, the Italians used poison gas and air power against the valiant but outgunned defense of the Ethiopians; they also skilfully played upon provincial rivalries which Haile Selassie had neither the time nor the resources to overcome. By April 1936, Italian forces had reached Lake Tana while driving westward from Harrar. On May 3, 1936, Haile Selassie left Addis Ababa for Djibouti, where a British frigate took him to Jerusalem. On May 5th, Marshal Pietro Badoglio entered the capital, and four days later Italy formally annexed the last independent African territory (excepting, perhaps, the ambiguously independent Republic of Liberia).

On June 30, 1936, Haile Selassie ad-dressed the League of Nations in Geneva. He spoke in Amharic, but his message was abundantly clear: the League could support one of its members, on the principle of collective security, or it could countenance international lawlessness. (Haile Selassie: At The League of Nations June 30, 1936). The League had the choice of accepting its obligations or of suffering dishonor. It chose dishonor. Britain and France recognized the Italian protectorate in Ethiopia; the United States and Russia refused. The League of Nations was destroyed as an international agency. The diminutive but courageous figure of Haile Selassie pleading for the cause of his nation inspired the highest tribute which the influential *Time* magazine could bestow on an individual:

"blind sympathy for uncivilized Ethiopia throughout the civilized world. In the wake of the world's grandiose Depression, with millions of white men uncertain as to the benefits of civilization, 1935 produced a peculiar Spirit of the Year in which it was felt to be a crying shame that the Machine Age seemed about to intrude upon Africa's last free unscattered and simple people. They were *ipso facto* Noble Savages, and the noblest Ethiopian of them all naturally emerged as Man of the Year."[1]

In June 1936, the Italians combined all of their holdings in the Horn of Africa—Eritrea, Ethiopia, and Italian Somaliland—into a single administrative unit that was divided into six provinces and placed under the governorship of Marshal Rodolfo Graziani. Although Graziani proclaimed Ethiopia "pacified," in fact the Ethiopians continued to resist. The Italians, in turn, escalated their reprisals. When an attempt was made to assassinate Graziani on February 19, 1937, over 30,000 Ethiopians were killed in retaliation; the educated class was particularly singled out for execution. In spite of his tough policies,

[1] *Time*, vol. xxvii, no. 1, January 6, 1936, p. 13.

Graziani failed to quell the mounting Ethiopian insurgency. The Italian government sought to mollify the Ethiopians by the appointment of the Duke of Aosta as Viceroy. He was instructed to be more conciliatory toward the Ethiopians, and to embark upon an ambitious program of agricultural development and public works. The program is now best remembered for the construction of an improved road system.

The efforts of the Duke of Aosta, however, proved unsuccessful. Despite his attempt to isolate the core of resistance, the Christian Amhara, by granting privileges to the Muslim Galla and Somali peoples, during the spring of 1938 a revolt erupted in Gojam, led by the Committee of Unity and Collaboration. The committee was made up largely of educated youths who had escaped Graziani's reprisals of the previous year and who strongly supported the emperor. Despite his efforts to rally the League of Nations to honor its pledge of collective security, Haile Selassie was unable to gain the support of Britain and France until the outbreak of World War II suddenly made him a natural ally against the Axis powers.

The Italian fleet in the eastern Mediterranean endangered Britain's strategic link to the Orient, the Suez Canal. Meanwhile, Italian forces were moving on Cairo from Libya and threatening Khartoum as well as menacing British control of the Nile waters in the Sudan and controlling the Red Sea from Ethiopia. Great Britain suddenly needed Haile Selassie and his insurgents in the highlands as much as the emperor had needed British power, which had been denied him in 1936. Relying on skilful defensive maneuvers by the few thousand men of the Sudan Defence Force, the British mobilized an expedition which invaded Eritrea and Ethiopia. In cooperation with the Ethiopian resistance, they defeated the Italians at the decisive battle of Keren. On May 5,

1941—five years to the day after its occupation by the Italians—Haile Selassie entered Addis Ababa, and by the end of the month the isolated Italian forces under the Duke of Aosta officially surrendered at Amba Alage.

In his speech celebrating independence and his restoration as Emperor, Haile Selassie promised a new era in Ethiopian history—to be characterized by Christian ethics in government, liberty of conscience, and democratic institutions. The Allied powers, stricken by guilt at abandoning him to the Italians in 1936, were not about to question the pious platitudes which obscured the realities of the emperor's administration. Haile Selassie had no intention of relinquishing his autocratic powers; nor did the two great institutions of the state—the church and the aristocracy—expect to abandon their privileges. The traditions of the past combined with the centralizing policies of modernization, under an emperor checked only by the limitations of his resources, would inevitably come into conflict with the frustrated expectations of the younger generation seeking a share in government.

During the war years, Haile Selassie had been able to consolidate his imperial administration behind the protection of the British Occupied Enemy Territory Administration (OETA). OETA was withdrawn on December 17, 1944, leaving complete sovereignty to Ethiopia, and the emperor. Many seemingly progressive measures were instituted, but real change lagged far behind. Despite Haile Selassie's attempts to reform taxation, the main source of revenue for the state continued in fact to be the rural peasantry. The nobility successfully defended their tax privileges, with many gaining exemption from any taxation on their large land holdings. Slavery was officially abolished, but there was a fine line between involuntary servitude and "domestic servants" who were virtually indentured for life. In 1956, for the first time in sixteen centuries, the Ethiopian Orthodox Church obtained its independence when the patriarch of Alexandria agreed to the appointment by the emperor of an Ethiopian *abuna* (head of the Ethiopian Orthodox Church). Church lands were taxed, and new bishops appointed, but the essential structure of the Church remained the same. During these same years, the emperor played an increasingly influential role in the newly independent African states, mediating in several disputes, and becoming one of the principal architects of the Organization of African Unity. (*Charter of the Organization of African Unity* May 25, 1963).

In fact, Haile Selassie sought to achieve the impossible—the institution of administrative changes without undermining his personal political control. Any reform was adamantly resisted by the nobility, the great landholders, and the church—with whom the emperor was forced to make compromises at the expense of his centralizing policies. Increasingly, dissatisfaction with the political, social, and economic environment in Ethiopia began to smolder, fueled by the new educated élite. Its members, although they were mostly younger sons of the nobility, were deeply affected by less affluent educated Ethiopians, and by teachers who propounded revolutionary ideas about democracy. The emperor was unwilling or unable to satisfy the rising expectations of the young. In December 1960, the first manifestations of the growing discontent erupted in an attempted coup initiated in Addis Ababa by the commander of the Imperial Bodyguard and a handful of younger security officers and intellectuals. They had only a narrow base of support, and were crushed in a few days by the weight of a loyal army, nobility, and church. Although abortive, the coup destroyed the myth of the populace's loyalty to and love for the emperor, and for the remaining fourteen years Haile Se-

lassie was faced with a rising tide of opposition to his regime and to him personally.

The opposition came from virtually every quarter. The emperor's attempts at tax and land reform were vigorously opposed by the landowners and completely neutralized by a successful rebellion in Gojam in 1969. At the same time, student dissent, labor unrest, and numerous minor peasant insurrections kept up the pressure for internal reforms. Faced with mounting grievances from within, the emperor also had to contend with historic secessionist movements on his frontier— in Eritrea, the Ogaden, and the Haud.

Eritrea was to prove the most intractable and resilient challenge to the government, frustrating every attempt to incorporate it into the Ethiopian state. After innumerable commissions and resolutions, the United Nations General Assembly had approved a resolution, on September 15, 1952, which granted limited autonomy to Eritrea with a federal structure under the sovereignty of the emperor. This was ostensibly a victory for Haile Selassie, who immediately sought to undermine Eritrean autonomy by the appointment of Amharic officials, a move which virtually abrogated the Federation by 1962. The Eritrean opposition, although divided among various factions, was soon able to challenge the Ethiopian Army successfully. Today, after twenty-six years, the Eritrean revolt remains the longest sustained conflict in the world. In 1989, it continues unabated, seriously draining the resources of Ethiopia. While Eritrea has been successfully defending its integrity in the north, Ethiopia has also carried on other long-standing frontier wars in a fragile attempt to maintain its sovereignty over the Ogaden and the Haud against the contentions of the Somalis—who have historically claimed these regions. The dispute over these borderlands smolders to the present day.

By 1974, beset by opposition from

without and within, the emperor had become a beleaguered and aging figure poised between the conflicting forces of tradition and modernity. His failure to introduce meaningful economic and political reforms was exacerbated in the 1970s by increasing inflation and pervasive corruption, all dramatized by the destructive famine in Wallo and Tigray in 1973–74, which the government sought to conceal. The exposure of the famine in the world press not only proved humiliating to the Ethiopians, but demonstrated the moral bankruptcy of the regime. For years, Ethiopian politics had been dominated by the emperor, who served as a referee between conservative and liberal factions, neither of whom had the unity nor the strength to overcome the other, while he himself retained his power by playing one against the other. Any threat to the emperor's authority would have to come from another source—the army.

On January 12, 1974, Ethiopian troops in Nageli, in southern Ethiopia, mutinied against poor food and bad living conditions. News of the mutiny was spread rapidly by the army signal corps—precipitating numerous mutinies throughout the country and encouraging urban intellectuals and workers to riot in the streets of Addis Ababa and other towns. Ethiopia was thrown into six months of turmoil. Each group sought to take advantage of the chaos to improve its position. In March, the conservatives agreed to revise the constitution, but only so long as they remained in control. The intellectuals and workers failed to be mollified by salary increases and government control of food and gasoline prices. This left the army, which itself was deeply divided, to fill the vacuum by the formation, on June 28, 1974, of the Coordinating Committee of the Armed Forces, the Police, and the Territorial Army (the *Derg*), with Major Mengistu Haile Mariam as Chairman.

At first the *Derg* sought to maintain the outward symbols of the parliamentary constitutional monarchy, but by August the *Derg* had become increasingly militant. During the ensuing weeks, numerous steps were taken to denigrate the emperor, particularly in regard to his inactivity during the famine, and to isolate him from his bodyguard, the Crown Council, and his palace and private treasury. On September 12, 1974, Haile Selassie was officially dethroned and confined under house arrest. The *Derg* adopted the name of the Provisional Military Administrative Council (PMAC); the council consisted of some 120 members under the chairmanship of General Aman.

The subsequent history of the PMAC was characterized by intensive internal strife in the capital and the imposition of *Yé-Itiopia Hibretesebawinet* (Ethiopian Socialism) on the countryside. The leadership of General Aman, who was not only an Eritrean but also was opposed to the mass arrest of aristocrats and important government officials of the former monarchy, was challenged by the intellectuals and labor who demanded a "people's government." General Aman was killed resisting arrest on November 23, 1974, and his successor, General Tefari Banti, was a mere figurehead; the Vice-Chairman, Major Mengistu, emerged at the head of Ethiopian affairs. His accession to power symbolized the revolutionary changes which had swept over the Ethiopia of the Solomonic dynasty. His mother came from one of the linguistic groups known as *Shankala* (blacks) or *Baria* (slaves) by the Amhara. He had attended the Holeta Military School and had twice visited the United States for military training; his lack of university education was more than compensated for by the intelligence and cunning which enabled him to survive the struggles within the *Derg*.

Despite the kaleidoscopic rivalries within the *Derg*, the PMAC managed to launch a radical scheme of reform nationalizing all rural and urban land, abolishing tenancy, granting power to the farmers through peasant associations, and organizing the urban proletariat into cooperative societies known as *kabeles*. Early in 1975, banks, industries, and commercial companies were nationalized; only retail trade remained privately owned. The PMAC even sought to resolve the Eritrean problem with a series of military expeditions culminating in the massive attack in 1976 by some 40,000 Amhara and Tigrayan Christian peasants, all of whom were disastrously defeated by the Eritreans. Nor were the Eritreans the only people in revolt. By 1976, all of Ethiopia's fourteen administrative provinces were faced with rebellions to which Mengistu and the PMAC responded with massive counter-terrorism, including the deposition of the *Abuna* of the Ethiopian Orthodox Church.

In December 1976, Mengistu faced his most severe challenge from within the PMAC. The council members sought to diffuse power by restructuring the organization as a three-tiered system and awarding greater power to a secretary-general than to Vice-Chairman Mengistu. A series of power struggles ensued until February 11, 1977, when the PMAC was reorganized with only one vice-chairman, Mengistu, who took charge of all the armed forces, including peasant militias, urban defense squads, and the army. He also became Chairman of the powerless Civilian Council of Ministers, and Head of State. Ethiopia had become not a people's republic, but a military dictatorship under Haile Mariam Mengistu who rules relentlessly to this day. (The Derg and Mengistu Haile Mariam: *Unity: Foundation of our Independence and Strength* May 1, 1988).

## EAST AFRICA SINCE INDEPENDENCE

On December 9, 1961, Tanganyika became the first of the three countries of East Africa to become independent, taking the name of the United Republic of Tanzania upon its merger with Zanzibar on April 26, 1964. Uganda soon followed, becoming independent on October 9, 1962; Kenya declared its independence on December 12, 1964. Three principal issues have dominated the history of these East African states ever since: regional cooperation; national integration; and economic and social justice.

The search for regional unity was the product of history and geography. Since Great Britain occupied Egypt and the Suez Canal in 1882, the fundamental principle which had determined British policy in Eastern Africa was the protection of the waters of the Nile and their sources in East Africa. The very existence of Egypt, and British sovereignty there, were dependent on the control of the river. Britain's diplomatic and military resources were thus directed to East Africa and its interior to ensure British domination of the Nile Basin and its life giving waters. Consequently, Uganda, which contained one of the major sources of the Nile, assumed a strategic importance out of all proportion to its beauty as "the pearl of Africa." Determined to preserve the water so needed by Egypt, Britain declared Uganda a crown colony in 1894. By so doing she inevitably intertwined the complementary territories of the East African Protectorate (Kenya) by the Uganda railway from Mombasa to Lake Victoria including, after the First World War, the former German colony of Tanganyika at that time a mandate of the League of Nations.

Britain's annexation of East Africa to the empire was a political realization of the region's geographical unity. Like most boundaries dividing African states, those in East Africa between Tanzania, Uganda, and Kenya were quite arbitrary, drafted on maps in the state rooms of London and Berlin. The geographic coherence of East Africa from the Sudan and Ethiopia to the north, Zaire to the west, and Mozambique to the south complemented British hegemony. Eventually the British established regional agencies; unfortunately the narrow nationalism of the East African leaders has steadily dismembered them. Prior to independence the East African Economic Community had achieved a degree of economic integration unique in Africa. The essential elements of this unity were the existence of a common market, common currency, a similar tax structure, and an integrated system of railways, harbors, airways, posts, and telecommunications. There was thus free movement not only of goods, but also of labor and capital, which flowed back and forth across perfunctory frontiers. The East African community also protected nascent industries with a common imperial tariff.

This remarkable experiment in regional cooperation did not withstand the "winds of change" blowing with the hurricane force of independence throughout East Africa. The economic integration forged by the British collapsed before the determination of the African states throughout the continent to defend their newly acquired sovereignty over fiscal, monetary, and commercial policies, and the, perceived or real, unequal distribution of economic benefits among the independent East African states. Kenya, for example, appeared to the other countries to have prospered more than Uganda or Tanzania because of its dominant position in the East African Economic Community, but in reality its wealth was due to its fertility, to the productivity of its peasant agriculture, and to the revenue from white settler plantations. Not surprisingly, Uganda and Tanzania demanded modifications in the operation of the Community; they were met with cold indifference by Kenya, and soon resulted in the organization's demise.

With the collapse of the British vision of a Greater East Africa, each state turned within itself in search of national unity in a genuine desire to forge a suitable balance between the deep-seated loyalty to each ethnic group by its members and the allegiance demanded by the new nation. This dilemma, common to every independent African nation, was intertwined with the structure of the party system adopted by the nationalists in each of the East African states during their campaigns for independence. In Tanzania, the concept of the two-party system, as represented by the parliamentary model of Great Britain, was regarded with suspicion. It was felt, especially by the leading Tanganyikan intellectual and politician, Julius Nyerere, that such a system could only create class antagonism. Upon returning from Great Britain, Nyerere dominated the Tanganyika African National Union (TANU), arguing articulately that only a single party committed not only to independence but also to African socialism—which predicated a classless society—could achieve both. The United Nations had inherited the mantle of responsibility for the Mandate of Tanganyika abandoned by the League of Nations. With its support, Julius Nyerere, as the leader of TANU, became Prime Minister of the self-governing territory. Tanzania became independent on December 9, 1961; it was declared a republic on December 9, 1962, with Nyerere as its president.

In Kenya, the dynamics of a one-party state were driven not by romantic visions of a classless society, but by the realities of Kenya's tribal antagonisms. In February 1960, the Lancaster House Conference in London agreed upon a new constitution for Kenya, which guaranteed an African-elected majority in the Legislative Council; the intention was for the government of Kenya to evolve from self-government to independence. The rapid advance toward independence that had characterized the Tanganyika Mandate under the single-party, TANU, was forestalled by the rivalry between the two, primarily ethnic, parties in Kenya: the Kenya African National Union (KANU), led by Jomo Kenyatta and dominated by the Kikuyu; and the Kenya African Democratic Union (KADU), a coalition of rural and pastoral groups led, however, by Oginga Odinga and his Luo followers. Politics became driven by ethnic rivalries. The conflicts were only partially resolved by the national elections in 1963, in which KANU won a majority. Kenya became self-governing on June 1, 1963; it became an independent republic on December 12, 1964, with Jomo Kenyatta as its first president.

Independence, however, did not end the ethnic and political rivalries within Kenya. The defection, in March 1966, of thirty KANU members to KADU led Oginga Odinga to transform KADU into a new party—the Kenya People's Union (KPU). The KPU's influence, however, steadily declined in contrast to the growing power of KANU, which was led by the charismatic Kenyatta. (Oginga Odinga: *Not Yet Uhuru* October 25, 1969). Suddenly, in July 1969, the popular Luo minister of economic planning, Tom Mboya, was assassinated by a Kikuyu. The assassination precipitated smouldering ethnic animosities between Luo and Kikuyu. These hostilities provided a pretext for the Kikuyu-dominated government of Kenyatta to proscribe the KPU, imprison Odinga, and establish a one-party state in Kenya which has remained in power to the present day.

During the halcyon years of Kenyatta's rule, Kenya prospered as a model of a multi-ethnic state, but during his declining years, sharp divisions began to emerge in Kenya politics. These involved two main groups, the so-called "inner circle" and "outer circles" that maneuvered for power in anticipation of the death of the Mwalimu. The inner circle, unofficially known as KANU "A",

was led by the Foreign Minister Dr. Njoroge Mungai and was closely associated with the Kenyatta family. The rival group, also unofficially called KANU "B", was led by the Attorney General (later Minister of Constitutional Affairs during Moi's Presidency) Charles Njonjo, himself a Kikuyu from Kiambu. Included in this group were Mwai Kibaki, Minister of Finance and Planning (later Vice-President), a Kikuyu from Nyeri, and Vice-President Daniel Arap Moi from the Tugen, one of the smallest of the Kalenjin tribes.

As early as October 1976, the Mungai group began a campaign to table a bill which would amend the provision in the constitution that permitted the Vice-President automatically to succeed the President for ninety days, in the event of the President's death. Mungai and his followers feared that any acting President, even in office for only ninety days, might be tempted to invoke emergency powers either to perpetuate his own rule or to detain prospective candidates for the office. The bill would have, in effect, blocked Vice-President Moi from succeeding Kenyatta after his death on August 27, 1978. As Attorney General, Charles Njonjo ruled that discussion of the matter was a criminal offense—a position he steadfastly defended, thus enabling the succession of Arap Moi as president without open conflict between the rival Kikuyu factions. To assure his acceptance as Kenyatta's successor, President Moi continued the policy of his predecessor, as reflected in the "Nyayo" (footsteps) philosophy, which is often interpreted to mean "love," "peace," and "unity."

In Uganda, the problem of national integration proved more intractable than in any other of the East African territories. Although the Uganda National Congress (UNC) had been founded in 1952 as a national party, the traditional privileged position of Buganda remained as a serious historical obstacle to a united

Uganda. By 1959, the UNC had dissolved into rival parties. The most influential was the Uganda People's Congress (UPC), led by Apollo Milton Obote, whose supporters were mostly from districts outside of Buganda. The principal rival of the UPC was the Democratic Party (DP). The DP was a coalition based more on opportunism than on reality. It soon disintegrated in the struggle between the Baganda—represented by their party, the *Kabaka Yekka* (The King Only), whose titular leader was the Kabaka Sir Edward Mutesa II—and the other ethnic groups in Uganda. An unholy alliance between the UPC and the *Kabaka Yekka* was consummated to obtain the independence of Uganda on October 9, 1962, but thereafter politics in Uganda plunged into ethnic chaos. The Prime Minister, Apollo Milton Obote, suspended the constitution in March 1966, abolishing the federal relationship of Buganda and the other interlacustrine kingdoms and converting Uganda into a unitary state.

Obote's assumption of power, however, was the beginning of his own destruction. The Baganda never accepted the abolition of their kingdom, and, in retaliation, Obote sought to crush the Baganda by terror. The kabaka was expelled, and dissident Baganda were either eliminated or imprisoned. An attempt on Obote's life in December 1969, presumably by supporters of the Kabaka, only intensified the reign of terror. Opposition leaders of every ethnic group were arrested, and all parties were banned except the UPC. Uganda had, like Kenya and Tanzania, become a one-party state. Obote justified his authoritarian rule on the grounds that the creation of a united socialist Uganda required him to dismantle the kingdom of Buganda, which he regarded as a capitalist anachronism.

While regional cooperation was dying, and national integration was symbolized by the emergence of the one-party state,

these were issues created by the politicians and the privileged. To the mass of East Africans, the struggle for equality in education, medical care, and the civil service was a practical reality, of far greater importance in their daily lives than the machinations of politicians. Segregation of whites, Indians, Arabs, and Africans in schools, hospitals, and the bureaucracy gradually began to disappear. Scholarships for study abroad were no longer based on racial quotas. In the civil service, the policy of Africanization opened the more responsible offices to Africans. A uniform salary scale for all races, as well as other symbols of colonial rule, outwardly trivial but psychologically pervasive, were eliminated.

The governments of the three East African states emphasized the importance of frugality and hard work in building nations independent of neo-imperialism. Often enshrouded in political rhetoric and slogans, the appeal was more genuine than cynical, more sincere than opportunistic. In Tanzania, the emphasis on "freedom," "work," and "self-help," known as *Ujamaa* (all together), formed the foundation of the Arusha Declaration in January 1967, which required equality and self-denial of government civil servants in emulation of the hard-working peasantry. The nationalization of banks, commercial firms, and industry was also declared; the goal was to eliminate class privilege and protect Tanzania from foreign control of its economy. (Julius K. Nyerere: *The Arusha Declaration January 29, 1967*). Although he pursued the goals of *Ujamaa* tenaciously after nearly a quarter of a century of unquestioned leadership, Julius Nyerere decided to step down as President of Tanzania on November 5, 1985. He was succeeded by Ali Hassan Mwinyi, President of Zanzibar and Vice-President of the Republic, elected by delegates to a special Congress of the ruling Revolutionary Chama Cha Mapinduzi (CCM) Party. Although Julius

Nyerere remained Secretary of the party, his retirement as President marked the end of an era. Nyerere was the last of the founders of the East African independencies; his departure from office symbolized the transfer of power and ideas to a new generation.

In Kenya, nationalization was not regarded so much as a means to protect the nation from neo-imperialists, as a way to transfer foreign resources to Kenyan nationals, instead of to the state—and specifically to the leading officials of the Kikuyu-dominated KANU. The government, under the guise of African socialism, encouraged its citizens to participate in the economy of the country, but in reality this meant the Africanization of Kenyan capitalism.

In Uganda, the first government of Milton Obote (1962–67) was not unfavorably disposed to capitalism, although the language of African socialism was employed in public pronouncements, Obote's own ideological position was still ambiguous, if not incoherent, perhaps because he was surrounded in his own party by strong supporters of private enterprise. Moreover, the predominance of Buganda in Uganda was based on the commitment of the agricultural élite of Buganda to petty capitalism, and on investment accumulated by individual private initiative. The state, in fact, provided incentives in the form of tax relief and subsidies to energetic entrepreneurs.

The attempt on Obote's life in December 1969 provided a pretext to crush the Baganda economically as well as politically. As the opposition parties were banned, the government, on December 18, 1968, also announced the "Move to the Left" symbolized by *The Common Man's Charter* (Apollo, Milton Obote, *The Common Man's Charter*). The Charter contained several rather general propositions about the economic future of Uganda, which it declared should be vested in the majority. The government would have

the right to nationalize not only the corporate sector, but private enterprises, *mailo* (private) holdings in Buganda, and freehold land at any time for the benefit of the people. On May 1, 1970, May Day, President Obote proclaimed the *Nakivubo Pronouncement*, declaring that all import and export business (except oil) would be a monopoly of the state. This, however, was the extent of Obote's "Move to the Left," which he was forced to modify when faced with the combined opposition of the large corporations. With his base of support eroded in the former kingdoms, in the middle class, and in the business community, there was little opposition when his regime was overthrown. On January 25, 1971, Major General Idi Amin Dada, Commander-in-Chief of the Ugandan army, toppled the government while Obote was attending the Commonwealth Conference in Singapore.

The Second Republic of Uganda was proclaimed on March 17, 1971, by Idi Amin, the new President. Idi Amin Dada, a Kakwa from the West Nile Province, had virtually fought his way to command the Uganda army (he was a champion boxer). Unsophisticated, semi-literate, he admired force and used it ruthlessly against his opponents, real or imagined. Supported by the army, which he handsomely rewarded in pay and privileges, he systematically slaughtered over half a million Ugandans, expelled all Asian non-citizens in August 1972, and earned the opprobrium of the international community. He was finally overthrown by a combined force of Ugandan exiles and the Tanzanian army on April 11, 1979.

The downfall of Amin was preceded by a coalition of all the political forces opposed to his regime. In 1978, an "Ad Hoc Committee for the Promotion of Unity Among Ugandans" was established. The committee subsequently organized, on January 1, 1979, a meeting of seven Ugandan exile groups to discuss unification with the intention of overthrowing Idi Amin. A "Consultative Committee" of ten members was established to seek out other groups and to convince them of the need for concerted action. The result was the Moshi Conference of March 4, 1979. The conference was attended by twenty-two different groups, all of whom were united by their common opposition to Amin's regime. Within six weeks, the Moshi alliance, with the support of Tanzania, had overthrown Amin. He was replaced, on April 13, 1979 by the Uganda National Liberation Front (UNLF) government, with Professor Yusufu Lule, a Muganda, as the "consensus" President.

Once Amin, the common enemy, had been driven into exile, the various factions within the UNLF began to maneuver for power. This led to the unceremonious ouster within a few months of Yusufu Lule, a man who regarded himself as representing the more conservative, moderate Ugandans. He was replaced by Godfrey Binaisa, who was in turn replaced within the year by a Military Commission that served as an interim government pending the results of national elections to be held in December 1980. The Military Commission consisted of Paulo Muwanga (Chairman), Yoweri Museveni (Vice-Chairman), Major General Tito Okello, Brigadier Oyite Ojok, Colonel Omaria, and Colonel Maruru.

Meanwhile Milton Obote had returned home from exile in Tanzania in May 1980, and on December 15, 1980, he seized power as President of Uganda with the support of Julius Nyerere and Tanzanian troops. Obote's return did not go unopposed, and armed opposition soon broke out in the Luwero triangle—the area formed by Luwero, Mubende and Mpigi districts of Buganda, the heartland of the former kingdom. Once again in the history of Uganda, the role of Buganda, "the Buganda Question" in any proposed political settlement, emerged to challenge Obote's government. The regime was eventually swept away by a military coup led by General Tito Okello on July 27, 1985.

After protracted negotiations, the military government of Okello signed a peace accord with the most powerful insurgent movement, the National Resistance Movement/National Resistance Army (NRM/NRA), led by Yoweri Museveni, on December 17, 1985, in Nairobi. The agreement, however, was a fragile document soon repudiated by the Free Uganda National Army (FUNA) and the Uganda National Rescue Fund (UNRF). Moreover, the NRA supporters of Museveni did not want an agreement that seemed to give away so much to Okello's government. Museveni himself refrained from going to Kampala to assume the Vice-Chairmanship of the Military Council as stipulated in the Nairobi agreement, and on January 25, 1986, his NRA forces marched into Kampala, overthrew the government of General Tito Okello, and began the Presidency of Yoweri Museveni.

# 1 ANONYMOUS

## PERIPLUS OF THE ERYTHRAEAN SEA

*Probably written about 100* A.D. *at Alexandria, "The Periplus of the Erythraean Sea" was a merchant's guide to the Red Sea and Indian Ocean ports. It is generally accepted as the earliest firsthand account of the East African coast to have survived to the present.*

· · ·

From Tabai after 400 stades sailing is a promontory towards which the current runs, and the market-town of Opone. . . . It produces cinnamon, both the *aroma* and *moto* varieties, as well as the better sort of slaves, which are brought to Egypt in increasing numbers, and much tortoise-shell of better quality than elsewhere.

Voyages from Egypt to all these further market-towns are made in the month of July, that is *Epiphi.* The ships are usually fitted out in the inner [Red Sea] ports of Ariake and Barugaza; and they bring the further market-towns the products of these places: wheat, rice, ghee, sesame oil, cotton cloth (both the *monache* and the *sagmatogene*), girdles, and honey from the reed called *sakchari.* Some make voyages directly to these market-towns, others exchange cargo as they go. The country has no sovereign but each market-town is ruled by its own chief.

After Opone the coast veers more towards the south. First there are the Small and Great Bluffs of Azania and rivers for anchorages for six days' journey southwestwards. Then come the Little and the Great Beach for another six days' journey, and after that in order the Courses of Azania, first that called Sarapion, the next Nikon, and then several rivers and other anchorages one after the other, separately a halt and a day's journey, in all seven, as far as the Pyralaae Islands and the island called Diorux [the Chan-

nel]. Beyond this, slightly south of southwest after a voyage of two days and nights along the Ausanitic coast, is the island of Menouthesias some 300 stades from the land. It is flat and wooded. There are many rivers in it, and many kinds of birds and the mountain tortoise. There are no wild animals at all except the crocodile, but they never attack men. In this place there are small sewn boats and dug-outs, which they use for fishing and for catching tortoise. In this island they fish in a peculiar way with wicker baskets, which they fasten across where the tide goes out.

Two days' sail beyond the island lies the last mainland market-town of Azania, which is called Rhapta, a name derived from the small sewn boats [ραπτων πλοιαριων]. Here there is much ivory and tortoise-shell.

Men of the greatest stature, who are pirates, inhabit the whole coast and at each place have set up chiefs. The Chief of the Ma'afir is the suzerain, according to an ancient right which subordinates it to the kingdom which has become the first in Arabia. The people of Mouza hold it in tribute under his sovereignty and send there small ships, mostly with Arab captains and crews who trade and intermarry with the mainlanders of all the places and know their language.

Into these market-towns are imported the lances made especially for them at Mouza, hatchets, swords, awls, and many kinds of small glass vessels; and at some places wine and not a little wheat, not for trade but to gain the goodwill of the barbarians. Much ivory is taken away from these places, but it is inferior in quality to that of Adulis, and also rhinoceros horn

From "The Periplus of the Erythraean Sea," in G. S. P. Freeman-Grenville, *The East African Coast: Select Documents from the First to the Earlier Nineteenth Century* (Oxford: Clarendon Press, 1962), pp. 1–2. Reprinted by permission of the Clarendon Press, Oxford.

and tortoise-shell, different from that of India, and a little coconut oil.

And these, I think, are the last of the market-towns of Azania on the mainland lying to the right of Berenice; for after all these places the ocean curves westwards and runs along the regions of Ethiopia, Libya and Africa, stretching out from the south and mingling with the western sea.

# 2 EZANA
## THE DESTRUCTION OF KUSH

*During the eighth century* B.C., *the land south of Aswan known as Kush established its independence from Egypt and, by the mid-seventh century* B.C., *had asserted its hegemony over lower Egypt. Driven from Egypt by the Assyrians, the kings of Kush retreated to Nubia, where they continued to rule over the middle Nile for another thousand years, preserving their own unique Egyptian-Nubian culture. Soon after the retreat from Egypt, the capital of Kush was moved from Napata southward to Meroe near Shendi, where Kush was increasingly exposed to the African cultures farther south and west. In the Christian era, Kush slipped into a gradual decay that ended in 350 A.D. when the King of Aksum, Ezana, destroyed Meroe and sacked the decrepit riverain towns. Ezana recorded his destruction of Kush in one of the longest inscriptions to have survived from the Aksumite kingdom of Abyssinia.*

1. By the power of the Lord of Heaven, Who in heaven and upon earth is mightier than everything which exists,
2. Ezana, the son of Ella Amida, a native of Halen, king of Aksum and of
3. Hemer (Himyar), and of Raydan, and of Saba, and of Salhen, and of Seyamo, and of Bega, and of
4. Kasu (the Meroites), King of Kings, the son of Ella Amida, who is invincible to the enemy.
5. By the might of the Lord of Heaven, Who hath made me Lord, Who to all eternity, the Perfect One,
6. reigns, Who is invincible to the enemy, no enemy shall stand before

me, and after me no enemy shall follow.
7. By the might of the Lord of all, I made war upon Noba, for the peoples had rebelled and
8. had made a boast of it. And "they (the Axumites) will not cross the river Takkaze (Atbara)," said the peoples
9. of Noba. And they were in the habit of attacking the peoples of Mangurto, and Khasa, and Barya, and the blacks,
10. and of making war upon the Red peoples. And twice and thrice had they broken their solemn oaths, and had
11. killed their neighbours mercilessly, and they had stripped bare and stolen the properties of our deputies and messengers which I had
12. sent to them to inquire into their

The inscription is found in L. P. Kirwan, "A Survey of Nubian Origins," *Sudan Notes and Records,* 20 (1937), 50–51. Reprinted by permission of the publisher and the Royal Geographical Society.

thefts, and had stolen from them
13. their weapons of defence. And as I had sent warnings to them and they would not harken to me, and they refused to cease from their evil deeds,
14. and then betook themselves to flight, I made war upon them. And I rose in the might of the Lord of the
15. Land, and I fought with them on the Takkaze (Atbara), at the ford of Kemalke. Thereupon they took flight, and would not
16. make a stand. And I followed after the fugitives for twenty and three days,
17. killing some and making prisoners others, and capturing spoil wherever I tarried. Prisoners and
18. spoil my people who had marched into the country brought back to me. Meanwhile I burnt their towns, both those built of bricks and those
19. built of reeds, and my soldiers carried off its food, and its copper, and its iron, and its
20. brass, and they destroyed the statues of their houses (i.e. temples), and the treasuries of food, and the cotton trees, and
21. cast them into the River Seda (Nile).
28. And I came to Kasu (Meroe) and I fought a battle and made prisoners of its people at

29. the junction of the rivers Seda and Takkaze. And the day after I arrived I sent out
30. to raid the country, the army Mahaza, and the army Hara, and Damawa, and Falha and Sera
31. upstream of Seda (i.e. towards the modern Khartoum), and the cities built of bricks and those of reeds. The names of the cities
32. built of bricks were Alwa (near Khartoum) and Daro. And they killed, and captured prisoners, and cast people into the water. . . .
34. . . . And after that I sent the army of Halen, and the army of Laken
35. . . . down the Seda (i.e. north of the junction of the Nile with the Atbara) against the towns of the Noba which are made of reeds—4
36. towns—Negus—I. The towns built of bricks which the Noba had taken
37. were Tabito—I—and Fertoti—I. And my peoples arrived at the frontier of the Red Noba and they returned safe and sound,
38. having captured prisoners and slain the Noba and taken spoil from them by the might of the Lord of Heaven.
39. And I planted a throne in that country at the place where the Rivers Seda and Takkaze join. . . .

# 3  COSMAS INDICOPLEUSTES
## TRADE IN ETHIOPIA

*The Christian Topography of Cosmas Indicopleustes was written in 547 A.D., when the Mediterranean world was just entering the Middle Ages. Cosmas attempted to establish that the world is flat by citing Greek authors and the Scriptures. Cosmas himself did visit Ethiopia, and his work is one of the few accounts that describe a barren period in East African history.*

From Cosmas Indicopleustes, *The Christian Topography of Cosmas, an Egyptian Monk,* trans. and edited by J. W. McCrindle (London: Hakluyt Society, 1897), pp. 49–54.

If one measures in a straight cord line the stages which make up the length of the earth from Tzinitza to the west, he will find that there are somewhere about four hundred stages, each thirty miles in length. The measurement is to be made in this way: from Tzinitza to the borders of Persia, between which are included all Iouvia,[1] India, and the country of the Bactrians, there are about one hundred and fifty stages at least; the whole country of the Persians has eighty stations; and from Nisibis to Seleucia[2] there are thirteen stages; and from Seleucia to Rome and the Gauls and Iberia, whose inhabitants are now called Spaniards, onward to Gadeira, which lies out towards the ocean, there are more than one hundred and fifty stages; thus making altogether the number of stages to be four hundred, more or less. With regard to breadth: from the hyperborean[3] regions to Byzantium there are not more than fifty stages. For we can form a conjecture as to the extent of the uninhabited and the inhabited parts of those northern regions from the Caspian Sea, which is a gulf of the ocean. From Byzantium, again, to Alexandria there are fifty stages, and from Alexandria to the Cataracts thirty stages, from the Cataracts to Axomis, thirty stages;[4] from Ax-

omis to the projecting part of Ethiopia, which is the frankincense country called Barbaria, lying along the ocean, and not near but at a great distance from the land of Sasu which is the remotest part of Ethiopia, fifty stages more or less; so that we may reckon the whole number of stages at two hundred more or less; and thus we see that even here the divine scripture speaks the truth in representing the length of the earth to be double its breadth; *For thou shalt make the table in length two cubits and in breadth one cubit,* a pattern, as it were, of the earth.

The region which produces frankincense is situated at the projecting parts of Ethiopia, and lies inland, but is washed by the ocean on the other side. Hence the inhabitants of Barbaria, being near at hand, go up into the interior and, engaging in traffic with the natives, bring back from them many kinds of spices, frankincense, cassia,[5] calamus,[6] and many other articles of merchandise, which they afterwards send by sea to Adule, to the country of the Homerites, to Further India, and to Persia. This very fact you will find mentioned in the Book of Kings, where it is recorded that the Queen of Sheba, that is, of the Homerite country, whom afterwards our Lord in the Gospels calls the Queen of the South, brought to Solomon spices from this very Barbaria, which lay near Sheba on the other side of the sea, together with bars of ebony, and apes and gold from Ethiopia which, though separated from Sheba by the Arabian Gulf, lay in its vicinity. We can see again from the words of the Lord that he calls these places the ends of the earth, saying: *The Queen of the South shall rise up in judgment with this generation and*

---

[1] This would mean the country of the Huns.
[2] Nisibis, the capital of Mygdoniia, was, after the time of Lucullus, considered the chief bulwark of the Roman power in the East. It was an ancient, large, and populous city, and was for long the great northern emporium of the commerce of the East and West. It was situated about two days' journey from the head waters of the Tigris in the midst of a pleasant and fertile plain at the foot of Mount Masius. The Seleucia here referred to was situated on the Tigris about 40 miles to the north-east of Babylon, from the ruins of which it was mainly constructed: just as, afterwards, its own ruins served to build Ctesiphon. Next to Alexandria, it was the greatest emporium of commerce in the East.
[3] Far northern regions (ed.).
[4] Axomis (Auxume in Ptolemy) is the modern Axum, the capital of Tigre. In the early centuries of our era it was a powerful State, possessing nearly the whole of Abyssinia, a portion of the south-west Red Sea coast and north-western Arabia. It was distant from its seaport, Adule, which was situated near Annesley Bay, about 120 miles, or an eight days' caravan journey. It was the chief centre of the trade with the interior of Africa. The Greek lan-

guage was understood and spoken, both by the court and the numerous foreigners who had either settled in it or who resorted to it for trading purposes. . . . Christianity was introduced into Axum in the fourth century by Oedisius and Frumentius, the latter of whom was afterwards appointed its first bishop. Sasu, which is next mentioned, is near the coast, and only 5° to the north of the equator.
[5] A kind of cinnamon (ed.).
[6] Reed used as a pen (ed.).

*shall condemn it, for she came from the ends of the earth to hear the wisdom of Solomon*—Matt. xii, 42. For the Homerites are not far distant from Barbaria, as the sea which lies between them can be crossed in a couple of days, and then beyond Barbaria is the ocean, which is there called Zingion. The country known as that of Sasu is itself near the ocean, just as the ocean is near the frankincense country, in which there are many gold mines. The King of the Axomites accordingly, every other year, through the governor of Agau,[7] sends thither special agents to bargain for the gold, and these are accompanied by many other traders—upwards, say, of five hundred—bound on the same errand as themselves. They take along with them to the mining district oxen, lumps of salt, and iron, and when they reach its neighbourhood they make a halt at a certain spot and form an encampment, which they fence round with a great hedge of thorns. Within this they live, and having slaughtered the oxen, cut them in pieces, and lay the pieces on the top of the thorns, along with the lumps of salt and the iron. Then come the natives bringing gold in nuggets like peas, called *tancharas,* and lay one or two or more of these upon what pleases them— the pieces of flesh or the salt or the iron, and then they retire to some distance off. Then the owner of the meat approaches, and if he is satisfied he takes the gold away, and upon seeing this its owner comes and takes the flesh or the salt or the iron. If, however, he is not satisfied, he leaves the gold, when the native seeing that he has not taken it, comes and either puts down more gold, or takes up what he had laid down, and goes away. Such is the mode in which business is transacted with the people of that country, because their language is different and interpreters are hardly to be found. The time they stay in that country is five days more or less, according as the natives more or less readily coming forward buy up all their wares. On the journey homeward they all agree to travel well-armed, since some of the tribes through whose country they must pass might threaten to attack them from a desire to rob them of their gold. The space of six months is taken up with this trading expedition, including both the going and the returning. In going they march very slowly, chiefly because of the cattle, but in returning they quicken their pace lest on the way they should be overtaken by winter and its rains. For the sources of the river Nile lie somewhere in these parts, and in winter, on account of the heavy rains, the numerous rivers which they generate obstruct the path of the traveller. The people there have their winter at the time we have our summer. It begins in the month Epiphi of the Egyptians and continues till Thoth,[8] and during the three months the rain falls in torrents, and makes a multitude of rivers all of which flow into the Nile.

The facts which I have just recorded fell partly under my own observation and partly were told me by traders who had been to those parts.

---

[7] The Agau people is the native race spread over the Abyssinian plateau both to east and west of Lake Tana. . . .

[8] From July to September.

# 4  TUAN CH'ÊNG-SHIH
## CHINA'S DISCOVERY OF AFRICA

*Although China had long had contacts with the world beyond her frontiers, intercourse with the countries beyond Asia was encouraged during the T'ang Dynasty (618–907 A.D.) by a long period of peace and the cosmopolitan outlook of China's rulers. The selection below is from the* Yu-yang-tsa-tsu, *a general book of knowledge, written by the Chinese scholar Tuan Ch'êng-shih (d. 863 A.D.).*

It is, however, in the T'ang period that the first definite information appears in Chinese sources on the countries beyond India, and what is to the point here, on Africa. There is a curious work, written by the scholar Tuan Ch'êng-shih, who died in A.D. 863, called the *Yu-yang-tsa-tsu.* This book was published in the *Chin-tai-pi-shu* by Mao Chin (1598–1657). The antiquity of the text is guaranteed by the *Hsin T'ang-shu,* by Ou-yang Hsiu, completed in 1060, which has an abridged extract of it. From the chapter in which a number of exotic plants are described, it is clear that part of his information is derived from priests of *Fu-lin,* that is Ta-ch'in or the Roman Orient and Magadha in India. Hirth has called attention to this text; in his translation, however, there are a few curious errors which make a new translation necessary.

The text runs: "The country of Po-pa-li is in the southwestern sea. (The people) do not eat any of the five grains but eat only meat. They often stick a needle into the veins of cattle and draw blood which they drink raw, mixed with milk. They wear no clothes except that they cover (the parts) below their loins with sheepskins. Their women are clean and of proper behaviour. The inhabitants themselves kidnap them, and if they sell them to foreign merchants, they fetch several times their price. The country produces only ivory and ambergris.[1] If Persian merchants wish to go into the country, they collect around them several thousand men and present them with strips of cloth. All, whether old or young draw blood and swear an oath, and then only do they trade their products. From olden times on they were not subject to any foreign country. In fighting they use elephants' tusks and ribs and the horns of wild buffaloes as lances and they wear cuirasses [2] and bows and arrows. They have twenty myriads of foot soldiers. The Arabs make frequent raids upon them."

What is this country? Hirth first identified it with Berbera, on the Somali coast. This identification is confirmed by an important notice in a work about which we shall have to say a little more presently. It is the *Chu-fan-chih,* written by Chao Ju-kua, a Commissioner of foreign trade at Ch'üan-chou in Fukien province. It was completed in 1226. About one-third of its contents is drawn from an earlier work, the *Lingwai-tai-ta,* written by Chou Ch'ü-fei in 1178. This book has a note on a country called Pi-pa-lo which runs as follows:

"The country of Pi-pa-lo has four chou (departmental cities) and for the rest (the people) are all settled in villages which each try to gain the supremacy over the others by violence. They serve Heaven and do not serve the Buddha (presumably meaning that they are Mohammedans). The country produces many camels and sheep and they have camels' meat and

From J. J. L. Duyvendak, *China's Discovery of Africa* (London: Arthur Probsthain, 1949), pp. 12–15, 22–24. Reprinted by permission.
[1] A substance used in perfumes (ed.).

[2] A piece of close-fitting armor for protecting the breast and back; it was originally made of leather (ed.).

milk as well as baked cakes as their regular food. The country produces dragon's saliva (ambergris), big elephants' tusks, and big rhinoceros horns. Some elephants' tusks weigh more than 100 catty [3] and some rhinoceros horns more than 10 catty. There is also much putchuk, liquid storax gum, myrrh, and tortoise-shell which is extremely thick, and which (people from) other countries all come to buy. 'Among the products there is further the so-called camel-crane (i.e. the ostrich, called by the Persians *ushturmurgh* and by the Arabs *teir-al-djamal,* both meaning "camel-bird"), whose body to the crown is 6 or 7 feet high. It has wings and can fly, but not to any height.' Among quadrupeds there is the so-called *tsu-la* (giraffe), striped like a camel and in size like an ox. It is yellow in colour. Its front legs are 5 feet high and its hind legs are only 3 feet. Its head is high up and is turned upwards. Its skin is an inch thick. There is also a mule with red, black, and white stripes wound as girdles around the body. Both (these kinds) are animals of the mountain wilds. They are occasional variations of the camel. The inhabitants are fond of hunting and from time to time they catch them with poisoned arrows."

The *Hsin T'ang-shu,* as I said, reproduces part of the notice on Berbera of the *Yu-yang-tsa-tsu.* It also has a short entry on another African territory, which so far as I am aware has not been noticed in this connection, viz. on Ma-lin, that is Melinda. The text says: "South-west from Fu-lin (that is the country of the Roman Orient of which 'Ch'ih-san,' Alexandria, is indicated as the western border), after one traverses the desert for two thousand miles is a country called Ma-lin. It is the old P'o-sa. Its people are black and their nature is fierce. The land is pestilentious and has no herbs, no trees, and no cereals. They feed the horses on dried fish; the people eat *hu-mang;* the

hu-mang is the Persian date. They are not ashamed of debauching the wives of their fathers or chiefs, they are (in this respect) the worst of the barbarians. They call this: to seek out the proper master and subject. In the seventh moon they rest completely (i.e. Ramadan). They (then) do not send out nor receive (any merchandise) in trade and they sit drinking all night long."

· · ·

There is a short note on Ts'eng-po, identified with Zanguebar, which is not particularly interesting, and one on K'un-lun Ts'eng-ch'i which deserves our attention. It is in the section dealing with countries on the sea.

" 'K'un-lun Ts'eng-ch'i is in the southwestern sea. It is adjacent to a large island in the sea. There are regularly great p'êng birds. When they fly they obscure the sun for a short time. There are wild camels, and if the p'êng birds meet them, they swallow them up. If one finds a feather of the p'êng bird, by cutting the quill, one can make a water-jar of it. The products of the country are big elephants' tusks and rhinoceros' horns.'

In the west 'there is an island in the sea on which there are many savages. Their bodies are black as lacquer and they have frizzled hair. They are enticed by (offers of) food and then captured' and sold 'as slaves to the Arabic countries, where they fetch a very high price. They are employed as gate-keepers, and it is said that they have no longing for their kinsfolk.' "

There can be little doubt that the island mentioned is Madagascar. The p'êng bird is the legendary rukh, and perhaps it was the presence of the now extinct dodo which is at the origin of the story that it was found there. Marco Polo says that it can swallow an elephant. Yule explains the story of the quills as the fronds of the raphia palm; Ferrand identifies it with the use made of the *langana* (Malgash), a big bamboo, about 15 centimeters in diameter and 2 meters long, in which the knots have been perforated with the exception

---

[3] A unit of weight used in China that is generally equal to $1^1/3$ pounds avoirdupois (ed.).

of the one at the end, so as to turn it into a water vessel. These *langana* are particularly used by the coast tribes of Madagascar.

The capturing of slaves brings up an interesting question. Chou Ch'ü-fei inserts another sentence: "thousands of them are sold as foreign slaves."

It is certain that some of these slaves came to China. Foreign slaves were designated by various names. K'un-lun-nu, K'un-lun slaves is one of them. The word *k'un-lun* has had an interesting history. Used early on as the name of the fabulous mountains in the West, the home of Hsi-wang-mu, the word originally seems to mean the round vault of the sky, in which as it were, these gigantic Tibetan mountains seem to lose themselves. Etymologically, it is certainly connected with the binom *hun-lun,* "chaos." The K'un-lun mountains are also identified with the Anavatapta mountain and the Sumeru in India, well known in Buddhist literature. Now the Chinese have applied the term *k'un-lun* to the peoples, mostly of the Malay race, whom they found at the ends of the earth. At first chiefly confined to the races of the South-West, later, as the geographic knowledge of the Chinese expanded, the same term was applied to the native races of the countries around the Indian Ocean, including the Negroes.

We also find Seng-chih-nu, slaves from Seng-chih, which undoubtedly is the same as Ts'eng-ch'i, as transcription of Zanggi, the general Arabic word for Negroes. In the name of the country K'un-lun Ts'eng-ch'i (k'i), we may therefore recognize the country of the blacks, Zanzibar, prefixed by the appellation K'un-lun, a curious, though perhaps accidental, reminder of the Malay origin of the inhabitants of Madagascar.

Slaves are further called: *kuei-nu,* "devil-slaves," *yeh-jen,* "wild men," *hei-hsiao-ssŭ,* "black servants," *fan hsiao-ssŭ,* "barbarian servants," or *fan-nu,* "barbarian slaves." These names may sometimes have designated Malay slaves in general, but often they undoubtedly refer to Negro-slaves. We hear about them quite early: the priest Tao-an is called K'un-lun-tzŭ, "the K'un-lun," or the Ch'i-tao-jen, "the lacquered monk," because he was so dark in spite of his being a northern Chinese. The later consort of Emperor Chien-wen of the Chin dynasty was nicknamed "K'un-lun" by the courtiers, because she was tall and of a dark colour. The *P'ing-chou-k'o-t'an* writes: "In Kuang-chou most of the wealthy people keep devil-slaves. They are very strong and can lift (weights of) several hundred catties. Their language and tastes are unintelligible. Their nature is simple and they do not run away. They are also called 'wild men.' Their colour is black as ink, their lips are red and their teeth white, their hair is curly and yellow. There are males and females (*N.B.:* the term for animals is used). They live in the mountains (or islands) beyond the seas. They eat raw things. If, in captivity, they are fed on cooked food, after several days they get diarrhoea. This is called 'changing the bowels.' For this reason they sometimes fall ill and die; if they do not die one can keep them, and after having been kept a long time they begin to understand people's language, although they themselves cannot speak it. There is one kind of wild men near the sea who can enter the water without blinking their eyes. They are called 'K'un-lun slaves.' "

That the slave-trade, whether of Negroes or other tribes of the Indian Ocean was pretty extensive also appears from a notice in the *Ling-wai-tai-ta:* "The people of Chan-ch'eng (Champa) buy male and female slaves; and the ships carry human beings as cargo." Chao Ju-kua adds that a boy was priced at 3 taels of gold or the equivalent in aromatic wood. Slaves were also used on board ships for mending a leaky ship from the outside under water.

There is a strange pathos in the thought of these melancholy, silent, black slaves, who were supposed to have no longing for their home, in medieval China, used as doorkeepers.

# 5  JOÃO DE BARROS
## THE FOUNDING OF KILWA

*In 1532 João de Barros became factor (agent) of the India House in Lisbon and thus had access to all the documents and correspondence of Portuguese officials who were under the authority of the Viceroy of the Indies.  He does not indicate whether the* Chronica dos Reyes de Quiloa *was written in Arabic or was translated therefrom.*

*The Arabic version was presented in 1877 to the British Consul at Zanzibar, Sir John Kirk, by Sultan Sayyid Barghash.  The author is unknown, but from clues in the text, G. S. P. Freeman-Grenville concludes that the author was born in 1499 and that his family came from Malindi.  The chronicle may have been composed about 1520.*

*The two accounts are presented below for comparison.*

## DE BARROS' VERSION

According to what we learn from a Chronicle of the Kings of this town, a little more than seventy years after the towns of Mogadishu and Barawa were built, which, as we have already seen, were the first towns on this coast, and nearly four hundred years after the era of Muhammad, there reigned in the town of Shiraz, which is in Persia, a Moorish King named Sultan Hocen.

At his death he left seven sons. One of these, named, Ale, was held in little esteem by his brothers, because he was begotten by his father by one of his slaves of Abyssinian race, whereas their mother was descended from the Princes of Persia. But whatever he may have lacked by reason of his origin, he made up for it in character and wisdom. In order to escape the scorn and ill treatment of his brothers, he resolved to find a new place to dwell in, where he might live with better fortune than he had amongst his own people. He was already married, and gathered together his wife, sons, family and some other people, who wished to follow him in the enterprise, and embarked in two ships at the island of Ormuz, and, because of the reports of gold to be found on the coast of Zanzibar, came thither.

From G. S. P. Freeman-Grenville, *The Medieval History of the Coast of Tanganyika, with special reference to recent archaeological discoveries* (London: Oxford University Press, 1962), pp. 75–78, 84–86. Reprinted by permission.

## ARABIC VERSION

Chapter One: The first man to come to Kilwa and found it, and his descent from the Persian kings of the land of Shiraz.

Historians have said, amongst their assertions, that the first man to come to Kilwa came in the following way.  There arrived a ship in which there were people who claimed to have come from Shiraz in the land of the Persians.  It is said there were seven ships: the first stopped at Mandakha; the second at Shaughu; [1] the third at a town called Yanba; the fourth at Mombasa; [2] the fifth at the Green Island (of Pemba); the sixth at the land of Kilwa; and the seventh at Hanzuan.  They say all the masters of these six ships were brothers, and that the one who went to the town of Hanzuan was their father.  God alone knows all truth!

I understand from a person interested in history, whom I trust, that the reason for their leaving Shiraz in Persia was that their Sultan one day dreamed a dream. He was called Hasan (sc. Husain) ibn Ali: he was the father of these six men and the seventh of those who left.  In his dream he saw a rat with an iron snout gnawing holes in the town wall.  He interpreted the

[1] Mandhakha has not been identified, nor Shaughu; Yanba could be Jambe (Yambe) Island, off Tanga harbour, but, if so, the list is out of order.
[2] The text has the Arabic word, which strictly is Mafia, but Mombasa seems more logical if the list is in order since the next place mentioned is certainly Pemba.  Hanzuan, the last place named is presumably Yohana in the Comoro Islands.

Having come to the settlements of Mogadishu and Barawa, as he was of Persian origin and belonged to a sect of Mahamed which, as we have previously seen, was different from that of the Arabs, and as his intention was to found his own settlement of which he could be lord, and not be the subject of any other person, he sailed down the coast until he came to the port of Kilwa. Seeing from the situation and position of the land, which was surrounded by water, that he could live secure from the insults of the Kafirs, who inhabited it, he bought it from them at the price of some cloth, and, because, of the reasons he gave them, they crossed over to the mainland. After this, when they had abandoned the place, he began to fortify it, not only against them, in case they showed any malice, but also against various Moorish towns in the neighbourhood and against some Moors who inhabited certain islands called Songo and Xanga,[3] and who ruled the land up to Mompana about twenty leagues from Kilwa. As he was a wise man and of great courage, in a short time he fortified himself so that the place became a noble settlement, to which he gave the name it now bears. He began to rule over his neighbours, and sent his son, a goodly young man, to rule over the island of Monfia and other islands nearby. His descendants, who succeeded him, called themselves kings, as he did.

dream to prophesy the ruin of their country. When he had made certain that his interpretation of the dream was correct, he told his sons. He convinced them that their land would not escape destruction, and asked their advice. They said they left their decision to God and his Prophet (may he be exalted!), and to their father.

Their father said he intended to leave the land and go to another. His sons retorted: How can we go? Will the amirs and wazirs and the council agree to your departure, which involves the breaking of the cord that binds the kingdom together? He answered his sons and said: I have a stratagem by which we can escape. Tomorrow I shall summon all of you and the wazirs and amirs and the council. He said to his eldest son: I shall insult you before them all. When you have heard me show anger, strike me as though you were filled with rage. I shall grow angry on that account, and shall make it an excuse to leave the land. In this way, if God wills, we shall be able to depart.

Next day he summoned all his sons, and all the wazirs, amirs and the council, and they consulted together about the matters for discussion before them. The father spoke abusively of his eldest son, who thereupon struck him before them all. His father was angry and said: I will not remain in a land where I have been insulted like this. And the rest of his sons and all the people said: We will avenge you on your son and kill him. He answered: I am not satisfied. And they said: What will you? He replied: Only leaving this land will satisfy me.

And they all agreed to leave with their sultan. He got ready with his household and some of his amirs, wazirs and subjects. They took the road to the ports, and, embarking in seven ships, set sail. So they travelled under God's guidance to the lands of the Swahili coasts, where the ships dispersed, each going to the place already mentioned. It is strong evidence that they were kings in their own country,

[3] Both of these islands are in the Kilwa creek.

and a refutation of those who deny it. God alone knows all truth!

When they arrived in the ship which went to Kilwa, they found it was an island surrounded by the sea, but that at low water it was joined to the mainland so that one could cross on foot. They disembarked on the island and met a man who was a Muslim, followed by some of his children. It is said his name was Muriri wa Bari. They found there one mosque said to be the one he is buried in, and which is called Kibala.[4]

They asked the Muslim about the country and he replied: The island is ruled by an infidel from Muli,[5] who is king of it; he has gone to Muli to hunt, but will soon return. After a few days the infidel returned from Muli and crossed to the island at low tide. The newcomer and he met together, and Muriri acted as interpreter. The newcomer to Kilwa said: I should like to settle on the island: pray sell it to me that I may do so.

The infidel answered: I will sell it on condition that you encircle the island with coloured clothing. The newcomer agreed with the infidel and bought on the condition stipulated. He encircled the island with clothing, some white, some black, and every other colour besides. So the infidel agreed and took away all the clothing, handing over the island and departing to Muli. He concealed his real intention of returning with troops to kill the newcomer and his followers and to take their goods by force. The Muslim warned the purchaser and said: He is very fond of this island and will undoubtedly return to despoil you and yours of all your possessions and kill you. You must find some stratagem to be safe from his evil intention.

So they set themselves to the task and dug out the creek across which in former

[4] The term means the niche in a mosque which indicates the direction of Mecca, and in Swahili the north, since Mecca is northwards from the coast.
[5] The word evidently means mainland as distinct from an island. It has been shown that the word derives from Avestic through Pehlevi.

After his death he was succeeded by his son Ale Bumale, who reigned 40 years. As he had no sons, his nephew, Ale Busoloquete, inherited Kilwa, being the son of his brother who was in Mafia. He did not remain in power for more than four years and a half.

He (Ale Busoloquete) was succeeded by Daut, his son, who was driven out of Kilwa in the fourth year of his reign by Matata Mandalima, who was king of Xanga and his enemy, and Daut took refuge in Monfia, where he died. Matata left in Kilwa his nephew, named Ale Bonebaquer, who after two years was driven out by the Persians of Kilwa. In his place they put Hocen Soleiman, a nephew of the

times men passed at low tide between the mainland and the island. The tide filled it and did not recede again. Some days later the infidel came from Muli to the point from which he was wont to cross. He saw the tide was up; and waited in the usual way for it to ebb until he could cross; but the water remained up and did not go down at all. Then he despaired of seizing the island and was sorry at what he had done. He went home full of remorse and sorrow.

The first king of the land was Sultan Ali ibn al-Husain ibn Ali surnamed Nguo Nyingi. And this was in the middle of the third century after the flight of the Prophet-Peace upon him! This king ruled Kilwa and then went to Mafia, for the island pleased him. He put in charge of it his son Muhammad ibn Ali, who was known as Mkoma Watu.

Muhammad ibn Ali ruled for two and a half years, and after his death his third brother Bashat ibn Ali succeeded him. He was the first independent king of Mafia after his father died. He ruled four and a half years and then died.

The first man to come to Kilwa ruled forty years. After his death Ali ibn Bashat ibn Ali ruled for four and a half years. He took precedence over his paternal uncles Sulaiman ibn Ali, al-Hasan ibn Ali and Daud ibn Ali. When he died his uncle Daud ibn Ali ruled in his stead for two years. Then he went to Mafia to visit his father's grave. He liked Mafia and settled there, and gave his kingdom to his son Ali ibn Daud ibn Ali ibn al-Husain. He was the last of the seed of the first man to come to Kilwa. God knows best!

Chapter Two: The disturbance in the affairs of the kingdom of Kilwa and the Matamandalin.

These, the people of Shagh, fought a great war with the people of Kilwa, and conquered the country.[6] They took over the government and appointed to rule one of themselves named Khalid ibn Bakr.

[6] The people of Shagh were probably inhabitants of Songo Mnara Island (ed.).

deceased Daut.   He reigned sixteen
years. . . .

After two and a half years the people of
Kilwa united to depose him and banish
him from the country. They expelled him
without injuring him in any way, and
made him return to his own land.

Then al-Hasan ibn Sulaiman ibn Ali the
founder of Kilwa ruled for twelve years.
The Matamandalin attacked for a second
time and conquered the country.  And
they set up a man named Muhammad ibn
al-Husain al-Mandhiri, who reigned for
twelve years, and the name of the Matamandalin was mentioned in the Friday
prayers.  All these things happened after
the flight of Sultan al-Hasan to the land
of Zanzibar.

Then the people of Kilwa gathered
together to get rid of the Matamandalin.
They agreed that the matter of setting up
a king was not one for their sons, but that
they would depute it to them to do it for
them.  So they called all the young men
together and said: Are you content that
your king should have been deposed?
They all answered together: No! Then
they said to the young men: Make up your
minds and swear allegiance to the son of
your king.

So a thousand young men met, and did
as they were asked: they swore allegiance
to the sultan's son.  Then they went to the
house of the Amir (sc. Muhammad ibn
al-Husain) and seized him and put him in
fetters.  Then they sent the young men
with their king with a message to his
deposed father the sultan who had fled to
Zanzibar, so that he might come and receive the land from his son. He returned
from Zanzibar in six ships; and, when he
arrived at Kilwa, the Amir broke out and
went down to the strand to oppose him.
Then the young men slew the Amir. Thus
he took control of the country and ruled
for fourteen years before he died.

(Sc. al-Hasan ibn Sulaiman reigned sixteen years) and was succeeded by Ale
Bem Daut, his nephew, who reigned sixty
years, and was succeeded by his grandson
of the same name.

The inhabitants rose against him because he was a wicked man, and threw him alive into a well, after he had reigned six years.

They put in his place his brother Hasan Ben Daut, who reigned for twenty-four years.

After him there reigned Soleiman for two years. He was of royal descent. The inhabitants cut off his head because he was a very bad king.

He was succeeded by al-Hasan ibn Daud ibn Ali the founder of Kilwa, and at that time he was seventy years of age. And he reigned over his kingdom seventy years more. (End of Ch. II).

# 6  IBN BATTUTA
## THE EAST AFRICAN COAST IN 1331

*The celebrated Muslim traveler Ibn Battuta (1304–1368/9) traversed nearly the whole of the Muslim world and beyond during his many years of wandering. Born in Tangiers, he made the first of his four pilgrimages to Mecca when he was twenty-one; thereafter, his passion was to "travel throughout the earth," never twice by the same road. His second journey took him through southern Iraq and southwest Persia, then to Tabriz and north-western Mesopotamia. He subsequently traveled along the Red Sea, down the East African coast, and returned via the Persian Gulf. His fourth journey took him to Constantinople and from there to India, where he arrived in September 1333. He resided in India for several years in the service of the Sultan, traveling to China on the latter's behalf in 1342. Ibn Battuta then returned to the West, visiting Andalusia and the western Sudan. The account of this intelligent and perceptive observer provides an invaluable picture of the East African coast in 1331.*

I travelled from the city of Adan by sea for four days and arrived at the city of Zaila, the city of the Barbara,[1] who are a people of the negroes,[2] Shafiites in rite. Their country is a desert extending for two months' journey, beginning at Zaila and ending at Maqdashaw. Their cattle are camels, and they also have sheep which are famed for their fat. The inhabitants of Zaila are black in colour, and the majority of them are Rafidis.[3] It is a large city with a great bazaar, but it is in the dirtiest, most disagreeable, and most stinking town in the world. The reason

From *The Travels of Ibn Battuta, A.D. 1325–1354,* trans. and edited by H. A. R. Gibb (New York: Cambridge University Press, 1962), II, 373–382. Reprinted by permission of Cambridge University Press on behalf of *The Hakluyt Society.* In this selection inserts bracketed into the text are those of H. A. R. Gibb.

[1] Zaila, on a sandy spit on the Somali coast due south of Aden, was included at this time in the Ethiopian kingdom of Awfat or Ifat. . . .

By the term *Barbara* the Arabic geographers apparently mean the Hamitic tribes who are neither Abyssinian (*Habash*) nor negroes (*Zinj*), and more especially the Somalis, although Ibn Battuta here includes them among the negroes. . . .

[2] Arabic *Zinj* or *Zanj,* a term ultimately derived from Persian or Sanskrit, probably in the language of the seamen of the Persian Gulf.

[3] I.e., Shiites, probably of the Zaidi sect.

for its stench is the quantity of its fish and the blood of the camels that they slaughter in the streets. When we arrived there we chose to spend the night at sea in spite of its extreme roughness, rather than pass a night in the town, because of its filth.

We sailed on from there for fifteen nights and came to Maqdashaw, which is a town of enormous size.[4] Its inhabitants are merchants possessed of vast resources; they own large numbers of camels, of which they slaughter hundreds every day [for food], and also have quantities of sheep. In this place are manufactured the woven fabrics called after it, which are unequalled and exported from it to Egypt and elsewhere. It is the custom of the people of this town that, when a vessel reaches the anchorage, the *sumbuqs,* which are small boats, come out to it. In each *sumbuq* there are a number of young men of the town, each one of whom brings a covered platter containing food and presents it to one of the merchants on the ship saying "This is my guest," and each of the others does the same. The merchant, on disembarking, goes only to the house of his host among the young men, except those of them who have made frequent journeys to the town and have gained some acquaintance with its inhabitants; these lodge where they please. When he takes up residence with his host, the latter sells his goods for him and buys for him; and if anyone buys anything from him at too low a price or sells to him in the absence of his host, that sale is held invalid by them. This practice is a profitable one for them.

When the young men came on board the vessel in which I was, one of them came up to me. My companions said to him "This man is not a merchant, but a doctor of the law," whereupon he called out to his friends and said to them "This

is the guest of the qadi." There was among them one of the qadi's men, who informed him of this, and he came down to the beach with a number of students and sent one of them to me. I then disembarked with my companions and saluted him and his party. He said to me "In the name of God, let us go to salute the Shaikh." "And who is the Shaikh?" I said, and he answered, "The Sultan," for it is their custom to call the sultan "the Shaikh." Then I said to him "When I am lodged, I shall go to him," but he said to me, "It is the custom that whenever there comes a jurist or a sharif or a man of religion, he must first see the sultan before taking a lodging." So I went with him to the sultan, as they asked.

*Account of the Sultan of Maqdashaw.*[5] The sultan of Maqdashaw is, as we have mentioned, called only by the title of "the Shaikh." His name is Abu Bakr, son of the shaikh Omar; he is by origin of the Barbara and he speaks in Maqdishi, but knows the Arabic language. One of his customs is that, when a vessel arrives, the sultan's *sumbuq* goes out to it, and enquiries are made as to the ship, whence it has come, who is its owner and its *rubban* (that is, its captain), what is its cargo, and who has come on it of merchants and others. When all of this information has been collected, it is presented to the sultan, and if there are any persons [of such quality] that the sultan should assign a lodging to him as his guest, he does so.

When I arrived with the qadi I have mentioned, who was called Ibn al-Burhan, an Egyptian by origin, at the sultan's residence, one of the serving-boys came out and saluted the qadi, who said to him "Take word to the intendant's office and inform the Shaikh that this man has come

---

[4] Mogadishu was founded in the tenth century as a trading colony by Arabs from the Persian Gulf, the principal group being from al-Hasa. . . .

[5] The various Arab tribes occupied different quarters in Mogadishu (hence presumably its expansion), but recognized the supremacy of the tribe of Muqri, who called themselves Qahtanis, i.e. south-Arabians, and furnished the qadi of the city. The sultanate seems to have emerged only towards the end of the thirteenth century, and the most noted of its sultans was this Abu Bakr b. Fakhr al-Din.

from the land of al-Hijaz." So he took the message, then returned bringing a plate on which were some leaves of betel and areca nuts. He gave me ten leaves along with a few of the nuts, the same to the qadi, and what was left on the plate to my companions and the qadi's students. He brought also a jug of rose-water of Damascus, which he poured over me and over the qadi [i.e. over our hands], and said "Our master commands that he be lodged in the students' house," this being a building equipped for the entertainment of students of religion. The qadi took me by the hand and we went to this house, which is in the vicinity of the Shaikh's residence, and furnished with carpets and all necessary appointments. Later on [the serving boy] brought food from the Shaikh's residence. With him came one of his viziers, who was responsible for [the care of] the guests, and who said "Our master greets you and says to you that you are heartily welcome." He then set down the food and we ate. Their food is rice cooked with ghee, which they put into a large wooden platter, and on top of this they set platters of *kushan*.[6] This is the seasoning, made of chickens, fleshmeat, fish and vegetables. They cook unripe bananas in fresh milk and put this in one dish, and in another dish they put curdled milk, on which they place [pieces of] pickled lemon, bunches of pickled pepper steeped in vinegar and salted, green ginger, and mangoes. These resemble apples, but have a stone; when ripe they are exceedingly sweet and are eaten like [other] fruit, but before ripening they are acid like lemons, and they pickle them in vinegar. When they take a mouthful of rice, they eat some of these salted and vinegar conserves after it. A single person of the people of Maqdashaw eats as much as a whole company of us would eat, as a mat-

ter of habit, and they are corpulent and fat in the extreme.

After we had eaten, the qadi took leave of us. We stayed there three days, food being brought to us three times a day, following their custom. On the fourth day, which was a Friday, the qadi and students and one of the Shaikh's viziers came to me, bringing a set of robes; these [official] robes of theirs consist of a silk wrapper which one ties round his waist in place of drawers (for they have no acquaintance with these), a tunic of Egyptian linen with an embroidered border, a furred mantle of Jerusalem stuff, and an Egyptian turban with an embroidered edge. They also brought robes for my companions suitable to their position. We went to the congregational mosque and made our prayers behind the *maqsura*.[7] When the Shaikh came out of the door of the *maqsura* I saluted him along with the qadi; he said a word of greeting, spoke in their tongue with the qadi, and then said in Arabic "You are heartily welcome, and you have honoured our land and given us pleasure." He went out to the court of the mosque and stood by the grave of his father, who is buried there, then recited some verses from the Quran and said a prayer. After this the viziers, amirs, and officers of the troops came up and saluted him. Their manner of salutation is the same as the custom of the people of al-Yaman; one puts his forefinger to the ground, then raises it to his head and says "May God prolong thy majesty." The Shaikh then went out of the gate of the mosque, put on his sandals, ordered the qadi to put on his sandals and me to do likewise, and set out on foot for his residence, which is close to the mosque. All the [rest of the] people walked barefoot. Over his head were carried four canopies of coloured silk, with the figure of a bird in gold on top of each canopy.[8] His gar-

---

[6] *Kushan* is probably a term of the Persian Gulf seamen for seasonings of meat and vegetables, resembling curries, served with rice. The origin may be related to Persian *gushtan*, glossed as "meats and fruit pulps."

[7] The enclosure in the congregational mosque reserved for the ruler.
[8] Ibn Battuta does not call these by the name of the ceremonial parasol, *jitr*, the use of which had been

ments on that day were a large green mantle of Jerusalem stuff, with fine robes of Egyptian stuffs with their appendages underneath it, and he was girt with a waist-wrapper of silk and turbaned with a large turban. In front of him were sounded drums and trumpets and fifes, and before and behind him were the commanders of the troops, while the qadi, the doctors of the law and the sharifs walked alongside him. He entered his audience-hall in this disposition, and the viziers, amirs and officers of the troops sat down in a gallery there. For the qadi there was spread a rug, on which no one may sit but he, and beside him were the jurists and sharifs. They remained there until the hour of the afternoon prayer, and after they had prayed it, the whole body of troops came and stood in rows in order of their ranks. Thereafter the drums, fifes, trumpets and flutes are sounded; while they play no person moves or stirs from his place, and anyone who is walking stands still, moving neither backwards nor forwards. When the playing of the drum-band comes to an end, they salute with their fingers as we have described and withdraw. This is a custom of theirs on every Friday.

On the Saturday, the population comes to the Shaikh's gate and they sit in porticoes outside his residence. The qadi, jurists, sharifs, men of religion, shaikhs and those who have made the Pilgrimage go in to the second audience-hall, where they sit on platforms prepared for that purpose. The qadi will be on a platform by himself, and each class of persons on the platform proper to them, which is shared by no others. The Shaikh then takes his seat in his hall and sends for the qadi, who sits down on his left; thereafter the jurists enter, and the principal men amongst them sit down in front of the

Shaikh, while the remainder salute and withdraw. Next the sharifs come in, their principal men sit down in front of him, and the remainder salute and withdraw. If they are guests, they sit on the Shaikh's right. Next the shaikhs and pilgrims come in, and their principal men sit, and the rest salute and withdraw. Then come the viziers, then the amirs, then the officers of the troops, group after group, and they salute and withdraw. Food is brought in; the qadi and sharifs and all those who are sitting in the hall eat in the presence of the Shaikh, and he eats with them. If he wishes to honour one of his principal amirs, he sends for him, and the latter eats with them. The rest of the people eat in the dining-hall, and the order of eating is the same as their order of entry into the Shaikh's presence. The Shaikh then goes into his residence, and the qadi, with the viziers, the private secretary, and four of the principal amirs, sits for deciding cases among the population and petitioners. Every case that is concerned with the rulings of the Divine Law is decided by the qadi, and all cases other than those are decided by the members of the council, that is to say, the viziers and amirs. If any case calls for consultation of the sultan, they write to him about it, and he sends out the reply to them immediately on the reverse of the document as determined by his judgment. And this too is their fixed custom.

I then sailed from the city of Maqdashaw, making for the country of the Sawahil [Coastlands], with the object of visiting the city of Kulwa in the land of the Zinj people. We came to the island of Mambasa, a large island two days' journey by sea from the Sawahil country.[9] It has no mainland territory, and its trees are the banana, the lemon, and the citron. Its people have a fruit which

---

apparently introduced by the Fatimid caliphs of Egypt and spread to all parts of the Muslim world. But apart from the fact of the four "canopies" (qibab), it is difficult to see how these differed from the parasols, especially as the latter too were often surmounted by the figure of a bird.

[9] *Sahil*, literally "coastland," meant in maritime usage a port serving as an entrepôt for the goods of its hinterland . . . Mombasa is separated from the mainland only by a narrow strait, but Ibn Battuta apparently means that it is two days sailing time from the "Coastlands" properly so called, i.e. the trading ports to the southward.

they call *jammun*, resembling an olive and with a stone like its stone. The inhabitants of this island sow no grain, and it has to be transported to them from the Sawahil. Their food consists mostly of bananas and fish. They are Shafiites in rite, pious, honourable, and upright, and their mosques are of wood, admirably constructed. At each of the gates of the mosques there are one or two wells (their wells have a depth of one or two cubits), and they draw up water from them in a wooden vessel, into which has been fixed a thin stick of the length of one cubit. The ground round the well and the mosque is paved; anyone who intends to go into the mosque washes his feet before entering, and at its gate there is a piece of thick matting on which he rubs his feet. If one intends to make an ablution, he holds the vessel between his thighs, pours [water] on his hands and performs the ritual washings. All the people walk with bare feet.

We stayed one night in this island and sailed on to the city of Kulwa, a large city on the seacoast,[10] most of whose inhabitants are Zinj, jet-black in colour. They have tattoo marks on their faces, just as [there are] on the faces of the *Limis* of Janawa.[11] I was told by a merchant that the city of Sufala[12] lies at a distance of half a month's journey from the city of Kulwa, and that between Sufala and Yufi, in the country of the Limis, is a month's journey; from Yufi gold dust is brought to Sufala.[13] The city of Kulwa is one of

the finest and most substantially built towns; all the buildings are of wood, and the houses are roofed with *dis* reeds. The rains there are frequent. Its people engage in *jihad*, because they are on a common mainland with the heathen Zinj people and contiguous to them, and they are for the most part religious and upright, and Shafiites in rite.

*Account of the Sultan of Kulwa.* Its sultan at the period of my entry into it was Abul-Muzaffar Hasan, who was called also by the appellation of Abul-Mawahib, on account of the multitude of his gifts and acts of generosity. He used to engage frequently in expeditions to the land of the Zinj people, raiding them and taking booty, and he would set aside the fifth part of it to devote to the objects prescribed for it in the Book of God Most High. He used to deposit the portion for the relatives [of the Prophet] in a separate treasury; whenever he was visited by sharifs he would pay it out to them, and the sharifs used to come to visit him from al-Iraq and al-Hijaz and other countries. I saw at his court a number of the sharifs of al-Hijaz, amongst them Muhammad b. Jammaz, Mansur b. Lubaida b. Abu Numayy, and Muhammad b. Shumaila b. Abu Numayy, and at Maqdashaw I met Tabl b. Kubaish b. Jammaz, who was intending to go to him. This sultan is a man of great humility; he sits with poor brethren, and eats with them, and greatly respects men of religion and noble descent.

*An anecdote illustrating his generosity.* I was present with him on a Friday, when he had come out [of the mosque] after the prayer and was proceeding to his residence. He was accosted by a poor brother, a Yamanite, who said to him "O Abul-Mawahib;" he replied "At your service, O faqir—what do you want?" The man said, "Give me those robes that you are wearing." He said "Certainly I shall give you them." The man said "Now," and he said "Yes, now," went back to the mosque and into the khatib's chamber, where he dressed in other garments, and having taken off those robes

[10] Kilwa (*Kulwa* is not otherwise attested), Quiloa of the Portuguese chronicles, now Kilwa Kisiwani in Tanganyika (8° 57′ S., 39° 34′ E.), 340 miles south of Mombasa. . . .

[11] *Limi* is a variant form of *Lamlam*, applied by the Arab geographers to the (supposedly cannibal) tribes of the interior. Janawa was the name given to the country of the pagan tribes south of the Muslim lands in West Africa, which passed into Portuguese and thence into English as Guinea.

[12] Sofala, at 20° 10′ S., 34° 42′ E., was the southernmost trading station of the Arabs in Africa, founded by colonists from Mogadishu.

[13] Yufi is the kingdom of Nupe in West Africa. This confusion between the gold dust of the Niger and the mined gold ore of Sofala and the assumption of a connection between them are probably due to some misunderstanding on Ibn Battuta's part.

he called to the poor brother "Come in and take them." So the faqir came in, took them, made a bundle of them in a kerchief, placed them on his head and went off. The population were loud in their gratitude to the sultan for the humility and generosity that he had displayed, and his son, who was his designated heir, took the clothing from the poor brother and gave him ten slaves in exchange. When the sultan learned of the gratitude expressed by the people to him for that action, he too ordered the faqir to be given ten head of slaves and two loads of ivory, for most of their gifts consist of ivory and it is seldom that they give gold. When this worthy and open-handed sultan died (God have mercy on him), he was succeeded by his brother Daud, who was of the opposite line of conduct. When a petitioner came to him he would say to him "He who gave is dead, and left nothing behind to be given." Visitors would stay at his court for many months, and finally he would make them some small gift, so that at last solicitors gave up coming to his gate.

## 7 DUARTE BARBOSA

## THE EAST COAST OF AFRICA AT THE BEGINNING OF THE SIXTEENTH CENTURY

*Duarte Barbosa was a Portuguese royal commercial agent whose account of the East African Coast concerns the years 1500 to 1518, the beginning of the Portuguese period. He describes the towns of the coast before the major impact of Portuguese control and influence had altered their character and affected their prosperity.*

### SOFALA

Having passed the Little Vciques, for the Indies, at xviii leagues from them there is a river which is not very large, whereon is a town of the Moors called Sofala, close to which town the King of Portugal has a fort. These Moors established themselves there a long time ago on account of the great trade in gold which they carry on with the Gentiles of the mainland: these speak somewhat of bad Arabic (garabia), and have got a king over them, who is at present subject to the King of Portugal. And the mode of their trade is that they come by sea in small barks which they call zanbucs (sambuk), from the kingdoms of Quiloa, and Mombaza, and Melindi; and they bring much cotton cloth of many colours, and white and blue, and some of silk; and grey, and red, and yellow beads, which come to the said kingdoms in other larger ships from the great kingdom of Cambay [India—ed.], which merchandise these Moors buy and collect from other Moors who bring them there, and they pay for them in gold by weight, and for a price which satisfies them; and the said Moors keep them and sell these cloths to the Gentiles of the kingdom of Benamatapa who come there laden with gold, which gold they give in exchange for the before mentioned cloths without weighing, and so much in quantity that these Moors usually gain one hundred for one. They also collect a large quantity of ivory, which is found all round Sofala, which they likewise sell in the great kingdom of Cambay at five or six

From Duarte Barbosa, *A Description of the Coasts of East Africa and Malabar in the Beginning of the Sixteenth Century*, trans. by Henry E. J. Stanley (London: Hakluyt Society, 1866), pp. 4–15, 19–21.

ducats [1] the hundred weight, and so also some amber, which these Moors of Sofala bring them from the Vciques. They are black men, and men of colour—some speak Arabic, and the rest make use of the language of the Gentiles of the country. They wrap themselves from the waist downwards with cloths of cotton and silk, and they wear other silk cloths above named, such as cloaks and wraps for the head, and some of them wear hoods of scarlet, and of other coloured woollen stuffs and camelets, and of other silks. And their victuals are millet, and rice, and meat, and fish. In this river near to the sea there are many sea horses, which go in the sea, and come out on land at times to feed. These have teeth like small elephants, and it is better ivory than that of the elephant, and whiter and harder, and of greater durability of colour. In the country all round Sofala there are many elephants, which are very large and wild, and the people of the country do not know how to tame them: there are also many lions, ounces, mountain panthers, wild asses, and many other animals. It is a country of plains and mountains, and well watered. The Moors have now recently begun to produce much fine cotton in this country, and they weave it into white stuff because they do not know how to dye it, or because they have not got any colours; and they take the blue or coloured stuffs of Cambay and unravel them, and again weave the threads with their white thread, and in this manner they make coloured stuffs, by means of which they get much gold.

## KINGDOM OF BENAMATAPA

On entering within this country of Sofala, there is the kingdom of Benamatapa, which is very large and peopled by Gentiles, whom the Moors call Cafers. These are brown men, who go bare, but covered from the waist downwards with coloured stuffs, or skins of wild animals; and the

[1] A ducat was a gold coin of varying value (ed.).

persons most in honour among them wear some of the tails of the skin behind them, which go trailing on the ground for state and show, and they make bounds and movements of their bodies, by which they make these tails wag on either side of them. They carry swords in scabbards of wood bound with gold or other metals, and they wear them on the left hand side as we do, in sashes of coloured stuffs, which they make for this purpose with four or five knots, and their tassels hanging down, like gentlemen; and in their hands azagayes, and others carry bows and arrows: it must be mentioned that the bows are of middle size, and the iron points of the arrows are very large and well wrought. They are men of war, and some of them are merchants: their women go naked as long as they are girls, only covering their middles with cotton cloths, and when they are married and have children, they wear other cloths over their breasts.

## ZINBAOCH

Leaving Sofala for the interior of the country, at xv days journey from it, there is a large town of Gentiles, which is called Zinbaoch; and it has houses of wood and straw, in which town the King of Benamatapa frequently dwells, and from there to the city of Benamatapa there are six days journey, and the road goes from Sofala, inland, towards the Cape of Good Hope. And in the said Benamatapa, which is a very large town, the king is used to make his longest residence; and it is thence that the merchants bring to Sofala the gold which they sell to the Moors without weighing it, for coloured stuffs and beads of Cambay, which are much used and valued amongst them; and the people of this city of Benamatapa say that this gold comes from still further off towards the Cape of Good Hope, from another kingdom subject to this king of Benamatapa, who is a great lord, and holds many other kings as his subjects, and many other lands, which extend far inland, both towards the Cape of Good Hope and towards Mozambich. And in this town he is each day served with large presents, which the kings and lords, his subjects, send to him; and when they bring them, they carry them bareheaded through all the city, until they arrive at the palace, from whence the king sees them come from a window, and he orders them to be taken up from there, and the bearers do not see him, but only hear his words; and afterwards, he bids them call the persons who have brought these presents, and he dismisses them. This king constantly takes with him into the field a captain, whom they call Sono, with a great quantity of men-at-arms, and amongst them they bring six thousand women, who also bear arms and fight. With these forces he goes about subduing and pacifying whatever kings rise up or desire to revolt. The said king of Benamatapa sends, each year, many honourable persons throughout his kingdoms to all the towns and lordships, to give them new regulations, so that all may do them obeisance, which is in this manner: each one of the envoys comes to a town, and bids the people extinguish all the fires that there are in it; and after they have been put out, all the inhabitants go to this man who has been sent as commissary, to get fresh fire from him in sign of subjection and obedience; and, whoever should not do this is held as a rebel, and the king immediately sends the number of people that are necessary to destroy him, and these pass through all the towns at their expense: their rations are meat, rice, and oil of sesame.

## RIVER ZUAMA

Leaving Sofala for Mozambich, at forty leagues from it, there is a very large river, which is called the Zuama; and it is said that it goes towards Benamatapa, and it extends more than 160 leagues. In the mouth of this river there is a town of the Moors, which has a king, and it is called Mongalo. Much gold comes from Benamatapa to this town of the Moors, by this river, which makes another branch which falls at Angos, where the Moors make use of boats (almadias), which are boats hollowed out from a single trunk, to bring the cloths and other merchandise from Angos, and to transport much gold and ivory.

## ANGOY

After passing this river of Zuama, at xl leagues from it, there is a town of the Moors on the sea coast, which is called Angoy, and has a king, and the Moors who live there are all merchants, and deal in gold, ivory, silk, and cotton stuffs, and beads of Cambay, the same as do those of Sofala. And the Moors bring these goods from Quiloa, and Monbaza, and Melynde, in small vessels hidden from the Portuguese ships; and they carry from there a great quantity of ivory, and much gold. And in this town of Angos there are plenty of provisions of millet, rice, and some kinds of meat. These men are very brown and copper coloured; they go naked from the waist upwards, and from thence downwards, they wrap themselves with cloths of cotton and silk, and wear other cloths folded after the fashion of cloaks, and some wear caps and others hoods, worked with stuffs and silks; and they speak the language belonging to the country, which is that of the Pagans, and some of them speak Arabic. These people are sometimes in obedience to the king of Portugal, and at times they throw it off, for they are a long way off from the Portuguese forts.

## MOZAMBIQUE ISLAND

Having passed this town of Anguox, on the way to India, there are very near to the land three islands, one of which is inhabited by Moors, and is called Mozambique. It has a very good port, and all the Moors touch there who are sailing to Sofala, Zuama, or Anguox. Amongst these Moors there is a sheriff, who governs them, and does justice. These are of the language and customs of the Moors of Anguox, in which island the King of Portugal now holds a fort, and keeps the said Moors under his orders and government. At this island the Portuguese ships provide themselves with water and wood, fish and other kinds of provisions; and at this place they refit those ships which stand in need of repair. And from this island likewise the Portuguese fort in Sofala draws its supplies, both of Portuguese goods and of the produce of India, on account of the road being longer by the mainland.

Opposite this island there are many very large elephants and wild animals. The country is inhabited by Gentiles, brutish people who go naked and smeared all over with coloured clay, and their natural parts wrapped in a strip of blue cotton stuff, without any other covering; and they have their lips pierced with three holes in each lip, and in these holes they wear bones stuck in, and claws, and small stones, and other little things dangling from them.

## ISLAND OF QUILOA

After passing this place and going towards India, there is another island close to the mainland, called Quiloa, in which there is a town of the Moors, built of handsome houses of stone and lime, and very lofty, with their windows like those of the Christians; in the same way it has streets, and these houses have got their terraces, and the wood worked in with the masonry, with plenty of gardens, in which there are many fruit trees and much water. This island has got a king over it, and from hence there is trade with Sofala with ships, which carry much gold, which is dispersed thence through all Arabia Felix, for henceforward all this country is thus named on account of the shore of the sea being peopled with many towns and cities of the Moors; and when the King of Portugal discovered this land, the Moors of Sofala, and Zuama, and Anguox, and Mozambique, were all under obedience to the King of Quiloa, who was a great king amongst them. And there is much gold in this town, because all the ships which go to Sofala touch at this island, both in going and coming back. These people are Moors, of a dusky colour, and some of them are black and some white; they are very well dressed with rich cloths of gold, and silk, and cotton, and the women also go very well dressed out with much gold and silver in chains and bracelets on their arms, and legs, and ears. The speech of these people is Arabic, and they have got books of the Alcoran, and honour greatly their prophet Muhamad. This King, for his great pride, and for not being willing to obey the King of Portugal, had this town taken from him by force, and in it they killed and captured many people, and the King fled from the island, in which the King of Portugal ordered a fortress to be built, and thus he holds under his command and government those who continued to dwell there.

## ISLAND OF MOMBAZA

Passing Quiloa, and going along the coast of the said Arabia Felix towards India, close to the mainland there is another island, in which there is a city of the Moors, called Mombaza,[2] very large and beautiful, and built of high and handsome houses of stone and whitewash, and with very good streets, in the manner of those of Quiloa. And it also had a king over it. The people are of dusky white, and brown complexions, and likewise the women, who are much adorned with silk and gold stuffs. It is a town of great trade in goods, and has a good port, where there are always many ships, both of those that sail for Sofala and those that come from Cambay and Melinde, and others which sail to the islands of Zanzibar, Manfia, and Penda, which will be spoken of further on. This Mombaza is a country well supplied with plenty of provisions, very fine sheep, which have round tails, and many cows,

2 Mombaza.

chickens, and very large goats, much rice and millet, and plenty of oranges, sweet and bitter, and lemons, cedrats, pomegranates, Indian figs, and all sorts of vegetables, and very good water. The inhabitants at times are at war with the people of the continent, and at other times at peace, and trade with them, and obtain much honey and wax, and ivory. This King, for his pride and unwillingness to obey the King of Portugal, lost his city, and the Portuguese took it from him by force, and the King fled, and they killed and made captives many of his people, and the country was ravaged, and much plunder was carried off from it of gold and silver, copper, ivory, rich stuffs of gold and silk, and much other valuable merchandize.

## MELINDE

After passing the city of Mombaza, at no great distance further on along the coast, there is a very handsome town on the mainland on the beach, called Melinde, and it is a town of the Moors, which has a king. And this town has fine houses of stone and whitewash, of several stories, with their windows and terraces, and good streets. The inhabitants are dusky and black, and go naked from the waist upwards, and from that downwards they cover themselves with cloths of cotton and silk, and others wear wraps like cloaks, and handsome caps on their heads. The trade is great which they carry on in cloth, gold, ivory, copper, quicksilver, and much other merchandise, with both Moors and Gentiles of the kingdom of Cambay, who come to their port with ships laden with cloth, which they buy in exchange for gold, ivory, and wax. Both parties find great profit in this. There are plenty of provisions in this town, of rice, millet, and some wheat, which is brought to them from Cambay, and plenty of fruit, for there are many gardens and orchards. There are here many of the large-tailed sheep, and of all other meats as above; there are also oranges, sweet and sour. This King and people have always been

very friendly and obedient to the King of Portugal, and the Portuguese have always met with much friendship and good reception amongst them.

## ISLAND OF SAN LORENZO

Opposite these places, in the sea above the Cape of the Currents, at a distance of eighty leagues, there is a very large island, which is called San Lorenzo, and which is peopled by Gentiles, and has in it some towns of Moors. This island has many kings, both Moors and Gentiles. There is in it much meat, rice, and millet, and plenty of oranges and lemons, and there is much ginger in this country, which they do not make use of, except to eat it almost green. The inhabitants go naked, covering only their middles with cotton cloths. They do not navigate, nor does any one do so for them; they have got canoes for fishing on their coast. They are people of a dark complexion, and have a language of their own. They frequently are at war with one another, and their arms are azagayes, very sharp, with their points very well worked; they throw these in order to wound, and carry several of them in their hands. They are very well built and active men, and have a good method of wrestling. There is amongst them silver of inferior quality. Their principal food is roots, which they sow, and it is called yname,[3] and in the Indies of Spain it is called maize. The country is very beautiful and luxuriant in vegetation, and it has very large rivers. This island is in length from the part of Sofala and Melinde three hundred leagues, and to the mainland there are sixty leagues.

## PENDA, MANFIA, AND ZANZIBAR

Between this island of San Lorenzo and the continent, not very far from it, are three islands, which are called one

[3] Root in the form of a gourd, composed of two bulbs, which grow one above the other, the larger one below the smaller one. It is cut into slices and eaten instead of bread. It throws out very large leaves, without fruit. . . .

Manfia, another Zanzibar, and the other Penda; these are inhabited by Moors; they are very fertile islands, with plenty of provisions, rice, millet, and flesh, and abundant oranges, lemons, and cedrats. All the mountains are full of them; they produce many sugar canes, but do not know how to make sugar. These islands have their kings. The inhabitants trade with the mainland with their provisions and fruits; they have small vessels, very loosely and badly made, without decks, and with a single mast; all their planks are sewn together with cords of reed or matting, and the sails are of palm mats. They are very feeble people, with very few and despicable weapons. In these islands they live in great luxury, and abundance; they dress in very good cloths of silk and cotton, which they buy in Mombaza of the merchants from Cambay, who reside there. Their wives adorn themselves with many jewels of gold from Sofala, and silver, in chains, ear-rings, bracelets, and ankle rings, and are dressed in silk stuffs: and they have many mosques, and hold the Alcoran of Mahomed.

## PATE

After passing Melinde, and going towards India, they cross the Gulf (because the coast trends inwards) towards the Red Sea, and on the coast there is a town called Pate, and further on there is another town of the Moors, called Lamon; all these trade with the Gentiles of the country, and they are strongly-walled towns of stone and whitewash, because at times they have to fight with the Gentiles, who live in the interior of the country.

## BRAVA

Leaving these places, further on along the coast is a town of the Moors, well walled, and built of good houses of stone and whitewash, which is called Brava. It has not got a king; it is governed by its elders, they being honoured and respectable persons. It is a place of trade, which has already been destroyed by the Portuguese, with great slaughter of the inhabitants, of whom many were made captives, and great riches in gold, silver, and other merchandise were taken here, and those who escaped fled into the country, and after the place was destroyed they returned to people it.

.   .   .

## KINGDOM OF PRESTER JOHN

Leaving these towns of the Moors and entering into the interior of the country, the great kingdom of Prester John is to be found, whom the Moors of Arabia call Abexi; [4] this kingdom is very large, and peopled with many cities, towns, and villages, with many inhabitants: and it has many kings subject to it and tributary kings. And in their country there are many who live in the fields and mountains, like Beduins: they are black men, very well made: they have many horses, and make use of them, and are good riders, and there are great sportsmen and hunters amongst them. Their provisions are flesh of all kinds, milk, butter, and wheaten bread, and of these things there is a great abundance. Their clothes are of hides because the country is wanting in cloths; and there is a law amongst them by which certain families and ranks of persons may wear cloths, and the rest of the people may wear only hides well dressed and tanned. Amongst them there are men and women who have never drunk water, but only milk, which greatly supports them, and quenches the thirst, on account of its being more healthy and substantial, and there is great abundance of it in the country. These people are Christians of the doctrine of the blessed Saint Bartholomew, as they say; and their baptism is in three kinds, of blood, fire, and water: that is to say, that they circumcise themselves, and mark themselves on the temples and forehead with fire, and also in water, like the Catholic Christians. Many of them are deficient in our true faith, because the country is very large, and whilst in the principal city of Babel

[4] Habeshy, Abyssinian.

Melech, where Prester John resides, they may be Christians, in many other distant parts they live in error and without being taught; so that they are only Christians in name.

## BABEL MELECH

In the interior of this country is the great city of Babel Melech, where Prester John holds his residence. The Moors call him the great King of the Habeshys: he is Christian, and lord of many extensive countries and numerous people, with whom he makes subject many great kings. He is very rich, and possesses more gold than any other prince. This Prester John holds a very large court, and he keeps many men at arms continually in his pay, whom he takes about with him. He goes out very rarely from his dwelling; many kings and great lords come to visit him. In this city a great feast takes place in the month of August, for which so many kings and nobles come together, and so many people that they are innumerable:

and on this day of the feast in August they take an image out of a church, which is believed to be that of Our Lady, or that of St. Bartholomew, which image is of gold and of the size of a man; its eyes are of very large and beautiful rubies of great value, and the whole of it is adorned with many precious stones of much value, and placing it in a great chariot of gold, they carry it in procession with very great veneration and ceremony, and Prester John goes in front of this car in another gold car, very richly dressed in cloth of gold with much jewellery. And they begin to go out thus in the morning, and go in procession through all the city with much music of all sorts of instruments, until the evening, when they go home. And so many people throng to this procession, that in order to arrive at the car of the image many die of being squeezed and suffocated; and those who die in this wise are held as saints and martyrs; and many old men and old women go with a good will to die in this manner.

# 8  FRANCISCO ALVAREZ
## THE LAND OF PRESTER JOHN

*Father Francisco Alvarez (d. c. 1540) was chaplin to the Portuguese mission that was led by Don Rodrigo de Lima and that visited Ethiopia during the years 1520 to 1525. At that time Abyssinia was still known as the land of Prester John, the legendary priest-king whose dominions were thought to be in Ethiopia and whose Christian subjects Portugal was anxious to support against the Muslims of Arabia and the Persian Gulf as part of the continuing Portuguese crusade against Islam.*

At a day's journey from this church of Imbra Christo are edifices, the like of which and so many, cannot, as it appears to me, be found in the world, and they are

From Father Francisco Alvarez, *Narrative of the Portuguese Embassy to Abyssinia During the Years 1520–1527*, trans. and edited by Lord Stanley of Alderley (London: Hakluyt Society, 1881), pp. 122–126, 240–245.

churches entirely excavated in the rock, very well hewn. The names of these churches are these: Emanuel, St. Saviour, St. Mary, Holy Cross, St. George, Golgotha, Bethlehem, Marcoreos, the Martyrs. The principal one is Lalibela. This Lalibela, they say, was a King in this same country for eighty years, and he was King before the one before mentioned who was named Abraham. This King ordered these edifices to be made. He does not lie in the church which bears his name, he lies in the church of Golgotha, which is the church of the fewest buildings here. It is in this manner: all excavated in the stone itself, a hundred and twenty spans in length, and seventy-two spans in width. The ceiling of this church rests on five supports, two on each side, and one in the centre, like fives of dice, and the ceiling or roof is all flat like the floor of the church, the sides also are worked in a fine fashion, also the windows, and the doors with all the tracery, which could be told, so that neither a jeweller in silver, nor a worker of wax in wax, could do more work. The tomb of this King is in the same manner as that of Santiago of Galicia, at Compostella, and it is in this manner: the gallery which goes round the church is like a cloister, and lower than the body of the church, and one goes down from the church to this gallery; there are three windows on each side, that is to say, at that height which the church is higher than the gallery, and as much as the body of the church extends, so much is excavated below, and to as much depth as there is height above the floor of the church. And if one looks through each of these windows which is opposite the sun, one sees the tomb at the right of the high altar. In the centre of the body of the church is the sign of a door like a trap door, it is covered up with a large stone, like an altar stone, fitting very exactly in that door. They say that this is the entrance to the lower chamber, and that no one enters there, nor does it appear that that stone or door can be raised. This stone has a hole in the centre which pierces it through, its size is three palms.[1] All the pilgrims put their hands into this stone (which hardly find room), and say that many miracles are done here. On the left hand side, when one goes from the principal door before the principal

chapel, there is a tomb cut in the same rock as the church, which they say is made after the manner of the sepulchre of Christ in Jerusalem. So they hold it in honour and veneration and reverence, as becomes the memory to which it belongs. In the other part of the church are two great images carved in the wall itself, which remain in a manner separated from it. They showed me these things as though I should be amazed at seeing them. One of the images is of St. Peter, the other of St. John: they give them great reverence. This church also possesses a separate chapel, almost a church; this has naves on six supports, that is, three on each side. This is very well constructed, with much elegance: the middle nave is raised and arched, its windows and doorways are well wrought, that is, the principal door, and one side door, for the other gives entrance to the principal church. This chapel is as broad as it is long, that is, fifty-two spans broad, and as many in length. It has another chapel, very high and small, like a pinnacle, with many windows in the same height: these also have as much width as length, that is, twelve spans. This church and its chapels have their altars and canopies, with their supports, made of the rock itself, it also has a very great circuit cut out of the rock. The circuit is on the same level as the church itself, and is all square: all its walls are pierced with holes the size of the mouth of a barrel. All these holes are stopped up with small stones, and they say that they are tombs, and such they appear to be, because some have been stopped up since a long time, others recently. The entrance of this circuit is below the rock, at a great depth and measure of thirteen spans, all artificially excavated, or worked with the pick-axe, for here there is no digging, because the stone is hard, and for great walls like the Porto in Portugal.

· · ·

The church of St. Saviour stands alone, cut out of a rock; it is very large. Its

---

[1] *Palmo,* measure of four inches.

interior is two hundred spans in length, and a hundred and twenty in width. It has five naves, in each one seven square columns; the large one has four, and the walls of the church have as much. The columns are very well worked, with arches which hang down a span below the vaulted roof. The vaulted roofs are very well worked, and of great height, principally the centre one, which is very high. It is of a handsome height; most of the ends are lower, all in proportion. In the principal height of these naves there is much tracery, such as . . . , or keystones, or roses, which they put on the vaults, on which they make roses and other graceful works. On the sides it has very pretty windows, with much tracery, long and narrow in the middle. Within and without, these are long, like the loopholes of a wall, narrow without and wide within; these are wide both within and without, and narrow in the middle, with arches and tracery. The principal chapel is very high, and the canopy over the altar is very high, with a support at each corner. All this is made from the rock itself. In the other naves they do not deck the chapels and altars with canopies like the high altar in its grandeur. The principal door has at each side many and large buttresses, and the door commences with very large arches, and goes on narrowing with other arches until they reach a small door, which is not more than nine spans high and four and a half wide. The side doors are in this manner, only that they do not commence with so much width, and they end with the width of the principal door. On the outside part of this church are seven buttresses with arches, which are twelve palms distant from the wall of the church, and from buttress to buttress an arch, and above the church, on these arches, a vault constructed in such manner that if it were built of pieces and soft stone it could not be straighter nor better constructed, nor with more work about it. These arches outside may be about the height of two lances. There is not any variation in the whole of this rock in

which this church stands; it all looks like one block of marble. The court or cloister which the church has round it is all worked with the same stone. It is sixty palms wide at each end, and in front of the principal church door quite a hundred palms. Above this church, where it should be roofed, there are on each side nine large arches, like cloisters, which descend from the top to the bottom, to the tombs along the sides, as in the other church. The entrance to this church is by a descent through the rock itself, eighty steps cut artificially in the stone, of a width that ten men can go side by side, and of the height of a lance or more. This entrance has four holes above, which give light to the passage above the edges. From this rock to the enclosure of the church is like a field; there are many houses, and they sow barley in it.

. . .

On the 4th day of the month of January Prester John sent to tell us to order our tents, both that of the church and our own, to be taken from this place to a distance of about half a league, where they had made a large tank of water, in which they were to be baptized on the day of the Kings, because on that day it is their custom to be baptized every year, as that was the day on which Christ was baptized. We took thither a small tent for resting in and the church tent. The next day, which was the vigil of the day of the Kings, the Prester sent to call us, and we saw the enclosure where the tank was. The enclosure was a fence, and very large, in a plain. He sent to ask us if we intended to be baptized. I replied that it was not our custom to be baptized more than once, when we were little. Some said, principally the ambassador, that we would do what His Highness commanded. When they perceived that, they came back again with another message to me, asking what I said as to being baptized. I answered that I had been already baptized, and should not be so again. They still sent word that if we did not wish to be baptized in their tank, they would send us water to our tent. To this the ambassador replied that it should be as His Highness ordered. The Franks and our people had arranged to give a representation of the Kings, and they sent to tell him of it. A message came that it pleased him, and so they got ready for it, and they made it in the inclosure and plain close to the King's tent, which was pitched close to the tank. They gave the representation, and it was not esteemed, nor hardly looked at, and so it was a cold affair. Now that it was night they told us to go to our tent, which was not far off. In all this night till dawn a great number of priests never ceased chaunting over the said tank, saying that they were blessing the water, and about midnight, a little earlier or later, they began the baptism. They say, and I believe that such is the truth, that the first person baptized is the Prester, and after him the Abima, and after him the Queen, the wife of the Prester. They say that these three persons wear cloths over their nakedness, and that all the others were as their mothers bore them. When it was almost the hour of sunrise, and the baptism in fullest force, the Prester sent to call me to see the said baptism. I went and remained there till the hour of tierce, seeing how they were baptized; they placed me at one end of the tank, with my face towards Prester John, and they baptize in this manner.

The tank is large, the bottom of it in the earth, and it is cut very straight in the earth, and well squared; it is lined with planks, and over the planks waxed cotton cloth is spread. The water came from a rivulet through a conduit, like those to irrigate gardens, and it fell into the tank through a cane, at the end of which was a bag that was full; because they strain the water which falls into the tank; and it was no longer running when I saw it: the tank was full of blessed water, as they said, and they told me that it contained oil. This tank had five or six steps at one end, and about three fathoms in front of these steps was the dais of Prester John, on which he

sat. He had before him a curtain of blue tafetan, with an opening of about a span, by which those who were baptized saw him, because he was with his face to the tank. In the tank stood the old priest, the master of the Prester, who was with me Christmas night, and he was naked as when his mother bore him (and quite dead of cold, because it was a very sharp frost), standing in the water up to his shoulders or thereabouts, for so deep was the tank that those who were to be baptized entered by the steps, naked, with their backs to the Prester, and when they came out again they showed him their fronts, the women as well as the men. When they came to the said priest, he put his hands on their head, and put it three times under the water, saying in his language: "In name of the Father, of the Son, and of the Holy Spirit," he made the sign of the cross as a blessing, and they went away in peace. (The "I baptize thee," I heard him say it.) If they were little people they did not go down all the steps, and the priest approached them, and dipped them there. They placed me at the other end of the tank, with my face looking to the Prester, so that when he saw the backs, I saw the fronts, and the contrary way when they came out of the tank. After a great number of baptized persons had passed, he sent to call me to be near him; and so near that the Cabeata did not stir to hear what the Prester said, and to speak to the interpreter who was close to me: and he asked me what I thought of that office. I answered him that the things of God's service which were done in good faith and without evil deceit, and in His praise, were good, but such an office as this, there was none in our Church, rather it forbade us baptizing without necessity on that day, because on that day Christ was baptized, so that we should not think of saying of ourselves that we were baptized on the same day as Christ; also the Church does not order this sacrament to be given more than once. Afterwards he asked whether we had it written in books not to be baptized more than once. I replied,

Yes, that we had, and that in the Creed, which was made at the Council of Pope Leon, with the three hundred and eighteen bishops, about which at times His Highness had questioned me, it was said: "Confiteor unum baptisma in remissionem peccatorum." Then they said to me that such was the truth, and so it was written in their books; but what were they to do with many who turned Moors and Jews after being Christians and then repented, and with others who did not believe well in baptism, what remedy would they have? I answered: For those who do not rightly believe, teaching and preaching would suffice for them, and if that did not profit, burn them as heretics. And so Christ spoke, and St. Mark wrote it: "Qui crediderit et baptizatus fuerit salvus erit, qui vero non crediderit condemnabitur." And as to those who turned Moors or Jews, and afterwards of their own free will recognised their error, and asked for mercy, the *Abima* would absolve them, with penances salutary for their souls, if he had powers for this, if not, let them go to the Pope of Rome, in whom are all the powers. And those who did not repent, they might take them and burn them, for such is the use in Frankland and the Church of Rome. To this there came the reply, that all this seemed to him good, but that his grandfather had ordained this baptism by the counsel of great priests, in order that so many souls should not be lost, and that it had been the custom until now; and he asked if the Pope would concede to the Abima to hold these powers, and how much it would cost him, and in how much time could they come. I answered him that the Pope desired nothing except to save souls, and that he would esteem it fortunate to send to him, the Abima, with such powers, and that it would only cost him the expenses of the journey, which would not be much, and also the letters of his powers: and that they could go and come through Portugal in three years: and by the road of Jerusalem, that I did not know it. To this there

came no answer except that I might go in peace to say mass. I said it was no longer time for saying mass, that midday was long passed. So I went to dine with our Portuguese and the Franks.

This tank was all closed in and covered over with coloured tent cloths, so well that more could not be said, and so well arranged, with so many oranges and lemons, and boughs suspended and so well disposed, that the boughs, oranges, and lemons appeared to have grown there, and that it was a well ordered garden. The large tent which was over the tank was long and . . . , and above covered with red and blue crosses of the fashion of the crosses of the order of Christ. This day, later in the afternoon, Prester John sent to call the ambassador and all his company. The baptism was already ended, and His Highness was still within his curtain where I left him. We entered there, and he at once asked the ambassador what he thought of it. He replied that it was very good, although we had not got such a custom. The water was then running into the tank, and he asked if there were here Portuguese who could swim. At once two jumped into the tank, and swam and dived as much as the tank allowed of. He enjoyed greatly, as he showed by his looks, seeing them swim and dive. After this he desired us to go outside and go to one end of the enclosure or circuit; and here he ordered a banquet to be made for us of bread and wine (according to their custom and the use of the country), and he desired us to raise our church tent and the tent we were lodging in, because he wished to return to his quarters, and that we should go in front of him because he was ordering his horsemen to skirmish in the manner in which they fight with the Moors in the field. So we went in front of him, looking at the said skirmish. They began, but soon there came such heavy rain that it did not allow them to carry out the skirmish which they had begun well.

# 9  JOÃO DOS SANTOS
## THE WAZIMBA

*"Ethiopia Oriental," by Father João dos Santos, is one of the most complete sources of written information on the peoples living in southeastern Africa in the late sixteenth century—Bantu, Arab, and Portuguese. Dos Santos resided at Sofala and traveled to the interior stations of Sena and Tete between 1586 and 1590, when the marauding Wazimba were sweeping through the region northward out of Central Africa.*

Opposite the fort of Sena, on the other side of the river, live some Kaffirs, lords of those lands, good neighbours and friends of the Portuguese, and always most loyal to them.[1] It so happened at the time I was there that the Muzimba Kaffirs, of whom I previously made mention, who eat human flesh, invaded this territory and made war upon one of these friendly Kaffirs, and by force of arms took from him the kraal in which he resided and a great part of his land, besides which they killed and ate a number of his people. The Kaffir, seeing himself thus routed and his power destroyed, proceeded to Sena to lay his trouble before the captain, who was then André de Santiago, and to beg for assistance in driving out of his house the enemy who had taken possession of it. The captain, upon hearing his pitiful request, determined to assist him, both because he was very friendly to us and because he did not wish to have so near to Sena a neighbour as wicked as the Muzimba.

Therefore, having made all necessary preparations for this war, he set out, taking with him a great number of the Portuguese of Sena with their guns and two pieces of heavy cannon from the fort. On arriving at the place where the Muzimbas were, they found them within a strong double palisade of wood, with its ramparts and loopholes for arrows, sur-

rounded by a very deep and wide trench, within which the enemy were most defiant. André de Santiago, seeing that the enterprise was much more formidable than he had anticipated and that he had brought with him but few men to attack so strong an enemy and his fortress, fixed his camp on the bank of a rivulet which ran by the place, and sent a message to the captain of Tete, Pedro Fernandes de Chaves, to come to his assistance with the Portuguese of Tete and as many Kaffir vassals of his fort as he could bring.

Pedro Fernandes de Chaves immediately prepared to go to the assistance of André de Santiago, and assembled more than a hundred men with their guns, Portuguese and half-castes, and the eleven vassal chiefs. They all crossed to the other side of the river and proceeded by land until they were near the place where the Muzimbas had fortified themselves. These had information of their approach, and greatly feared their arrival. For this reason they sent out spies secretly upon the road, that when they approached they might see them, and report concerning the men who were coming. And learning from these spies that the Portuguese were in front of the Kaffirs in palanquins and hammocks and not disposed in order of battle, they sallied out of their fortress by night secretly, without being heard by André de Santiago, and proceeded to conceal themselves in a dense thicket at about half a league's distance, through which the men of Tete would have to pass. When they were thus stationed the Portuguese came up nearly half a league in advance of the Kaffirs of their company,

From Friar João dos Santos, "Ethiopia Oriental," in George McCall Theal, *Records of South-Eastern Africa, Collected in Various Libraries and Archive Departments in Europe* (London, 1898), VII, 293–304.
[1] Sena is located on the Zambezi River, in Portuguese Mozambique (ed.).

quite unsuspicious of what might befall them in the thicket. Just as they were entering it the Muzimbas fell upon them suddenly with such violence that in a short time they were all killed, not one surviving, and when they were dead the Muzimbas cut off their legs and arms, which they carried away on their backs with all the baggage and arms they had brought with them, after which they returned secretly to their fortress. When the chiefs reached the thicket and found all the Portuguese and their captain dead, they immediately turned back from the place and retreated to Tete, where they related the lamentable event that had occurred.

At the time that preparations for this war were being made there was a friar of St. Dominic preaching at Tete, named Nicolau do Rosario, a native of Pedrogão, a man who had reached perfection in many virtues. The captain Pedro Fernandes and the Portuguese of Tete begged this friar to accompany them on the expedition, to receive confessions and administer the sacraments to those who required them. To this the father acceded, thinking that in doing so he was serving our Lord and showing friendship to the Portuguese, and therefore he accompanied them. In the ambush he was severely wounded, and seizing him yet alive the Muzimbas carried him away with them to put him to death more cruelly afterwards, which they did upon arriving at their fortress, where they bound him hand and foot to a tree and killed him with their arrows in the most cruel manner. This they did to him rather than to others because he was a priest and head of the Christians, as they called him, laying all the blame for the war upon him and saying that Christians did nothing without the leave and counsel of their cacis. And in this manner the father met his death with great constancy, never ceasing to preach in a loud voice and profess the faith of Christ, as I shall relate more in detail in another place.

These Zimbas, or Muzimbas, do not adore idols or recognise any God, but instead they venerate and honour their king, whom they regard as a divinity, and they say he is the greatest and best in the world. And the said king says of himself that he alone is god of the earth, for which reason if it rains when he does not wish it to do so, or is too hot, he shoots arrows at the sky for not obeying him; and although all these people eat human flesh, the king does not, to seem different from his vassals.

All these Kaffirs as a rule are tall, well-proportioned, and very robust. The arms they carry are battle-axes, arrows, assagais, and large shields with which they entirely cover themselves. These shields are made of light wood covered with the skins of wild animals which they kill and eat. They are in the habit of eating the men they kill in war, and drinking out of their skulls, showing themselves in this boastful and ferocious. If any of the Kaffirs of their tribe fall ill or are severely wounded in war, to save themselves the trouble of tending them they kill and eat them. They are addicted to many other brutalities similar to these, which I leave for the sake of brevity.

After the Zimbas had put Father Nicolau to death they rested during the remainder of that sad day, and on the night that followed they celebrated their victory and success, playing upon many cornets and drums, and the next day at dawn they all sallied out of their fortress, the chief clothed in the chasuble that the father had brought with him to say mass, carrying the golden chalice in his left hand and an assagai in his right, all the other Zimbas carrying on their backs the limbs of the Portuguese, with the head of the captain of Tete on the point of a long lance, and beating a drum they had taken from him. In this manner, with loud shouts and cries they came within sight of André de Santiago and all the Portuguese who were with him, and showed them all these things. After this they retired within their fortress, saying that what they had done to the men of Tete who had come to help their enemies, they would do to them, and that it was the flesh of those men that they were about to eat.

André de Santiago, who was waiting for Pedro Fernandes de Chaves with much anxiety, and who knew nothing of what had taken place, was greatly shocked, as also were all the other Portuguese, at this most horrible and pitiful spectacle, for which reason they decided to retreat as soon as night came on. In carrying this decision into execution they were in so great a hurry to reach the other side of the river that they were heard by the Muzimbas, who sallied out of their fortress and falling upon them with great violence killed many of them on the bank of the river. Among the slain was André de Santiago, who died as the valiant man he was, because it being within his power to escape he did not do so, but remained fighting and defending his companions on the bank, where he killed a great number of the Muzimbas before he was killed by them.

Thus these robbers and fierce Muzimbas killed one hundred and thirty Portuguese and half-castes of Tete and Sena and the two captains of these forts. This they accomplished with very little loss on their side, with their usual cunning, as they always took the Portuguese unawares, when they were unable to fight. This took place in the year 1592.

Great sorrow was felt at the death of Father Nicolau, whom all looked upon as a saint, and for all the Portuguese who lost their lives in this most disastrous war, both because some of them were married and left wives and children at these rivers, and because the Zimbas were victorious, more insolent than before, and were within fortifications close to Sena, where with greater audacity they might in the future do much damage to the Portuguese who passed up and down these rivers with their merchandise. For these reasons

Dom Pedro de Sousa, captain of Mozambique, determined to chastise these Zimbas, conquer them, and drive them from the vicinity of Sena. To do this he proceeded to the rivers of Cuama from Mozambique in the following year, 1593, accompanied by some soldiers from the said fortress, with whom he reached Sena.

After obtaining information of the condition of the Zimbas, he commanded all the necessary preparations to be made for this war, and assembled nearly two hundred Portuguese and fifteen hundred Kaffirs, with whom he crossed to the other side of the Zambesi and proceeded by land to the fortress of the Zimbas, where he formed a camp at the same place that André de Santiago had formed his. Then he commanded that the various pieces of artillery which he had taken with him for the purpose should be fired against the wall of the fortress, but this had no effect upon it, as it was made of large wood, strengthened within by a strong and wide rampart which the Zimbas had constructed with the earth from the trench.

Dom Pedro, seeing that his artillery had no effect upon the enemy's wall, determined to enter the fortress and take it by assault, and for this purpose he commanded part of the trench to be filled up, which was done with great difficulty and danger to our men, as the Zimbas from the top of the wall wounded and killed some of them with arrows. When this part of the trench was filled up, a number of men crossed over with axes in their hands to the foot of the palisade, which they began to cut down, but the Zimbas from the top of the wall poured so great a quantity of boiling fat and water upon them that nearly all were scalded and badly wounded, especially the naked Kaffirs, so that no one dared go near the palisade, because they were afraid of the boiling fat and through fear of certain iron hooks similar to long harpoons, which the Zimbas thrust through the loopholes in the wall and with which they wounded and caught hold of all who came near and pulled from within with such force that they drew them to the apertures, where they wounded them mortally. For this reason the captain commanded all the men to be recalled to the camp to rest, and the remainder of that day was spent in tending the wounded and the scalded.

The following day the captain commanded a quantity of wood and branches of trees to be collected, with which huge wickerwork frames were made, as high as and higher than the enemy's palisade, and he commanded them to be placed in front of the wall and filled with earth that the soldiers might fight on them with their guns, and the Zimbas would not dare to appear on the wall or be able to pour boiling fat upon the men cutting down the palisade. When this stratagem of war was almost in readiness, another peaceful or cowardly device was planned in the following manner. The war had lasted two months, for which reason the residents of these rivers, who were there rather by force than of their own free will, being away from their homes and trade, which is their profession, and not war, pretended to have received letters from their wives in Sena relating the danger they were in from a rebel Kaffir who they said was coming with a number of men to rob Sena, knowing that the Portuguese were absent, for which reason they ought immediately to return home. This false information was spread through the camp, and the residents of Sena went to the captain and begged him to abandon the siege of the Zimbas and attend to what was of greater importance, as otherwise they would be compelled to return to their homes and leave him.

Dom Pedro, seeing their determination and believing the information said to be given in the letters to be true, abandoned the siege and commanded the men to pass by night to the other side of the river and return to Sena, but this retreat could not be effected with such secrecy as to be unknown to the Zimbas, who sallied out of their fortress with great cries, fell upon the camp, killed some men who were still there, and seized the greater part of the baggage and artillery, that had not been taken away.

With this defeat and disappointment the captain returned to Sena, and thence to Mozambique, without accomplishing what he desired; and the Zimba's position was improved and he became more insolent than before. Nevertheless he offered peace to the Portuguese of Sena, saying that he never wished to be at war with them, and always desired their friendship and commerce, but that the Portuguese had unjustly made war upon him, without his having done them any injury, and that he had killed them in just defence, as he was compelled to do. Peace was conceded to him, I fancy, on account of the benefit that would result from it to the Portuguese of this river. The affairs of the country were in this condition when I left it to proceed to Mozambique.

A Muzimba Kaffir of the tribe of which I spoke in the last chapter, who was lord of a little kraal and had a few vassals, but who was most ambitious of human honour, meditating upon the means by which he might become a great lord and renowned in the world, decided that for this purpose it would be expedient to sally out of his country with an armed force and destroy, rob, and eat every living thing that came in his way. This his diabolical intention he made known to his vassals and other Muzimbas of the same tribe, to whom his design did not appear objectionable, because as they are usually addicted to idleness, robbery, and cannibalism, by it they had an opportunity offered to them of satisfying their cruel and depraved inclination. Their course of action having been decided upon and arranged, they sallied forth from their country and commenced expending their fury upon their neighbours; and they traversed all the kingdoms of Kaffraria, proceeding constantly towards the east.

Through these lands they marched, destroying and plundering all they found, and devouring every living thing, not only men, women, and children, but cattle, dogs, cats, rats, snakes, and lizards, sparing none except Kaffirs who came to them and wished to accompany them on this expedition, whom they admitted into their army. In this manner they assembled more than fifteen thousand warriors, with whom they laid waste all the lands they traversed, so that they appeared to be a cruel scourge and punishment that God chose to send to Kaffraria.

Having reached the island of Kilwa, which is close to the mainland and peopled by Moors, they saw that they could not enter it because of the sea by which it was surrounded. They therefore formed a camp upon the mainland, opposite the island, and besieged it for several months, devouring all the animals and crops that the Moors possessed upon the mainland, so that nothing from it could reach the island.

Meantime a Moor of the said island, moved by greed and ambitious of honour, proceeded secretly one night to the mainland, where the Muzimbas were stationed, by a ford, well known to him, where one could cross at low tide. On reaching the camp, he informed the Kaffirs who met him that he came from the island and wished to speak to the chief captain of the army upon a matter of great importance. Being taken by them and presented to the captain, he said: "Powerful captain, you must know that I am a native of this land and a resident of the island of Kilwa that you are besieging, and I know for certain that very soon you will be lord of it and will punish the people for not recognising you as the great lord that you are, and obeying you as is right. I, knowing this, have come to offer you the obedience that is your due, and further I wish to lead you into the island of Kilwa with all your army, by the ford by which I have come, which is well known to me, upon condition that you

will spare the lives of my relatives who are in the place and divide with me the spoils and riches which you seize in the island, and also that you will bestow upon me the lands there that I shall point out to you, as this is of little consequence to you and of great importance to me." The Zimba replied that he was well pleased, and that if he would lead him into the island with all his men, as he said he would do, he promised to perform what he desired.

Upon this all were disposed in order to cross the ford, and the Moor led them to it, going in front to show them the way. Thus they all reached the island after midnight, and seized the Moors who were asleep and unsuspicious of the treachery being enacted or of what was about to happen. The Muzimbas killed the greater number without any resistance, and the remainder they took prisoners and ate gradually while they remained there, so that they killed and ate more than three thousand Moors, men and women, among whom many were very beautiful and delicate; and they plundered the whole town of Kilwa, in which they found great spoils and riches. Of the Moors only those escaped who had time to flee to the thickets on the island, where they remained in hiding until the Muzimbas returned to the mainland, after which they went back to the town, which in former years was a most noble one, the residence of the kings of all that coast, and even at the present time the ruins of the vast and sumptuous mosques and dwelling-houses give proof of its former grandeur.

When the Muzimbas had nothing more to do in the island their captain sent for the Moor who had conducted them to it by the ford, who was yet alive with all his relatives, as the captain had commanded them to be guarded, not wishing any of them to be put to death as the others had been. When they were all assembled before him he turned to the Moor and said: "I do not wish, nor am I satisfied, that a creature as wicked as thou art should live any longer, as thou wert so cruel that for thy own interest thou deliveredst thy country and thy compatriots into the hands of their enemies." And turning to the Kaffirs he said: "Take this wicked man and all his family who are here present and bind them hand and foot and throw them into the sea to be eaten by the fishes, as it is not proper that any one belonging to so wicked a race should live, nor do I wish you to eat them, as their flesh must be poisonous." This command was forthwith carried into execution, a sentence which surely was not that of a barbarian such as this man was, but of a wise man, and which shows with what reason Alexander the Great said that he profited by the treachery of those who delivered cities to him, but that he hated the traitors.

When this war of Kilwa was thus concluded the Muzimba returned to the mainland by the same ford by which he had entered the island when he was guided by the Moor.

After Kilwa was destroyed, the Zimba continued his journey along the coast until he reached that part of the mainland which is opposite the island of Mombasa, where he fixed his camp on the shore and determined to enter the island as he had entered Kilwa, but he could not immediately do so, as at the same time four Turkish galleys from the straits of Mecca, of which I shall give more detailed information later on, had put in there. These Turks defended the entrance of the island against him and fought with him on many occasions, killing a number of men with their artillery fired from two galleys that they had stationed in the passage by which the Zimba wished to enter.

This contest was continued for several days, until it happened that Thomé de Sousa arrived from India with a powerful fleet to oppose these same galleys, and finding them in this strait he fought with them and captured them with all that they carried, taking the Turks who were in them prisoners, and also ravaged the is-

land of Mombasa. All this was accomplished in sight of the Muzimbas who were on the mainland, who marvelled much to see the wonders performed by the Portuguese, for which reason the Muzimba chief said that the Portuguese were the gods of the sea and he god of the land, and forthwith sent an ambassador to Thomé de Sousa to say that he was a friend of the Portuguese and did not wish to be at war with them, and that as they had completed their work with such honour he also wished to perform his, which had already occupied him a long time, and which was to enter the island and kill and eat every living thing he should find in it. This design he immediately carried into execution with the consent of the Portuguese, and entering the island he searched all the palm groves and thickets in it, where he found many Moors hiding, who had escaped from the town, of whom he killed and ate all he could seize. When this was done Thomé de Sousa with his fleet returned victorious to India, as I shall relate farther on, and the Zimba returned to the mainland and proceeded on his journey, marching with his army towards Melinde.

The king of Melinde was greatly alarmed by the intelligence he received of the approach of the Muzimbas, knowing the ruin they had caused in Kilwa and Mombasa; nevertheless he placed great confidence in the valour of Matheus Mendez de Vasconcellos, who was then captain of this coast, and was at the time in Melinde with only thirty Portuguese soldiers and merchants, who were prepared to defend the town until they died in combat. The Zimbas reached Melinde with great insolence and boastfulness, as men who had never feared any nation, and attacked the town with great fury. Although our soldiers killed many of them with their guns, some of them succeeded in entering at different parts of the wall, which was low, and were already almost masters of a rampart, while a fierce combat was raging on all sides. At this moment more than three thousand Kaffirs called Mosseguejos, friends of the king, came to the succour of Melinde. These Kaffirs, knowing how hard pressed their friend the king of Melinde was by the arrival of the Muzimbas, had come to succour and assist him.

These Mosseguejos are most valiant men, who love war, of whom I shall give more detailed information farther on.

Arriving then at this point of the combat, they attacked the Muzimbas in the rear with such courage and force that in a short time they assisted in defeating and putting them to flight. And as these Muzimbas were strangers and had committed so many barbarities and killed so great a number of people upon the roads and in the countries through which they had passed, the same was done to them in their flight, all that were found being put to death; only the chief and about one hundred men escaped, and these returned the same way they had come, keeping in one body, without again separating, until they were once more in their own country.

Thus was destroyed in the town of Melinde, by the help of the Mosseguejos, the host of Muzimbas that had sallied out of the land which extends along the river of Sena, and reached Melinde, which is a journey of about three hundred leagues, without encountering any resistance or finding any who could meet them in battle, but on the contrary the kraals and lands were abandoned when it was known that this cruel army of cannibals was about to pass through them.

What I have said here concerning the Kaffirs who inhabit the interior appears to me sufficient for the present. And as we began by describing the peculiarities of the river of Luabo, we should follow the river Quilimane until we reach the shore of the sea, saying something of its inhabitants.

# 10   GASPAR BOCARRO
## FROM TETE TO KILWA

*Gaspar Bocarro appears to have been the first European to travel overland from Tete on the Zambezi to Kilwa in 1616 through what is now the southern interior of Tanzania. The account of this journey appears in* Extractos da Decada, *by Antonio Bocarro, Keeper of the Archives and Chronicler of India at Lisbon from 1631 to 1649. In his official capacity, Bocarro had access to official correspondence from East Africa and India. The* Extractos *were dedicated to Philip III of Portugal (1621–1640) but were not actually printed by the Royal Academy of Sciences at Lisbon until 1876. Gaspar Bocarro may have been related to Antonio Bocarro. Gaspar performed the journey to ensure the safe passage of African silver to Portugal.*

At the time when Diogo Simoës sent the silver to His Majesty by means of the religious of Saint Dominic, who perforce had to pass by the fortress of Moçambique, and to go from thence to India, there were in the rivers of Cuama [1] certain persons dissatisfied with Diogo Simoës, who said openly that the Captain of Moçambique ought to seize the silver and send it on his own orders to His Majesty; and some wrote that this should be done.

From Sir John Gray, "A Journey by Land from Tete to Kilwa in 1616," in *Tanganyika Notes and Records,* 25 (1948), 40–45. Reprinted by permission of the Tanzania Society, Dar es Salaam.

[1] The name given at this date to the country in the region of the Zambesi delta.

When Diogo Simoës heard this, he was very angry. For this reason Gaspar Bocarro, a man of noble birth, brought up in the household of the Marquis of Ferreira, who had spent many years in these rivers, offered to make the journey by land from Tete [2] to the coast of Melinde [3] so that he could put Moçambique out of his way, and from the coast pass to Ormuz [4] and from there make his way by land to Spain,[5] and deliver the silver, which Diogo Simoës had given to him, to His Majesty: which journey he would make at his own expense, so as to serve the said lord: and he also would lend two thousand cruzados [6] to help to maintain the fort at Chicove,[7] for which no provision had come from India.

Diogo Simoës was pleased, accepted his offer, and received the said money, which Gaspar Bocarro gave him for the maintenance of the fort; then he delivered to him two frasilas [8] of silver ore, in one of which there was a small stone of pure silver, which appeared to have been smelted, but was pure in origin: (he also gave him) authenticated papers and credentials, so that he might deliver all to His Majesty. When this had been arranged and concluded, Gaspar Bocarro provided himself with necessaries for his very long and risky journey.

Gaspar Bocarro left Tete in March, 1616, taking in his company ten or twelve of his slaves. He crossed to the other side of the River Zambeze and made his way through the lands of Bororo. After two days' journeying he reached the village of Inhampury, where he bought a thousand bracelets of copper wire, which are made by the Cafres of this village, because they have plenty of copper there. These bracelets serve as money for petty expenses on all these roads in Cafraria. Bocarro gave Inhampury a present of some garments and beads, which came to seven cruzados. They left there and slept at Baue, a village of the same Inhampury, where one of his wives lived, to whom he gave another present, which was worth three cruzados. Thence they made their way for three days through thickets and desert land to Danda, a town subject to Muzura, who is the biggest Cafre Lord in all the lands of Bororo. To the governor of this town Bocarro gave cloths and beads, which were worth two cruzados. After this they slept at Bunga, a large village, subject to Muzura, where he gave the governor one cruzado's worth of cloth and beads. Thence Gaspar Bocarro sent Muzura word of his coming and sent ahead of him a present, which the Cafres call "the mouth," consisting of cloth and beads, which were worth five cruzados. On reaching the town, in which he dwelt and which is called Marauy, he went to see Muzura and gave him garments, and beads, and silk cloths, which were worth seventy cruzados. He also gave him his bed which included the hangings, a bolster of damask, and linen sheets, because it was a heavy weight to carry such a bed on the shoulders for such a long journey. Muzura gave Bocarro two tusks of ivory, which were worth eighteen cruzados, and a black woman, and food during the fifteen days that he stayed there (and he also gave) to all his people plenty of millet, rice, hens, capons, cows and figs, and he also gave him three Cafres, who were his subjects and were to act as guides and to guard them safely when passing through his lands.

With these three guides Bocarro left

[2] A town about 270 miles up the Zambesi, where at this date there was a fort.
[3] In contemporary Portuguese letters and chronicles the coast between Cape Delgado and Cape Guardafui is usually referred to as "the coast of Malindi." . . .
[4] An island at the entrance to the Persian Gulf, which was at this date in the possession of the Portuguese.
[5] Portuguese historians call the period 1580–1640 "the Spanish captivity," it being the period during which their country was ruled by the kings of Spain. At this date Philip III of Portugal (1598–1621) was also Philip IV of Spain.
[6] The cruzado was valued at 400 reis. . . . at the beginning of the seventeenth century 400 reis were worth about 5s. 4d.
[7] On the banks of Zambesi above Tete.
[8] The frasila weighed 35–36 English pounds.

Muzura and slept at Moromba, a town of Muzura. He gave the governor thereof, who was called Inhamocumba, garments and beads, which were worth two cruzados, and he gave Bocarro three more Cafres to accompany him and to be his guides. Near this town of Moromba is the great river Manganja,[9] or lake which looks like a sea, from which flows the river Nhanha,[10] which enters the Zambesi below Sena,[11] where it is called the river of Chiry.[12] From Moromba Gaspar Bocarro set out with this three additional guides, and made his way alongside this river Nhanha, and slept on its shore, and on the following day crossed over to the other side in vessels belonging to the native Cafres.[13] (Then) he made his way North and slept at the town of Caramboe, a son of Muzura, to whom Bocarro gave garments and beads which were worth seven cruzados. Thence he dined at a village called Mocama and slept at another village called Mogombe, to the governor of which he gave cloths and beads which were worth one cruzado. There he slept on the confines of the lands of Muzura's son.

From here onward begin the lands which are called Manguro, and are subject to Chicoave, who is a friend and quasi-vassal of Muzura, for he is afraid of him. He began to make his way through these lands and slept at the village of Machambe, to whom he gave cloths and beads which were worth two cruzados. From there he slept at the village of Muzunguira, to whom he gave bracelets and beads which were worth one cruzado.

From there he slept at the town, in which dwelt Chicoave, the lord of these lands. Before he came to him he gave him in advance for "the mouth" one hundred bracelets, one cloth, and some beads, which were worth seven cruzados. When he spoke with this Cafre, he gave him another present, which was worth seven cruzados, and the Cafre gave him a tusk of ivory, which was worth three cruzados. Muzura sent this Cafre a present so that he might give the road and guides to Bocarro, and he gave him his son, who thenceforward accompanied him together with the other guides of Muzura. Thence he crossed a river called Ruambara, which he crossed in boats. After leaving the town of Chicoave he slept at the village Chipanga and after at the village of Changuessa, to whom he gave a cloth and a bundle of beads. Thence he slept in an uninhabited place and on the following day at the village of Mauano, to whom he gave a cloth and a necklace of beads. Thence slept at a village called Rupapa, the lord of which was Quitenga, to whom he gave three cloths and twenty bracelets. From there he slept in a thicket and on the following day proceeded along the river Rofuma[14] to the village of Muangongo, to whom he gave fifty bracelets, two necklaces of beads, a machira,[15] and a cloth. He ferried Gaspar Bocarro and all his people in his boat to the other bank of the river and accompanied them for three days.

The lord of the lands, which extend from this river Rofuma as far as the salt sea, is Manhanga. Leaving this river Bocarro slept at the house of Darama, to whom he gave six bracelets and a few beads. Thence he slept at the village of Davia, to whom he gave twenty bracelets and a necklace of beads. From there he slept in the town in which dwells Manhanga, the lord of these lands. Before he came to him, Bocarro sent in advance to

[9] "Manganja" appears to be a Portuguese corruption of some Bantu word which has "nyanja" (cf. Note 10) as one of its roots. Manganja is clearly identifiable with Lake Nyassa.
[10] Apparently the common Bantu word "nyanja" meaning an expanse of water such as a lake.
[11] A town about 150 miles up the Zambesi, where at this date the Portuguese had a fort.
[12] Sc. the Shire, which flows out of Lake Nyassa and joins the Zambesi a little below Sena.
[13] Bocarro evidently made his crossing in the upper reaches of the Shire very close to its exit from Lake Nyasa, but never actually reached that lake.

[14] Sc. the Rovuma.
[15] "A sort of cloak or upper garment worn by the Cafres."

acquaint him as to his coming, and sent as "the mouth" two hundred bracelets and a machira. When he came to him, he gave him a further six hundred bracelets. Muzura likewise sent this Cafre a hundred bracelets, and a machira, and a black girl, so that he might make the roads through his lands free to Bocarro. He (sc. Manhanga) gave Bocarro a tusk of ivory and sent to Muzura a present of garments, which had come there from the coast of Melinde,[16] because this Cafre is obedient to Muzura. Here Muzura's three guides returned, and also the three guides of Inhamocumba, the governor of Moramba, and also Chicoave's son. From here Bocarro travelled onwards with guides, who were given to him by Manhanga and to whom he gave forthwith twenty bracelets. They made their way for seven days through country, which was uninhabited, because it had been destroyed by the Zimbas, who passed that way making war. At the end of seven days they reached the village of Chiponda, brother of Manhanga, to whom he gave fifty bracelets and a machira; and he (sc. Chiponda) gave him a small tusk of ivory; and he also gave him another Cafre to act as his guide and to accompany him on the road from there to the seashore, to whom Bocarro gave twenty bracelets. From there they made their way for four days through desert lands, and at the end of that time came to the village of Ponde, to whom they gave a few beads. Thence they went to the village of Morengue, to whom they gave a machira and a few beads. Thence they travelled through desert land for four days and came to Bucury, a village of

Moors,[17] where they slept. The next day they came to the shore of the salt sea at the hour of midday. From there they embarked and passed over to the island of Quiloa,[18] which is opposite to the shore, where were the factor and other Portuguese, who made Bocarro their guest.

The inhabited lands along this road abound in foodstuffs, that is to say, millet, rice, fruits, hens, sheep, cows and goats, all of which are cheap. Gaspar Bocarro spent fifty three days on the road and also spent more than one hundred and fifty cruzados in presents and for his own food and for the food which he gave to the people who accompanied him on the road. Though Gaspar Bocarro spent fifty three days on the road with all his servants, they (sc. the servants) were able to return from Quiloa to Tete, travelling light, in no more than twenty-five days.

At Quiloa Bocarro took ship for his voyage to Ormuz. On reaching Mombaça he heard that the roads in Persia were being obstructed by the Shah, and the land was at war. Therefore he decided to return to Moçambique and thence to the rivers of Cuama, where he arrived safely.

I have written all the details of this journey, the names of the villages and the lands, and their lords, and the expenses incurred by Gaspar Bocarro, because, if any one in time to come wishes to make this journey, the adventurer, who makes it, may know about the road and the expense.

---

[16] Probably from Kilwa Kisiwani.

[17] Like other Portuguese chroniclers Bocarro used the word Moor (Mouro) to distinguish the coast inhabitant of mixed Arab and African blood from the pure Arab from Asia.
[18] Kilwa Kisiwani was at this date ruled by a "Moorish" Sultan, who was independent of the Portuguese, but was on friendly terms with them.

## 11  FATHER LOBO
### PORTUGUESE MISSIONARIES IN ETHIOPIA

*Father Jeronimo Lobo (1593–1678) left Portugal for Goa, India, in 1622. After residing in India for a year, during which he completed his studies in divinity, he received letters from Ethiopia proclaiming that the Emperor of Ethiopia had been converted to the Church of Rome and desired Roman Catholic missionaries. Father Lobo was among the eight Jesuit priests who were selected to go to Ethiopia and administer to the emperor. At the time, Ethiopia was in constant revolt; after an appropriate flirtation with Roman Catholicism, the emperor returned to the Coptic (Egyptian Christian) Church in 1632.*

I continued two years at my residence in Tigre [in northern Ethiopia—ed.], entirely taken up with the duties of the mission, preaching, confessing, baptising, and enjoyed a longer quiet and repose than I had ever done since I left Portugal. During this time one of our fathers, being always sick, and of a constitution which the air of Abyssinia was very hurtful to, obtained a permission from our superiors to return to the Indies. I was willing to accompany him through part of his way, and went with him over a desart, at no great distance from my residence, where I found many trees loaded with a kind of fruit, called by the natives Anchoy, about the bigness of an apricot, and very yellow, which is much eaten without any ill effect. I therefore made no scruple of gathering and eating it, without knowing that the inhabitants always peeled it, the rind being a violent purgative; so that, eating the fruit and skin together, I fell into such a disorder as almost brought me to my end. The ordinary dose is six of these rinds, and I had devoured twenty.

I removed from thence to Debaroa, fifty-four miles nearer the sea, and crossed in my way the desart of the province of Saraoe. The country is fruitful, pleasant, and populous. There are greater numbers of Moors in these parts than in any other province of Abyssinia; and the Abyssins of this country are not much better than the Moors.

From Father Jerome Lobo, *A Voyage to Abyssinia,* translated by Samuel Johnson (London: A. Bettesworth and C. Hitch, 1735), pp. 125–131.

I was at Debaroa when the persecution was first set on foot against the Catholics. Sultan Segued, who had been so great a favourer of us, was grown old, and his spirit and authority decreased with his strength. His son, who was arrived at manhood, being weary of waiting so long for the crown he was to inherit, took occasion to blame his father's conduct, and found some reason for censuring all his actions; he even proceeded so far as to give orders sometimes contrary to the emperor's. He had embraced the Catholic religion, rather through complaisance than conviction or inclination; and many of the Abyssins, who had done the same, waited only for an opportunity of making public profession of the ancient erroneous opinions, and of re-uniting themselves to the church of Alexandria. So artfully can this people dissemble their sentiments, that we had not been able hitherto to distinguish our real from our pretended favourers; but as soon as this prince began to give evident tokens of his hatred, even in the life-time of the emperor, we saw all the courtiers and governors, who had treated us with such a shew of friendship, declare against us, and persecute us as disturbers of the public tranquillity; who had come into Ethiopia with no other intention than to abolish the ancient laws and customs of the country, to sow divisions between father and son, and preach up a revolution.

After having borne all sorts of affronts and ill-treatments, we retired to our house at Fremona, in the midst of our country men, who had been settling round about us a long time, imagining we should be more secure there, and that, at least during the life of the emperor, they would not come to extremities, or proceed to open force. I laid some stress upon the kindness which the viceroy of Tigre had shown to us, and in particular to me; but was soon convinced that those hopes had no real foundation, for he was one of the most violent of our persecutors. He seized upon all our lands, and advancing with his troops to Fremona, blocked up the town. The army had not been stationed there long before they committed all sorts of disorders; so that one day a Portuguese, provoked beyond his temper at the insolence of some of them, went out with his four sons, and wounding several of them, forced the rest back to their camp.

We thought we had good reason to apprehend an attack; their troops were increasing, our town was surrounded, and on the point of being forced. Our Portuguese therefore thought, that without staying till the last extremities, they might lawfully repel one violence by another; and sallying out, to the number of fifty, wounded about threescore of the Abyssins, and had put them to the sword, but that they feared it might bring too great an odium upon our cause. The Portuguese were some of them wounded, but happily none died on either side.

Though the times were by no means favourable to us, every one blamed the conduct of the viceroy; and those who did not commend our action, made the necessity we were reduced to of self-defence an excuse for it. The viceroy's principal design was to get my person into his possession, imagining, that if I was once in his power, all the Portuguese would pay him a blind obedience. Having been unsuccessful in his attempt by open force, he made use of the arts of negociation, but with an event not more to his satisfaction. This viceroy being recalled, a son-in-law of the emperor's succeeded, who treated us even worse than his predecessor had done.

When he entered upon his command, he loaded us with kindnesses, giving us so many assurances of his protection, that, while the emperor lived, we thought him one of our friends; but no sooner was our protector dead, than this man pulled off his mask; and quitting all shame, let us see that neither the fear of God nor any other consideration was capable of restraining him, when we were to be distressed. The persecution then becoming general, there was no longer any place of security for us in Abyssinia; where we were looked upon by all as the authors of all the civil commotions; and many councils were held to determine in what manner they should dispose of us. Several were of opinion, that the best way would be to kill us all at once; and affirmed, that no other means were left of re-establishing order and tranquillity in the kingdom.

Others, more prudent, were not for putting us to death with so little consideration; but advised, that we should be banished to one of the isles of the lake of Dambia, an affliction more severe than death itself. These alledged, in vindication of their opinions, that it was reasonable to expect, if they put us to death, that the viceroy of the Indies would come with fire and sword to demand satisfaction. This argument made so great an impression upon some of them, that they thought no better measures could be taken than to send us back again to the Indies. This proposal, however, was not without its difficulties; for they suspected, that when we should arrive at the Portuguese territories, we would levy an army, return back to Abyssinia, and under pretence of establishing the Catholic religion, revenge all the injuries we had suffered.

While they were thus deliberating upon our fate, we were imploring the succour of the Almighty with fervent and humble supplications, intreating him, in the midst of our sighs and tears, that he would not suffer his own cause to miscarry; and that however it might please him to dispose of our lives, which we prayed he would assist us to lay down with patience and resignation, worthy of the faith for which we were persecuted, he would not permit our enemies to triumph over the truth.

Thus we passed our days and nights in prayers, in affliction and tears, continually crowded with widows and orphans that subsisted upon our charity, and came to us for bread, when we had not any for ourselves.

While we were in this distress, we received an account that the viceroy of the Indies had fitted out a powerful fleet against the king of Mombaza, who, having thrown off the authority of the Portuguese, had killed the governor of the fortress, and had since committed many acts of cruelty. The same fleet, as we were informed, after the king of Mombaza was reduced, was to burn and ruin Zeila, in revenge of the death of two Portuguese Jesuits who were killed by the king in the year 1604. As Zeila was not far from the frontiers of Abyssinia, they imagined that they already saw the Portuguese invading their country.

The viceroy of Tigre had enquired of me, a few days before, how many men one India ship carried; and being told that the compliment of some was a thousand men, he compared that answer with the report then spread over all the country, that there were eighteen Portuguese vessels on the coast of Adel; and concluded, that they were manned by an army of eighteen thousand men. Then considering what had been achieved by four hundred, under the command of Don Christopher de Gama, he thought Abyssinia already ravaged, or subjected to the king of Portugal. Many declared themselves of his opinion, and the court took its measures with respect to us from these uncertain and ungrounded rumours. Some were so infatuated with their apprehensions, that they undertook to describe the camp of the Portuguese, and affirmed that they had heard the report of their cannons.

All this contributed to exasperate the inhabitants, and reduced us often to the point of being massacred. At length they came to a resolution of giving us up to the Turks, assuring them that we were masters of a vast treasure; in hope, that after they had inflicted all kinds of tortures on us, to make us confess where we had hid our gold, or what we had done with it, they would at length kill us in rage for the disappointment. Nor was this their only view, for they believed that the Turks would, by killing us, kindle such an irreconcilable hatred between themselves and our nation, as would make it necessary for them to keep us out of the Red sea, of which they are entirely masters: so that their determination was as politic as cruel. Some pretend, that the Turks were engaged to put us to death as soon as we were in their power.

## 12  JAMES BRUCE
### SHEIK ADLAN AND THE BLACK HORSE CAVALRY OF SENNAR

*James Bruce of Kinnaird (1730–1794) spent the early part of his life in study and travel. He was appointed British Consul in Algiers, but determined to seek the source of the Nile, which had baffled men for centuries, he visited Ethiopia in 1769. Here he found the origins of the Blue Nile. Although Pedro Paez had arrived at the same source over 150 years before in 1618 and although that source was but the beginning of one branch of the Nile River,*

*Bruce's* Travels to Discover the Source of the Nile, 1768–73 *stimulated others to the Nile origins. Moreover, his narrative of his travels remains one of the few eighteenth-century descriptions of Ethiopia and the Funj kingdom of Sennar in the Sudan. The Funj were a mysterious people whose origins are unknown but who suddenly appeared on the Blue Nile in 1504 and established their capital at Sennar. Having been converted to Islam, the Funj asserted their hegemony over the middle Nile and reached the height of their power in the seventeenth century. At the time Bruce visited Sennar in 1772, the Funj kingdom was in decline, yet the Black Horse Cavalry of Sheik Adlan appeared to the traveler as impressive as its reputation.*

It was not till the 8th of May I had my audience of Shekh Adelan at Aira, which is three miles and a half from Sennaar; we walked out early in the morning, for the greatest part of the way along the side of the Nile, which had no beauty, being totally divested of trees, the bottom foul and muddy, and the edges of the water, white with small concretions of calcareous earth, which, with the bright sun upon them, dazzled and affected our eyes very much.

We then struck across a large sandy plain, without trees or bushes, and came to Adelan's habitation; two or three very considerable houses, of one storey, occupied the middle of a large square, each of whose sides was at least half of an English mile. Instead of a wall to inclose this square, was a high fence or impalement of strong reeds, canes, or stalks of dora (I do not know which), in fascines strongly joined together by stakes and cords. On the outside of the gate, on each hand, were six houses of a slighter construction than the rest; close upon the fence were sheds where the soldiers lay, the horses picqueted before them with their heads turned towards the sheds, and their food laid before them on the ground; above each soldier's sleeping-place, covered only on the top and open in the sides, were hung a lance, a small oval shield, and a large broad-sword. These, I understood, were chiefly quarters for couriers, who,

From James Bruce, *Travels to Discover the Source of the Nile, 1768–73* (Edinburgh: Archibald Constable and Co., and Manners and Miller, 1813), VI, 359–365.

being Arabs, were not taken into the court or square, but shut out at night.

Within the gate was a number of horses, with the soldiers barracks behind them; they were all picqueted in ranks, their faces to their masters barracks. It was one of the finest sights I ever saw of the kind. They were all above sixteen hands high, of the breed of the old Saracen horses, all finely made, and as strong as our coach horses, but exceedingly nimble in their motion; rather thick and short in the forehand, but with the most beautiful eyes, ears, and heads in the world; they were mostly black, some of them black and white, some of them milk-white, foaled so, not white by age, with white eyes and white hoofs, not perhaps a great recommendation.

A steel shirt of mail hung upon each man's quarters, opposite to his horse, and by it an antelope's skin, made soft like shamoy, with which it was covered from the dew of the night. A head-piece of copper, without crest or plumage, was suspended by a lace above the shirt of mail, and was the most picturesque part of the trophy. To these was added an enormous broad-sword, in a red leather scabbard; and upon the pummel hung two thick gloves, not divided into fingers as ours, but like hedgers gloves, their fingers in one poke. They told me, that, within that inclosure at Aira, there were 400 horses, which, with the riders, and armour complete for each of them, were all the property of Shekh Adelan, every horseman being his slave, and bought with his money. There were five or six (I know not which) of these squares or inclosures, none of them half a mile from the other, which contained the king's horses, slaves, and servants. Whether they were all in as good order as Adelan's I cannot say, for I did not go further; but no body of horse could ever be more magnificently disposed under the direction of any Christian power.

Adelan was then sitting upon a piece of the trunk of a palm-tree, in the front of one of these divisions of his horses, which he seemed to be contemplating with pleasure; a number of black people, his own servants and friends, were standing around him. He had on a long drab-coloured camblet gown, lined with yellow sattin, and a camlet cap like a head-piece, with two short points that covered his ears. This, it seems, was his dress when he rose early in the morning to visit his horses, which he never neglected. The Shekh was a man above six feet high, and rather corpulent, had a heavy walk, seemingly more from affectation of grandeur, than want of agility. He was about sixty, of the colour and features of an Arab, and not of a Negro, but had rather more beard than falls to the lot of people in this country; large piercing eyes, and a determined, though, at the same time, a very pleasing countenance. Upon my coming near him, he got up; "You that are a horseman," says he without any salutation, "what would your king of Habesh give for these horses?" "What king," answered I, in the same tone, "would not give any price for such horses, if he knew their value?" "Well," replies he, in a lower voice, to the people about him, "if we are forced to go to Habesh, as Baady was, we will carry our horses along with us." I understood by this he alluded to the issue of his approaching quarrel with the king.

We then went into a large saloon, hung round with mirrors and scarlet damask; in one of the longest sides, were two large sofas covered with crimson and yellow damask, and large cushions of cloth of gold, like to the king's. He now pulled off his camlet gown and cap, and remained in a crimson sattin coat reaching down below his knees, which lapped over at the breast, and was girt round his waist with a scarf or sash, in which he had stuck a short dagger in an ivory sheath, mounted with gold; and one of the largest and most beautiful amethysts upon his finger that ever I saw, mounted plain, without any diamonds, and a small gold ear-ring in one of his ears.

"Why have you come hither," says he to me, "without arms and on foot, and without attendants?" *Yagoube.* "I was told that horses were not kept at Sennaar, and brought none with me." *Adelan.* "You suppose you have come through great dangers, and so you have. But what do you think of me, who am day and night out in the fields, surrounded by hundreds and thousands of Arabs, all of whom would eat me alive if they dared?" I answered, "A brave man, used to command as you are, does not look to the number of his enemies, but to their abilities; a wolf does not fear ten thousand sheep more than he does one." *Ad.* "True; look out at the door; these are their chiefs whom I am now taxing, and I have brought them hither that they may judge from what they see whether I am ready for them or not." *Yag.* "You could not do more properly; but, as to my own affairs, I wait upon you from the king of Abyssinia, desiring safe conduct through your country into Egypt, with his royal promise, that he is ready to do the like for you again, or any other favour you may call upon him for." He took the letter and read it. *Ad.* "The king of Abyssinia may be assured I am always ready to do more for him than this. It is true, since the mad attempt upon Sennaar, and the next still madder, to replace old Baady upon the throne, we have had no formal peace, but neither are we at war. We understand one another as good neighbours ought to do; and what else is peace?" *Yag.* "You know I am a stranger and traveller, seeking my way home. I have nothing to do with peace or war between nations. All I beg is a safe conduct through your kingdom, and the rights of hospitality bestowed in such cases on every common stranger; and one of the favours I beg is, your acceptance of a small present. I bring it not from home; I have been long absent from thence, or it would have been better." *Ad.* "I'll not refuse it, but it is quite unnecessary. I have faults like other men, but to hurt, or ransack strangers, was never one of them. Mahomet Abou Kalec, my brother, is, however, a much better man to strangers than I am; you will be lucky if you meet him here; if not, I will do for you what I can, when once the confusion of these Arabs is over."

I gave him the Sherriffe's letter, which he opened, looked at it, and laid by without reading, saying only, "Aye, Metical is a good man, he sometimes takes care of our people going to Mecca; for my part, I never was there, and probably never shall." I then presented my letter from Ali Bey to him.[1] He placed it upon his knee, and gave a slap upon it with his open hand. *Ad.* "What! do you not know, have you not heard, Mahomet Abou Dahab, his Hasnadar, has rebelled against him, banished him out of Cairo, and now sits in his place? But, don't be disconcerted at that; I know you to be a man of honour and prudence; if Mahomet, my brother, does not come, as soon as I can get leisure I will dispatch you." The servant that had conducted me to Sennaar, and was then with us, went forward close to him, and said, in a kind of whisper, "Should he go often to the king?" "When he pleases; he may go to see the

town, and take a walk, but never alone, and also to the palace, that, when he returns to his own country, he may report he saw a king at Sennaar, that neither knows how to govern, nor will suffer others to teach him; who knows not how to make war, and yet will not sit in peace." I then took my leave of him; but there was a plentiful breakfast in the other room, to which he sent us, and which went far to comfort Hagi Ismael for the misfortune of his patron, Ali Bey. At going out, I took my leave by kissing his hand, which he submitted to without reluctance. "Shekh," said I, "when I pass these Arabs in the square, I hope it will not disoblige you if I converse with some of them out of curiosity?" *Ad.* "By no means, as much as you please; but don't let them know where they can find you at Sennaar, or they will be in your house from morning till night, will eat up all your victuals, and then, in return, will cut your throat, if they can meet you upon your journey."

I returned home to Sennaar, very well pleased with my reception at Aira. I had not seen, since I left Gondar, a man so open and frank in his manners, and who spoke, without disguise, what apparently he had in his heart; but he was exceedingly engaged in business, and it was of such extent that it seemed to me impossible to be brought to an end in a much longer time than I proposed staying at Sennaar. The distance, too, between Aira and that town was a very great discouragement to me. The whole way was covered with insolent, brutish people; so that every man we met between Sennaar and Aira produced some altercation, some demand of presents, gold, cloth, tobacco, and a variety of other disagreeable circumstances, which had always the appearance of ending in something serious.

[1] Ali Bey was an eighteenth-century Mamluk ruler of Egypt (ed.).

# 13  JOHN LEWIS BURCKHARDT

## SHENDI

*John Lewis Burckhardt (1784–1817) was born in Lausanne and was educated at several European universities. As an employee of the Association for Promoting the Discovery of the Interior Parts of Africa, he traveled in Asia Minor, Egypt, and the Sudan. At the end of 1813 Burckhardt crossed the Nubian Desert and arrived in 1814 at Shendi, the important caravan center and market town on the Middle Nile. He continued his journey eastward from Shendi to Sawakin on the Red Sea. Burckhardt died from dysentery in Cairo in October 1817 at the age of thirty-three.*

*Shendi in 1814 was ruled by Nimr Muhammad Nimr (1785–1846) of the Jaaliyin Arabs. Nimr spent his youth in exile among the Batahin and then returned to Shendi, where he was declared* mek, *or king, in 1802. He ruled Shendi until 1822, when he opposed the invasion of the forces of Muhammad Ali of Egypt by assassinating the viceroy's son and commander of the invading army, Ismail. Punitive expeditions from Egypt forced Mek Nimr to flee from Shendi; he took up exile on the Ethiopian frontier, where he became a redoubtable warlord until his death in 1846. His descendants were granted amnesty in 1865 and subsequently returned to Shendi.*

Next to Sennaar, and Kobbe (in Darfour), Shendy is the largest town in eastern Soudan, and larger, according to the report of the merchants, than the capitals of Dongola and Kordofan. It consists of several quarters, divided from each other by public places, or markets, and it contains altogether from eight hundred to a thousand houses. It is built upon the sandy plain, at about half an hour's walk from the river; its houses are similar to those of Berber; but it contains a greater number of large buildings, and fewer ruins. The houses seldom form any regular street, but are spread over the plain in great disorder. I nowhere saw any walls of burnt bricks. The houses of the chief, and those of his relatives, contain courtyards twenty feet square, inclosed by high walls, and this is the general description of the habitations of Shendy. The government is in the hands of the Mek; the name of the present chief is Nimr, i.e. Tiger. The reigning family is of the same tribe as that which now occupies the throne of Sennaar, namely, the Wold Adjib, which, as far as I could understand, is a branch

of the Funnye. The father of Nimr was an Arab of the tribe of Djaalein, but his mother was of the royal blood of Wold Adjib; and thus it appears that women have a right to the succession. This agrees with the narrative of Bruce, who found at Shendy a woman upon the throne, whom he calls Sittina (an Arabic word, meaning our Lady). The Mek of Shendy, like the Mek of Berber, is subject to Sennaar; but, excepting the purchase money paid for his government, on his accession, and occasional presents to the king and vizier [1] of Sennaar, he is entirely independent, and governs his district, which extends about two days journey farther to the south, quite at his own pleasure.

Before the arrival of the Mamelouks in Dongola, Mek Nimr had been for many years in continual warfare with the Arabs Sheygya, who had killed several of his relatives in battle, and, by making inroads into his dominions with large parties of horsemen, had repeatedly laid waste the whole western bank of the river. The Sheygya made peace with him, in order more effectually to oppose the Mame-

---

From John Lewis Burckhardt, *Travels in Nubia* (London: J. Murray, 1822), pp. 247–256, 263–266.

[1] The vizier of Sennaar, of the Adelan family, is said to be the real master there, while the king has a mere shadow of authority.

louks, when his own brother, to whom the command of the western bank had been entrusted, declared against him, and they have now carried on war for several years, with little success or loss on either side, as they are separated from each other by the river, and can never pass it but in small parties.

The government of Shendy is much to be preferred to that of Berber: the full authority of the Mek is not thwarted by the influence of powerful families, which in these countries tends only to insecurity, nor has he adopted that system of rapacity which makes Berber so justly dreaded by strangers. His absolute power is owing to the diversity of Arab tribes inhabiting Shendy, none of which is strong enough to cope with his own family and its numerous branches. The largest of these tribes are the Nimrab, Nayfab, and Djaalein, the greater part of whom still lead the Bedouin life. The most respectable class of the inhabitants of Shendy are the merchants, amongst whom are great numbers of foreign settlers from Sennaar, Kordofan, Darfour, and Dongola: the last are the most numerous, and they occupy an entire quarter of the town, but their nation is less esteemed than any other. They are reproached with inhospitality, and their avarice has become proverbial; the broker business, which is almost exclusively in their hands, has added to the odium of their name, so that an Arab of Shendy considers it as an insult to be called a Dongolawy, a name here considered as equivalent to that of Jew in Europe.

Commerce flourishes at Shendy, because the Mek does not extort any taxes from the merchants, which many people assured me he dared not do from his fear of the vizier of Sennaar. I am not able to judge how far this may be true; but the fact is, that caravans pay nothing whatever by way of duty; they generally make up a small present to the Mek, in order to enjoy his particular protection, and add something further for one of his brothers,

who is a principal man in the place. Our party of Ababdes sent him a small parcel of soap and sugar, of which my quota amounted to half a dollar. I did not hear of any subordinate offices in the government of Shendy, and the Mek seems to unite all the branches of authority in his own person. His relatives are the governors of villages; and his court consists of half a dozen police officers, a writer, an Imam, a treasurer, and a body-guard, formed principally of slaves. The character of the people is much the same as that of the inhabitants of Berber. They are kept in some order, it is true, by the Mek; but wickedness and injustice govern all their conduct, for they know that the law can do little more than endeavour to prevent crimes, and that it very seldom punishes them. Nightly robbers, drunken people who have assaulted strangers, thieves detected in the market, &c. &c. are often carried before the Mek, but he is generally satisfied with imprisoning them for two or three days; and I did not hear a single instance of his having ordered any person to be put to death, or even flogged, although such crimes as I have mentioned were committed daily during my stay at Shendy. The delinquents were permitted to return quietly to their homes, on paying a small fine to the Mek and his people. I was told that at Kordofan thieves are always punished with death.

Debauchery and drunkenness are as fashionable here as at Berber; the latter, I think, is even more common. No night passed without my hearing the loud songs of some Bouza meeting, though our quarter, that of the Dongolawy, who are too avaricious to be addicted to these vices, was one of the quietest. At Berber public women were constantly seen in the street; at Shendy I very seldom met any of them, though within the inclosures of the houses they are almost as numerous as at Berber.

The dress, habits, and manners of the inhabitants of Shendy are the same as those of the places last described, and appear to prevail as far as Darfour, and

Sennaar. I observed more well-dressed people at Shendy than at Berber, and clean linen was much oftener seen. Gold being a very current article in the Shendy market, the women have more frequently golden rings at their noses and ears than those of Berber; the people also possess more wealth. It is not uncommon to see a family possessed of a dozen slaves, acting as servants in the house, and labourers in the field.

The people of Shendy, like those of Berber, are shepherds, traders, and husbandmen. Agriculture, however, seems to be little thought of by the inhabitants themselves, being chiefly left to the Arab peasants of the vicinity; the cultivable soil in the neighbourhood of the city is narrow; but to the north and south of it are some fine arable plains. Water-wheels are common; they are erected generally on those parts of the high banks, which the most copious inundations of the river cannot overflow; by means of them the cultivators raise one winter-crop; but they are too lazy to bestow the labour necessary for watering the soil a second or third time, as is done in the most elevated parts of Upper Egypt, where also the river very seldom rises high enough to overflow the banks. Dhourra [millet—ed.] is the chief produce; Dokhen and wheat are sown in small quantities, the former for the consumption of the western traders who visit Shendy, the latter almost exclusively for the families of the great. Large quantities of onions, some red pepper (brought from Kordofan), Bamyes, chick-peas, Meloukhye, and Tormos,[2] are always found in the market either green or dried. During the inundation some water-melons and cucumbers are sown, but for the use only of the Harem of the Mek.

The cattle are very fine; and the inhabitants say that their size and quality continue to increase, in proportion as you ascend the river. I saw no domestic animals that are not common in Egypt. Elephants are first met with at Abou Heraze, two or three days to the north of Sennaar; and they have never been known to pass to the northward of that district, which is bounded by a chain of mountains six or eight hours in breadth, reaching close to the river. I was told that tigers are frequently seen in the Wadys east of Shendy. In the mountains of Dender, a district towards the Atbara, and six or eight journies south-east of Shendy, the giraffa is found. It is hunted by the Arabs Shukorein and Kowahel, and is highly prized for its skin, of which the strongest bucklers are made. I frequently saw mountain-goats of the largest size brought to the market of Shendy; they have long horns bending to the middle of the back; their flesh is esteemed a great dainty. They call them Areal, a name given in Syria to the red deer. In Upper Egypt they are called Teytal and in Syria Beden. They are caught by the Djaalein Bedouins in nooses, in the same manner as they catch ostriches, which are also very common in this neighbourhood. The ostrich-feathers however are inferior to those of the western deserts. Those most esteemed in Egypt are from Kordofan and Darfour, which the caravans from the latter place bring to Siout. The Djaalein peasants bring the feathers to the market in bundles, good and bad together, and exchange them for Dhourra. Their price, when I was at Shendy, was about one-tenth of what they would bring at Cairo, where the best kinds, in 1812, sold at two hundred and eighty piastres per pound. The Pasha of Egypt has lately included them among the articles monopolized by him.[3]

---

[2] In Egypt, the meal of the Tormos is used as a substitute for soap in washing the head and body.

[3] The trade in ostrich-feathers is one of the most complicated in the markets of Africa: at Cairo the feathers are assorted into several different qualities, and parcels are made up by the Jews, (who alone understand the trade well,) containing portions of every kind. Each parcel of ten pounds weight must contain one pound of the finest and whitest sort, one pound of the second quality, also white, but of a smaller size, and eight pounds of the sorts called

The hippopotamus is not common at Shendy, though it occasionally makes its appearance there; during my stay there was one in the river in the vicinity of Boeydha, which made great ravages in the fields. It never rose above water in the day-time, but came on shore in the night, and destroyed as much by the treading of its enormous feet, as it did by its voracity; the people have no means of killing them. At Sennaar, where hippopotami are numerous, they are caught in trenches, slightly covered with reeds, into which they fall during their nightly excursions. It is generally said that no musketball can bring them to the ground, unless they are hit in the vulnerable spot, which is over the ear. The whips called Korbadj, which are formed of their skins, are made at Sennaar, and on the Nile, above that place; the skin, immediately after being taken off, is cut into narrow strips, about five or six feet in length, gradually tapering to a point: each strip is then rolled up, so that the edges unite, and form a pipe, in which state it is tied fast and left to dry in the sun. In order to render these whips pliable, they must be rubbed with butter or grease. At Shendy they are sold at the rate of twelve or sixteen for a Spanish dollar; in Egypt, where they are in general use, and the dread of every servant and peasant, they are worth from half a dollar, to a dollar each. In colder climates, even in Syria, they become brittle, crack, and lose their elasticity.

Crocodiles are very numerous about Shendy. I have generally remarked that these animals inhabit particular parts of the Nile, from whence they seldom appear to move; thus, in Lower Egypt, they have entirely disappeared, although no reasonable cause can be assigned for their not descending the river. In Upper Egypt, the neighbourhood of Akhmim, Dendera, Or-

ment, and Edfou, are at present the favourite haunts of the crocodile, while few are ever seen in the intermediate parts of the river. The same is the case in different parts of Nubia towards Dongola. At Berber nobody is afraid of encountering crocodiles in the river, and we bathed there very often, swimming out into the midst of the stream. At Shendy, on the contrary, they are greatly dreaded; the Arabs and the slaves and females, who repair to the shore of the river near the town every morning and evening to wash their linen, and fill their waterskins for the supply of the town, are obliged to be continually on the alert, and such as bathe take care not to proceed to any great distance into the river. I was several times present when a crocodile made its appearance, and witnessed the terror it inspired; the crowd all quickly retiring up the beach. During my stay at Shendy, a man who had been advised to bathe in the river, after having escaped the small-pox, was seized and killed by one of these animals. At Sennaar crocodiles are often brought to market, and their flesh is publicly sold there. I once tasted some of the meat at Esne, in Upper Egypt; it is of a dirty white colour, not unlike young veal, with a slight fishy smell; the animal had been caught by some fishermen in a strong net, and was about twelve feet in length. The Governor of Esne ordered it to be brought into his court-yard, where more than an hundred balls were fired against it without effect, till it was thrown upon its back, and the contents of a small swivel discharged at its belly, the skin of which is much softer than that of the back. Fish are very seldom caught by the Arabs at Shendy. Nets appear to be unknown, but children often amuse themselves in angling with hooked nails.

The produce of the fields of Shendy and its neighbourhood is not sufficient for the supply of the population, the wants of which are much increased by the continual arrival of caravans. Dhourra is imported principally from Abou Heraze, in the route to Sennaar. A caravan of more

Jemina, Bajoca, Coda, and Spadone, the last of which is black, and of little value. The market-price of white sorted feathers is at present (1816) two hundred and eighty piastres per rotolo, or pound, or two thousand eight hundred piastres, each parcel of ten pounds.

than three hundred camels arrived from thence with Dhourra during my stay at Shendy, and the price, which, on our arrival, was at the rate of one dollar for twelve measures, fell to twenty measures per dollar. The price of grain varies almost daily, the market being affected by the arrival of every caravan of traders, who always buy up a considerable quantity for the food of the slaves and camels. The Mek also monopolizes the corn-trade as much as he can. At Abou Heraze and Sennaar, Dhourra is said to be in great plenty: forty measures being sold for a dollar. This grain is of the same shape and size as that of Shendy and Upper Egypt; but it is of an ash gray colour; it is said to be less nourishing, and of course is less esteemed than the other.

Horses are more numerous here than at Berber. The Mek, it is said, can raise within Shendy itself from two to three hundred horsemen. According to the custom of the Eastern Arabs, the Djaalein Bedouins ride mares in preference to stallions; but the latter are preferred by the inhabitants of the town. The Mek's brother, Ras Saad ed Dyn, had a horse for which he had given in the southern districts thirteen slaves; it surpassed in beauty any other horse I ever remember to have seen. At a public festival on the occasion of the circumcision of one of Mek Nimr's sons, all the horsemen of Shendy met, and accompanied the family of the chief through the town, their horses prancing about. They appeared to me but very indifferent horsemen; none attempted any of the manoeuvres for which the Mamelouks are so famous; they contented themselves with galloping backwards and forwards, nor did I see one bold rider amongst them. It is in this cavalry, however, that the Mek places his chief strength, and it decides the fate of all the battles he is obliged to fight with his enemies. The saddles, and bridles, as well as the stirrups, in which they place the great toe only, are the same as those used at Berber and by the Arabs Sheygya, who appear to be as celebrated for their horsemanship in this country as the Mamelouks once were in Turkey. Mek Nimr has about twenty firelocks, which he has either bought or taken from Egyptian traders; with these he arms his favourite slaves, but few of them have courage sufficient to fire them off, and there are none who dare take an aim by placing the gun against the shoulder. The sight of it alone generally frightens the enemy, and so far it fully answers their purpose, for it is always the wish of both parties to finish the battle with as little bloodshed as possible, because the law of retaliation is in full force amongst these Arabs. Several of Mek Nimr's musquets are either broken, or so much rusted, as to make them unserviceable, and nobody could be found to clean and mend them. Having been seen one day cleaning my gun, I was supposed to be skilful in this art, and serious proposals were made to me, to enter into the Mek's service as gunsmith. He offered me one male and two female slaves, and as much Dhourra as I might want for their maintenance; and it was with difficulty that I could persuade the slaves who made me the proposal in the name of their master, that I knew nothing of the business of a gunsmith. Travellers in these countries ought to avoid showing their capacity in the most trifling things that may be of use or afford pleasure to the chiefs, who will endeavour to force them into their service. Not having succeeded in prevailing upon me to remain, the Mek wished at least to have my gun. He sent for it, and kept it for several days; and upon my urgent entreaties to have it returned to me, he sent me four Spanish dollars, ordering his slaves at the same time to carry me several dishes of bread and meat from his own kitchen. Upon complaining to some of the inhabitants of this treatment, they replied, that having now eaten of the Mek's food I had become his friend, and that it would therefore be a disgrace to me to make any difficulty in parting with my gun. I was very sorry to lose it, especially when I considered in what countries I still intended to travel; but in my present circumstances four dollars were not be despised. Seeing no chance therefore of either getting back my gun, or obtaining a higher price for it, I accepted the Mek's four dollars with many professions of thanks.

It will appear very singular that firearms are not more frequently met with here, as they may so easily be imported. But the fact is, that traders are afraid to carry them, lest they should excite the cupidity of some or other of the chiefs; and it is not to be supposed, that until they are more numerous, they can be taken to market like other goods, or be paid for at a regular price. To the country people, who seldom visit the towns where traders make any stay, a musquet is an object of the greatest terror, and will frighten away dozens of them. A Djaalein Arab, who had some ostrich-feathers to sell, came one day to the house where I lodged, to barter with my companions for his feathers. The moment he espied my gun standing in the corner of the room, he got up, and desired it might be removed, for that he did not like to remain near so deadly an instrument.

.   .   .

On the great market days, which are every Friday and Saturday, several thousands of people resort to Shendy from the distance of three or four days; the greater part of whom bring cattle for sale. Judging from the individuals I saw in the market, all these Arabs appear to be entirely of the same race, excepting only that the true Djaalein Bedouins who come from the eastern desert are much fairer-skinned than the inhabitants of the banks of the Nile, which arises probably from their taking greater care not to mix in concubinage with the Negro race. I was much struck with the physiognomy of many of these Djaaleins, who had exactly the countenance and expression of features of the Bedouins of eastern Arabia; their beards are even shorter, and thinner.

Some individuals of a tribe of Djaalein who border, to the south, upon the Shukorye, appeared at the market with hats on their heads, made of reeds; they were high and pointed, with broad brims, and were tied under the chin with a leather thong. They are worn both by men and women.

About four or five hundred camels, as many cows, a hundred asses, and twenty or thirty horses, were on sale on the great market-days. Every merchant then takes his stand in one of the open shops, or in the open market, and exposes part of his merchandize; for even the richest traders are not ashamed of trafficking in the minutest detail. The Egyptian, Souakin, Sennaar, and Kordofan merchants form separate corps, in the midst of which is a great circle of slaves, thus exposed for sale. The country people bring to market mats, baskets, ox hides, and other skins, coarse pottery, camel saddles, wooden dishes, and other articles of their own manufacture, &c. About a dozen shoemakers, or rather sandal-makers, from the country, work for these two days in the market, and will make a pair of sandals at an hour's notice. The works in leather are very prettily done. The leather is tanned with the Garadh or pulse of the acacia; the Bedouins about Sennaar are said to be the most skilful in its preparation. Leather sacks are likewise sold here; they serve for the transport of every kind of baggage and merchandize, excepting Dhourra, gum arabic, and salt, which are carried in baskets. Many blacksmiths repair to Shendy from the country; they make and sell the small knives generally worn among these people. The knives are about eight inches long, and are worn in a leather scabbard tied over the left elbow: they are two-edged, like those worn by the Berabera.

The market is so crowded, and the dust and heat are so great, during the mid-day hours, which is the favourite time for transacting business, that I was unable to remain in the market-place many hours together, and always left one of my companions in charge of the little I had to sell. In different parts of the place are stationed peasants with jars of water, which they sell to the thirsty, at the rate of a handful of Dhourra for as much water as two persons can drink. Several of the Fakys [holymen—ed.] have water-cisterns in the courtyards of their houses, which are always kept full, and at which every one may drink gratis. Many of them have likewise small chapels annexed to their dwellings. There is no mosque in the whole place.

The only artizans I saw at Shendy were blacksmiths, silversmiths, who work very coarse ornaments for the women, tanners, potters, and carpenters. If a house is to be built, the owner, his relatives, and slaves, with a few labourers, execute the masonry, and the carpenter is only called in to lay the roof and make the doors. Like the Bedouins of the desert, these Arabs are their own artizans upon all ordinary occasions.

There are no weavers at Shendy, but all the women and grown up children, and many of the men, are seen with a distaff constantly in their hands, spinning cotton yarn, which they sell to the people of Berber. The distaff, Mugzil, resembles that used in Egypt and Syria. Cotton is cultivated in this neighbourhood, and is a general produce of all the countries on the banks of the Nile, although nowhere in any great quantity, except at Damer and about Sennaar.

The wholesale trade at Shendy is principally conducted through the agency of brokers. Most of these are Dongolawy, who seem, in general, to be the most acute and intelligent traders of this part of the country. A caravan no sooner arrives, than every merchant's house is crowded with brokers; but the avidity and parsimony of all parties are too great to allow them to bring their transactions to a speedy conclusion. Even after the bargain is made, each party endeavours to cheat the other before the goods are delivered and the money paid. In addition to this, every attempt to enter into an engagement of any importance becomes known all over the place, and the jealousy of the traders often prevents its taking place. No merchandize has its fixed price; there is no such thing as a price current; every one sells according to the prospect he has of cheating the buyer and bribing the broker. The purchase money, or, in cases of barter, its equivalent in merchandize, is almost always immediately paid down; the longest credit I have witnessed is a couple of days; and it is evident, on the termination of every commercial transaction, that the buyer and seller reciprocally entertain suspicions of each other's honesty. To oblige a debtor to settle his accounts, recourse is generally had to the slaves of the Mek, who act as police officers; but a man who is unprotected, and without friends, is sure to lose the greater part of his goods, if he allows them to go out of his hands without immediate payment.

# 14  JOHN HANNING SPEKE
## UNYAMWEZI AND BUGANDA

*John Hanning Speke (1827–1864) arrived in Zanzibar with Richard Burton in 1856 for the purpose of finding the inland sea of Ujiji in East Africa. During the expedition the two explorers reached Lake Tanganyika, and while Burton was recovering from an illness at Tabora, Speke wandered off to the north, where he saw the waters of Lake Victoria. Speke jumped to the conclusion that he had discovered the source of the Nile. To prove this assumption, he returned to East Africa in 1860 and, accompanied by J. A. Grant, traversed the Unyamwezi country of what is now western Tanzania and visited Uganda on the west and the northern shore of Lake Victoria. He was the first European to visit the powerful interlacustrine kingdom of Buganda, and his reports of the richness of the country and the prospects for "Christianity, Commerce, and Civilization" encouraged others to follow. Speke and Grant reached Gondokoro on the Upper Nile in 1863. They had contributed much to Europe's geographical knowledge of the interior of eastern Africa but had failed to resolve completely the question of the Nile source.*

U-n-ya-muezi—Country of Moon—must have been one of the largest kingdoms in Africa. It is little inferior in size to England, and of much the same shape, though now, instead of being united, it is cut up into petty states. In its northern extremities it is known by the appellation U-sukuma—country north; and in the southern, U-takama—country south. There are no [written—ed.] historical traditions known to the people; neither was anything ever written concerning their country, as far as we know, until the Hindus, who traded with the east coast of Africa, opened commercial dealings with its people in slaves and ivory, possibly some time prior to the birth of our Saviour, when, associated with their name, Men of the Moon, sprang into existence the Mountains of the Moon. These Men of the Moon are hereditarily the greatest traders in Africa, and are the only people who, for love of barter and change, will leave their own country as porters and go to the coast, and they do so with as much zest as our country-folk go to a fair. As far back as we can trace they have done this, and they still do it as heretofore. The whole of their country ranges from 3000 to 4000 feet above the sea-level—a high plateau, studded with little outcropping hills of granite, between which, in the valleys, there are numerous fertilising springs of fresh water, and rich iron ore is found in sandstone. Generally industrious—much more so than most other ne-

groes—they cultivate extensively, make cloths of cotton in their own looms, smelt iron and work it up very expertly, build tembes to live in over a large portion of their country, but otherwise live in grass huts, and keep flocks and herds of considerable extent.

The Wanyamuezi, however, are not a very well-favoured people in physical appearance, and are much darker than either the Wazaramo or the Wagogo, though many of their men are handsome and their women pretty; neither are they well dressed or well armed, being wanting in pluck and gallantry. Their women, generally, are better dressed than the men. Cloths fastened round under the arms are their national costume, along with a necklace of beads, large brass or copper wire armlets, and a profusion of thin circles, called sambo, made of the giraffe's tail-hairs bound round by the thinnest iron or copper wire; whilst the men at home wear loin-cloths, but in the field, or whilst travelling, simply hang a goat-skin over their shoulders, exposing at least three-fourths of their body in a rather indecorous manner. In all other respects they ornament themselves like the women, only, instead of a long coil of wire wound up the arm, they content themselves with having massive rings of copper or brass on the wrist; and they carry for arms a spear and bow and arrows. All extract more or less their lower incisors, and cut a ∧ between their two upper incisors. The whole tribe are desperate smokers, and greatly given to drink.

On the 24th, we all, as many as were left of us, marched into the merchants'

From John Hanning Speke, *Journal of the Discovery of the Source of the Nile* (Edinburgh and London: Willam Blackwood and Sons, 1863), pp. 84–88, 273–279.

depot, S. lat. 5° 0′ 52″, and E. long. 33° 1′ 34″, escorted by Musa, who advanced to meet us, and guided us into his tembe, where he begged we would reside with him until we could find men to carry our property on to Karague. He added that he would accompany us; for he was on the point of going there when my first instalment of property arrived, but deferred his intention out of respect to myself. He had been detained at Kaze ever since I last left it in consequence of the Arabs having provoked a war with Manua Sera, to which he was adverse. For a long time also he had been a chained prisoner; as the Arabs, jealous of the favour Manua Sera had shown to him in preference to themselves, basely accused him of supplying Manua Sera with gunpowder, and bound him hand and foot "like a slave." It was delightful to see old Musa's face again, and the supremely hospitable, kind, and courteous manner in which he looked after us, constantly bringing in all kind of small delicacies, and seeing that nothing was wanting to make us happy. All the property I had sent on in advance he had stored away; or rather, I should say, as much as had reached him, for the road expenses had eaten a great hole in it.

Once settled down into position, Sheikh Snay and the whole conclave of Arab merchants came to call on me. They said they had an army of four hundred slaves armed with muskets ready to take the field at once to hunt down Manua Sera, who was cutting their caravan road to pieces, and had just seized, by their latest reports, a whole convoy of their ammunition. I begged them strongly to listen to reason, and accept my advice as an old soldier, not to carry on their guerilla warfare in such a headlong hurry, else they would be led a dance by Manua Sera, as we had been by Tantia Topee in India. I advised them to allow me to mediate between them, after telling them what a favourable interview I had had with Manua Sera and Maula, whose son was at that moment concealed in Musa's tembe. My advice,

however, was not wanted. Snay knew better than any one how to deal with savages, and determined on setting out as soon as his army had "eaten their beef-feast of war."

On my questioning him about the Nile, Snay still thought the Nyanza was the source of the Jub river,[1] as he did in our former journey, but gave way when I told him that vessels frequented the Nile, as this also coincided with his knowledge of navigators in vessels appearing on some waters to the northward of Unyoro. In a great hurry he then bade me good-bye; when, as he thought it would be final, I gave him, in consideration for his former good services to the last expedition, one of the gold watches given me by the Indian Government. I saw him no more, though he and all the other Arabs sent me presents of cows, goats, and rice, with a notice that they should have gone on their war-path before, only, hearing of my arrival, out of due respect to my greatness, they waited to welcome me in. Further, after doing for Manua Sera, they were determined to go on to Ugogo to assist Salem bin Saif and the other merchants on, during which, at the same time, they would fight all the Wagogo who persisted in taking taxes and in harassing their caravans. At the advice of Musa, I sent Maula's son off at night to tell the old chief how sorry I was to find the Arabs so hotheaded I could not even effect an arrangement with them. It was a great pity; for Manua Sera was so much liked by the Wanyamuezi, they would, had they been able, have done anything to restore him.

. . .

Next day, after crossing more of those abominable rush-drains, whilst in sight of the Victoria Nyanza, we ascended the most beautiful hills, covered with verdure of all descriptions. At Meruka, where I put up, there resided some grandees, the

[1] The Jub is the largest river known to the Zanzibar Arabs. It debouches on the east coast north of Zanzibar, close under the equator.

chief of whom was the king's aunt. She sent me a goat, a hen, a basket of eggs, and some plantains, in return for which I sent her a wire and some beads. I felt inclined to stop here a month, everything was so very pleasant. The temperature was perfect. The roads, as indeed they were everywhere, were as broad as our coach-roads, cut through the long grasses, straight over the hills and down through the woods in the dells—a strange contrast to the wretched tracks in all the adjacent countries. The huts were kept so clean and so neat, not a fault could be found with them—the gardens the same. Wherever I strolled I saw nothing but richness, and what ought to be wealth. The whole land was a picture of quiescent beauty, with a boundless sea in the background. Looking over the hills, it struck the fancy at once that at one period the whole land must have been at a uniform level with their present tops, but that, by the constant denudation it was subjected to by frequent rains, it had been cut down and sloped into those beautiful hills and dales which now so much pleased the eye; for there were none of those quartz dykes I had seen protruding through the same kind of aqueous formations in Usui and Karague; nor were there any other sorts of volcanic disturbance to distort the calm quiet aspect of the scene.

From this, the country being all hill and dale, with miry rush-drains in the bottoms, I walked, carrying my shoes and stockings in my hands, nearly all the way. Rozaro's "children" became more and more troublesome, stealing everything they could lay their hands upon out of the village huts we passed on the way. On arrival at Sangua, I found many of them had been seized by some men who, bolder than the rest, had overtaken them whilst gutting their huts, and made them prisoners, demanding of me two slaves and one load of beads for their restitution. I sent my men back to see what had happened, and ordered them to bring all the men on to me, that I might see fair play. They, however, took the law into their own hands, drove off the Waganda villagers by firing their muskets, and relieved the thieves. A complaint was then laid against Nyamgundu by the chief officer of the village, and I was requested to halt. That I would not do, leaving the matter in the hands of the governor-general, Mr. Pokino, whom I heard we should find at the next station, Masaka.

On arrival there at the government establishment—a large collection of grass huts, separated one from the other within large enclosures, which overspread the whole top of a low hill—I was requested to withdraw and put up in some huts a short distance off, and wait until his excellency, who was from home, could come and see me; which the next day he did, coming in state with a large number of officers, who brought with them a cow, sundry pots of pombe [beer—ed.], enormous sticks of sugar-cane, and a large bundle of country coffee. This grows in great profusion all over this land in large bushy trees, the berries sticking on the branches like clusters of holly-berries.

I was then introduced, and told that his excellency was the appointed governor of all the land lying between the Katonga and the Kitangule rivers. After the first formalities were over, the complaint about the officers at Sangua was preferred for decision, on which Pokino at once gave it against the villagers, as they had no right, by the laws of the land, to lay hands on a king's guest. Just then Maula arrived, and began to abuse Nyamgundu. Of course I would not stand this; and, after telling all the facts of the case, I begged Pokino to send Maula away out of my camp. Pokino said he could not do this, as it was by the king's order he was appointed; but he put Maula in the background, laughing at the way he had "let the bird fly out of his hands," and settled that Nyamgundu should be my guide. I then gave him a wire, and he gave me three large sheets of mbugu, which he said I should require, as there were so many watercourses to cross on the road I was going. A second day's halt was necessitated by many of my men catching fever, probably owing to the constant crossing of those abominable rush-drains. There was no want of food here, for I never saw such a profusion of plantains anywhere. They were literally lying in heaps on the ground, though the people were brewing pombe all day, and cooking them for dinner every evening.

After crossing many more hills and miry bottoms, constantly coming in view of the lake, we reached Ugonzi, and after another march of the same description, came to Kituntu, the last officer's residence in Uddu [a province of Buganda—ed.]. Formerly it was the property of a Beluch named Eseau, who came to this country with merchandise, trading on account of Said Said, late Sultan of Zanzibar; but having lost it all on his way here, paying mahongo, or taxes, and so forth, he feared returning, and instead made great friends with the late king Sunna, who took an especial fancy to him because he had a very large beard, and raised him to the rank of Mkungu. A few years ago, however, Eseau died, and left all his family and property to a slave named Uledi, who now, in consequence, is the border officer.

I became now quite puzzled whilst thinking which was the finest spot I had seen in Uddu, so many were exceedingly beautiful; but I think I gave the preference to this, both for its own immediate neighbourhood and the long range of view it afforded of Uganda [Buganda—ed.] proper, the lake, and the large island, or group of islands, called Sese, where the king of Uganda keeps one of his fleets of boats.

Some little boys came here who had all their hair shaved off excepting two round tufts on either side of the head. They were the king's pages; and, producing three sticks, said they had brought them to me from their king, who wanted three charms or medicines. Then placing one stick on the ground before me, they said, "This one is a head which, being affected by dreams of a deceased relative, requires re-

lief;" the second symbolised the king's desire for the accomplishment of a phenomenon to which the old phalic worship was devoted; "and this third one," they said, "is a sign that the king wants a charm to keep all his subjects in awe of him." I then promised I would do what I could when I reached the palace, but feared to do anything in the distance. I wished to go on with the march, but was dissuaded by Nyamgundu, who said he had received orders to find me some cows here, as his king was most anxious I should be well fed. Next day, however, we descended into the Katonga valley, where, instead of finding a magnificent broad sheet of water, as I had been led to expect by the Arabs' account of it, I found I had to wade through a succession of rush-drains divided one from the other by islands. It took me two hours, with my clothes tucked up under my arms, to get through them all; and many of them were so matted with weeds, that my feet sank down as though I trod in a bog.

The Waganda all said that at certain times in the year no one could ford these drains, as they all flooded; but, strangely enough, they were always lowest when most rain fell in Uganda. No one, however, could account for this singular fact. No one knew of a lake to supply the waters, nor where they came from. That they flowed into the lake there was no doubt—as I could see by the trickling waters in some few places—and they lay exactly on the equator. Rising out of the valley, I found all the country just as hilly as before, but many of the rush-drains going to northward; and in the dells were such magnificent trees, they quite took me by surprise. Clean-trunked, they towered up just as so many great pillars, and then spread out their high branches like a canopy over us. I thought of the blue gums of Australia, and believed these would beat them. At the village of Mbule we were gracefully received by the local officer, who brought a small present, and assured me that the king was in a nervous state of excitement, always asking after me. Whilst speaking he trembled, and he was so restless he could never sit still.

Up and down we went on again through this wonderful country, surprisingly rich in grass, cultivation, and trees. Watercourses were as frequent as ever, though not quite so troublesome to the traveller, as they were more frequently bridged with poles or palm-tree trunks.

This, the next place we arrived at, was Nyamgundu's own residence, where I stopped a day to try and shoot buffaloes. Maula here had the coolness to tell me he must inspect all the things I had brought for presentation to the king, as he said it was the custom; after which he would hurry on and inform his majesty. Of course I refused, saying it was uncourteous to both the king and myself. Still he persisted, until, finding it hopeless, he spitefully told Nyamgundu to keep me here at least two days. Nyamgundu, however, very prudently told him he should obey his orders, which were to take me on as fast as he could. I then gave Nyamgundu wires and beads for himself and all his family round, which made Maula slink farther away from me than ever.

The buffaloes were very numerous in the tall grasses that lined the sides and bottoms of the hills; but although I saw some, I could not get a shot, for the grasses being double the height of myself, afforded them means of dashing out of view as soon as seen, and the rustling noise made whilst I followed them kept them on the alert. At night a hyena came into my hut, and carried off one of my goats that was tied to a log between two of my sleeping men.

During the next march, after passing some of the most beautifully-wooded dells, in which lay small rush-lakes on the right of the road, draining, as I fancied, into the Victoria Lake, I met with a party of the king's gamekeepers, staking their nets all along the side of a hill, hoping to catch antelopes by driving the covers with dogs and men. Farther on, also, I came on a party driving one hundred cows, as a present from Mtesa to Rumanika, which the officers in charge said was their king's return for the favour Rumanika had done him in sending me on to him. It was in this way that great kings sent "letters" to one another.

# 15  SIR SAMUEL BAKER
## KHARTOUM AND THE NILOTIC SLAVE TRADE

*Born into a wealthy British family, Samuel White Baker (1821–1893) settled in Ceylon, where he established an agricultural colony and devoted himself to hunting. Thereafter he traveled widely, principally for the purpose of making hunting trips. Anxious to participate in the search for the Nile sources, he and his beautiful Hungarian wife, Florence Ninian von Sass (d. 1916), arrived in Cairo in 1861 and traveled up the Nile to spend a year in the Sudan hunting along the Abyssinian frontier. In 1862 they reached Khartoum, where they intended to prepare for an expedition to the upper White Nile. At that time, Khartoum was the capital of the Egyptian Sudan. The city had steadily increased in size and had become an outpost of Europe and the Middle East on the periphery of tropical Africa, through which passed the slaves who had been taken from the Nile tributaries far to the south. The Bakers proceeded slowly up the Nile, met Speke and Grant returning from their exploration of the Nile sources at Lake Victoria, and then pressed on to Bunyoro. They discovered Lake Albert in 1864.*

From Sir Samuel White Baker, *The Albert N'Yanza: Great Basin of the Nile* (London: Macmillan, 1879), pp. 7–16.

Khartoum is situated in lat. 15° 29', on a point of land forming the angle between the White and Blue Niles at their junction. A more miserable, filthy, and unhealthy spot can hardly be imagined. Far as the eye can reach, upon all sides, is a sandy desert. The town, chiefly composed of huts of unburnt brick, extends over a flat hardly above the level of the river at high-water, and is occasionally flooded. Although containing about 30,000 inhabitants, and densely crowded, there are neither drains nor cesspools: the streets are redolent with inconceivable nuisances; should animals die, they remain where they fall, to create pestilence and disgust. There are, nevertheless, a few respectable houses, occupied by the traders of the country, a small proportion of whom are Italians, French, and Germans, the European population numbering about thirty. Greeks, Syrians, Copts, Armenians, Turks, Arabs, and Egyptians, form the motley inhabitants of Khartoum.

There are consuls for France, Austria, and America, and with much pleasure I acknowledge many kind attentions, and assistance received from the two former, M. Thibaut and Herr Hansall.

Khartoum is the seat of government, the Soudan provinces being under the control of a Governor-general, with despotic power. In 1861, there were about six thousand troops quartered in the town; a portion of these were Egyptians; other regiments were composed of blacks from Kordofan, and from the White and Blue Niles, with one regiment of Arnouts, and a battery of artillery. These troops are the curse of the country: as in the case of most Turkish and Egyptian officials, the receipt of pay is most irregular, and accordingly the soldiers are under loose discipline. Foraging and plunder is the business of the Egyptian soldier, and the miserable natives must submit to insult and ill-treatment at the will of the brutes who pillage them *ad libitum.*

In 1862, Moosa Pasha was the Governor-general of the Soudan. This man was a rather exaggerated specimen of Turkish authorities in general, combining the worst of Oriental failings with the brutality of a wild animal.

During his administration the Soudan became utterly ruined; governed by military force, the revenue was unequal to the expenditure, and fresh taxes were levied upon the inhabitants to an extent that paralysed the entire country. The Turk never improves. There is an Arab proverb that "the grass never grows in the footprint of a Turk," and nothing can be more aptly expressive of the character of the nation than this simple adage. Misgovernment, monopoly, extortion, and oppression, are the certain accompaniments of Turkish administration. At a great distance from all civilization, and separated from Lower Egypt by the Nubian deserts, Khartoum affords a wide field for the development of Egyptian official character. Every official plunders; the Governor-general extorts from all sides; he fills his private pockets by throwing every conceivable obstacle in the way of progress, and embarrasses every commercial movement in order to extort bribes from individuals. Following the general rule of his predecessors, a new governor upon arrival exhibits a spasmodic energy. Attended by cavasses and soldiers, he rides through every street of Khartoum, abusing the underlings for past neglect, ordering the streets to be swept, and the town to be thoroughly cleansed; he visits the market-place, examines the quality of the bread at the bakers' stalls, and the meat at the butchers'. He tests the accuracy of the weights and scales; fines and imprisons the impostors, and institutes a complete reform, concluding his sanitary and philanthropic arrangements by the imposition of some local taxes.

The town is comparatively sweet; the bread is of fair weight and size, and the new governor, like a new broom, has swept all clean. A few weeks glide away, and the nose again recalls the savoury old times when streets were never swept, and filth once more reigns paramount. The town relapses into its former state, again the false weights usurp the place of honest measures, and the only permanent and visible sign of the new administration is the *local tax*.

From the highest to the lowest official, dishonesty and deceit are the rule—and each robs in proportion to his grade in the Government employ—the onus of extortion falling upon the natives; thus, exorbitant taxes are levied upon the agriculturists, and the industry of the inhabitants is disheartened by oppression. The taxes are collected by the soldiery, who naturally extort by violence an excess of the actual impost; accordingly the Arabs limit their cultivation to their bare necessities, fearing that a productive farm would entail an extortionate demand. The heaviest and most unjust tax is that upon the "sageer," or water-wheel, by which the farmer irrigates his otherwise barren soil.

The erection of the sageer is the first step necessary to cultivation. On the borders of the river there is much land available for agriculture; but from an almost total want of rain the ground must be constantly irrigated by artificial means. No sooner does an enterprising fellow erect a water-wheel, than he is taxed, not only for his wheel, but he brings upon himself a perfect curse, as the soldiers employed for the collection of taxes fasten upon his garden, and insist upon a variety of extras in the shape of butter, corn, vegetables, sheep, &c. for themselves, which almost ruin the proprietor. Any government but that of Egypt and Turkey would offer a bonus for the erection of irrigating machinery that would give a stimulus to cultivation, and multiply the produce of the country; but the only rule without an exception is that of Turkish extortion. I have never met with any Turkish official who would take the slightest interest in plans for the *improvement* of the country, unless he discovered a means of filling his private purse. Thus in a country where

Nature has been hard in her measure dealt to the inhabitants, they are still more reduced by oppression. The Arabs fly from their villages on the approach of the brutal tax-gatherers, driving their flocks and herds with them to distant countries, and leaving their standing crops to the mercy of the soldiery. No one can conceive the suffering of the country.

The general aspect of the Soudan is that of misery; nor is there a single feature of attraction to recompense a European for the drawbacks of pestilential climate and brutal associations. To a stranger it appears a superlative folly that the Egyptian Government should have retained a possession, the occupation of which is wholly unprofitable; the receipts being far below the expenditure, "malgré" the increased taxation. At so great a distance from the sea-coast and hemmed in by immense deserts, there is a difficulty of transport that must nullify all commercial transactions on an extended scale.

The great and most important article of commerce as an export from the Soudan, is gum arabic: this is produced by several species of mimosa, the finest quality being a product of Kordofan; the other natural productions exported are senna, hides, and ivory. All merchandise both to and from the Soudan must be transported upon camels, no other animals being adapted to the deserts. The cataracts of the Nile between Assouan and Khartoum rendering the navigation next to impossible, the camel is the only medium of transport, and the uncertainty of procuring them without great delay is the trader's greatest difficulty. The entire country is subject to droughts that occasion a total desolation, and the want of pasture entails starvation upon both cattle and camels, rendering it at certain seasons impossible to transport the productions of the country, and thus stagnating all enterprise. Upon existing conditions the Soudan is worthless, having neither natural capabilities nor political importance; but there is, nevertheless, a reason that first prompted its occupation by the Egyptians, and that is in force to the present day. *The Soudan supplies slaves.*

Without the White Nile trade Khartoum would almost cease to exist; and that trade is kidnapping and murder. The character of the Khartoumers needs no further comment. The amount of ivory brought down from the White Nile is a mere bagatelle as an export, the annual value being about £40,000.

The people for the most part engaged in the nefarious traffic of the White Nile are Syrians, Copts, Turks, Circassians, and some few *Europeans.* So closely connected with the difficulties of my expedition is that accursed slave-trade, that the so-called ivory trade of the White Nile requires an explanation.

Throughout the Soudan money is exceedingly scarce and the rate of interest exorbitant, varying, according to the securities, from thirty-six to eighty per cent.; this fact proves general poverty and dishonesty, and acts as a preventive to all improvement. So high and fatal a rate deters all honest enterprise, and the country must lie in ruin under such a system. The wild speculator borrows upon such terms, to rise suddenly like a rocket, or to fall like its exhausted stick. Thus, honest enterprise being impossible, dishonesty takes the lead, and a successful expedition to the White Nile is supposed to overcome all charges. There are two classes of White Nile traders, the one possessing capital, the other being penniless adventurers; the same system of operations is pursued by both, but that of the former will be evident from the description of the latter.

A man without means forms an expedition, and borrows money for this purpose at 100 per cent. after this fashion. He agrees to repay the lender in ivory at one-half its market value. Having obtained the required sum, he hires several vessels and engages from 100 to 300 men, composed of Arabs and runaway villains from distant countries, who have found an asylum from justice in the obscurity of Khartoum. He purchases guns and large quantities of ammunition for his men, together with a few hundred pounds of glass beads. The piratical expedition being complete, he pays his men five months' wages in advance, at the rate of forty-five piastres (nine shillings) per month, and he agrees to give them eighty piastres per month for any period exceeding the five months advanced. His men receive their advance partly in cash and partly in cotton stuffs for clothes at an exorbitant price. Every man has a strip of paper, upon which is written by the clerk of the expedition the amount he has received both in goods and money, and this paper he must produce at the final settlement. The vessels sail about December, and on arrival at the desired locality, the party disembark and proceed into the interior, until they arrive at the village of some negro chief, with whom they establish an intimacy. Charmed with his new friends, the power of whose weapons he acknowledges, the negro chief does not neglect the opportunity of seeking their alliance to attack a hostile neighbour. Marching throughout the night, guided by their negro hosts, they bivouac within an hour's march of the unsuspecting village doomed to an attack about half an hour before break of day. The time arrives, and, quietly surrounding the village while its occupants are still sleeping, they fire the grass huts in all directions, and pour volleys of musketry through the flaming thatch. Panic-stricken, the unfortunate victims rush from their burning dwellings, and the men are shot down like pheasants in a battue, while the women and children, bewildered in the danger and confusion, are kidnapped and secured. The herds of cattle, still within their kraal or "zareeba," are easily disposed of, and are driven off with great rejoicing, as the prize of victory. The women and children are then fastened together, the former secured in an instrument called a sheba, made of a forked pole, the neck of the prisoner fitting into the fork, secured by a cross piece lashed behind; while the wrists, brought together in advance of the body, are tied to the pole. The children are then fastened by their necks with a rope attached to the women, and thus form a living chain, in which order they are marched to the head-quarters in company with the captured herds.

This is the commencement of business: should there be ivory in any of the huts not destroyed by the fire, it is appropriated; a general plunder takes place. The trader's party dig up the floors of the huts to search for iron hoes, which are generally thus concealed, as the greatest treasure of the negroes; the granaries are overturned and wantonly destroyed, and the hands are cut off the bodies of the slain, the more easily to detach the copper or iron bracelets that are usually worn. With this booty the *traders* return to their negro ally: they have thrashed and discomfited his enemy, which delights him; they present him with thirty or forty head of cattle which intoxicates him with joy, and a present of a pretty little captive girl of about fourteen completes his happiness.

But business only commenced. The negro covets cattle, and the trader has now captured perhaps 2,000 head. They are to be had for ivory, and shortly the tusks appear. Ivory is daily brought into camp in exchange for cattle, a tusk for a cow, according to size—a profitable business, as the cows have cost nothing. The trade proves brisk; but still there remain some little customs to be observed—some slight formalities, well understood by the White Nile trade. The slaves and two-thirds of the captured cattle belong to the trader, but his men claim as their perquisite one-third of the stolen animals. These having been divided, the slaves are put up to public auction among the men, who purchase such as they require; the amount being entered on the papers (serki) of the purchasers, to be reckoned against their

wages. To avoid the exposure, should the document fall into the hands of the Government or European consuls, the amount is not entered as for the purchase of a slave, but is divided for fictitious supplies—thus, should a slave be purchased for 1,000 piastres, that amount would appear on the document somewhat as follows:—

| Soap | 50 | Piastres. |
|------|-----|-----------|
| Tarboash (cap) | 100 | |
| Araki | 500 | |
| Shoes | 200 | |
| Cotton Cloth | 150 | |
| | 1,000 | |

The slaves sold to the men are constantly being changed and resold among themselves; but should the relatives of the kidnapped women and children wish to ransom them, the trader takes them from his men, cancels the amount of purchase, and restores them to their relations for a certain number of elephants' tusks, as may be agreed upon. Should any slave attempt to escape, she is punished either by brutal flogging, or shot or hanged, as a warning to others.

An attack or razzia, such as described, generally leads to a quarrel with the negro ally, who in his turn is murdered and plundered by the trader—his women and children naturally becoming slaves.

A good season for a party of a hundred and fifty men should produce about two hundred cantars (20,000 lbs.) of ivory, valued at Khartoum at £4,000. The men being paid in slaves, the wages should be *nil*, and there should be a surplus of four or five hundred slaves for the trader's own profit—worth on an average five to six pounds each.

The boats are accordingly packed with a human cargo, and a portion of the trader's men accompany them to the Soudan, while the remainder of the party form a camp or settlement in the country they have adopted, and industriously plunder, massacre, and enslave, until their master's return with the boats from Khartoum in the following season, by which time they are supposed to have a cargo of slaves and ivory ready for shipment. The business thus thoroughly established, the slaves are landed at various points within a few days' journey of Khartoum, at which places are agents, or purchasers waiting to receive them with dollars prepared for cash payments. The purchasers and dealers are, for the most part, Arabs. The slaves are then marched across the country to different places; many to Sennaar, where they are sold to other dealers, who sell them to the Arabs and to the Turks. Others are taken immense distances to ports on the Red Sea, Souakim, and Masowa, there to be shipped for Arabia and Persia. Many are sent to Cairo, and in fact they are disseminated throughout the slave-dealing East, the White Nile being the great nursery for the supply.

The amiable trader returns from the White Nile to Khartoum; hands over to his creditor sufficient ivory to liquidate the original loan of £1,000, and, already a man of capital, he commences as an independent trader.

Such was the White Nile trade when I prepared to start from Khartoum on my expedition to the Nile sources. Every one in Khartoum, with the exception of a few Europeans, was in favour of the slave-trade, and looked with jealous eyes upon a stranger venturing within the precincts of their holy land; a land sacred to slavery and to every abomination and villainy that man can commit.

# 16  GEORG SCHWEINFURTH
## KING MUNZA

*During his second sojourn in Africa, the botanist and traveler Georg Schweinfurth (1836–1925) spent three years (1868–1871) in the Upper Nile hinterland. His travels and work were a major contribution to European knowledge of the southern Sudan and the northeast Congo. He describes his visit to the powerful* Munza, *king of the Mangbettu people who inhabited the valley of the upper Uele River on the eastern reaches of the Congo basin.*

As we approached the huts, the drums and trumpets were sounded to their fullest powers, and the crowds of people pressing forward on either hand left but a narrow passage for our procession. We bent our steps to one of the largest huts, which formed a kind of palatial hall open like a shed at both ends. Waiting my arrival

From Dr. Georg Schweinfurth, *The Heart of Africa,* trans. by Ellen E. Frewer (New York: Sampson Low, Marston, Searle, and Rivington, 1874), II, 40–52.

here was one of the officers of state, who, I presume, was the master of the ceremonies, as I afterwards observed him presiding over the general festivities. This official took me by the right hand, and without a word conducted me to the interior of the hall. Here, like the audience at a concert, were arranged according to their rank hundreds of nobles and courtiers, each occupying his own ornamental bench and decked out with all his war equipments. At the other end of the building a space was left for the royal throne, which differed in no respect from the other benches, except that it stood upon an outspread mat; behind this bench was placed a large support of singular construction, resting as it seemed upon three legs, and furnished with projections that served as props for the back and arms of the sitter: this support was thickly studded with copper rings and nails. I requested that my own chair might be placed at a few paces from the royal bench, and there I took up my position with my people standing or squatting behind me, and the Nubian soldiers forming a guard around. The greater number of the soldiers had their guns, but my black squires, who had never before been brought face to face with so mighty a potentate, subsequently confessed to me that their hearts beat fast, and that they could not help trembling to think how a sign from Munza could have brought all our limbs to the spit.

For a considerable time I had to sit waiting in expectation before the empty throne. My servants informed me that Munza had attended the market in his ordinary costume, but that he had been seen to hasten home to his private apartments, where he was now undergoing a process of anointing, frizzling, and bedizening at the hands of his wives, in order that he should appear before me in the imposing splendour of his state attire. I had thus no other alternative than patiently to abide my time; for what could be more flattering to a foreign guest than for a king to receive him in his costliest toilet?

In the interval of waiting there seemed a continuous uproar. The fitful beating of kettle-drums and the perpetual braying of horns resounded through the airy building until it shook again, and mingling with the boisterous strains rose the voices of the assembled courtiers as they whiled away the time in loud and eager conversation. There was no doubt that I was myself the main cause of their excitement; for although I sat with my back to the majority, I could not be otherwise than quite aware that all eyes were intently fixed upon me. All, however, kept their seats at a respectful distance, so that I could calmly look about me and note down my observations of what I saw.

The hall itself was the chief object that attracted my attention. It was at least a hundred feet in length, forty feet high, and fifty broad. It had been quite recently completed, and the fresh bright look of the materials gave it an enlivening aspect, the natural brown polish of the woodwork looking as though it were gleaming with the lustre of new varnish. Close by was a second and more spacious hall, which in height was only surpassed by the loftiest of the surrounding oil-palms; but this, although it had only been erected five years previously, had already begun to show symptoms of decay, and being enclosed on all sides was dark, and therefore less adapted for the gathering at a public spectacle. Considering the part of Africa in which these halls were found, one might truly be justified in calling them wonders of the world; I hardly know with all our building resources what material we could have employed, except it were whalebone, of sufficient lightness and durability to erect structures like these royal halls of Munza, capable of withstanding the tropical storms and hurricanes. The bold arch of the vaulted roof was supported on three long rows of pillars formed from perfectly straight tree-stems; the countless spars and rafters as well as the other parts of the building being composed entirely of the leaf-stalks of the wine-palm (*Raphia vinifera*).[1] The floor was covered with a dark red clay plaster, as firm and smooth as asphalt. The sides were enclosed by a low breastwork, and the space between this and the arching

[1] This palm is found in every bank-forest in the Monbutto country, and its leaves vary from 25 to 35 feet in length: the midrib of the leaf (rhachis) is of a bright brown colour, and furnishes the most popular building material throughout Central Africa.

roof, which at the sides sloped nearly to the ground, allowed light and air to pass into the building. Outside against the breastwork stood crowds of natives, probably the "great unwashed" of the Monbuttoo, who were unable to obtain places within, and contented themselves with eagerly gazing through this opening at the proceedings. Officials with long sticks went their rounds and kept order among the mob, making free use of their sticks whenever it was necessary; all boys who ventured uninvited into the hall being vigorously beaten back as trespassers.

I had probably been left for an hour, and was getting lost in the contemplation of all the wonders, when a louder sound of voices and an increasing clang of horns and kettle-drums led me to suppose that there was an announcement of the approach of the king; but, no, this was only a prelude. The sovereign was still being painted and beautified by the hands of his fair ones. There was, however, a fresh and increasing commotion near the entrance of the hall, where a number of ornamental weapons was being arranged. Posts were driven into the ground, and long poles were fastened horizontally across them; then against this extemporized scaffolding were laid, or supported crosswise, hundreds of ornamental lances and spears, all of pure copper, and of every variety of form and shape. The gleam of the red metal caught the rays of the tropical noontide sun, and in the symmetry of their arrangement the rows of dazzling lance-heads shone with the glow of flaming torches, making a background to the royal throne that was really magnificent. The display of wealth, which according to Central African tradition was incalculable, was truly regal, and surpassed anything of the kind that I had conceived possible.

A little longer and the weapons are all arranged. The expected king has left his home. There is a running to and fro of heralds, marshals, and police. The thronging masses flock towards the entrance, and silence is proclaimed. The king is close at hand. Then come the trumpeters flourishing away on their huge ivory horns; then the ringers swinging their cumbrous iron bells; and now, with a long firm stride, looking neither to the right nor to the left, wild, romantic, picturesque alike in mien and in attire, comes the tawny Caesar himself! He was followed by a number of his favoured wives. Without vouchsafing me a glance, he flung himself upon his unpretending chair of state, and sat with his eyes fixed upon his feet. Mohammed had joined the retinue of his royal friend, and took up his position opposite me on the other side of the king on a stool that was brought for his accommodation. He also had arrayed himself in a suitable dress in honour of the occasion, and now sat in the imposing uniform of a commander of Arnauts.

I could now feast my eyes upon the fantastic figure of the ruler. I was intensely interested in gazing at the strange weird-looking sovereign, of whom it was commonly reported that his daily food was human flesh. With arms and legs, neck and breast, all bedizened with copper rings, chains, and other strange devices, and with a great copper crescent at the top of his head, the potentate gleamed with a shimmer that was to our ideas unworthy of royalty, but savoured far too much of the magazines of civic opulence, reminding one almost unavoidably of a well-kept kitchen! His appearance, however, was decidedly marked with his nationality, for every adornment that he had about him belonged exclusively to Central Africa, as none but the fabrications of his native land are deemed worthy of adorning the person of a king of the Monbuttoo.

Agreeably to the national fashion a plumed hat rested on the top of his chignon, and soared a foot and a half above his head; this hat was a narrow cylinder of closely-plaited reeds; it was ornamented with three layers of red parrots' feathers, and crowned with a plume of the same; there was no brim, but the copper crescent projected from the front like the vizor of a Norman helmet. The muscles of Munza's ears were pierced, and copper bars as thick as the finger inserted in the cavities. The entire body was smeared with the native unguent of powdered camwood, which converted the original bright brown tint of his skin into the colour that is so conspicuous in ancient Pompeian halls. With the exception of being of an unusually fine texture, his single garment differed in no respect from what was worn throughout the country; it consisted of a large piece of fig bark impregnated with the same dye that served as his cosmetic, and this, falling in graceful folds about his body, formed breeches and waistcoat all in one. Round thongs of buffalo-hide, with heavy copper balls attached to the ends, were fastened round the waist in a huge knot, and like a girdle held the coat, which was neatly-hemmed. The material of the coat was so carefully manipulated that it had quite the appearance of a rich *moiré antique*. Around the king's neck hung a copper ornament made in little points which radiated like beams all over his chest; on his bare arms were strange-looking pendants which in shape could only be compared to drumsticks with rings at the end. Halfway up the lower part of the arms and just below the knee were three bright, horny-looking circlets cut out of hippopotamus-hide, likewise tipped with copper. As a symbol of his dignity Munza wielded in his right hand the sickle-shaped Monbuttoo scimitar, in this case only an ornamental weapon, and made of pure copper.

As soon as the king had taken his seat, two little tables, beautifully carved, were placed on either side of his throne, and on these stood the dainties of which he continually partook, but which were carefully concealed by napkins of fig bark; in addition to these tables, some really artistic flasks of porous clay were brought in, full of drinking water.

Such was Munza, the autocrat of the Monbuttoo, with whom I was now

brought face to face. He appeared as the type of those half-mythical potentates, a species of Mwata Yanvo or Great Makoko, whose names alone have penetrated to Europe, a truly savage monarch, without a trace of anything European or Oriental in his attire, and with nothing fictitious or borrowed to be attributed to him.

He was a man of about forty years of age, of a fair height, of a slim but powerful build, and, like the rest of his countrymen, stiff and erect in figure. Although belonging to a type by no means uncomely, his features were far from prepossessing, but had a Nero-like expression that told of *ennui* and satiety. He had small whiskers and a tolerably thick beard; his profile was almost orthognatic, but the perfectly Caucasian nose offered a remarkable contrast to the thick and protruding negro lips. In his eyes gleamed the wild light of animal sensuality, and around his mouth lurked an expression that I never saw in any other Monbuttoo, a combination of avarice, violence, and love of cruelty that could with the extremest difficulty relax into a smile. No spark of love or affection could beam forth from such features as his.

A considerable time elapsed before the king looked directly at the pale-faced man with the long hair and the tight black clothes who now for the first time appeared before him. I held my hat in my hand, but no greeting had as yet taken place, for, observing that everyone kept his seat when the king entered the hall, I had done the same, and now waited for him to address me. The wild uproar of the cannibals still continued, and Munza, sitting in a careless attitude, only raised his eyes now and then from their fixed stare upon the ground as though to scan the whole assemblage, but in reality to take stray glances at my person, and in this way, little by little, he satisfied his curiosity. I could not help marvelling at the composure of this wild African, and wondering where in the world he could have learnt his dignity and self-posses-sion.

At length the monarch began to ask me some questions. They were fluently trans-lated into the Zandey dialect by the chief interpreter, who always played a principal part in our intercourse with the natives. The Niam-niam [Azande—ed.] in their turn rendered the sense to me in Arabic. The conversation, however, was of the most commonplace character, and re-ferred neither to the purpose of my com-ing nor to the country from which I came. Munza's interrogations brought to my mind the rough reception afforded to Reinhold Forster, the companion of the renowned Captain Cook, by Frederick the Great, who bluntly asked him if he had ever seen a king? "Yes, your Majesty," was the answer, "several; two tame and three savage." Munza appeared ex-tremely anxious to keep up to an Oriental measure the principle of *nil admirari*; nothing could disturb his composure, and even at my subsequent visits, where there was no state ceremonial, he maintained a taciturnity nearly as resolute.

My servants now brought forth the presents I had brought and spread them at the king's feet. These consisted, in the first place, of a piece of black cloth, a telescope, a silver platter, and a porcelain vase; the silver was taken for white iron, and the porcelain for carved ivory. The next gift was a real piece of carved ivory, brought as a specimen to show the way in which the material is employed; there was a book with gilt edges, a gift which could not fail to recall to my mind the scene in which Speke describes Kamrasi's first lesson in the Bible; then came a dou-ble mirror, that both magnified and re-duced what it reflected; and last, though by no means least, was a large assortment of beads of Venetian glass, including thirty necklaces, composed of thirty dis-tinct pieces, so that Munza was in posses-sion of more than a thousand separate beads. The universal principle followed by the Nubians forbade that any presents

of firearms should be made to native rul-ers. Munza regarded all these offerings with great attention, but without commit-ting himself to any audible expression of approval. Not so his fifty wives, who were seated on stools arranged behind his throne; they gave frequent half-sup-pressed utterances of surprise, and the double mirror was passed admiringly from hand to hand, its contortions elicit-ing shouts of delight.

There were fifty of these ladies present: they were only the most intimate, or wives of the first rank, the entire number of court ladies being far larger. Except in the greater elegance of their attire, they de-parted in no way from the fashion of the country, the description of which must be deferred for the present.

After a time Munza turned his atten-tion to his refreshments. As far as I could distinguish them, they consisted of lumps of plantain-meal and tapioca piled on leaves, of dried plantains, and of a fruit which to my surprise I immediately recognised as the cola-nut of the west. From this rosy-shelled kernel the king cut a few slices, and chewed them in the inter-vals of smoking his tobacco. His pipe, in the shape of an iron stem six feet long, was handed to him by a chibbukchak, who was in attendance for that purpose. Very remarkable was the way in which Munza smoked. To bring himself into the correct position he threw himself far back in his seat, supported his right elbow on the arm-rest, put one leg across the other, and with his left hand received the pipe-stem. In this attitude he gravely took one long inhalation, then, with a haughty gesture, resigned his pipe to the hands of his at-tendant and allowed the smoke slowly to reissue from his mouth. It is a habit among Turks of rank to smoke thus by taking only two or three inhalations from a pipe handed to them by their servants; but where, again, may I ask, could this cannibal prince have learnt such a cus-tom?

To my request for a cola-nut the king

responded by graciously passing me a specimen with his own hand. Turning to Mohammed, I expressed my surprise at beholding this fruit of the far west amongst the Monbuttoo; I told him of its high value as a spice in Bornoo, where it is worth its weight in silver, and I went on to say that it confirmed my impression that the Welle was identical with the river of Baghirmy, called the Shary, and that this nut accordingly came to me like a key to a problem that I was seeking to solve. Then again addressing Munza, I made him understand that I knew the fruit, and pointing in the direction of Lake Tsad, I told him that there it was eaten by the great people of the country. I hoped in this way to induce him to give me some information on the subject; but he had made up his mind to be astonished at nothing, nor could I ever even on future occasions draw him into a geographical discussion. All that I could learn was that the cola-nut grew wild in the country, and that it was called "nangweh" by the natives, who were accustomed to chew it in the intervals of their smoking.

The performances that had been prepared for our entertainment now commenced. First of all a couple of hornblowers stepped forward, and proceeded to execute solos upon their instruments. These men were advanced proficients in their art, and brought forth sounds of such power, compass, and flexibility that they could be modulated from sounds like the roar of a hungry lion, or the trumpeting of an infuriated elephant, down to tones which might be compared to the sighing of the breeze or to a lover's whisper. One of them, whose ivory horn was so huge that he could scarcely hold it in a horizontal position, executed rapid passages and shakes with as much neatness and decision as though he were performing on a flute.

Next appeared a number of professional singers and jesters, and amongst them a little plump fellow, who acted the part of a pantomime clown, and jumped about and turned somersaults till his limbs looked like the arms of a windmill; he was covered from head to foot with bushy tufts and pigtails, and altogether his appearance was so excessively ludicrous that, to the inward delight of the king, I burst into a hearty fit of laughter. I called him a court fool, and in many respects he fully deserved the title. I hardly know why the Nubians should have drawn my attention, as though to something quite new, to the wooden Monbuttoo scimitar that he wore in his girdle. His jokes and pranks seemed neverending, and he was permitted to take liberties with every one, not excepting even Munza himself; and amongst other tricks he would approach the king with his right hand extended, and just as Munza had got hold of it, would start backwards and make off with a bound. A short time before he appeared, some freshly baked ears of maize, the first of the season, had been laid before me; of this delicacy the fool, with the most comical gestures, made me comprehend that he wished to partake; I therefore took up some detached grains, and threw them, one by one, into his open mouth; he caught them with a snap, and devoured them with such comical grimaces, that the performance called forth a roar of applause from the whole assembly.

The next episode consisted of the performances of a eunuch, who formed a butt for the wit of the spectators. How Munza had come into possession of this creature, no one seemed to know, and I could only learn that he was employed in the inner parts of the palace. He was a fat grotesque-looking figure, and when he sang looked exactly like a grunting baboon; to add to the oddity of his appearance, Munza, as though in mockery of his Nubian guests, had had him arrayed in a red fez, and thus he was the only one in all the immense concourse of natives who had anything foreign in his attire.

But the most important part of the programme was reserved for the end: Munza was to make an oration. Whilst all the audience remained quietly seated on their stools and benches, up jumped the king, loosened his coat, cleared his throat, and commenced his harangue. Of course I could not understand a single word, and a double interpretation would have been worse than useless: but, from what I could see and hear, it was evident that Munza endeavoured to be choice and emphatic in his language, as not only did he often correct himself, but he made pauses after the sentences that he intended to be impressive, to allow for the applause of his auditors. Then the shout of "Ee, ee, tchupy, tchupy, ee, Munza, ee," resounded from every throat, and the musical instruments caught up the strain, until the uproar was truly demoniacal. Several times after this chorus, and as if to stimulate the tumult, Munza uttered a stentorian "brrr—" [2] with a voice so sonorous that the very roof vibrated, and the swallows fled in terror from their nests in the eaves.

The kettle-drums and horns now struck up a livelier and more rhythmical strain, and Munza assumed a new character and proceeded to beat time with all the solemnity of a conductor. His *bâton* was something like a baby's rattle, and consisted of a hollow sphere of basket-work filled with

[2] It may interest the reader to learn that in the Shamane prayers "brrr—" is synonymous with "hail," and I have little doubt that it here meant some sort of applause, as it was always the signal for the repetition of the hymn in celebration of the glories of Munza.

pebbles and shells, and attached to a stick.[3]

The discourse lasted full half an hour, during which time I took the portrait of the king. . . . Hunger at length compelled me to take my leave of the sovereign and retrace my steps to the camp. At parting Munza said to me, "I do not know what to give you in return for all your presents; I am sorry I am so poor and have nothing to offer you." Fascinated by his modesty and indulging the idea that it was only a preface to a munificent gift worthy of royalty, I replied, "Don't mention that: I did not come for what I could get; we buy ivory from the Turks, and pay them with yellow lead and white iron, and we make white stuffs and powder and guns for ourselves. I only ask for two things: a pig (*Potamochoerus*) and a chimpanzee."

"You shall certainly have them," said Munza; but I was thoroughly deceived, and, in spite of my repeated reminders, neither pig nor chimpanzee ever appeared.

As I left the hall the king commenced a new oration. As for myself, I was so thoroughly fatigued with the noise and tumult, that I was glad to spend the remainder of this memorable day quietly in my tent.

[3] A similar contrivance is used on the river Gabon on the West Coast.

# 17   SALIM AL-MAZRUI
## THE SULTAN AND MOMBASA

*Only one example of a long and illustrious poetic tradition,* Utendi wa al-Akida *was written by Abdallah ibn Maseed ibn Salim al-Mazrui (1797–1894). This heroic poem concerns the conflict between al-Akida, the* Wali *(Governor) of Mombasa and the Sultan of Zanzibar, Sayyid Barghash. Acting on the complaints of the people of Mombasa, the sultan deposed al-Akida, who was finally driven from Fort Jesus in 1875 with the assistance of two British men-of-war.*

From Abdallah ibn Maseed ibn Salim al-Mazrui, "Utendi wa al-Akida," in Lyndon Harris, *Swahili Poetry* (Oxford: Clarendon Press, 1962), pp. 131, 133, 135, 137, 139, 141, 143. Reprinted by permission of the Clarendon Press, Oxford.

First in the Name of God        if you want
the truth        the Swahili        country
is no place for us to live in.

Ruler, our ruler        ruler born in our
country        how could anything be
withheld        from him that he could
not seize?

But the year is not good        it is like a
day of awakening        to sorrow and
repentance        listen, brethren.

It is a year beginning unluckily        and
ending with deception        a year of
much trouble        as you will see for
yourselves.

It came in with strife        want of friendli-
ness        and destruction of souls
all, I say, without cause.

In these last days of the good old world
a subject cannot be allowed        to
quarrel with his Sultan        and go un-
punished.

The tale of Bakhashweini        I will relate
exactly        understand that its beginning        is the strife that you know of.

The Wali was a man        beloved by the
people        a man in whom the Sultan
had great confidence.

But there is no ruler        who is loved by
all        there is sure to come an evil
person        who seeks to do him ill.

And so Muhammad        was slandered to
the Sultan        and the friction increased        until discord flared up.

Our great lord sent        his special minister        to investigate the reports
that had reached him.

When the ship arrived        it brought the
reply        there was nothing more to
say        the Sultan was angry.

The man in the ship        was Muhammad
b. Suleiman        the Sultan's envoy
he it is who was on board.

When he landed at the Customs        and
came up the steps        all the Kilindini
people        followed him in a crowd.

The elders of the town        told Said (the
Sultan)        al-Akida is a bad man
it is better to beware of him.

He asked, What is the matter?        What
has he done?        Whatever (he may

have done) in his own home Dauani
he cannot deal threateningly with me.

The elders were silent        not knowing
what to think        they kept on hesitat-
ing        till the great man was annoyed.

He asked them what was the matter
what had they to say        Say what you
have to        and I will consider it.

We have only one thing to say        Our
wish is this        that you take away
from us the trouble        that has come
upon us.

What        Bakhashweini        deserves        is
known to God Almighty        may the
Lord God curse him        and deliver us
all from him.

The Sultan's command        was to go to
the Court        five and fifty        soldiers were waiting there.

The Wali was sent for        he came in a
rage        when he arrived he saw how
it was        and sat down in his place.

He was handed a letter        which he
took hurriedly        he grasped it
and tore it open.

When he opened it        he saw the order
which had been written        that he
should leave the Fort        and live
there no more.

Then he spoke        with his tongue and
said        I am going for the keys
and I will bring them all here.

He went off, I tell you        he went off
arrogantly        just after midday
and barricaded himself within.

He sent forth the Khalifa        Go and
capture Mustafa        face death itself
to bring him to me.

Go quickly, sergeant        and arrest the
Baluchis [1]        then tell him (Mustafa)
Shishi anti, it is Arabic.

Go, Al-Adwan        my brave lion        I
have none like you        among all my
soldiers.

So shall I remove doubt        entirely from
my heart        I will seize the Baluchis
women as well as men.

Then spoke al-Adwani        al-Akida,

---

[1] An inhabitant of Baluchistan (ed.).

what is the matter?      Grieve not so
much      I will take the Baluchis.
I will seize the Baluchis      and put them
in chains      in the cell of Wadi
Mataka      there will I put them.
He set off to do so      going in a hurry
when he got there (he found him) eating rice      and Mustafa was en-
chained.
Rifles were fired      some people hid
themselves      As the Jemadari
crouched down      he was hit by a
bullet.
Alas this destruction      we are a famous
people      but because we are divided
(lit. in two ranks)      that is why we
are destroyed.
Ramadhani Kazabeka      these are the
things you wanted      there is no escape from them now      for they have
come upon us.
Mustafa was imprisoned      he was almost slain by the sword      but God
protected him      and he was put in
a cell.
The people of Bakhashweini      called
out in the Fort      Who is it today?
who is it?·      Who (dares) to approach
us?
Never, never      far be it from me
I will prefer death      rather than be
forced out (of the Fort).
I will not agree to come out      to force
me out will be difficult      even
though you may collect riches      I
will not accept them.
I was born in the Fort      The Kilindi
folk      and all who are in the town
I am familiar with them all.
I ask the people of Mombasa      Why
should war come?      When you are
all entangled      you are all involved
in trouble.
Tell Sheikh Suud      the son of the Sai-
yids      because so much is involved
he can by no means disentangle affairs.
For he is as my father      the husband
of my mother      he has spun this web
around me      until I have been
deposed.

He left to go to Mgau      and I thought
·nothing of him      not realizing he
was bent on mischief      going to tell
tales.
He involved me in discord      and it
stuck hard      so that I had nothing
to say      that I could make up before
the Sultan.
I appeared before the Sultan      without
getting my intention      like a corrupt
slave      who had done wrong.
I grieve for my efforts      in striving with
people      when lo a pot (of trouble)
very big indeed was being brewed for
me.
I said to myself      I will not leave Zanzibar      and I saw that I was in danger      of losing Mombasa.
When I was in Zanzibar      I thought I
would not come      I will not return
(but) I came      and I reached Mombasa.
I am expecting some people      they are
elders of the town      but they do not
come to me      I would give them
money (if they came).
I would grant them a share      of what
God gave to me      I should give it to
my companions      for them to use.
When I get the townspeople      it would
be for me a matter of questioning
like Rambi Saji      so great is my anger.
Salimu make ready      so that we may
die like men      even if it be by daylight      fear not, it is all the same.
Let Salimu stay right there      . that is
where I am coming      let me fly
round him like a bat      till he knows
not where to go.
Muhammad remained      in the Fort
with the crowd      of men and women
and refused to open the gate.
There went to him groups      of good
and honourable men      (to beg him)
to cease from his folly      but he
refused their counsel.
Muhammad declared      I will not go
back on what I have decided      about
the gate have no doubt      I am not

the one to open it.

He drove them from the Fort      the poor Baluchis      in humiliation and sorrow      they were scattered about the villages.

The news spread      and reached Zanzibar      The Sultan pondered      how to get him out by a trick.

After a few days      there came good gifts      and a pledge of peace then he came out of the Fort.

After the day's round      there arrived Seif the Sour      with his akida Mataru      and an army of soldiers.

And Muhammad realized      that this is war indeed      without doubt he will be captured      unless he defends himself.

He said I must      get the town on my side      I will not rejoice the enemy and consent to be tricked.

Bakhashweini proclaimed      that of the soldiers of the Fort      none must remain in the town      after the setting of the sun

He had a consultation      with his brothers and other faithful men      they spoke boastfully      and this is what they said.

We have placed the cannons in position our guns are set      only he who is a fool      will dare to come to us.

Every sensible man      even though he be strong      would be only a fool to come upon us so.

For this is a great loss      which follows along with great gain      and I call upon all Muslims (lit. the family of the Mother of Cities)      to come and join us here.

Do not think it is like Gaeti      who was not equal to death      I tell you without hiding anything      I will certainly face it.

You will see regiment upon regiment on the highway like smoke      Do not think this is boasting      what I am telling you.

Everyone who is first      with moaning and anguish      with twenty-four

pounds of chains      that is what I shall put him in.

To every man who is my enemy      I shall change into a leopard for him it is because he does not know me that he trifles with me.

This is how they talked      Muhammad and his brother      and all who followed along with them      were of the same mind.

But this is a gamble      and those who sleep must not sleep      they must keep watch      till the morning comes.

He opened the gate      (and said) what I say is no lie      I have no need of idle words      all I want I shall do.

He poured out his carriers      saying, Today is the day      Do not think there is a journey ahead      for we are going into the town.

What I say is true      the road was filled with smoke      we saw hosts of men and lo they were the enemy.

Now look after yourselves      it is not night but day      let us go forth like noblemen      let there be no running away.

They were like locusts      and they destroyed the town      and they behaved with violence      intent on evil.

An Englishman arrived      and gave him good advice      and he said I will not listen      to anything you say to me.

The European was vexed      and said to him sharply      You do not like my words      not one do you hear.

The Admiral spake      Now what advice should we give in Zanzibar      about what should be done?

I will arrange for gunboats      to creep up by sea      he has chosen evil and he must suffer for it.

I shall attack him with shell      but I shall not aim to hit      the shot shall pass as a sign      perhaps he will give up.

He took it in jest      the Fort had no sign (of damage)      those inside rejoiced and blessed their good fortune.

Another shell came over     and hit the
target      and it caused great damage
and lives were lost.
He lowered the flag      hoisting another
at once      to show them a signal
that we have surrendered.
The firing ceased      the young men
made ready      and came ashore to
look      and entered the Fort.
Muhammad came out      his heart was
very cold      I want your promise
Admiral, that you will do something
for me.
I want you to stand surety for me      and
leave me in the Fort      or if we go to
the Sultan      when we arrive inter-
cede for me.
The Admiral explained      If I go to the
Sultan      and you are not in my
hands      that would be wrong.
Let us go on board      and sail at once
when we get to the Sultan      I shall
find something to say.

They went down to the shore      and
went on board      when they reached
Zanzibar      he told him not to worry.
He went ashore      and went to the Sultan      (who was told) Muhammad is
inside      Sir, I have brought him to
you.
We have come according to promise
do not refuse my request      he is under arrest      and now I ask pardon
for him.
What you ask has been granted      and
I will follow your counsel      you have
got him out of the      difficulties
which surrounded him.
Do not keep him in Zanzibar      I fore-
see danger there for him      for he is
a mischievous person      and will
harm my subjects.
Now I have come to the end      my tale
is finished      I have said all there is
to say      and there is nothing left to
say.

# 18  SIR APOLO KAGWA
## COURT LIFE IN BUGANDA

*In an attempt to improve on the description of the* Baganda *by a missionary, the Reverend
John Roscoe,* * *Sir Apolo Kagwa (d. 1927), Regent and Prime Minister of Buganda, wrote*
The Customs of the Baganda *in Luganda in 1918 during the early part of the reign of
Kabaka* Daudi Chwa. *In this work Kagwa recalls the enthronement of Kimera in 1910
and the pomp and ceremony of the courts of the kabakas (kings) of Buganda.*

The next morning Kibale, Mpewo clan,
and Nakatanza, Lugave clan, came to the
palace and knocked at the door of the
king's house. At eight o'clock a council

From Sir Apolo Kagwa, *The Customs of the
Baganda,* trans. by Ernest B. Kalibala and edited by
May Mandelbaum Edel (New York: Columbia University Press, 1934), pp. 63–67, 170–173. Reprinted
by permission.
* John Roscoe, *The Baganda* (London: Macmillan,
1911).

was held by the provincial chiefs to lay
plans for the enthronement. Mugema,
who tied the knot in the king's barkcloth
on the right shoulder, demanded the right
to tie the one on the left shoulder. This
caused a disagreement in the council. It
was finally settled against Mugema by the
men of the royal family. Then the chiefs
went to the royal palace.
Kabumba, of the Lugave clan, brought

the carpet and Kiini, of the Mamba clan, the tanner, brought the skins of lions, leopards, hyenas, and cows. Apolo Kagwa escorted the king and his sister, Djuma Katebe. He headed the procession, carrying the king's spears and shields. He marched at the right of the king because he is next to the king and insures his peace. At the palace gate Mugema led the king to the throne and placed him on it. He then placed the barkcloth on the king and knotted it on the right shoulder, as an indication that the king was the owner of the country. He laid a calfskin over the barkcloth because Kimera wore a calfskin. Then he said, "You will perform all the acts and duties befitting a king."

The Kasudju knotted a barkcloth on the king's left shoulder which meant, "You are His Majesty who rules over all other officials and men." On top of this he put a leopard skin meaning,"A king is the leopard; the common people are squirrels." Then he too said, "You will perform all the acts and duties befitting a king."

Kakinda, of the Kobe clan, brought a differently decorated barkcloth and this was placed over all the other ceremonial robes. This was several yards long and was wrapped from the right shoulder around the body and back again.

Then the Mukwenda, Sabagabo, brought a shield and two spears and handed them to the king. This meant that the king would overthrow his enemies. Kadjubi tied a string of sparkling beads about the king's left arm as a memorial to Wanyana, saying, "You are Kimera." Segulu, of the Lugave clan, put a bracelet on the king's right hand to show that he among the princes was the king elect. Namutwe, assistant Sekibobo, handed a bow and arrow to the king to assure him of his jurisdiction over the subjugated Basagala. Those who remember Greek history know that there was a king who had a slave remind him about his victory over the Athenians at all his meals (sic!).

Kaima by virtue of his office of chief in charge of the weapons brought a bow and arrow to the king. Then Masembe came and stood before the king with a milk jar. Mugema introduced him, saying, "This is your head herdsman who takes care of Namala's cow from which your great-great-grandfather, Kimera, drank his milk." Then the king touched the jar and Masembe took it away. Sebalidja, the head shepherd, brought a brass milk jar, and handed it to Mpiŋga, who had been Kimera's shepherd. Mpiŋga introduced him to the king, saying, "When milking my cow Mbulide, given me by Kimera, I use this jar."

Luboyera, of the Butiko clan, brought a beer jar known as Mwendanvuma, saying, "This is the jar in which I make your beer." Kalinda presented the type of jar in which the king's drinking water is kept, saying, "This is your water jar."

Semwaŋga and Kabogoza, Ŋoŋge clan, the barkcloth makers, brought a mallet, saying, "This is the mallet upon which your barkcloths are made." Segirinya, Ŋgo clan, brought the iron tool used in engraving the crown and royal stick. He presented this to the king, saying, "This is omuindu.[1] I use it to adorn your crown and to fashion your walking sticks." Walukaga, of the Kasimba clan, a blacksmith, brought a hammer, saying, "With this I make the spear with which you conquer." Mutalaga, of the Nvuma clan, another blacksmith, brought a dagger. He gave it to Kasudju, who gave it to the king saying, "Whoever rebels against you, you will destroy with this dagger."

Then Mugema introduced the chief royal drums, known as Mudjaguzo. Kaula, of the Lugave clan, brought the drumsticks and Kasudju gave them to the king. The king beat the drum. Kimomera, of the Butiko clan, the assistant drummer, gave the king another pair of drumsticks and the king beat on another drum known as Namanyonyi.

[1] A stick with branches.

Muyandja, of the Nyonyi clan, brought an axe and said, "This is your axe Naŋkuŋga that builds your boats." Omusoloza,[2] of the Nyonyi clan, presented the king with two pieces of firewood, and said, "These two pieces of wood keep the fire in Gombolola, whence you obtain the ashes to smear yourself for war."

This ended the introductory ceremony. Several others followed.

Sekaiba, of the Mbogo clan, came covered with a barkcloth known as "Throne" and carried the king on his shoulders for about twenty feet, while the princesses and the huge crowd that had assembled paid homage to the enthroned king. They shouted and gave the yells of their clans. Then the prime minister with a shield and two spears escorted the king to his dwelling house. Here the relatives of the king offered him gifts. They came in order, his grandfather, then his aunts, his sisters, brothers and the other princes. They were required to stand at the end of the carpet and introduce themselves formally.

After that another group of kinsmen came. This comprised the children of the princesses. They adorned their heads in the proper fashion and came singing beautiful melodies. The king gave them a bull and bade them farewell. His mother's relatives also offered gifts, and introduced themselves. Before the conclusion of the ceremony his grandfathers of the Ŋoŋge clan, the grandfathers of

### Sir Apolo Kagwa

Tcwa I of the Ŋgeye clan, and those of Kimera of the Nsenene clan, in the order named, introduced themselves.

.    .    .

The men who served the various chiefs on their estates were mostly young men. It was they who were the most energetic and successful in the looting campaigns the king ordered from time to time against

[2] Tax-collector.

the neighbors. When the booty was brought home the chief selected that which pleased him most from among the loot of his subordinates, and so became a rich man. The king might show favoritism and assign his favorite chiefs to frequent and lucrative campaigns.

This custom may have had something to do with the Baganda ignorance of trading. They were used to use force to get anything they desired, or else to receive it from the king as a gift. Those who were appointed to the various estates cultivated them by means of the peasants, who moved wherever they pleased. They very commonly went to the estate of a newly appointed chief who they thought might be honored with presents and booty. This meant that there was very great instability, the great mass of the peasantry shifting about and chiefs long established being left alone with their wealth.

.    .    .

The following account gives an idea of the pomp of the King of Buganda and of his power in governing. When the king was about to appear, that is, to open the parliament [the Buganda parliament or *lukiko*—ed.], there was an overwhelming display. All people who were in their houses remained indoors; those in the street kneeled down; and all the drums, trumpets, and every sounding instrument was used to proclaim his majesty's approach. There was a band of executioners who walked near his majesty, ready to imprison and if necessary to kill any person who was found guilty of any sort of offense. When a verdict was passed in the parliament, the guilty person was quickly enveloped in a multitude of ropes; even if he tried to plead for mercy, it was impossible that his majesty should hear him because he was almost choked to death.

There were many who, in order to gain recognition, told lies about other chiefs, so that they might lose their offices. It was not until Mutesa [1856–1884—ed.] that that kind of system was done away with.

When one person accused another, the king sent for the accused person and told him that such and such a thing had been said about him. Mutesa was against people who told him untruths. He demanded the truth of the accused. If the man was guilty and told the truth, he was soon acquitted. If he lied and witnesses were produced who certified as to his guilt, he was finally killed.

When the king walked for exercise, there were many people about him. If he came to a place where there was no road, the people soon made one for him. During his journeys, all doorkeepers were required to carry their doors with them. When the king rested, they enclosed him with the doors and guarded him. To understand the kingly power it should be said that he was a law unto himself, an absolute monarch. The following were the king's palace officers.

| | |
|---|---|
| Kauta | Chef |
| Seruti | Butler |
| Kaula | Drummer |
| Nsandja | King's priest, who guarded all his horns |
| Banda | Potter |
| Omukweya | King's head carrier during the journeys |
| Omusoloza | Man in charge of fire wood. |

There was also the executioner's division. All these and many other petty divisions made up the king's household and contributed to his pomp. Sabakaki was the title of a person who was the head of the king's palace, including the division of the king's pages. He was promptly obeyed in everything he said. In the division of the king's pages there were about one thousand young men appointed by various chiefs to serve his majesty in the palace. They were under a chief named Sabawali.

Next to the king came his prime minister. He too was honored. When his drums sounded, all chiefs hurried to his palace to go with him to the king's court. The prime minister walked very slowly to give the people a chance to join him. When he reached the court he sat down to render judgment. When the king appeared to open the court, the prime minister presented the cases. Those who appealed to his majesty were given a chance to present their own cases. The prime minister had two assistants to help him dispose of the cases. One assistant was in Maseŋgere and the other in Gombolola in the outer royal court. The communication between his majesty and the prime minister was carried on by means of constant messengers, a man and a woman from the prime minister and a messenger from the king. The prime minister's messengers kept the king acquainted with what was going on in the country at large and the king's messenger kept the prime minister informed of the latest decisions or suggestions or new decrees issued by the king. Oftentimes there was concerted action, for they respected each other. If the king wished to do anything or to order something from his estates, the word went through the prime minister. The prime minister's messenger working with the king's messenger were certain to bring anything from any part of the country, but one without the other could do nothing.

All chiefs, high or low, when they visited the capital, brought news, or something to give to the king. First they reported to the prime minister and got his assent. All secrets to be told the king went through the prime minister, and vice versa. When the king decided to appoint another prime minister, he stopped the prime minister's reception of all important and secret messages. Instead he designated Kimbugwe, the king's twin guard, to receive information concerning state affairs pending the appointment of the new prime minister. When the new prime minister was to be charged with state affairs, . . . the king stood outside the parliament house with his scepter; a group of chiefs selected as candidates faced him. Then the king gave his scepter to the man he designated as prime minister, saying, "Go and judge my Buganda country." The newly appointed chief repeated the oath of allegiance, saying, "I shall render justice." After which he left and entered his official residence and the king returned to his palace. The prime minister never gave thanks or knelt down as did other chiefs.

All Saza [county—ed.] chiefs were equally powerful in their respective counties. No messenger of whatever nature could travel in a county without a Saza chief's messenger to accompany him. If the king's and the prime minister's messengers were sent to Muwemba to assist Mukwenda in buying cows for the king, they couldn't bring anything unless they had with them a Saza chief's messenger. They were regarded as thieves. This is one point to show how well Buganda was governed. The Baganda, as far back as can be remembered, have been an obedient and well-governed people, respecting their king, chiefs, and country. This may account for the respect and encouragement with which the British Government has consented to regard the native system of government.

# 19  RECORDS OF MAJI MAJI
## THE MAJI MAJI REBELLION, 1905–1907

*On a fateful morning in July 1905 the men of Matumbi in southeast Tanganyika rebelled against the German administration of German East Africa. They had been forced by Arab government agents,* akidas, *to cultivate cotton for negligible wages, to the neglect of their own subsistence cultivations. A stateless society, the Matumbi resented the authoritarian imposition of colonial rule which sought to draft them into the colonial economic order. Without a traditional structure of centralized leadership the Matumbi resistance rallied around the prophet Kinjikitile Ngwale who, possessed by the spirit of Hongo, a subordinate to Bokero, the principal deity of the stateless peoples of southern Tanganyika, became the locus of grievances whose loyalty he insured by distributing sacred water,* maji, *accompanied by a ritual, whose origins appear to have come from the Southern Sudan, and which would guarantee the insurgents protection against the bullets of the European rifles. Under the leadership of Kinjikitile, who took the title of Bokero, the cult, known in history as Maji Maji, swept through southern Tanganyika mobilizing the disparate clans against the German administration until ruthlessly suppressed in 1907. The saga of this African resistance is recorded in the writings and memories of the participants.[1]*

Our news is this, that the Germans treat us badly and oppress us much, because it is their will.

*So wrote an eighteen-year-old schoolgirl from Chiwata in southern Tanzania in 1898. Thirteen years before, German adventurers had claimed a protectorate in East Africa. They had fought their way inland along the caravan routes, establishing garrisons of* askari *at key points, recognising or deposing tribal leaders, and creating an administration of subordinate staff called* akidas *and* jumbes. *By the late 1890s Tanzania was an occupied country:*

Here at Chiwata there is a court every Wednesday, and many people are beaten and some are imprisoned by order of the German Government. But we, who have for so long been used to govern ourselves, find the laws of these Germans

very hard, especially the taxes, because we black people have no money, our wealth consists of millet, maize, oil, and groundnuts, etc. Here at Chiwata two houses have been built, one for the court and one for the prison.

*This was the situation throughout southern Tanzania at the turn of the century. In Matumbi, north-west of Kilwa, the Germans appointed an agent to rule. In 1897 he demanded that the Matumbi should pay him tax. They refused:*

Then when that European arrived he asked, "Why did you not answer the call by drum to pay tax?" And they said, "We do not owe you anything. We have no debt to you. If you as a stranger want to stay in this country, then you will have to ask us. Then we will ask of you an offering to propitiate the gods. You will offer something and we will propitiate the gods on your behalf; we will give you land and you will get a place to stay in. But it is not for us as hosts to give you the offering. That is quite impossible."

*The Matumbi resisted and were defeated. Soon afterwards, the Germans began to seek profit from south-eastern Tanzania by forcing*

From *Records of the Maji Maji Rising,* eds., G. C. K. Gwassa and John Iliffe (Nairobi: East African Publishing House, 1967), Historical Association of Tanzania, Paper No. 4, pp. 3–30.
[1] *Records of the Maji Maji Rising* has been elucidated by the editors, so rather than delete their editorial comments, I have retained them to make the records themselves more meaningful. Robert O. Collins, ed.

*the people to grow cash crops for export to Europe. A few German settlers established cotton plantations in Matumbi, while smaller plots were laid out by the jumbes and akidas. The Matumbi were forced to work in the fields, and their hatred grew:*

The cultivation of cotton was done by turns. Every village was allotted days on which to cultivate at Samanga Ndumbo and at the Jumbe's plantation. One person came from each homestead, unless there were very many people. Thus you might be told to work for five or ten days at Samanga. So a person would go. Then after half the number of days another man came from home to relieve him. If the new man did not feel pity for him, the same person would stay on until he finished. It was also like this at the Jumbe's. If you returned from Samanga then your turn at the Jumbe's remained, or if you began at the Jumbe's you waited for the turn at Samanga after you had finished. No woman went unless her husband ran away; then they would say she had hidden him. Then the woman would go. When in a village a former clan head [*Mpindo*] was seized to go to cultivate he would offer his slave in his stead. Then after arriving there you all suffered very greatly. Your back and your buttocks were whipped, and there was no rising up once you stooped to dig. The good thing about the Germans was that all people were the same before the whip. If a jumbe or akida made a mistake he received the whip as well. Thus there were people whose job was to clear the land of trees and undergrowth; others tilled the land; others would smooth the field and plant; another group would do the weeding and yet another the picking; and lastly others carried the bales of cotton to the coast beyond Kikanda for shipping. Thus we did not know where it was taken. Then if that European gave out some bakshishi to the akida or jumbe they kept it. We did not get anything. In addition, people suffered much from the cotton, which took three months [to ripen] and was picked in the fourth. Now digging and planting were in the months of Ntandatu and Nchimbi, and this was the time of very many wild pigs in this country. If you left the chasing of the pigs to the woman she could not manage well at night. In addition, they [the pigs] are very stubborn at that period and will not move even if you go within very close range. Only very few women can assist their husbands at night and these are the ones with very strong hearts. There were just as many birds, and if you did not have children it was necessary to help your wife drive away the birds, while at the same time you cleared a piece of land for the second maize crop, because your wife would not have time. And during this period they still wanted you to leave your home and go to Samanga or to work on the jumbe's plantation. This was why people became furious and angry. The work was astonishingly hard and full of grave suffering, but its wages were the whip on one's back and buttocks. And yet he [the German] still wanted us to pay him tax. Were we not human beings? And Wamatumbi, especially the Wawolo [highlanders], since the days of old, did not want to be troubled or ruled by any person. They were really fierce, ah! Given such grave suffering they thought it better for a man to die rather than live in such torment.

Thus they hated the rule which was too cruel. It was not because of agriculture, not at all. If it had been good agriculture which had meaning and profit, who would have given himself up to die? Earlier they had made troubles as well, but when he began to cause us to cultivate cotton for him and to dig roads and so on, then people said, "This has now become an absolute ruler. Destroy him."

*A settler named Steinhagen—Bwana Kinoo—owned the cotton plantation at Samanga. This is how the work was organised:*

During the cultivation there was much suffering. We, the labour conscripts, stayed in the front line cultivating. Then behind us was an overseer whose work it was to whip us. Behind the overseer there was a jumbe, and every jumbe stood behind his fifty men. Behind the line of jumbes stood Bwana Kinoo himself. Then, behold death there! And then as you till the land from beginning to end your footprints must not be seen save those of the jumbe. And that Selemani, the overseer, had a whip, and he was extremely cruel. His work was to whip the conscripts if they rose up or tried to rest, or if they left a trail of their footprints behind them. Ah, brothers, God is great—that we have lived like this is God's Providence! And on the other side Bwana Kinoo had a bamboo stick. If the men of a certain jumbe left their footprints behind them, that jumbe would be boxed on the ears and Kinoo would beat him with the bamboo stick using both hands, while at the same time Selemani lashed out at us labourers.

*There were European planters in Matumbi, but elsewhere along the southern coast cash crops were grown on communal plots supervised by akidas and headmen. These plots were established between 1902 and 1905 by European-controlled district development committees called "Communes". Two officials of the Dar es Salaam Commune described how the plots were organised in Uzaramo:*

When and how were the village plots organised?

Village plots were set up in each akida's and headman's area early in 1902 (September–October). Bushland was mainly chosen. The people were consulted in choosing the post. Each headman made a plot for his area in the neighbourhood of his headquarters. The principle was that every 30–50 men were to cultivate 2½ acres. . . . Where pos-

sible, the advice of the natives was obtained as to the crop to be grown. So far as possible, one crop was to be grown on each plot, according to the type of soil. Some 2,000 acres were cleared and cultivated. The size varied from 2½ to 35 acres; the average was about 12½ acres.

In 1903–04 it was ordered that each village plot should be extended by at least a quarter. The total area in that year came to 3,215 acres. Maize, millet, simsim, groundnuts, rice, chiroko, and coconut palms were grown during 1902–03. Cotton was added in 1903–04.

No extension took place in 1904–05, but the cultivation of other crops was abandoned in favour of cotton.

What was the labour situation and the supervision?

. . . According to returns by the headmen, the number of able-bodied men amounted to:

| 1902–03 | c. | 25,00 men |
| 1903–04 | c. | 26,000 men |
| 1904–05 | c. | 25,000 men |

During the last year, women and children had to be brought in to help, since the men frequently refused to work.

In Herr von Geibler's opinion, two days' work a week, as proposed by the District Office order, was insufficient from the start; 50–100 per cent more had to be worked from the first. When cotton became a main crop, continuous work was sometimes necessary. . . .

The akidas were relied upon to report on the condition of the plots, and they were also responsible for punishing those whom the headmen reported as refractory workers. There was no European control of this—who among the natives worked, and for how many days—although agricultural students (some of them children) were sent out, each with a note-book, to judge the condition of the plots and the work performed, and to report to the District Officer. Only once a year did a European visit the plots, to measure them out and select the land. No lists of workers were kept anywhere; the profits were distributed only according to the total numbers. Work on most of the plots was *flatly* refused during 1904–05. The headmen complained that they no longer had the people in hand. The officials of the Commune believed at the time that they could detect a state of ferment.

Were refractory workers punished, and by whom?

Last year (1904–05), following reports from the akidas and from Sergeant Holzhausen, who was sent to inspect the headmen, numerous headmen were punished by the District Office with imprisonment in chains or solitary confinement for totally neglecting their village plots as a result of the natives' refusal to work. The last, in June, was headman Kibasila, who got one month in chains.

What were the financial returns?

*1902–03:* . . . Total receipts: Shs. [Shillings] 25,580. . . . Gives an average
      per headman: Shs. 47.75
        per worker: 35 cents.

*1903–04:* . . . Very bad harvest as a result of drought. . . .
    Total receipts: Shs. 17,528 from 178 plots totalling 3,170 acres. 178 headmen and 26,186 workers were engaged in production. Mode of distribution:
    ½ to workers
    ¼ to commune
    ¼ to headmen

. . . The last payment to the headmen and people took place early in October 1903, following the distribution plan of 1902–03.

No subsequent distribution took place.

*Forced cultivation of unprofitable cash crops was a widespread grievance in southern Tanzania, but it was not the only one. Each area had its own sufferings. The Matumbi, for example, hated the Arab akidas and the askari whom the Germans set over them:*

Another reason again had its origin in ruling, that was the second reason: the rule of Arabs which arose from the German Government when it ruled this country and brought Arab akidas. Since the days of old, Wamatumbi had refused to be ruled. Those Arabs had failed in the past to penetrate into this country, because they had been completely barred from coming to capture people to enslave them. But when they got work as akidas they began to seize people and reduce them to slavery; in fact they practised complete fraud and extortion and tortured them unjustly. Thus there was one akida at Kibata, another akida at Chumo, another akida at Miteja, another akida at Kinjumbi, and one at Samanga. An African akida was the Yao at Kitambi's. And an akida of the tribe of the Bajuni, a person from Lamu, was there at Ngarambi. Now all these oppressed the Wamatumbi very much because they now had their opportunity. Thus when the troubles of Maji Maji started they [the Wamatumbi] immediately joined, saying, "We had better join so that we can drive off those enemies in order that we may get happiness".

There was every kind of suffering. The askari were a calamity. You carried a heavy load. He did not assess your strength to carry the load. If it were too heavy for you you carried it until you died. Then when the askari was within distance he sent a bullet to the nearest jumbe. On receiving that bullet, the jumbe had to fetch a very beautiful woman and slaughter a chicken or goat for him. Without these things he would be in trouble. All people were barbarians to the askari. A small mistake would be punishable with twenty-five strokes.

*Behind all these particular grievances lay the fact of alien rule:*

All these are words that buzz like bees. If you had experienced it, you would have known how grave it was. To be chained, to be shot with bullets in the crown of one's head and in one's chest, while in addition you carried loads as the great eye of heaven rose up! Alas, such was life, and those iron chains were many—he made them in his own country. Better remove such suffering; fight him off so that the loads are carried by the askari themselves.

*"Better remove such suffering"—but how was this to be done? The Germans had defeated every tribe that had resisted their invasion. The tribes were small and divided. They had no weapons to match the rifles of the German troops:*

They waited for a long period because they were afraid. How could one clan face the Germans alone and not be wiped out? There had to be many.

It is true they were ruled for a very long time before they rose in arms against the Germans. The problem was how to beat him really well. Who would start? Thus they waited for a long time because there was no plan or knowledge. Truly his practices were bad. But while there were no superior weapons should the people not fear? Everywhere elders were busy thinking, "What should we do?"

*The people waited and suffered, conscious of their disunity and the military strength of their rulers. Then, in the year 1904, a prophet arose. His name was Kinjikitile. Near his home at Ngarambe there was a pool in a tributary of the River Rufiji. Kinjikitile was possessed by the spirit Hongo who dwelt in the pool:*

He was taken by an evil spirit one day in the morning at about nine o'clock. Everyone saw it, and his children and wives as well. They were basking outside when they saw him go on his belly, his hands stretched out before him. They tried to get hold of his legs and pull him but it was impossible, and he cried out that he did not want [to be pulled back] and that they were hurting him. Then he disappeared in the pool of water. He slept in there and his relatives slept by the pool overnight waiting for him. Those who knew how to swim dived down into the pool but they did not see anything. Then they said, "If he is dead we will see his body; if he has been taken by a beast or by a spirit of the waters we shall see him returned dead or alive." So they waited, and the following morning, at about nine o'clock again, he emerged unhurt with his clothes dry and as he had tucked them the previous day. After returning from there he began talking of prophetic matters. He said, "All dead ancestors will come back; they are at Bokero's in Rufiji Ruhingo. No lion or leopard will eat men. We are all the Sayyid Said's, the Sayyid's alone." The song ran: "We are the Sayyid's family alone. Be it an Mpogoro, Mkichi, or Matumbi, we are all the Sayyid Said's." The lion was sheep, and the European was red earth or fish of the water. Let us beat him. And he caught two lions which he tethered with a creeper, and people danced Likinda before those two lions. They remained harmless. Then word of this new man spread afar.

*Kinkikitile taught that Africans were one*

*and that his medicine—the maji of the rising's name—was stronger than European weapons. His teaching spread among the people living around the River Rufiji. It reached the Matumbi through a whispering campaign they called Njwiywila:*

Njwiywila meant secret communication such as at a secret meeting. At that time if you listened to Njwiywila you paid one pice. That was the meaning of Njwiywila. The message in Njwiywila was like this: "This year is a year of war, for there is a man at Ngarambe who has been possessed—he has Lilungu. Why? Because we are suffering like this and because . . . we are oppressed by the akidas. We work without payment. There is an expert at Ngarambe to help us. How? There is Jumbe Hongo!" This Njwiywila began at Kikobo amongst the Kichi, for they were very near Kinjikitile. It spread to Mwengei and Kipatimu and to Samanga. But the people of Samanga did not believe quickly. It spread quickly throughout Matumbi country and beyond. In the message of Njwiywila was also the information that those who went to Ngarambe would see their dead ancestors. Then people began going to Ngarambe to see for themselves.

*Pilgrims began to flock to Ngarambe early in 1905. A German officer later described these pilgrimages. He was probably wrong to think they were engineered by a conspiracy of chiefs:*

The chiefs of the Matumbi and Kichi Hills spread it among their people that a spirit, living in the form of a snake in the Pangani Rapids on the River Rufiji, had given a magic medicine to a medicine man living in Ngarambe who had assumed the title Bokero (intermediary between men and the spirit). The medicine would free those who possessed it from all agricultural cares. Further, it would confer prosperity and health, would pro-tect them from famine and sickness, and would especially protect the fields against devastation by wild pigs. It guaranteed a good harvest, so that in future people would no more need to perform wage labour for foreigners in order to obtain accustomed luxuries (cloth, beads, etc.). Finally—and here mention was made only of the warfare customary between natives—the medicine would also give invulnerability, acting in such a way that enemy bullets would fall from their targets like raindrops from a greased body. It would strengthen women and children for the flight customary in wartime, with the associated hardships and privations, and protect them from being seized by the victorious attackers, who were accustomed to take women and children with them as booty. The medicine consisted of water, maize, and sorghum grains. The water was applied at Ngarambe by pouring it over the head and by drinking. It was also handed out in small bamboo stems, to be hung round the neck. The women were to set the grains in the fields they cultivated, in order to obtain a good harvest and keep away the wild pigs. The men were to put one of each sort into the powder of each shot, thus achieving accuracy of aim.

The business appeared completely harmless, and was understood in a rather hazy way by the many people who made pilgrimage to the medicine man. In no way secretly, but publicly and without ceremony, great crowds of people—some of as many as 300 adults were observed—made their way to the medicine man under the eyes of the Arabs, Indians, and coastal people who were all later to suffer.

*The Matumbi recall the joy which Kinjikitile inspired. They also recall that the pilgrims danced likinda—a dance of war:*

It was like a wedding procession, I tell you! People were singing, dancing, and ululating throughout. When they arrived at Ngarambe they slept there and danced likinda, everyone in his own group. The following morning they received medicine and returned to their homes.

*From the beginning, Kinjikitile's message promised aid against European rule. As the people flocked to Ngarambe, so the militancy of the movement grew. Finally, some time during 1905, Kinjikitile sent representatives through the surrounding country to mobilise and train the people. To Nandete, in Matumbi, he sent a man whose title was Mpokosi:*

The song of Mpokosi during likinda was in the Ngindo language. He used to take his fly-whisk and his calabash container for medicine, and he went around sprinkling them with medicine. It was like military drilling with muzzle-loaders, and under very strict discipline. Thus Mpokosi would say:

"Attention!"
"We are at attention."
"What are you carrying?"
"We are carrying peas."
"Peas? Peas of what type?"
"Creeping peas."
"Creeping?"
"Creeping."

And so on as they marched, until Mpokosi ordered:

"Attention!"
"We are at attention."
"Turn towards Donde country [inland]."
(The warriors turned.)
"Turn towards the black water [the ocean]."
(They obeyed.)
"Destroy the red earth?"
"Destroy!"
"Destroy?"
"Destroy!"

And so on as they advanced as if to shoot.

During that time they were dressed in their military attire called Ngumbalyo. Further, each one was told where to go or the day to start drilling. Thus all gathered at Nandete for this type of likinda. The song was entirely in riddles. Thus the question "what are you carrying?" meant "what do you want to do?" The answer "we are carrying peas" meant "we are carrying bullets", and they used peas in their guns during drilling. "Creeping peas" are those that creep, and it meant that they were marching to the battlefield. "Creeping, creeping"—that was walking, that is military marching. "Destroy the red earth"—that meant tear the European apart or destroy him.

And as they returned from Nampuru to their camp they sang many times, "Let us fight him today". They sang the same song as they marched to the battlefield.

*Kinjikitile prepared the people for war. He promised them protection against European weapons. He offered them leadership, organisation, unity. But he told them not to fight until he gave the order. By July 1905 no order had come, and the Matumbi were impatient:*

At Ngarambe he told them, "The Germans will leave. War will start from up-country towards the coast and from the coast into the hinterland. There will definitely be war. But for the time being go and work for him. If he orders you to cultivate cotton or to dig his road or to carry his load, do as he requires. Go and remain quiet. When I am ready I will declare the war." Those elders returned home and kept quiet. They waited for a long time. Then the elders wondered. "This mganga said he would declare war against the Germans. Why then is he delaying? When will the Europeans go? After all, we have already received the medicine and we are brave men. Why should we wait?" Then the Africans asked themselves, "How do we start the war? How do we make the Germans angry? Let us go and uproot their cotton so that war may rise."

Only a few shoots of cotton were affected, not the whole field. . . . Ngulumbalyo Mandai and Lindimyo Machela uprooted the first two shoots. Then Jumbe Mtemangani [of Nandete] sent a letter to Kibata through his wife Namchanjama Niponde. She was to report to the akida. People of Nandete had refused to be sent by Mtemangani to Kibata. The people had returned home to prepare for war. We waited for the akida or his spies to come to Nandete. Then we were ready. War broke out.

They heard that cotton had been uprooted in Wolo [Nandete]. The Arab at Kibata told Jumbe Kapungu to send his wife to investigate the reports of cotton uprooting. Jumbe Kapungu refused, saying, "If you have heard they have uprooted cotton you must realise that this is the beginning of war. So how can I send a woman to make enquiries? . . . So my grandfather [Kapungu] and my father left for Wolo accompanied by others. They went up to Mundi at Kulita's. On seeing Kapungu, Kulita told him to hide himself, for if the Matumbi heard he was there they would slaughter him. At six in the evening the Matumbi called on Kulita and said, "We have heard that the red earth is here. Is this true?" Kulita denied it, saying, "I cannot support the red earth." At the first cock Kulita escorted Kapungu and his men back to Kibata. But the Matumbi had caught wind that agents of the akida had come. So from Kipepele Hill onwards Kapungu was hotly pursued by the Matumbi. Near Mwando Hill Kapungu declared, "I cannot go on running like a woman. Here we will face them." They fought for two hours until two in the afternoon. Kapungu's slave Manyanya fell dead. Ka-

pungu and his friends ran back into Kibata.

There at Kibata they began to fight. They fought for a whole week. Then the Arab ran out of ammunition. His village was surrounded by warriors. Then those jumbes who had gone to rescue him arranged for his escape to Miteja and thence to Kilwa. Then they plundered the shops and all property. But Kinjikitile had told them not to plunder. That was their mistake.

*It was the last week of July 1905, and the Matumbi were at war. The news spread rapidly among the people of the Rufiji Valley who had already heard Kinjikitile's message. Early in August the people of Kichi, southern Uzaramo, western Uluguru, and Ungindo joined the war. Watching it spread, the German Chief Secretary thought he detected skilled military planning:*

The development of the movement was undoubtedly controlled in a logical manner by good strategists. Many suspect that discharged askari were behind it, while others point to an Arab as the leader. The Acting District Officer of Kilwa believes that headman Abdalla Kitambi a Ngindo, is to be seen as the leading spirit. His residence is at Mtumbei, at the south-western foot of the Matumbi Hills, near Hopfer's cotton plantation. I have been told that Abdalla was once an akida under Kilwa District Office and enjoyed great confidence there. Later, on grounds unknown to me, he was removed from his office as akida. At all events, he possesses an accurate knowledge of German administrative methods and of the availability and disposition of military and police resources in Kilwa and the other coastal stations. The systematic manner in which the rising was planned and expanded over widely separated areas demonstrates how well the leaders knew the disproportion between the real physical resources of the administration and what it had been in the habit of demanding from the natives. In my opinion, the outbreak of the rising was made possible chiefly by the fact, which can no longer be doubted, that the more perceptive among the coloured peoples had seen through and correctly weighed the government's bluff in holding whole tribes in check with a handful of men.

*The Chief Secretary was probably mistaken. The peoples around the Rufiji seem to have joined because many were closely related to the Matumbi and shared many of their grievances and their religious beliefs. For example, the Zaramo believed that they must obey a spirit named Kolelo, a messenger of God. Many identified Kolelo with the spirit Hongo by whom Kinjikitile was possessed. First Kolelo, and then the God who had sent him, promised the Zaramo victory:*

In the year 1905 . . . Kolelo also concerned himself with politics. He (i.e. naturally the Zaramo who honour him) clearly decided that there were other needs to satisfy besides famine, and so the xenophobic movement of that year at first simply associated itself closely with Kolelo's name. Kolelo had forbidden the further payment of taxes to the white foreigners; in mid July a great flood would come and destroy all whites and their followers. Later it was said that the earth would open and swallow them, that no bullets but only water would come from the soldiers' guns, seven lions would come and destroy the enemy, "be not afraid, Kolelo spares his black children".

Soon, however, other voices intervened. Now it was not Kolelo who cared for his children, but God himself, who had previously sent Kolelo. Kolelo, however, had not adequately fulfilled his task, so that God himself now appeared.

Clearly linked to his new situation was everything said at the time about the resurrection of the dead, since according to Zaramo conceptions only God himself, and not Kolelo, has unlimited power over life and death. It was later said that before the rising chief Kibasila of Kisangire, subsequently the main ringleader in Uzaramo, was won for their cause by the discontented spirits in the Matumbi Hills by a sham resurrection. He was said to have first become fully convinced of the rightness of the rebel cause when they showed him a man who had seen a remarkable likeness to his dead father.

*The movement had begun in answer to the religious message of a prophet. The power of the maji—power over European weapons—depended on religious faith. And as the movement expanded away from the Rufiji Valley during August and September, it was again carried by prophets. These men called themselves hongo, messengers. They carried maji which they administered to the people. They promised unity and invulnerability. They called on all black men to rise against European rule. Theirs' was a revolutionary, or more accurately a millennial, message, a promise to rid the world of the evils of witchcraft and European rule. It is likely that the people of southern Tanzania had heard such millennial teachings before, but only as attacks on witchcraft. Now this religious tradition was mobilised against the Germans. It was a revolutionary message because established leaders who opposed it often found themselves swept aside by the force of popular belief. The following account of a hongo comes from a remote area, Uvidunda. It is unsympathetic, but it shows very clearly the millennial character of the movement:*

In that year there arrived in the country a certain man, a great deceiver, called Hongo. . . . Hongo asked the people whether they were prepared to sit down under the European order to pay the tax of three rupees every year and they answered that they could not help themselves, for how could they fight the Europeans with their guns when they themselves had only spears. Hongo then explained his troublesome teaching to them. He said that he was a son of God and that with his help they would be able to defeat the Europeans for he had a medicine which resisted the penetration of their bullets, and in fact they would not be able to fire at all as their bullets would turn into water. . . .

All the Jumbes and old men went to Ngwira [the Vidunda chief] to tell him that a great witch doctor Hongo had come to free them from the yoke of the Europeans and they repeated Hongo's words to him. But Ngwira was very angry when he heard these words for he realized that he was an impostor, seeking to destroy the country. Ngwira told them that he had travelled to Kilosa, Morogoro, he had seen the ocean, he had walked to Tanga, Dar es Salaam and Tabora and everywhere he had seen the strength of the Europeans. Hongo must be driven right away before he could destroy the country. The D.C., Kilosa, was prepared to find them work so that they would be able to get the money for their tax, and although it was certainly hard, no good would come of trying to fight the Europeans.

But the Jumbes and old men paid no attention to his wise words for they were bent on a course of folly and they went to the elders and relatives of Ngwira to persuade them that they must convince Ngwira of the wisdom of following Hongo. His relatives refused at first for they had been bought by the Europeans and received much money but eventually they, too, changed their minds.

Hongo appointed himself chief of the district. In Vidunda there was a certain Arab trader and Hongo ordered that he should be caught and beheaded as he was the servant of the Europeans. He was wounded but slipped from the hands of his enemies and ran away to Ngwira who hid him in his house and after a few days sent him secretly to Kilosa to give the news to the D.O. that the country

was being perverted by Hongo. Then Hongo gave orders that every man must anoint himself with his Usinga medicine; anyone who refused was to be caught and killed. People began to fear that they would be called witches and all the people of Kidodi and the people of Jumbe Kulumzima went to Hongo to receive his medicine. When they had been anointed with it, he lay in the road and ordered that everyone should jump over him without touching him and if anyone touched him he should be killed. . . .

Then Hongo expounded his taboos which were as follows:—No white magic or witchcraft was to be performed, no charms or medicines of any kind must be kept in their houses but all destroyed by fire. No meat was to be eaten unless it had been slaughtered by cutting the throat. If anyone wanted meat he was to go into the bush, catch rats and cut their throat. If it had not been cut at the throat it was unlawful meat and must be thrown away. It was against the law to drink strong drink or beer of "kimela" because these drinks had the colour of blood. It was strictly forbidden to perform the marriage ceremony until the war was finished. When a man met one of his friends his greeting must be "Pyuu, Pyuu", and the friend must answer the same words. They must call Europeans not "Europeans" but "Warautumbuchere" because their stomachs must be speared. Every man that had been anointed was to pay a present of three pence to Hongo. Every man was to sew one pesa into the fold of his loincloth, for this would sharpen his intelligence, and to wear on his head a turban made from the leaves of a castor oil plant tied up with string, and two stalks of mtama, because thus the Europeans would not be able to see him. . . .

When Hongo saw that his strength was increasing and that many people were following him, he gathered them together to go and take Kilosa.

*By the end of August the movement had spread southwards into the Lukuledi Valley, westwards to the Mahenge Plateau and the valley of the Kilombero. Everywhere the millennial message was carried by hongo. When they arrived in Undamba in the Kilombero Valley, they met the opposition of the local chief, Undole:*

Bwana Undole heard of the approaching war of Maji Maji while he was staying at Kumwembe village. . . . The war had already reached Mngeta, which was near Merera [Undole's capital]. When the news was announced, Undole sent one of the elders to Mngeta to investigate. On arrival, the envoy luckily met the people who had brought the maji medicine. The natives of Mngeta had already taken the maji and wore small pieces of reed on their heads. They advised the visitor to take the maji as well. But the visitor wanted first to know what was the meaning of drinking the maji. They told him, "We drink this maji medicine so that European and local wars will not harm us. If by bad luck war comes, bullets and spears will not harm us. Bullets and spears will not penetrate our skins." And they told him many more things in order to attract him. The man liked their news and wished to get the medicine. They told him, "If you want the medicine you must pay two cents." He paid the cents to those with the medicine, for that was what it cost. After he had drunk the medicine they tied small pieces of reed around his head and made him wear one cent and told him he could return home. "That is the sign of comradeship. When you reach home tell all the people that they must dress like you. Those who will not dress like this will be taken for Swahili and will be killed." He bade his hosts farewell and returned to Merera.

When he arrived home he explained to his master all that he had seen. . . . Further, he told him how the maji comrades had promised to visit his country.

After Undole had been told the news, the following morning he called a meeting of all elders and courtiers and explained to them the conditions regarding the maji. When the heads of the country arrived he harangued them, saying, "I do not want to hear that in my country there are people who drink the maji. Further, I do not like to invite the maji carriers into my country. Maji Maji is a sham medicine brought by the Ngindo from Mponda's. And if you agree to drink the maji do not complain to me later, for neither I nor my children will agree to take this maji. Europeans do not want this nonsense." . . .

After they had finished their business in Mngeta, the waganga of the maji proceeded to Mzee Masalika at Mkaja. There they cheated people, including Masalika who was made to drink the maji of immortality [maji ya uzima]. His people also took the maji although Undole had tried very hard to prevent that. The waganga then left for Makuwa's at Lugoda. . . . He drank the maji as well.

*Few rulers were strong enough to resist the teaching, and many were anxious to follow it. The Ngoni chiefs, for example, joined early in September when the maji was brought to Songea by Ngindo hongo led by Omari Kinjala. Here, as a mission teacher explained, one problem was to bring Christian converts into the movement:*

When I saw that it was not safe for me out in the open, I slept in the hut of an Ngoni who had not yet taken the medicine. I could not sleep, however, because the yells and "Saidi!" greetings of the Ngoni roused me from my sleep. A few even came into the hut, but they were friends of mine who were fond of me. They had taken the medicine already and urged me to go there as well. "If you go there," they said, "no harm will come to you. If you do not, you will be killed. But you need not go yourself; we will bring you medicine. Only you must not leave the hut tomorrow until we arrive, for the country now belongs to Hongo, and everything which the Ngoni seize they must bring to Hongo—it does not belong to them. Everything will now follow Ngoni custom. They will kill everyone they find with European clothes. Therefore, our friend, take our advice, then you will live."

*August 1905 was the month of victories. By its end, German forces existed only on the coast and in the four powerful military stations at Mahenge, Kilosa, Iringa, and Songea. If they were to win, the Maji Maji fighters had to capture these stations. On 30 August, the Mbunga and Pogoro peoples tried to take Mahenge. A missionary described this greatest single action of the rising. In Mahenge boma, the day had begun with executions:*

Scarcely were the five condemned men hanging on the trees when a messenger rushed in with the news that the enemy were approaching. Everyone made for the post allotted to him and peered out in the direction of Isongo, from which they were supposed to be coming. We did not have to wait long before catching sight of the first groups. These groups halted in sight of the boma, probably waiting for each other. Shortly after seven o'clock they advanced on the boma in close columns. There must have been over a thousand men. Since they came to make an end of all of us, we had to defend ourselves and take part in the firing, which opened on the attackers at about a thousand metres. Two machine-guns, Europeans, and soldiers rained death and destruction among the ranks of the advancing enemy. Although we saw the ranks thin, the survivors maintained order for about a quarter of an hour, marching closer amidst a hail of bullets. But then the ranks broke apart and took cover behind the numerous small rocks. Now and again a group rushed out on to the road, lifted one of the fallen, and quickly fled

again behind the rocks. Scurrying from rock to rock, they made their retreat. Then suddenly the cry rang out: "New enemy on the Gambira side!" Everyone looked in that direction, and there thick clouds of smoke were rising from our three schools and a second column of at least 1,200 men was advancing towards us. Fire was opened upon them immediately. The enemy sought to reach Mahenge village at the double. There they were hidden by the houses and stormed up the road towards the boma. As soon as they reappeared within range they were met by deafening fire. The first attackers were only three paces from the firing line when they sank to the ground, struck by deadly bullets. Those behind them lost courage, turned, and scattered. Fortunately, the attack had been beaten off. When no more enemy could be seen, the Station Commander climbed down from the top of the boma tower, from which he "had commanded the defence", and distributed champagne.

*The failure to take Mahenge was the turning point of the rising. New German forces moved into the liberated areas. First to rise, the Matumbi were also the first to suffer:*

They surrounded the German stockade in many files. The Maji Maji warriors shot several times but the Germans did not reply. . . . Then at five in the morning the European ordered his askari to fire as the Matumbi tried to break into the stockade. Oh so many people died that day! For they had not known what a machine-gun was. They thought that the Germans had run out of ammunition and were beating empty tins to frighten them away. Thus the stubborn ones received bullets, some in their legs, others in their backs, and others in their noses. Far too many people died that day. Great mourning followed in the whole Matumbi country. From then on they fought in small groups, waylaying the German askari.

And they were severely beaten as the machine-gun helped the Germans very much. They fought up to five in the evening. When they realised they were being killed in numbers, they fled, crying, "Kinjikitile, you have cheated us".

*In Liwale it was the same:*

After the war streams of blood remained. The whole area between the boma and the Liwale River was covered with blood and the river itself was all blood. They had said that the gun would spurt water! But it was all lies. After that nobody had any desire to fight the Europeans. They said, "Those Wamatumbi cheated us. They said the European's gun would not fire, but how is it that we are now being wiped out?" So when we heard that the Europeans were coming to Liwale we hid ourselves in the bush.

*By October 1905, three months after the rising had started, German forces were gaining the initiative. Now the Maji Maji fighters had to defend themselves by guerrilla action. The terms of surrender were harsh:*

The following terms of submission, either for individuals or for whole areas, are to be imposed according to circumstances:
1. The surrender of ringleaders and witch-doctors.
2. The surrender of all firearms, bows, arrows, and spears. If necessary, pressure may be exerted on the people by arresting the headmen until the required weapons have been surrendered. . . .
3. Besides the tax which he normally pays, every man who submits is to pay a fine of three rupees. In cases where this is not available, the man is to be required to perform paid labour for a productive enterprise of a public corporation, in order to earn the fine. . . .
The requirement of fines does not prejudice the right of military com-

manders to require especially refractory tribes to perform compulsory labour, e.g. to construct fortifications. . . .
4. Major sultans and other influential tribal leaders who declare the submission of the native communities they rule are to be required to provide contingents of several hundred men for punitive and compulsory labour for the government on the coast. The punitive labour will last three to six months for each contingent.

*To surrender was bitter, and a reign of terror began in the villages:*

An order was issued that the natives should capitulate because they could not fight the Europeans. Some agreed to surrender and went to Kibata. Their guns and spears were destroyed and they were given pieces of white cloth to be used as the flag of peace. The white flags were to be fixed on the tops of their houses or in the ground before their homes. On the other hand some people hated and killed those who had capitulated too soon. So the business of Maji Maji began again. And more askari swarmed the country. . . . Askari were then sent to villages to seize food and people's grain. However, it was better if white rather than black askari came to the village. These African askari killed everyone, children, elders, and women. They ripped open pregnant women and left them to die. And sometimes they did worse things which I cannot tell here for they were really terrible.

*As well as the askari, the Maji Maji fighters faced the auxiliaries whom the Germans recruited from tribes which did not join the rising. The following account is by a man from eastern Uhehe who fought against the rising in the Kilombero Valley:*

Jumbe Pangamasasi, the jumbe of Muhanga, brought the news. Then we went at night to tell the Europeans that Pangamasasi had brought news that the Vahonga had reached his country; they told him to drink the medicine, now he refused—Pangamasasi has come to break the news here. We set off; when we set off we journeyed until we arrived at Muhanga. They said, "The enemies are at Mungeta" [in the Kilombero Valley at the foot of the Uzungwa escarpment]. We set off at midnight. We went right over the hill; by the time it had dawned we had descended on the other side. Those Vahonga had run away; they said, "Here it is too near the hill, the people will run into the hills, we will not kill many people." Then they withdrew; they went to the marsh, they went right into the elephant grass. We met at Kapalala. Now when we reached them at Kapalala, we found some asleep; the whole army had gone to lie in ambush in the grass there, and then some said, "We shall go in the morning to our friends"— actually, it is those whom we found asleep, and then we captured them. When we had caught those people we said, "Where is the battle?" They said, "The battle is on the path which goes to Ifakara." Our leader, Bwana Fungashenzi, said—he said, "I do not want to go there, I want to go to Mudemu" [an Mbunga headman]. We returned on the road to Ifakara. Now we are going to Mudemu. We went there, and then we heard the noise coming from behind. We said, "People are coming shouting behind; where have they come from, these people?"—and we passed on. The European said, "Hi, you will go with soldier Mpandajumula; he will fire a gun. After that man has fired a gun the Vambunga will run away. You, you will run after them, you will go, you will run after them with stabbing spears only."

We started at a run; we are running, we are running, after not a long time our leader said "Eeep!" and we stood still. He said, "Stop. I see a lot of enemies." We stopped. We saw those people were

emerging; he saw them and said, "All to the right". We went to the right, and then we just lay down, we lay in the grass. When we lay there in the grass they began, but did not see us. Then they looked; now they are looking at the European's shoeprints, the shoeprints of the soldiers; they were not on the road. Again they returned; they were moving back and forth in a group, they returned. They are looking for shoeprints; there were none there. Actually, we had hidden, we were there, we were there in the grass where we were lying. The European then saw that they were really all gathered together; the people gathered together were many. He passed behind, we saw he had gone to the back. He said, "Lez ali!" and they lifted their guns to their shoulders. "Fiya!"—uwoo. After the guns had sounded, then they all came together, the enemy, they were coming, now they were coming towards us. Then they reached us—soldier Majilali Daudi, they stabbed him, they reached another soldier, Lisasi, whom they speared—then, "Kais malis, malis!" Thus he has given the order, now we are running away, we are going into the grass, we go into the grass, because here in the open space we shall all be finished. We entered the elephant grass. The commander turned. He said, "Eep!" Thus they all turned and put their guns to their shoulders. Now the Vambunga are trying to come, they are following the tracks which we had made. It strikes, he is on the ground; it strikes, he is on the ground. They try to come, they are unable to pass on the side. The Vambunga failed completely. Now the battle was getting hot. We shot, they were quite finished; they tried to run away out there and we ourselves went out. As we looked we saw they were quite finished.

*To the Germans, the leaders of the rising were rebels to be executed. So it was in Matumbi:*

This is how it took place. We, the children, were called on the day of execution. We stood in the front line. Behind us stood women, and lastly adult men in the third row. Then they brought the victim with much fuss after a trumpet had been blown. They made him stand before three piled up empty boxes. Then the Bwana Mkubwa descended from his seat and stood before us to give reasons for the execution of that man. Then he would say in a typical German accent, "Do you hear, you children?" And we would answer, "Yes, Your Greatness." Then he asked the women, "Do you all hear, you women?" And they answered, "Yes, Your Greatness." He asked the adult men and they answered in the same manner, "Yes, Your Greatness." Then he ordered a sergeant to make the victim mount the three boxes. He climbed, and they put a rope round his neck. The boxes beneath his feet were pushed away and he hung and died. I saw three such cases with my own eyes.

*On 27 February, 1906, forty-eight Ngoni leaders died on the scaffold in Songea, among them Nkosi Mputa Gama, paramount chief of southern Ungoni. Fr. Johannes Häfliger was with them before their death:*

The District Officer let Fr. Johannes know that the sultans were to be hanged today. He could if necessary see for himself whether any of them wished to be baptised. (For Fr. Johannes had previously sought permission from the District Officer to baptise them if possible.) Fr. Johannes therefore went into the gaol, or rather into the passage between the gaols, in which the condemned men were lodged. They had just received sentence, and things in the gaol were therefore animated. Each still had commissions for his dependents to carry out. As soon as Fr. Johannes set foot in the place, some of those he knew came to him and asked him to undertake these commissions, which he said he was prepared to do. Then he asked some who had already received a certain amount of instruction at Peramiho, "Do you not wish to be baptised before you die?" They asked, "Can we do that?" When they were assured of this, many raised their hands and called out, "I want to be baptised, and I, and I!" A few who had not as yet received any instruction asked what this was all about. Fr. Johannes told them that if they would only be quiet he would explain it to them. Mputa himself then demanded silence, and Fr. Johannes instructed them briefly in the essential truths and on baptism and contrition. Then he asked who wanted to be baptised. Thirty-one men declared themselves ready for baptism, among them Sultan Mputa. Seventeen men, among whom were numbered a few Muslims, wished to know nothing of baptism. Despite exhortation, Mpambalyoto said briefly, I will die a pagan. Msimanimoto, a chief from the neighbourhood of Peramiho, also wanted to know nothing of baptism, for he protested that he would die blameless, he had done no wrong. Even those who had taken part in the attack on Kigonsera offered themselves for baptism, although they had not previously received instruction. Some—Fratera, for example—showed themselves especially pleased that they could still be baptised. One asked whether he would truly rise again. The District Officer had allowed half an hour, but not all had been baptised when this expired, so that he extended it slightly. When all were baptised, they were called out in threes and their hands bound. Then they were led out to the gallows, which were alongside the gaol, outside the boma. Some took leave of Fr. Johannes with the words, "Until we meet again." As he went out, Mputa, who showed genuine contrition, said in his bad Swahili, "But Kinjala led me astray."

The mood of the condemned men varied. Some cheered themselves with the fact that they could at least all die together. Kasembe declared: "Why should we fear to die? My father is dead, my mother is dead; now do I merely follow them." A few began to tremble somewhat as they were called out and bound. Others sat quietly by, and one could see from their behavior that they were grieved and reluctant to die. On the whole, the business sat lightly on many, who chattered and laughed as at any other time. One asked Fr. Johannes for a pinch of snuff. Since he had none, he applied to Sergeant Leder, who stood watch, to get some from the guard. At this others also wanted snuff, but no more could be obtained. Some began to sing as they were led out. A few, however, cursed the District Officer especially. Mpambalyoto declared that Chabruma would soon come to revenge them. Several asked Fr. Johnannes to tell their families to bury them themselves, to buy cloth for the purpose and to wrap them in it. Bonjoli flatly demanded that Fr. Johannes should arrange it so that he was not hanged—from now on he would be true. Fratera prayed aloud the "Our Father" and "Hail Mary", and said, after he had been instructed, that at the end he would pray, "Jesus, Saviour, receive my spirit." For one the affair went on too long. He wanted to be led out before his turn. Fr. Johannes remained in the gaol until all had been led out, exhorting them to prayer and to a sense of contrition.

Thus many found at the end a merciful death, many who otherwise stood in grave peril of being lost eternally. God be thanked for it.

A vast crowd had naturally assembled outside to be witnesses of the "spectacle".

At evening the hanged men were buried in a large common grave.

*The great men of Ungoni were dead, but other men were fighting for their lives in guerrilla warfare throughout the south:*

The war is going on just the same; the Wamakonde are to the north of Chitangali river; they have rebelled again in these days, and the fighting is there. I think it will be many days before the fighting ceases, for the rebels on every side would rather die than be under the Germans, and many of them have died and their wives and children have been taken for spoil, but they will not leave off fighting.

*German forces had no military answer to guerrilla warfare. Instead, they used famine. One commander had recommended this as early as October 1905:*

In my view only hunger and want can bring about a final submission. Military actions alone will remain more or less a drop in the ocean. The people will be compelled to abandon their resistance completely only when the food supplies now available have been consumed, their houses have been destroyed by constant raids, and they have been deprived of the opportunity to cultivate new fields.

*Some officers saw famine as a final solution to the threat of revolt. Captain Richter in Songea believed this:*

When Fr. Johannes drew the District Officer's attention to the possibly imminent famine, he replied: That's right, the fellows can just starve. We shall be sure to get food for ourselves. If I could, I would even prevent them from planting anything. This is the only way that we can make the fellows sick of war.

*Nine years before, a schoolgirl in Chiwata had expressed her bitterness at German rule. Now, a married woman, she recorded the horror of starvation:*

We and all the people in our village are in the same condition, we are suffering from famine. Since my birth I have never seen such scarcity. I have seen famine but not one causing people to die. But in this famine many are dying, some are unable to do any work at all, they have no strength, their food consists of insects from the woods which they dig up and cook and eat. Some they eat without cooking. Many have died through eating these things from the woods and wild fruits. Some do not die at once but when they taste good food like millet, maize, or beans, etc., which is their usual food, at once their bodies swell and they feel ill and die, but some recover.

*For many peoples, as for the Matumbi, the famine marked the end of a way of life:*

There came three years of famine. Those who survived did so by Providence. . . . It was extremely fierce famine and people denied their children and wives. It was only those who really loved each other who remained together. And even these cooked their food under strict regulations, like this: Down in the cooking pot was the child's food, over which were laid pieces of wood. Above these sticks was put the wife's food, and more sticks were placed. The food of the husband came on top. During eating they followed a similar procedure. The husband started first. When he reached the sticks he knew his wife's food lay immediately below the sticks and that his share stopped above them. In the same way, when the wife reached the sticks she knew that only the child's share remained. On the other hand, if they did not love each other everyone went his way struggling to survive. That is why some men had to marry the same woman twice, for they had deserted them during the famine. When he searched for his former wife her parents asked him, "Where did you leave her?" So he had to pay dowry again. This famine was called Fugufugu. There has never been the like either before or after Maji Maji. Other famines are merely babes before

the famine after Maji Maji. People died in multitudes and bodies were left to rot as there was nobody able to bury them. People slept in the open for there were no houses, and lions ate one after the other. There was no seed to plant. During famine we ate insects. . . . Before the war the population was very dense and it was very difficult to find a piece of land on which to grow food. If you got a small piece of land you thanked God— there were too many people. Now, alas, you only see much bush everywhere.

*Those who had fought and suffered turned in bitterness on their leaders. Matumbi elders sang this song:*

> The swindle of Kinjikitile
> He deceived people
> To go to Ngarambe
> To drink the maji.

*For the educated men of the time, Maji Maji was a hideous lesson in European strength. Three years after the end of the rising, a teacher wrote to celebrate the birthday of the German Kaiser:*

For what reason do the people celebrate this festival? . . . The Lord God gives the Kaiser strength and power to accomplish all that happens in the land, and to govern and order all things so that they continue in peace. . . . As an example I take this land of German East Africa, our land, the land of the black people. Formerly its condition was one of injustice. The man with power treated unjustly the man who had none. . . . But now there is peace everywhere. There is none who terrorises, for all are under the Kaiser's rule. . . . If anyone will not keep the peace and live peacefully in his land—if he seeks to disturb the country—that man will be severely punished, for the Kaiser lacks nothing, he has many soldiers. His strength and power are great. You have seen how those rebels, the Maji-Maji or Hongo-Hongo people, were defeated in the years 1905 and 1906!

*Fifty years passed before articulate Tanzanians expressed another view of the rising in public. Addressing the United Nations in 1956, President Nyerere recognised the impact of the rising on the generation that followed, but he also claimed it as an inspiration to Tanzanian nationalism—an inspiration which belonged truly to the people:*

There was no nationalist movement, no nationalist agitators, no westernised demagogues, or subversive Communists who went about the country stirring up trouble against the Germans. The people fought because they did not believe in the white man's right to govern and civilize the black. They rose in a great rebellion not through fear of a terrorist movement or a superstitious oath, but in response to a natural call, a call of the spirit, ringing in the hearts of all men, and of all times, educated or uneducated, to rebel against foreign domination. It is important to bear this in mind . . . in order to understand the nature of a nationalist movement like mine. Its function is not to create the spirit of rebellion but to articulate it and show it a new technique.

The struggle against the Germans proved to our people the futility of trying to drive out their masters by force.

*And what of the people themselves? They also saw a connection between Maji Maji and nationalism, and at first their feelings were mixed:*

The movement of Kinjikitile and his maji went around like TANU. You know that when TANU started secretaries and other leaders were posted all over the country? In Dar es Salaam TANU had already been known. Kinjikitile's words were known in Ngarambe and they spread through extensive lands by Jujila or Mtemela. It is true that a source of salvation cannot hide itself from the people. . . .

When TANU began some people cried, "This is how Maji Maji began. We failed to drive away the Europeans by war. How can we do this by a mere fifty cents? Do not believe these, they are cheats. It is another Kinjikitile." Not all accepted the news of maji. But those who did not suffered as well. The Maji Maji warriors hated and killed them, and the German askari did not discriminate—he killed every African he came across. This was similar to TANU. Some have joned, others have not, but we are all independent. Is this not so?

*Indeed it was so, and with independence men began to think again about the rising. It is well to end where the story of Maji Maji began, in Matumbi:*

Their camp was there at Madukani. That was the headquarters of the war itself. It would be fitting if that place were honoured with a national flag. For that was the beginning of freedom.

# 20 RUHANANTUKA
## FLIGHT OF THE EKIRIMBI

*The Bahima were the cattle owners and warriors of the Ankole kingdom in what is now Uganda, and poetry was part of their traditional way of life. The poem that follows concerns the flight of a group of Bahima, the Ekirimbi, from Karagwe in the early years of the twentieth century. The poem was composed by one of them, Ruhanantuka, and although it appears to be a description of battle, no actual fighting took place between the Ekirimbi and the German authorities who opposed their move.*

1. I Who Give Courage To My Companions!

2. I Who Am Not Reluctant In Battle made a vow!

3. I Who Am Not Reluctant In Battle made a vow at the time of the preventing of the elephants [1] and with me was The Tamer Of Recruits;

4. I Who Am Not Loved By The Foe was full of anger when the enemy were reported.

5. I Who Am Vigilant called up the men at speed together with The Pain Bringer;

6. I found The Giver Of Courage in secret conference.

7. I Whose Decisions Are Wise, at me they took their aim and with me was Rwamisooro;

8. I Who Overthrow The Foe returned to the fight as they attacked us.

9. I Who Am Nimble withstood the bullets together with The Lover Of Battle;

10. I Who Am Invincible appeared with The Infallible One.

11. I Who Grasp My Weapons Firmly was sent in advance to Ruyanja together with The Overthrower;

12. I Who Seek No Avoidance Of Difficulties drew my bow.

13. I Who Do Not Tremble prepared to shoot together with The One Who Draws Tight His Bow;

14. I Who Crouch For The Attack, they brought me back for my sandals together with The Tall One;

15. I Who Do Not Disclose My Plans fought furiously and with me was The Brave One;

16. I Who Do Not Miss The Mark crossed over noiselessly together with The Spear Thrower.

17. I Who Am Not Reluctant In Battle was with The One Eager For Plunder;

18. I Who Attack On All Sides appeared with The One Who Exhausts The Foe.

19. I Who Move Forward To The Attack took the track of the Ekirimbi together with The Bringer Of Sorrow;

20. I Who Am In The Forefront Of The Battle tracked them down at Migyera together with The One Who Depends Not On The Advice Of Others.

21. At Kashaka, my rattle bell rang out and with me was Rwamisooro;

22. At Rubumba, I found their courage deserting them.

23. I Whose Aid Is Sought was assailed by bullets which left me unscathed and with me was The Fortunate One;

24. I Who Stand Firm In Battle defeated them utterly and so did The One Who Needs No Protection.

25. I Who Am Clear Headed faced the

From H. F. Morris, *The Heroic Recitations of the Bahima of Ankole* (Oxford: Clarendon Press, 1964), pp. 52, 54, 56, 58, 60, 62, 64. Reprinted by permission of the Clarendon Press, Oxford.
[1] I.e. at midnight, at which time it is often necessary to prevent the elephants from destroying the crops.

spears together with The Ceaseless Fighter;

26. I Who Am Agile came up alongside them and with me was Katwaza.

27. I Who Am Eager For Battle made a vow on an anthill [2] with The Tamer of Recruits;

28. I Who Am Not Disobeyed broke my bow in my impatience.

29. I Who Retaliate, they singled me out as I was fighting along with The Infallible One;

30. I Who Am Vigilant enticed them out from their camps and so did Katemba.

31. I Who Am Praised, with The Saviour Of The Warriors, gathered them together from whence they had fled;

32. I Who Attack Unprovoked was feared in the fight and so was Katemba.

33. I Who Fight Alone strove with men swift of foot and so did Katemba;

34. I Who Am Eager For Battle, with The One Who Seeks No Help, captured a slave girl.

35. I heard your cries, You Who Seek No Help;

36. I Who Encourage My Companions,
37. I Who Fight Unceasingly, with The Seeker Of The Foe, carried off all their cattle.

38. At Karambi, I and The Scourge Of The Warriors rejected the counsels of the middle-aged; [3]

39. At Rufunda, they sent me off and I outpaced them.

40. I Who Am Not Rejected came to their aid along with The Fortunate One;

41. I Who Am Eager To Attack was refreshed by the battle and so was He Who Draws Tight His Bow.

42. I Who Am Capable, with Rugumba,

attacked the enemy in their flight and with us was The Scatterer Of The Foe;

43. I Who Depend Not On The Advice of Others fell upon them unexpectedly.

44. I Who Prepare For Battle pushed my way to the enemy's rear and with me was The Bringer of Sorrow;

45. I Who Am Moved To Anger attacked the enemy host together with Runyamosho.

46. I The Angry One fought with great fury and so did He Who Is Of Steel;

47. He Who Is Not Disobeyed, along with Rwamisooro, stood fast beside me;

48. I Who Am Second To None, they could not pass me by as they sought me.

49. I Who Go To War, I Who Am Agile and He Who Is Led To Battle,
50. He Whose Appearance Is Pleasing, He Who Presses To The Battle's Fore, He Who Gets Ready To Shoot,
51. He Who Is Truculent and He Who Swells The Number Of The Warriors gave the foe no pause for breath.

52. I Who Am Agile, with Rwamisooro, passed over to the band of twenty; [4]

53. At Rushojwa, I had refused to leave and so had The Tamer Of The Recruits;

54. At Rugomerwa, we set off and they returned there.

55. I Who Do Not Miss The Mark outstripped those who were well armed together with The One Eager For Plunder;

56. I Who Incapacitate The Foe stood firm in the marketplace.

57. I Who Am Not Put To Flight passed on to the battle at Rufunza and so did Katemba;

58. I Who Do Not Tremble set to work with my spear.

---

[2] It was customary for an anthill to be adapted as a platform for chiefs to stand or sit on.
[3] Presumably because the advice given was one of caution.

[4] Warriors fought in small groups of ten or twenty or so.

59. At Kanyabihara, I turned them back with the spear together with The Tracker;

60. At Ibaare, I got before them to the cattle and He Who Draws Tight His Bow was with me;

61. I Who Do Not Ask For Help stood fast in the narrow way.

62. I Who Am Not Alarmed By The Footsteps Of The Plunderers with The One Unyielding Before Heroes,

63. I Who Am Agile completed the warriors' numbers.

64. I Who Surprise The Foe went ahead of those not yet in the fight and so did He Who Is Led To Battle;

65. I Who Do Not Despise Myself found them in flight.

66. I Who Am Invisible drove them off at dawn with The Pain Inflicter On Warriors;

67. I Who Fight Alone, my swiftness took me into the enemy's midst.

68. I Who Fight Alone, it took me into their midst along with Katemba;

69. I Who Devote Myself To Battle was wearied by the use of the bow;

70. I Who Am Well Armed with The One Who Is Not Disobeyed,

71. I Who Go To War, when I looked back, they stood motionless.

72. Without thought for myself, I gathered the warriors from Misheenyi and with me was He Who Frustrates The Foe;

73. I Who Cannot Be Dissuaded From Battle drove off the enemy hosts.

74. I Who Fight Alongside My Comrades scattered the foe and He Who Is Agile was with me;

75. I Who Am Hot For Battle overcame their artillery along with The Scourger.

76. I Who Do Not Lose Heart vanquished the rifles of the Baziba [5] and so did The Overthrower;

77. I Who Do Not Disclose My Plans stood fast with The Infallible One;

78. I Who Go To War pressed on to the fore of the battle.

79. I Who Have The Scars Of Battle, with The Overthrower, crossed over the bodies slain by The Vehement Assailant;

80. I Who Am Eager For Battle returned home undefeated.

81. At Kanshengo, I was amongst crowds and with me was The Tamer Of Recruits;

82. I told The Giver Of Courage the secrets of fighting and also The One Who Plants His Spear Firmly.

83. I, with The One Who Is Quick To Vanquish, made a vow in the royal enclosure;

84. I Who Drive The Foe Before Me visited Big Boots [6] and with me was The Irresistible One.

[5] Strictly speaking, the Baziba are the inhabitants of the small chieftainship of Kiziba in the north of Bukoba District, Tanganyika, but the Banyankore often apply the word indiscriminately to all inhabitants of this district.

[6] The nickname of Big Boots was given to Nuwa Mbaguta, the Enganzi of Ankole from about 1894 till 1937, on account of the large boots which he was in the habit of wearing.

# 21 ERNEST LINANT DE BELLEFONDS
## KABAKA MUTESA I

*Ernest Linant de Bellefonds was the son of his more famous father, Louis-Maurice-Adolphe Linant de Bellefonds, by his Abyssinian mother. He joined C. G. ("Chinese") Gordon as an administrator in Equatoria in 1874 after the death of his brother, Auguste-Édouard, from malaria. After the failure of a mission by the American Charles Chaillé-Long to bring Buganda within the sphere of the Egyptian Government, Gordon sent Linant to Buganda to negotiate an agreement whereby the Kabaka Mutesa I (b. Mukabaya, 1838–1884) would recognize Egyptian sovereignty. He arrived at Rubaga with a small force of Egyptian troops in April 1875, only to discover that the American explorer Henry Morton Stanley had preceded him by five days. Impressed by Stanley's large and well-equipped expedition, Mutesa ignored Linant's proposal to place Buganda under Egyptian suzerainty. He sent Linant back to Gordon bearing Stanley's famous letter, in which Mutesa appealed to the British public for Christian missionaries to be sent to Buganda. Upon his return to Gondokoro, Linant and a detachment of some forty troops of the Egyptian army were annihilated on August 4, 1875, by the Moogie clan of the Bari people.*

*21, 22, 23 April*—I have had many different discussions with M'Tesa during the last three days. Our conversation had dwelled on all the different powerful forces of the world in turn: America, England, France, Germany, Russia, the Ottoman Empire, constitutions, government, military might, production, industry and religion.

The King's sister was present at these sessions. The daughters and sisters of the King never go on foot; they are always carried by their slaves.

*25th April*—M'Tesa summoned me at eleven o'clock at the same time as the Fakir of the Xoderia. Our talk therefore was exclusively about the Koran. The poor Fakir was at a loss as to how to answer all the King's questions. I had to give him some help.

I informed the King of the system of trade by means of money. The value of all goods is based on the tallari. This system makes trade and transactions easier.

*27th April*—In answer to all M'Tesa's questions concerning the earth, the sun, the moon, the stars and the sky and in order to make him understand the movements of the heavenly bodies, I had to make shapes on a board, the heavenly bodies being represented by little glass balls. The lecture took place today. The gathering was not very large. The two viziers Katikiro* and Chambarango,* four leading officers, the two scribes and a few favourites. The four cardinal points, the rotation of the earth, its movement round the sun, night and day, the seasons, the movement of the moon round the earth and its phases (which I did by means of a mirror) and the general movement of our system in space.

M'Tesa grasped everything perfectly. We were seated on the ground in a circle and there was a very friendly atmosphere. I have never seen M'Tesa so happy. It was the first time that we had spoken to each other directly without using interpreters, and this is against all the laws of etiquette. M'Tesa himself explained afterwards to the wonderstruck gathering. What was so surprising was that M'Tesa was able to inspire in his associates and in many of his people this quest for understanding, for self-instruction and for knowledge. There is great rivalry among them and they are very eager to improve. They are an inquiring, observant, intelligent people with minds longing for the learning of white people whose superiority they recognize; and with the help of a mission having farmers, carpenters and smiths amongst them, these Gandas will soon become an industrial people. This being so, Ganda would be the centre of civilization of all this part of Africa. . . .

I left the King at two o'clock after we had arranged to meet again at four. The same people were there as in the morning. The talk was of Genesis, M'Tesa had the story of Genesis from the Creation to the Flood taken down on a writing-tablet. We parted at nightfall. M'Tesa is spellbound and I shall be able to obtain all I want from him. . . .

*17th May*—Yesterday and today we had long discussions with M'Tesa concerning the duties of man towards himself and towards his neighbour. I gave him various precepts, a mixture of Socrates' philosophy and Christian morality. What troubled the King most is knowing what paradise, hell and the angels are composed of. Where are they set and what sort of joy and punishment await us after death? Is it true that the body lives again after death? If this is so and given that the body is matter, should not God then have a body? . . .

*26 May*— . . . In as much as M'Tesa believes himself to be of divine essence, so he is led by pride and vanity to continually brag and boast, and this makes him look ridiculous and sets people against him. In spite of his faults, he is certainly the most intelligent African living between Sobat* and Lake Ukerewe.* He learns about the customs, habits and governments of every country and all this not merely out of idle curiosity, but with the idea of becoming better informed and of bringing about some useful reforms in his own country.

Thanks to him, the people of Uganda are today as much above the other tribes I have visited, as civilized Europe is above the Bedouin Arabs, those primitive nomads of the desert.

The self-esteem of M'Tesa is extreme. He is very concerned about what the civilized world thinks of him and his greatest ambition, and very laudable it is, is that his name should go down in posterity. He wants history to think of him as the founder of the human race.

'I am called M'Tesa,' he said one day, 'which means in Ganda language, *reformer, benefactor.* I want history to say of me one day that if I had not been given that name at my birth, posterity would give it to me at my death.'

From E. Linant de Bellefords, 'Itinéraire et Notes. Voyage de service fait entre le poste militaire de Fatiko et la capitale de M'Tesa, roi d'Uganda. Fevrier—Juin 1875', *Bulletin Trimestriel de la Société Khédiviale de Geographie du Caire*, ser. I, 1876–7, pp. 58–52, 73, 81–2. D.A. Low, *The Mind of Buganda* (Berkeley and Los Angeles: University of California Press, 1971), pp. 2–4. Reprinted by permission of the University of California Press.

*Katikiro:* chief minister.
*Chambarango:* Kyambalango, a county chief.
*Sobat:* the river Sobat now in the Sudan.
*Ukerewe:* an island at the south end of Lake Victoria.

# 22 MOHAMMED ABDILLE HASAN
## THE SAYYID'S REPLY

*Between 1895 and 1899, Sayyid Mohammed Abdille Hasan, commonly known as the Mad Mullah, urged the Muslim Somali of Berbera to reform. In 1899 he and his followers retreated inland from Berbera, where Sayyid Mohammed forced his reforming tenets on the Somali and declared a jihad, or holy war, against the infidels or those who refused to accept his teachings. Between 1901 and 1904, British and Ethiopian expeditions failed to curtail his operations. He moved for a time into Italian Somaliland, but in 1909 he was back in British territory and remained in virtual control of the hinterland until sufficient British forces were released by the conclusion of World War I to crush him. Throughout his long struggle against the British, Sayyid Mohammed employed poetry as an effective instrument to counter British charges against him. As a master of invective, ridicule, and scorn, he defended himself in poems such as the one that follows.*

1. Concerning your plea "Do not incite the Ogaadeen against us" I also have a complaint.
2. The people of the Ethiopian region [1] look for nothing from you,
3. So do not press my claim against them.
4. Do not claim on my behalf the blood money which they owe me.
5. I will myself seek to recover the property and the loot which they have seized.
6. Were I to leave a single penny with them my pledge would be perverted.
7. What I claim from you is only what you yourself owe me;
8. Since you are the government the responsibility is yours,
9. Can you disclaim those whom you tricked into attacking me?
10. Do they not swim in the prosperity which they have gained from what they devoured of mine?
11. Do they not drive their livestock from the valley of 'Aado to the west?
12. What did they seek from the lands between Burao and your stations?
13. Had you a pact with them by God and by consent?
14. Or did thirst drive them mad? Fools easily lose their way.
15. And afterwards was it not into your pockets that you poured the wealth?
16. Did you not enter the amounts of the booty in your printed books and cash ledgers?
17. And have you not openly admitted this in the full light of day?
18. Are not these spoils laden upon you as upon a burden-donkey?
19. That is my statement: if you are honest with me what can you answer?
20. What profit will you gain by denial? I have clearly established my case.
21. Concerning your plea: "Do not incite the Ogaadeen against us" I also have a complaint.
22. As to your statement "We have not seen the sailing ship" [2] I also have a complaint.
23. Why are you tiring yourself out,[3] working your wiles?
24. Do you not get weary with pointless talk?
25. Who rules the sea and controls the sails and holds of ships?

From Mohammed Abdille Hasan, "The Sayyid's Reply," in B. W. Andrzejewski and I. M. Lewis, *Somali Poetry and an Introduction* (Oxford: Clarendon Press, 1964), pp. 74, 76, 78, 80, 82. Reprinted by permission of the Clarendon Press, Oxford.
[1] Mainly of the Ogaadeen clan.

[2] Here the Sayyid refers to his claim that one of his dhows had been intercepted by the British.
[3] Lit. "Why are you dying, running fast with deceit?"

26. The Italians are your followers, the foundlings whom you drive with you;

27. Had they not been led by you they would not have come to Dannood,

28. They would not have sent an expedition to Doollo and 'Iid;

29. They would not have sent their armies against me.

30. They would not have harassed me with assaults at daybreak.

31. I had no issue with the Italians until you summoned them to your aid.

32. It was you who intrigued and plotted with them;

33. It was you who said "Join us in the war against the Dervishes;"

34. And they did not say "Leave us, and stop conspiring with us;"

35. Did you never tire of these evil machinations?

36. Was it not through these schemes that the landings at Obbia took place?

37. Did they not greatly aid you with their arms and supplies?

38. You fools, those who attacked yesterday on your side

39. Will they not strike at me from the back if we fight tomorrow?

40. Will they be prevented from attacking me, by disclaiming their bond with you? [4]

41. It is you who lead to pasture these weaker infidels;

42. Can I distinguish between you and your livestock?

43. As to your statement "We have not seen the sailing ship," I also have a complaint.

44. As to the raiders of whom you talk, I also have a complaint.

45. It is you who have oppressed them and seized their beasts,

46. It is you who took for yourselves their houses and property,

47. It is you who spoilt their settlements and defiled them with ordure,

48. It is you who reduced them to eating the tortoise and beast of prey;

49. This degradation you brought upon them.

50. If they (in turn) become beasts of prey and loot you

51. And steal small things from the clearings between your huts,

52. Then they were driven to this by hunger and famine;

53. Do not complain to me and I will not complain to you.

54. If you do not accept my statement,

55. And unless your servants confuse you with lies,

56. That I harboured them, or that I sent them against you,

57. Bring me clear evidence; otherwise it is you who are guilty of the sin.

58. As to the raiders of whom you talk, I also have a complaint.

59. Concerning your demand "Turn aside from the Warsangeli," I have a complaint.

60. If they prefer you, then they and I shall be at variance:

61. It is not in my nature to accept people who cringe to you.

62. But if they are Dervishes, how can I turn aside from them?

63. Do you also share their ancestry from Daarood Ismaaiil? [5]

64. Are you trying to steal towards me through my ancestor's genealogy?

65. Of late have you not turned them into gazelles,[6] (fugitive and homeless)?

---

[4] Lit. "Will they become fenced off by (the words) '(You) are not my company (or allies)?' "

[5] Daarood Ismaaiil, the eponymous ancestor of the Daarood clans to which the Sayyid belongs and which include the Warsangeli. The Sayyid refers to the fact that while the Warsangeli are of one blood with him, the British have no connexion with them, and therefore in Somali values, no claims upon their loyalty.

[6] Lit. "Did you not turn them into Speke's gazelles (deero) and Soemering's gazelles ('awl)." In our interpretation gazelles symbolize here living in deserted places, away from human habitations, in constant fear and always on the move. We have also heard of another possible interpretation of this line: the Sayyid apparently refers to the internal split which occurred among the Warsangeli, when those

66. Have you not seen how they loathe you?
67. For have you not seized their shops and stored their goods in your houses?
68. Have you not set fire to their ships so that smoke rose from them?
69. You, with your filthy genitals, have you not hanged their men?
70. They soon found out that you would have no mercy on them.
71. You are against both worship and the Divine Law.
72. You are building a mat partition between them and the streams of Paradise and Heaven.
73. You are casting them into the raging fury and fumes of Hell.
74. Do they not see how deceitful you are?
75. Or are they well pleased with your prevarication?
76. Will they be divorced from their womenfolk and wives? [7]

77. Concerning your demand "Return the camels," I have a complaint. [8]
78. I also have suffered damage and loss;
79. You threw me on the ground and skinned my knee,
80. It was you who snatched the camels as they grazed,
81. It was you who scattered the white-turbanned army,
82. It was I who was first hammered at Gallaadi and experienced your bitterness;
83. A fool understands nothing, but the warning did not elude me.
84. The tethering rope with which you bound Iise [9] was meant for me,

---

who sided with him would no longer associate with those who opposed him. The two different species of gazelle mentioned in this line live in separate herds.

[7] This passage is very obscure. Literally it means:

---

"Are they divorcing their womenfolk, they have divorced their wives?" Most probably this amounts to a rhetorical question "Are they becoming apostates from Islam?" According to oral traditions the Sayyid declared that marriages of those men who refused to follow him became void on the legal grounds of apostasy from Islam. Their wives were therefore automatically divorced and were bound to leave them.

[8] The reference here is to livestock seized from the clans friendly to the British by the Sayyid's forces.

[9] Iise was the captain of the dhow referred to in line 22 and allegedly captured by the British.

## 23  LORD DELAMERE
# WHITE MAN'S COUNTRY

*Hugh Cholmondeley (1870–1931), Lord Delamere, was born in Cheshire, England, educated at Eton, and first visited the Kenya highlands in 1897 while on a hunting trip. Captivated by the region, he returned and settled in Kenya in 1903. As the leading pioneer of white settlement in East Africa, Lord Delamere devoted the remainder of his life to making the Kenya highlands a white man's country. In the two letters that follow, he discusses two principal interests of the European settler in East Africa: land and the Indian immigrants, both of which became a persistent source of tension between the Africans and the Europeans. The Europeans contested African claims that the land occupied by white settlers rightfully belonged to the Africans but at the same time feared economic competition from Indian traders.*

*September 2nd,* 1903
NAIROBI

At the present time, for an agricultural farmer with a small capital, the staple product is potatoes. They grow extremely well here for several years *without* manure. The crop varies between two to ten tons to the acre. Through freights from Nairobi to the South African ports run three pounds a ton. Prices there vary from £8:10:0 to £13:10:0 a ton.

This harvest some settlers are sending potatoes direct through to Johannesburg and expect good results. Last season (there are two in a year) all the crop practically was sent to the South African ports and to Zanzibar, Mozambique, &c., and realised good prices. The only difficulty is getting the potatoes to market.

All the men worth their salt at present in the country are writing home to their relations and friends to join them. There are four settlers within short distance of Nairobi who have lately got out their brothers. Now these are men practically without capital and they evidently think it good enough. There are three dairy farmers not far from Nairobi who are doing well chiefly with native cows, although there are now two or three bulls in the country.

From Elspeth Huxley, *White Man's Country: Lord Delamere and the Making of Kenya* (London, 1935), I, 108–110, 206–208. By permission of author, Chatto & Windus, and Frederick A. Praeger.

A man called Sandbach Baker who was formerly a Manchester cotton merchant and went broke gambling on cotton is one of the dairy farmers. His wife told Lady Delamere the other day that if she had sufficient cows she could sell 1000 lbs. of butter a month in Nairobi and Mombasa. Of course that is only a small thing, but it is an opening for one or two at the present time. As soon as we can get a refrigerating plant going, which I think will be very shortly, there should be as good a sale for butter and cheese as from New Zealand. The drawback to cattle is the danger of occasional outbreaks of rinderpest.

Another opening in a small way at present, and later for export, is fruit. There is only one man in the country at present who grows fruit to any extent, because settlers go in for potatoes which bring a quick return. He grows excellent apples, plums, greengages, Japanese plums, strawberries, &c., and gets rid of the small amount he can grow in the country without trouble, and there is a demand for considerably more. Fruit at present of course fetches more or less fancy prices, but that would hardly continue when any amount was grown.

With potatoes to keep a man going, coffee promises a certain high return with the cheap land and labour procurable. Several settlers are at present growing it as fast as they can. It grows *extraor-*

*dinarily* well and badly cleaned coffee in the parchment has been valued at 70 to 80 shillings a hundredweight. I am sure that there is a fortune in coffee for a man who is willing to lay out a little money or who chooses to start small and work hard himself. Coffee at its high price is not touched by freight, and for good class coffee which we can certainly grow here there is an unlimited market in London. I have gone carefully into coffee estimates with settlers here and I am sure it is a first rate speculation, absurdly easy to grow—grows here like a weed.

I believe myself that money is to be made out of sheep. Grazing land, which is said by New Zealanders and others to be first class, can be hired on a 99 years' lease (which will almost certainly be convertible some day into freehold) up to 10,000 acres at a ha'penny an acre per annum. I intended to write a pamphlet for publication but my eyes have been giving me a lot of trouble lately and I have been unable to do more than begin it.

I have got my 100,000 acres of land but not at the place I originally intended, but I think at a better, though a little further from the coast. I have been unable to get a freehold but have got a 99 years' lease at ¹/₂ d. an acre per annum. My own opinion is that land will carry four or five sheep to the acre, but one cannot tell till one tries.

Besides coffee, tobacco and cotton appear to offer a good return.

Cotton has been produced (only in experimental plots) which has been valued by the Oldham Chamber of Commerce at 6d. a pound, or a penny more than middling American on the same day. With land and labour as cheap as they are, this should give a good return.

At present there is *no* one in the country with *any* capital except myself and some of the coast merchants, so none of these things are being developed except on a small scale, but it must be remembered that directly money is made land is sure to go up largely in value. At the present time the land here seems to me absurdly cheap. A South African who has had much experience was here the other day and said he wouldn't take 20 acres in South Africa for one here. My own opinion is that there is a fortune for any of the early-comers that are worth anything. Of course, if markets and so on were all fixed, land could not be got at the price, or anything like it.

. . .

*August,* 1907

Personally I can imagine no argument [he wrote] which is capable of justifying unchecked immigration of Asiatics into a country which we all of us hope may some day be part of a United South Africa, a great white colony stretching from the Cape to the Zambesi and governed for His Majesty by a true Afrikander bond.

Supposing that Indian immigration is allowed into South Africa it must carry with it that freedom which is one of the boasts of the British Empire. Indian colonists must be allowed to enter freely into competition in all trades and to hold land there. There is therefore only one choice before the Imperial Government. To choose whether South Africa is to be a colony of men of our own race holding the same ideals of civilisation and religion as ourselves, or whether it is to become an Asiatic colony peopled by a race whose civilisation is decadent and at its best stopped short of European civilisation, whose ideals and religion are totally different from our own and above all a people who undoubtedly, and I think naturally, look forward to a day when they can throw off the yoke of their white conquerors. . . .

In all new countries the backbone of the country is the small man, the white colonist with small means, but there is no place for him in a country when once the Asiatic is there. I have some years' experience myself of the newest of the colonies of the Crown in Africa and I know from personal observation and knowledge that every two or three Indians in the country mean the loss of a white colonist. There is no place for the small white man arriving in the country. All the vegetable growing for the towns is done by Indians, all the butchers with one or two exceptions are Indians, all the small country stores are kept by Indians and most of the town shops, all the lower grade clerks are Indians, nearly all the carpentry and building is done by Indians. They thus fill all the occupations and trades which would give employment to the poorer white colonists, especially those arriving new in the country.

That is what Indian immigration means in the early days of a very new country in Africa. It means that if open competition is allowed the small white colonist must go to the wall.

What is the next stage in the history of a country which has once allowed Asiatic immigration to get a foothold? The small man having been pretty well squeezed out, planters and farmers employ Indian labour, and then comes the stage that Natal has reached to-day when the Asiatics are as numerous as the white colonists and when they own large areas of land and businesses all over the country. White colonists will not go to a country which is filled with Asiatics, and the Asiatics go on increasing.

This shows again that it lies with the Imperial Government to-day to say whether Africa is to become a white daughter colony or an Asiatic granddaughter colony, to use an expression of Mr. Winston Churchill's.

And what does Indian immigration mean to the native? Because surely in Africa, in his own country, his rights both at the present time and in the future should be safeguarded. Admitting that at present he is lazy and relatively so well off that work has no particular attraction for him, will it always be so? Increasing as they do owing to cessation of wars and other benefits of civilisation, will they not be forced by circumstances into the life of the country and have to work for a living like European or Asiatic? And is his birthright, the right to work for a living in his own land, to be taken away from him? Is it only Europeans who are affected by Asiatic competition? I should say that the Indian took the place of the African quite as much as that of the European.

And later on will it not be worse, when the African has been brought by education and training to a point where he will be able to take positions of trust and responsibility? Are these all to be taken away beforehand and given to the Asiatic? And to put the matter on a higher plane. Should not the African be protected from the decadent civilisation of India and from the influence of its Hindu religion? Is it desirable that such religions should be introduced among the African natives who are like children and capable of easily absorbing impressions?

Is the introduction of Hindu rites and practices among the natives of Africa to be calmly viewed by all the great missions which have hundreds of earnest men teaching the ideals of our own religion to the natives all over Africa?

I am fain to admit that all civilisation has a deteriorating effect on a certain proportion of natives, but in the case of the evils caused by contact with Europeans, wise laws can be enacted to prevent such evils. I submit that no government of Europeans can make laws to check the evils arising from the mixture of African and Asiatic, because the average European is incapable of understanding the mind of the Asiatic, nor can laws be enforced except by public opinion.

This I consider one of the greatest evils of Asiatic immigration into a country governed by Europeans—that owing to a lack of understanding of the Asiatic and the impossibility of getting European police capable of dealing with Asiatic crime, Asiatic police have to be employed, and only those who have seen the methods of bribery and corruption of Indian police, even when dealing with their own people, know the harm done by allowing Indian police to have control over natives.

Time after time I have heard a native say they have been stopped by an Indian policeman and when I asked them how they got away they always said, "Oh, of course I gave him something."

I earnestly hope that the very powerful missionary organisations in Africa will take this matter up. It is a thing to be remembered that public opinion sooner or later asserts itself among our own people to do the right thing by the people of the country.

# 24 THE DEVONSHIRE WHITE PAPER
## THE INDIANS IN KENYA

*In Kenya, as in South Africa, Indian immigrants were regarded with suspicion and even hostility by the European community. After World War I, Indians in Kenya began to demand equal representation with the Europeans on the Legislative Council, the end of segregation, and the right to acquire land in the highlands. Both the Indians and the European settlers sent delegations to London to plead their respective causes. In presenting their case to the Colonial Secretary, the Duke of Devonshire, both sides stressed their desire to maintain native interests. In this way both sides, but particularly the European deputation led by Lord Delamere, who emphasized the virtues of British as against Indian traditions in guiding the Africans, overplayed their hand by providing a welcome way of escape for the British government, which in 1923, in a White Paper issued by the Colonial Secretary, the Duke of Devonshire, promptly proclaimed that the interests of the African were paramount in Kenya. Kenya was not in the future to become another Rhodesia.*

## GENERAL STATEMENT OF POLICY

The general policy underlying any decision that may be taken on the questions at issue must first be determined. It is a matter for satisfaction that, however irreconcilable the views of the European and Indian communities in Kenya on many points may be, there is one point on which both are agreed, namely, the importance of safeguarding the interests of the African natives. The African population of Kenya is estimated at more than 2¹/₂ millions; and according to the census

From *Indians in Kenya Memorandum* (London: Her Majesty's Stationery Office, 1923), pp. 9–12. Reprinted by permission.

of 1921, the total numbers of Europeans, Indians and Arabs in Kenya (including officials) were 9,651, 22,822 and 10,102 respectively.

Primarily, Kenya is an African territory, and His Majesty's Government think it necessary definitely to record their considered opinion that the interests of the African natives must be paramount, and that if, and when, those interests and the interests of the immigrant races should conflict, the former should prevail. Obviously the interests of the other communities, European, Indian or Arab, must severally be safeguarded. Whatever the circumstances in which members of these communities have entered Kenya, there will be no drastic action or reversal of measures already introduced, such as may have been contemplated in some quarters, the result of which might be to destroy or impair the existing interests of those who have already settled in Kenya. But in the administration of Kenya His Majesty's Government regard themselves as exercising a trust on behalf of the African population, and they are unable to delegate or share this trust, the object of which may be defined as the protection and advancement of the native races. It is not necessary to attempt to elaborate this position; the lines of development are as yet in certain directions undetermined, and many difficult problems arise which require time for their solution. But there can be no room for doubt that it is the mission of Great Britain to work continuously for the training and education of the Africans towards a higher intellectual moral and economic level than that which they had reached when the Crown assumed the responsibility for the administration of this territory. At present special consideration is being given to economic development in the native reserves, and within the limits imposed by the finances of the Colony all that is possible for the advancement and development of the Africans, both inside and outside the native reserves, will be done.

His Majesty's Government desire also to record that in their opinion the annexation of the East Africa Protectorate, which, with the exception of the mainland dominions of the Sultan of Zanzibar, has thus become a Colony, known as Kenya Colony, in no way derogates from this fundamental conception of the duty of the Government to the native races. As in the Uganda Protectorate, so in the Kenya Colony, the principle of trusteeship for the natives, no less than in the mandated territory of Tanganyika, is unassailable. This paramount duty of trusteeship will continue, as in the past, to be carried out under the Secretary of State for the Colonies by the agents of the Imperial Government, and by them alone.

## FUTURE CONSTITUTIONAL EVOLUTION

Before dealing with the practical points at issue directly connected with the claims of Indians, it is necessary, in view of the declaration of policy enunciated above, to refer to the question of the future constitutional evolution of Kenya.

It has been suggested that it might be possible for Kenya to advance in the near future on the lines of responsible self-government, subject to the reservation of native affairs. There are, however, in the opinion of His Majesty's Government, objections to the adoption in Kenya at this stage of such an arrangement, whether it take the form of removing all matters affecting Africans from consideration in the Council, or the appointment of the Governor as High Commissioner for Native Affairs, or provision for a special veto by the Crown on local legislation which touches native interests; and they are convinced that the existing system of government is in present circumstances best calculated to achieve the aims which they have in view, namely, the unfettered exercise of their trusteeship for the native races and the satisfaction of the legitimate aspirations of other communities resident in the Colony.

His Majesty's Government cannot but regard the grant of responsible self-government as out of the question within any period of time which need now to be taken into consideration. Nor, indeed, would they contemplate yet the possibility of substituting an unofficial majority in the Council for the Government official majority. Hasty action is to be strongly deprecated, and it will be necessary to see how matters develop, especially in regard to African representation, before proposals for so fundamental a change in the Constitution of the Colony can be entertained. Meanwhile, the administration of the Colony will follow the British traditions and principles which have been successful in other Colonies, and progress towards self-government must be left to take the lines which the passage of time and the growth of experience may indicate as being best for the country.

## PRACTICAL POINTS AT ISSUE

Turning now to the practical points at issue arising directly out of the claims of Indians domiciled in Kenya, these may be considered under the following heads—

Representation on the Legislative Council
Representation on the Executive Council
Representation on Municipal Councils
Segregation
Reservation of the Highlands for Europeans
Immigration

## REPRESENTATION ON THE LEGISLATIVE COUNCIL

(a) *Elective System*—In no responsible quarter is it suggested that the Indians in Kenya should not have elective representation upon the Legislative Council of the Colony. The point at issue is the method whereby such elective representation should be secured. There are two alternative methods—

(i) A common electoral roll

(ii) Communal franchise

Under the former system, Kenya would be divided up into a given number of constituencies, in each of which European and Indian voters on the roll would vote together at an election for candidates of either race, and the qualifications for admission to the voters' roll would be the same for Europeans and for Indians. Under the latter system, European and Indian constituencies would be demarcated independently, not necessarily coinciding in number or boundaries; the qualifications for admission to the voters' roll would not necessarily be the same for the two communities; and while Europeans would vote in the European constituencies for European candidates, Indians would vote in the Indian constituencies for Indian candidates.

As a variant of the former system, there is the common electoral roll with reservation of seats. This arrangement would involve the setting apart of a certain number of seats in a given constituency for candidates of a certain race; for example, in a constituency returning three members, with two seats reserved for Europeans and one for Indians, the two European candidates and the one Indian candidate highest in the poll would be elected, irrespective of the position in the poll of other candidates of either race.

The common electoral roll for all British subjects and British protected persons, with reservation of seats, was proposed in the Wood-Winterton report, and it was further suggested that the qualifications for voters should be such as to admit, if possible, ten per cent of the domiciled Indians to the register.

For the common electoral roll it is claimed that it would bridge the gap between the Europeans and Indians by giving a candidate of one race an incentive to study the needs and aspirations of the other race. Further, Indian sentiment, both in India and Kenya, strongly favours the common electoral roll, even though a communal franchise exists in India itself.

A communal franchise secures that every elector shall have the opportunity of being represented by a member with sympathies similar to his own, a consideration which in other Colonies has led the domiciled Indians to press for its adoption; it is well adapted to the needs of a country such as Kenya; no justification is seen for the suggestion that it is derogatory to any of the communities so represented, and it is believed that, so far from having a disruptive tendency, it would contract rather than widen the division between races in Kenya.

So far as Africans are concerned, a communal franchise provides a framework into which native representation can be fitted in due season.

From the point of view of the Indian residents themselves, this system permits of a far wider franchise being given than would be the case if a common electoral roll were introduced, and this alone should render it acceptable to all supporters of the Indian claims who have at heart the political development of the Indian people.

Finally, it allows of the immediate grant of electoral representation with a wide franchise to the other community in Kenya which is ripe for such institutions, the Arabs of the Coast.

These considerations were weighed before the Wood-Winterton report was drawn up; the recommendation then made turned largely on the desire to meet Indian feelings so far as conditions in Kenya would admit. The result of the reference to opinion in Kenya of the recommendation that a common electoral roll should be adopted, even though combined with a reservation of seats, was to show that the advantages claimed for the common electoral roll would in practice have been illusory. In the special conditions existing in Kenya it is clear that no candidate, European or Indian, could stand as an advocate of the interests of the other race without sacrificing the support of his own. If elections were to be fought on racial lines, as they undoubtedly would have been in Kenya, the main advantage claimed for the common electoral roll, namely, the bringing of the races nearer together, would be lost.

Having regard to all the circumstances, His Majesty's Government have decided that the interests of all concerned in Kenya will be best served by the adoption of a communal system of representation.

## 25   JOMO KENYATTA
## MEETING AT NYERI   JULY 26, 1952

*The Second World War was a great watershed in the evolution of Kenya. The many Africans (75,000) who had served in the British forces returned from overseas with a worldly outlook, imbued with universal ideas acquired through their association with many peoples from far-off lands. Within the colony, there were long-standing grievances about the alienation of land and the requirements of the settlers for African labour; the overseas experience of Kenyan soldiers gave them a new and more militant perspective on these questions. The discontent manifested itself in two forms: a revival of oathing among the Kikuyu; and the founding of the Kenya African Union (KAU) as a more demanding political party to replace the rather benign Kikuyu Central Association (KCA). Oathing ceremonies had been practiced by the Kikuyu for centuries, with different oaths for different needs; the practice was deeply embedded in Kikuyu culture and generally regarded by the colonial authorities as relatively harmless. The young militants of the KAU perceived in the custom of oathing a means of mobilizing the Kikuyu against the European presence, whether colonial or settler. The grievance over the alienation of land reached its most serious proportions at the meeting in Olenguruone between some 12,000 displaced Kikuyu from the highlands, who had settled in Masailand on the edge of the Mau plateau, and the colonial administration that refused to recognize their rights to the land upon which they had been squatters since the 1920s. Here in Olenguruone the oathing tradition of the Kikuyu was employed to ensure the unity of the Kikuyu people in their claims to the land of the Masai. The colonial administration ultimately prevailed and the "squatters" were evicted. However, the unity of the Kikuyu of Olenguruone cemented through oathing, took on a new dimension which was hostile, not only to the British administration, but to the European settler community. The settlers, by the displacement of the Kikuyu, had precipitated the Olenguruone dispute over Kenya's most precious commodity—land.*

*In the midst of this confrontation in September 1946, Jomo Kenyatta (1889–1978) returned from his long absence in England. He had been born an orphan at Mitumi, Kenya, and was educated at a Scottish mission school before becoming a herd boy. He joined the Kikuyu Central Association in 1922 and became its president. In 1929, during his term in this office, he made his first visit to Great Britain. He returned to England in 1931 as the representative of the KCA, and studied for a year at London University under the distinguished anthropologist, Professor B. Malinowski. During this period he wrote his well-known book,* Facing Mount Kenya *(1938), visited the Soviet Union on three separate occasions, and, on May 11, 1942, married an Englishwoman, Edna Grace Clarke. Upon returning to Kenya in 1946, he immediately involved himself in the Kenya African Union (KAU), which had been established on October 1, 1944 to represent African interests, following the suppression of the KCA. Always an enigma, or at least an ambiguous and equivocal figure, Kenyatta—who was elected president of the KAU on June 1, 1947—was increasingly caught up in the militancy of the younger members of the KAU, without, however, losing supreme control of the party. His relationship to the Mau Mau movement still remains a subject of controversy; in 1952 the colonial authorities tried and sentenced him to seven years hard labor for his presumed leadership of the terrorist Mau Mau movement. Although the Mau Mau were ultimately defeated, there no longer remained any doubt about the ultimate control of Kenya by the Africans; Kenyatta was released in 1958. Elected president of the Kenya African National Union, the successor of the KAU, in 1961, he became Prime Minister in 1963, and President of Kenya in December 1964. He remained in these offices until his death as a revered figure, the Mwalimu (teacher) of his people.*

*One of the crucial turning points in Kenyatta's career was the climatic meeting at Nyeri on July 26, 1952. Since April, Kenyatta had been making speeches throughout Kenya seeking to disassociate the KAU from the Mau Mau, while advocating the achievement of independence by peaceful means and hard work and the safeguarding of the integrity of the non-African peoples of Kenya. Over 50,000 people came to Nyeri, charged with fervor and emotion which Kenyatta found difficult to control, but from the Nyeri meeting there was no turning back on the road to independence.*

At 11 a.m. there were in the vicinity 20,000 Africans at the meeting. By 1 p.m. the attendance was estimated at 25,000. The meeting was held on an open flat, three miles out of Nyeri, bordering the Kikuyu Reserve and was an authorized meeting. Terence Patrick O'Brien, the suspect European Communist, was present and took photographs of the assembly.

Prominent African politicians present included Jomo Kenyatta, Ochieng Oneko, Anderson Wamuthenya, Morris

From "Kenya African Union Meeting At Nyeri: Report on Mass Meeting Held Between 11 a.m. and 3 p.m. on 26th July 1952 by Assistant Superintendent of Police, Nyeri," in *Historical Survey of the Origins and Growth of Mau Mau* (Her Majesty's Stationery Office [Cmnd. 1030], May 1960), App. F, pp. 301–08. This report in which this document is included in the appendices is frequently referred to as the "Corfield Report," referring to its principal author, F. D. Corfield.

Mwai, Samuel Kagotho, Henry Muoria, Henry Wambugu, Willy George and many others prominent in African politics and Trade Unionists from Nairobi and various K.A.U. branches in the country. The Transport and Allied Workers' Union, various sections of the old Labour Trade Union of East Africa and most African trading societies and organizations were represented. Jesse Kariuki interpreted from Kikuyu into Swahili.

### First Speaker—Jomo Kenyatta

"I am very pleased to come to Nyeri and see so many of you here at this meeting of K.A.U., but before we open the meeting, I appeal to you to sit down and keep quiet so that you can hear what we are going to say. (Considerable shouting and ill-behavior on the part of the crowd at this moment.) I want to explain to you that if you want self-Government you must first sit down and keep quiet. (Points to various groups who are standing and making a noise and admonishes them.) Our time at this meeting is limited and we office-bearers have travelled a long way to address you, and if you are going to waste the time of the meeting our purpose will be spoiled. Those who are continuing to make a noise must be removed from this meeting. I do not want any interruptions. Quiet, quiet. I am the leader of Mumbi and I ask you yet again to keep quiet. (Tremendous applause and the crowd becomes more orderly.) If one is born of Mumbi, sit down on this earth of ours and keep quiet, otherwise leave. Those of you who are near the main road will be covered in dust unless you sit down. (Applause, and the crowd is more or less quiet now.) What God has told me to say to you today I will now say, although our loudspeaker has not yet arrived from Nairobi. You are the earth and the earth is ours, so listen to me and do not interrupt any more. We will start this meeting with prayers. Our brother Wachira will say these prayers to you. I have asked

him to make our prayers very short as our time is restricted by Government." (Jeers.)

### Second Speaker—The Rev. Wachira

"Those who are despised are those who fight for freedom. God said that one man cannot knock down a wall and continue to freedom, but if people unite and push together they could break the wall and pass over the ground towards independence. May God be with us on this day. We are here to follow the principles of justice. May God lead us on to our goal. Jomo is a disciple of God who will lead you along the righteous path. In the name of Jesus Christ and the people of Mumbi, I give you my blessing." (Crowd hums three times the religious answer to such prayers, according to Kikuyu tradition.)

### Jomo Kenyatta Again

(He begins with his usual "eeeeee" which is characteristic of all his speeches, and this is given vociferous applause.)

"Time is limited and I am now starting. I want you to know the purpose of K.A.U. It is the biggest purpose the African has. It involves every African in Kenya and it is their mouthpiece which asks for freedom. (Applause.) K.A.U. is you and you are the K.A.U. If we unite now, each and every one of us, and each tribe to another, we will cause the implementation in this country of that which the European calls democracy. True democracy has no colour distinction. It does not choose between black and white. We are here in this tremendous gathering under the K.A.U. flag to find which road leads us from darkness into democracy. In order to find it we Africans must first achieve the right to elect our own representatives. That is surely the first principle of democracy. We are the only race in Kenya which does not elect its own representatives in the Legislature and we are going to set about to rectify this situation. (Applause.) We feel we are dominated by a handful of others who refuse to be just. (Applause. Jesse Kariuki is working the crowd up by translating Kenyatta's speech in such a way that he is conveying to the people an inference which Jomo Kenyatta does not convey.) God said this is our land. Land in which we are to flourish as a people. We are not worried that other races are here with us in our country, but we insist that we are the leaders here, and what we want we insist we get. We want our cattle to get fat on our land so that our children grow up in prosperity; we do not want that fat removed to feed others. (Applause.) He who has ears should now hear that K.A.U. claims this land as its own gift from God and I wish those who are black, white or brown at this meeting to know this. K.A.U. speaks in daylight. He who calls us the *Mau Mau* is not truthful. We do not know this thing *Mau Mau*. (Jeers and applause.) We want to prosper as a nation, and as a nation we demand equality, that is equal pay for equal work. Whether it is a chief, headman or labourer he needs in these days increased salary. He needs a salary that compares with a salary of a European who does equal work. We will never get our freedom unless we succeed in this issue. We do not want equal pay for equal work tomorrow—we want it right now. Those who profess to be just must realize that this is the foundation of justice. It has never been known in history that a country prospers without equality. We despise bribery and corruption, those two words that the European repeatedly refers to. Bribery and corruption is prevalent in this country, but I am not surprised. As long as a people are held down, corruption is sure to rise and the only answer to this is a policy of equality. If we work together as one, we must succeed.

Our country today is in a bad state for its land is full of fools—and fools in a country delay the independence of its people. K.A.U. seeks to remedy this situation and I tell you now it despises thieving, robbery and murder for these practices ruin our country. I say this because if one man steals, or two men steal, there are people sitting close by lapping up information, who say the whole tribe is bad because a theft has been committed. Those people are wrecking our chances of advancement. They will prevent us getting freedom. If I have my own way, let me tell you I would butcher the criminal, and there are more criminals than one in more senses than one. The policeman must arrest an offender, a man who is purely an offender, but he must not go about picking up people with a small horn of liquor in their hands and march them in procession with his fellow policemen to Government and say he has got a *Mau Mau* amongst the Kikuyu people. (Applause.) The plain clothes man who hides in the hedges must, I demand, get the truth of our words before he flies to Government to present them with false information. I ask this of them who are in the meeting to take heed of my words and do their work properly and justly. (Applause.) We are black people and when we achieve our freedom, we will also have police and plain clothes men.

Amongst you people before me are those future policemen and plain clothes men and informers whom I mention. I want, therefore, to teach you now that our Government will demand nothing short of fact and we will never have fitina-merchants. (Tremendous applause. This is obviously a crack against informers and I know the few African policemen here are feeling a little bit disturbed and uncomfortable.) We K.A.U. do not have divisions amongst our ranks. Each one of you may join. The only division and condition is that we refuse completely to enlist those who are not truthful. (The loud speaker arrives at this stage and is erected with considerable difficulty amongst the teeming masses.) I do not want you to associate yourselves with the present campaign of *fitina*—it is a salty campaign and it is harming us. (Applause.) Europeans are said to be the cleverest—they must therefore sift the information they get. (At this stage the crowd begins to get restless and there is a distinct change of attitude in Jomo Kenyatta. He appeals repeatedly to the masses to quieten down and Mr. Henderson sends him a message and tells him that unless he first brings his meeting to order he will not be permitted to make any more racial remarks.) Jomo Kenyatta agrees and takes considerable pains to quieten the masses. He leaves his platform and personally wanders about shaking his hand at the worst sections of the crowd. (After 15 minutes the crowd is pacified and Jomo returns to his platform.) Our friend Ochieng is here. Peter Mbiu is still in the United Kingdom. They went away because of our land hunger. I ask you to note that our land discussions are held in daylight. We want a commission in this country, a Royal Commission to enquire into the land problem. Anyone here who wants more land is to raise their right hand. (The whole meeting raises their hands, each individual raises both.) Now, who does not want more land and who is not supporting us over this land problem? (Nobody moves.) I think the Europeans here realize in their heart of hearts that our grievance is true. (Shouts of "What are they going to do about it?") Who of you are going to support K.A.U.? (All raise their hands and there is tremendous applause.) Is it your heart that supports the K.A.U., or is it merely your mouth? (Answer, "Our hearts" and the whole meeting rises and many start waving their arms about. Another seven minutes is taken to restore the crowd to order.) Then join us today in this union of ours. Do not be scared of the few policemen under those trees who are holding their rifles high in the air for you

to see. Their job is to seize criminals, and we shall save them a duty today. I will never ask you to be subversive (uses the English word which the meeting does not understand), but I ask you to be united, for the day of Independence is the day of complete unity and if we unite completely tomorrow, our independence will come tomorrow. This is the day for you to work hard for your country (applause), it is not words but deeds that count and the deeds I ask for come from your pockets. The biggest subscribers to K.A.U. are in this order. First, Thomson's Fall branch, second, Elburgon branch and third Gatundu branch. Do you, in Nyeri branch, want to beat them? (Answer, "Yes".) Then let us see your deeds come forth. (Applause. Samuel Kagotho now goes on to the platform and appeals to people to join the Union. Jomo tells the meeting that the most important points are to follow—this is calculated to hold the crowd, many of whom do not like subscribing—Samuel Kagotho tells the meeting where the different tables and K.A.U. clerks are to be found for those who wish to subscribe.)

*12.40 p.m.*

The K.A.U. flag is now hoisted and underneath it a piece of sugar cane is tied. (Sugar cane is used more or less consistently in *Mau Mau* oath ceremonies either at the entrance of oath huts or as an arch through which initiates are led. I take the introduction of this piece of sugar cane as a sign that those who go on to the platform and make speeches have themselves joined hands with *Mau Mau*. The production of this sugar cane piece is cheered by the whole meeting.)

### Jomo Kenyatta Again

"Eeeeeee" (the usual Jomo Kenyatta characteristic). "We now start our meeting (three distinct applauses and Jomo takes up his position under the K.A.U. flag holding the sugar-cane). (The crowd again is extremely restless and there are a

great many nasty cracks against Europeans from all over the arena, and thug
elements, some identified from Nairobi,
are trying to stir up the crowd on the
perimeter. Jomo again goes to great pains
to quiet the meeting and expressed to
me his amazement at the truculence of
some of the people. He makes a point of
saying that they cannot be K.A.U. members). Jomo continues: "I want to touch
on a number of points, and I ask you for
the hundredth time to keep quiet whilst
I do this. We want self-government, but
this we will never get if we drink beer. It
is harming our country and making people fools and encouraging crime. It is also
taking all our money. Prosperity is a pre-
requisite of independence and, more important, the beer we are drinking is
harmful to our birthrate. You sleep with a
woman for nothing if you drink beer. It
causes your bones to weaken and if you
want to increase the population of the
Kikuyu you must stop drinking." (Some
in the crowd shout that they want to hear
about land and not beer.) "I now want to
say this. If you are not in favour of the
K.A.U., and if you do not keep quiet
whilst I speak to you, leave this meeting.
Sit down and keep quiet. (At this stage
small groups begin to argue with one
another: 10 to 15 minutes pass before
Kenyatta can be heard speaking.) "I will
now tell you about our flag." (Tremendous applause and all Jomo can do is to
say that he will tell them about the flag
later. He directs all his office-bearers to
try and keep the crowd under control.
We are sitting in the middle and,
whereas before there was a few feet
space between us and the crowd, we are
now swamped with wriggling masses,
one of whom is even sitting on the back
of the chair on which I am sitting.)

### Next Speaker, Ebrahim, the African District Officer at Nyeri

"Ladies and gentlemen. I cannot say
much, except that this is the biggest
meeting I have seen in this District. I
want to ask Mr. Kenyatta what he is
going to do to stop *Mau Mau*." (This
causes such a state of affairs that I cannot
hear anything else Ebrahim says. He
leaves the platform a minute or two later
and Jomo Kenyatta replaces him.)

### Jomo Kenyatta Again

"Eeeeeee" (applause). "Quiet, because if you do not take my last warning
we will never be permitted to hold another K.A.U. meeting in this District.
Regarding Mr. Ebrahmi's speech, I do
not want you to think he is wrong, for if
there are two different types amongst a
single people, we separate unity. K.A.U.
is a good union and we do not want divided people. I think *Mau Mau* is a new
word. Elders do not know it. K.A.U. is
not a fighting union that uses fists and
weapons. If any of you here think that
force is good, I do not agree with you:
remember the old saying that he who is
hit with a *rungu* returns, but he who is hit
with justice never comes back. I do not
want people to accuse us falsely—that
we steal and that we are *Mau Mau*." (Tremendous applause.) "I pray to you that
we join hands for freedom and freedom
means abolishing criminality. Beer harms
us and those who drink it do us harm and
they may be the so-called *Mau Mau*."
(Tremendous applause. It is obvious that
Jomo is side-stepping denouncing *Mau
Mau*.) "Whatever grievances we have, let
us air them here in the open. The criminal does not want freedom and land—he
wants to line his own pocket. Let us
therefore demand our rights justly. The
British Government has discussed the
land problem in Kenya and we hope to
have a Royal Commission to this country
to look into the land problem very
shortly. When this Royal Commission
comes, let us show it that we are a good
peaceful people and not thieves and robbers. I am now going to ask Senior Chief
Nderi to say a few words to you. I expect
you to hear him and clap him when he
finishes.

## Senior Chief Nderi[1]

"Greetings to you all. *Wanyua* was the old greeting of the Kikuyu and I now say *Wanyua* to you. I am going to thank the organizers of this meeting for saying that bad things must stop. Do you like K.A.U. (answer 'Yes'.) Therefore you must do what Jomo says and stop doing bad things. I will tell you how the police have helped us during troubles in this District. Without the police you would have killed your leaders and possibly yourselves by causing the trouble. Our Government knows that you are hungry and it will feed you. (Terrific jeers.) Stop trouble in the district and let us come to an agreement. Land alone will not help us. (Jeers.) We also need education. That is what we are getting and this will bring us harmony. Let us dig hard in our *shambas* and help ourselves. Night-time activity is damning the Kikuyu people and this I have told Kenyatta. Nobody but Government can help us." (Nderi's speech has overcome the whole crowd and he is forced to sit down by barracking. The mood of the meeting is bad. I personally feel that all that remains is for the cooking pot to be brought on.)

## Jomo Kenyatta

(He again takes considerable pains to quiet the crowd, but he is not listened to. At this moment a few of the Emergency Company turret cars pass by on their way up to Nyeri for an exercise and this has a sobering-up effect although there were shouts of "Let them come." Jomo then continues.)

"Chief Nderi was only trying to show how the Kikuyu people can advance. Do not be cross with him. There are more than 100,000 Europeans in the United

Kingdom who have supported our Land Petition. Our land case is being well presented and I am now going to ask Ochieng to tell you what he and Peter Mbiu did in U.N.O. But first I will ask the *E.A. Standard* reporter who is here to come forward and see what the audience is so that he can tell everyone how the African feels." (The *E.A. Standard* reporter declines to get up and is jeered at mercilessly by the crowd, some of whom are shouting that he is yellow.) "Give Ochieng such applause that the ground beneath you splits in two."

## Ochieng Oneko[2]

"I am very pleased to be here to talk to you. I would be more pleased if everyone kept quiet. It is always said that there is noise and disturbance at African meetings, and I want to demonstrate that this theory is false. I have only a few minutes and can therefore only say a few words. Some laws of Kenya are bad and we want Government to know that we do not like them. (Crowd surges and speaker and Jesse Kariuki try to stop them. Jomo himself again goes into the crowd to try and pacify them.) "We do not want this meeting to turn into a riot. Sit down and keep quiet, I ask you, or we will not be permitted to hold another meeting." ("That does not matter" from the crowd. Mr. Henderson calls over Ochieng and tells him that the police are not very impressed with the conduct of the crowd and that unless order is restored he will not be permitted to speak. Eventually order is restored. Ochieng returns to the platform with a grin.) "You selected us to go as your representatives to the United Kingdom and U.N.O.

[1] Chief Nderi was the son of Chief Wangombe, about whom Jomo Kenyatta had written in a pamphlet entitled, "My People of KiKuyu: the Life of Chief Wangombe" (London: United Society for the Propogation of the Gospel, 1942). Kenyatta regarded Chief Wangombe as the very embodiment of the Kikuyu nation.

[2] Ochieng Oneko, a Luo militant, was removed from the executive committee of the KAU by the British authorities after the Emergency Proclamation of October 20, 1952, and arrested. Although his case was dismissed by the Supreme Court of Kenya, he was held in detention until after the Lancaster House Constitutional Conference conferred self-government on Kenya in 1963.

When the Europeans came to this country we were a peaceful people—tribal wars were merely minor disputes. The Europeans came here as our guests." (Terrific applause.) "This invitation has turned out to be false. They went for land and have established themselves in Kenya in such numbers that we suffered and this is why we went to the U.K. We do not want to be led. We want our own African Government and we will get it soon. We want the country to begin with peace between us, the Government and the European, but that peace can only come if we get justice. Before the European came, every African had sufficient land—that is not the case today. If we were to get education and advancement by losing land, then I wish we never get advancement. I wish to thank many of the British people in the United Kingdom who support us. Some ridicule Fenner Brockway, but I know he is our friend. We discussed in the U.K. the land problem with the Colonial Secretary and he promised he would send a Commission to this Country. We demand that the Commission not only looks into African land but compares African land to the White Highlands. We know a report on land is to come out from the Colonial Office and we must remain peaceful until we see how things go. We have had a measure of success. We are also completely against the system of appointment to Legislative Council. We must elect our own representatives for some of our members in Legislative Council are good, but due to the fact that they were nominated by Government, the time may come when others turn half-Government to major issues. We are also against some controls, particularly regarding the difference in price between European and African grown maize. When in the United Kingdom, we asked that such controls and laws be revoked. We have seen for too long that the European gets first place." (This speaker is stirring up the meeting and is obviously most dangerous.) "Regarding Trade Unionism—this is vital, for when the cost of living rises we must ensure that we are assisted in the same way as Europeans and that means equal pay for equal work. Then look at D.C.s' Offices. You see that an African is an "aaaaaaO". We only want an "O" and we refuse to listen to excuses from Government that the reason for these "a's" is that the African is not sufficiently responsible or suitable. Those Africans holding the titles "aaaaa" are doing the same work as D.C.s and P.C.s and should therefore be given this office. We told the Secretary of State this quite clearly. We want mass-education. A man without education is only half a man but we want the chance to learn properly. The Indians have most schools because they breed like locusts. We want co-operation and friendship between races but we do not want that friendship that resembles the friendship of the crocodile and the fish. We are a peaceful people and we will not chase the European away, but I assure you we will watch him most closely. Europeans are visitors and they know it, and those who are here know it—here at this meeting, but they will not admit it. They have to give us permission before we can go to the lavatory. If we want freedom we must hit back. I know we will get it. We will get it in the same way as the people in the Gold Coast and Nigeria. There is no doubt that we will get it. You and I will achieve it—the K.A.U.—a body for all Africans in Kenya. We must not discard our traditions for they are us. I do not want to hear a person calling himself Peter Johnston William Tableson for those are European names and every time we ask something or do something people overseas will say we are Europeans. If your name is Njeroge, we know you are a Kikuyu and you should be proud of it. If your name is Omolo you are a Luo, or Patel an Indian, or George a European." (Laughter at "George".) Then stick to your names and languages.

We learnt 'Yes, yes' and 'What there' which is English, only because we wanted to get trade, for in the trade world English is spoken. We do not copy our visitors. Regarding religion. We do not know God. What we know is *Ngai*. We believe in *Ngai* whether the missionaries say we are pagans or not. Are we not led by the God of Africa? We will wait in peace now for the developments regarding the Commission and I will then come back to tell you the news. I want you to love all Africans and I want tribes to get together. I said in Kiambu that I would marry a Kikuyu girl to show good relationship amongst tribes." (Three years ago this would have been taken by the Kikuyu as an insult for an uncircumcised Luo was the most despised thing imaginable to the Kikuyu. Today it is applauded.) "Freedom cannot come without suffering and unity. If you do not unite, you will be the person who is kicked in the backside and called 'Boy'. Laws were made for all Africans and if you bring tribal difficulties into the picture you will delay advancement. Europeans have complete unity and when I was in the United Kingdom I saw that. The European once ruled the European but then they got together. They will leave this country in time. Legislation will eventually cause that. Those who came to this country to eke out a living when they were kicked out of India will repeat the performance of evacuation in time. For the present I want no trouble, let us only trouble ourselves to get together. That is all I have to say." (This man, Ochieng, is obviously fanatically anti-British and speeches of this nature made to primitive masses are extremely harmful. The meeting is more or less an uproar now.)

## Jomo Kenyatta

(He returns to the platform to restore the masses to order.)

"You have, until now, done me a great favour in remaining quiet. Do not let people say we left this meeting like hungry hyenas. (After another 15 minutes the crowd was quiet.) Now, I will tell you about our flag. It has three colours as you see—black at the top, red in the middle and green at the bottom. Black is to show that this is for black people. Red is to show that the blood of an African is the same colour as the blood of a European and green is to show that when we were given this country by God it was green, fertile and good, but now you see the green is below the red and is suppressed. (Tremendous applause.) You also see on the flag a shield, a spear and an arrow. This means that we should remember our forefathers who used these weapons to guard this land for us. K.A.U. is marked on the flag. The 'U' is placed over the shield and indicates that the shield will guard the Union against all evils. The weapons do not mean that we should fight like our fathers. What could a spear do against an atom bomb. The weapon with which we will fight is justice and brains. The silver on the spear is the same colour as the silver on the shilling. That means our land was prosperous in the bygone days. Now do you approve of our flag? (Answer "Yes" amidst tremendous applause.) Does anyone not approve of it? If he does he is to stand up. (One poor misfortunate individual who misunderstood the question stands and is carried by the crowd over their heads to the perimeter and told to become a European.) God who gave us this land will see that this flag leads us throughout this land. (Applause.) We are to stop soon for these days everything depends on a permit. Nevertheless if we are given a permit whilst we are to be governed let us comply with it. Remember though that when we get our own Government there will not be permits. (Applause.) Those police armed in the trees came here to control Kenyatta's flock. Let us relieve them of a job today and disperse peacefully from this meeting. If you do not disperse peacefully and go back to your homes and shops in an orderly manner, you will do us a great disservice, for you will prevent the K.A.U. holding another meeting. Remember that he who hates another takes the snuff out of the other's nose. (This is a proverb which means that if one is permitted to do something and does not do it properly he will suffer by his actions.) I will end off the meeting by introducing Brother Kagia to you who will say a few words."

## Kagia

"I have never seen such a big meeting. We sent Ochieng and Peter Mbiu overseas because of land and because we are not allowed to elect our own representatives in Legislative Council. We were not robbed of our lands by guns but we were robbed by a very small group of Europeans. It was because they had complete control in Legislative Council that they got the land. They introduced laws like the Crown Lands Ordinance when we had no say in the Legislature. It was through Legislative Council that they took our lands away. That being so, Legislative Council could return lands to us today, and that is the reason why we want more representation in that Council. We do not trust some that are in Legislative Council, for as long as the African is nominated we will not be given more land. Our first essential is to get the elective system in operation and we then shall elect people who speak properly for us. We want the majority in Legislative Council for we are over 5,000,000 and this is our land. If we have suitable representation in Legislative Council there will be no need to go to the U.K. for our lands are not in the U.K. White people say that Legislative Council is reserved for people of learning, but that is not true and as Kwame Nkrumah in the Gold Coast said: 'The person who gets to Legislative Council is suitable providing he voices the feelings of his people whether he is literate or not.' I can tell you that the Gold Coast Government under Kwame has been praised, even by the Europeans themselves. If Asians are allowed to elect their own representatives, why not Africans? Are there not thousands of Asians uneducated? We want to dominate Legislative Council, and we will never stop until we do this. Let us bite this task with all our teeth and never let go." (Jomo Kenyatta has spent all the time taken by the speech of Kagia in trying to pacify the crowd and selected a number of *askaris* to penetrate the crowd and quieten them down.)

Next was Samuel Kagotho who sang a lengthy hymn praising Jomo Kenyatta as the leader under the flag and God's disciple to the African, and finally Jomo announces that he would close the meeting with a final resolution that the African be given freedom of assembly. This resolution was passed unanimously and the meeting ended. The subscriptions were considerable, but there was not time to count these.

The meeting dispersed without incident.

# 26  TOM MBOYA

## KENYA AS A NATION July 23, 1962

*Tom Mboya (1930–1969) was born on a sisal estate in the White Highlands of Kenya. Educated at Holy Ghost College, Mangu, he became a sanitary inspector in 1951. Like many others, he fell under the influence of Jomo Kenyatta and joined the Kenya African Union (KAU), of which he became Treasurer in 1953. When the KAU was proscribed during the Mau Mau disturbances, he turned his energy and his eloquence to organizing the African trade unions and becoming Secretary of the Kenya Federation of Labour; he was an outspoken advocate of independence. Although a Luo, Mboya was the principal rival of Oginga Odinga, the Luo Leader, whose more radical views he did not share. He received support from the United States and Great Britain as a counter to the Soviet Union's courtship of Odinga. Mboya's more moderate posture insured his credibility with the white Kenyans, as well as with Britain and the United States. This greatly contributed to his success at the constitutional conference held at Lancaster House in London in 1960. There he obtained important concessions for Africans, particularly regarding the sensitive issue of land reform. In May 1960, following the Lancaster House Conference, the Kenya African National Union (KANU) was formed from the remnants of the former KAU. Jomo Kenyatta served as its president; Tom Mboya was General Secretary and, during the subsequent transitional period of self-government, Minister of Labour. Upon the declaration of Kenya's independence from Britain on December 12, 1963, Mboya was installed as Minister of Justice and Constitutional Affairs (1963–64) in Kenyatta's government. He subsequently held the post of Minister for Economic Development and Planning, from 1964 until his tragic assassination by a Kikuyu on July 5, 1969, outside a pharmacy in Nairobi.*

*During his tenure as Minister of Labour, Mboya did much to allay the fears of Kenya's white minority—many of whom were preparing to leave Kenya upon its forthcoming independence. On July 23, 1962, at Eldoret, the bastion of white supremacy in the Highlands, he challenged the settlers about their commitment to the new Kenya. Many Europeans did leave Kenya when it became independent, but many others remained as Kenyan citizens, including such influential members of the settler community as Sir Michael Blundell, who served as a judge after independence, and Lord Delamere.*

I want to talk to you today about Kenya as a nation. Some of the things I shall have to say may not please you. But as farmers, you have grown used to a harsh enivornment, and everything you do or attempt is governed by the physical facts of life. I believe that if we are going to co-operate in the task of nation-building we must shed the fears and suspicions which have existed between our various communities for so long.

It is suggested by some people that there is no such thing as a Kenya nation.

From Tom Mboya, *The Challenge of Nationhood: A Collection of Speeches and Writings,* (London: Heineman Educational Books Ltd., 1970), pp. 41–47. Reprinted by permission.

All kinds of arguments and recriminations are thrown up to try to prove that any nationalist ambitions for Kenya must encounter more difficulties than could ever be overcome. Noisy minorities in all walks of life, both here and in their contact with overseas interests, keep plugging away at their 'no confidence' theme. Some people say that Kenya is heading for economic disaster and political chaos and tribal war.

Such people are not thinking from their heart or from their mind, but from their emotions and fears. Such people are not nation-builders; they are afraid and refuse to see their real duty in Kenya.

When I talk now about a 'Kenya nation', I am not speaking as a political romantic, but as a realist. Any sincere politician or leader must have some vision in front of him. There must be something much more than notoriety to attract him towards unceasing work, the bitterness of struggle, the temptations and the pressures. There must be a factor of dedication, an undeniable impulse to build and to serve. In this he must satisfy himself. There are very few other rewards.

It is not only the vision of the leaders that dictates our struggle. There are the deep-rooted aspirations of our people. These people may appear simple and uneducated; they may not be articulate but they are human beings and not stones. They have an inborn pride and a genuine desire for self-improvement and self-fulfilment. These are facts which may have dodged many people in the past but with which we all must reckon in the future. To ignore this force would be to lead to frustrations and explosions—indeed we have already had such an experience in Kenya.

It is not, however, the fear of this force that should dictate our decisions. There is the positive side of this force, namely, its ability to face the challenge of nation-building. We have to release this force of our people for new and constructive purposes. We have to harness the enthusiasm for self-improvement to form the spearhead in our efforts for nation-building.

What, after all, does it mean when people talk about 'the position of the Europeans' or 'the problem of farmers'? To me it only suggests one thing: that over the past few years, for some reason, the Europeans shut themselves inside a kind of thorn *boma* of traditional thinking, hoping either that this would insulate them from events outside, or, more recently, that somebody would produce large sums of money to move them safely and profitably out of Kenya. Despite wishful thinking and pious hopes Kenya has not stood still. History has caught up with many of our people and the fact of a Kenya nation has aroused varying degrees of outrage, or criticism, or patronising commentary, or enthusiasm and practical support. But, maybe because so much has happened so quickly, the fact of Kenya has not yet achieved widespread understanding.

Broadly speaking, it has been the tradition of some people, even some in Africa, to think of Africa in terms of Rider Haggard situations or *Sanders of the River*. If you expect me to be honest with you, you must be honest in return. And so you must admit that people—over the years —have set out to persuade themselves and others, that the Africans 'were perfectly happy' with their mud huts and *posho* and whatever work could be dragged out of them for pittance wages, until 'political agitators' started to stir them up with talk about 'education' and 'trade unions' and 'democracy'.

This attitude, expressed in this way, is written in the pages of our modern history. And on the foundation of this attitude had been built the view, which many must have encountered and shared, that the impudent emergence of African leadership—in this African country—was first rooted in desire for power, or wealth, or revenge. I've even heard it argued that the motive force was desire to be invited overseas, for social entertainment.

The real motive force was quite simple. Any phase of evolution must have its milestones of increasing maturity. Thus, a few years ago, and quite suddenly in the eyes of many Europeans, Kenya produced from the ranks of her people, African leaders equipped with sophistication and talent and national—as distinct from patriarchal—ambition. Their first objective, their first approach, was quite simply *equality*. That was the first moment of truth. It was a moment that called for goodwill, but instead it was generally greeted with rebuff. The ideas of race bedevilled Kenya then—the ideas of superiority and domination and privilege. There was no point of contact between black and white. There was not allowed to be any mingling of philosophies, any mutual exploration of background or purpose, any pooling of resources, any kind of common ground.

The missing link was the wisdom and foresight needed in these early days. Constructive ambition was turned into conflict. Racial attitude was matched by racial attitude. Many Europeans expected 'gratitude'.

In the period leading up to 1960, the daily and weekly press of Kenya was not of much help in bringing wisdom and foresight to bear. The principles and policies that were given at least their rough shape by a Lancaster House Conference of early 1960 came to many as a tremendous shock, from which some have never really recovered. Why was this? Because to a large extent the 'Wind of Change' had blown through Kenya unnoticed.

Relying on the local press many Europeans had been ill-prepared for Mr. Macleod's statements at Lancaster House. Their vision of Kenya was that of a marriage between South African apartheid policies and Sir Roy Welensky's policies. Perhaps this was the most revealing moment of our history. How so much can happen before our very eyes without our being able to comprehend it! It is this that explains the attitude and panic of those who ten years ago clamoured for independence for Kenya, but who are now preparing to desert Kenya on the eve of independence.

Think what has happened, despite this lesson of 1960. A fortnight ago Mr. Maudling was here, on a visit that proved very useful in many ways. Work has now started on constitutional drafting in the back-rooms of Westminster, and on papers flying to and fro between London and Nairobi. This simple fact represents

the wide measure of genuine agreement that exists in the country about one of the twin pillars of Kenya's independence: the constitution. We shall have elections in roughly six months' time, from which there will emerge a government of the people, to carry Kenya into independence in 1963.

The other twin pillar is that long-standing practical and emotional issue in Kenya, the land. We have come a long way here too, in terms of common sense, justice and national thinking, since the days when all political speeches on one side spoke of 'the anachronism' and on the other side of 'the sanctity' of the White Highlands.

One of the interpretations of the Colonial Secretary's recent announcement that Britain would finance as a first step a million-acre resettlement project, and then consider going further—is this: although the scale and the speed of this project have been criticised, it is going to mean that those European mixed farmers who want to leave, will be enabled to do so. And to anyone determined to leave I would say merely—in that historic House of Commons phrase—'in the name of God, go'. Kenya can do without anybody who has to be persuaded or cajoled to stay.

From this point that we've reached, the building of Kenya as a nation is going to be the biggest pioneering job in the history of Africa. You can't take up any compromise positon now. Either you're going to play your part wholeheartedly in the challenge of the future, or you're going to run away from it all.

We understand full well that almost all the productive capacity of Kenya has to spring from conservation and wise use of the land. We undestand the critical importance of agriculture, in its influence on living-standards and external trade, on urban growth and industrial development, on economic well-being and social contentment.

I see this, and want you to see it as

well, as a national contribution. And I also see this every achievement of the land, the agriculture, as the combined effort of ownership and management and labour. With my background, and in my particular present job, I am very conscious that our agriculture as a whole— the mixed farms and ranches and plantations—employ a labour force of something like a quarter of a million.

Sometimes, you know, I get it thrown at me by people who say that when all the Europeans have 'scrammed out of Africa'[1] these farm-workers will simply join the queue of unemployed and how do I like that? If we're going to be honest with each other, now and in the future, let us not shirk bringing out into the open all such attitudes and accusations.

People who say this kind of thing seem to me to combine vicious irresponsibility with a peculiar kind of despair. They can have no feeling for humanity, and no sense of national duty at all.

It is an odd moral outlook that would use unemployment as the currency in a game of politics. But Kenya now needs moral strength, and people of this kind are beyond the reach of any sympathy from me. Others tell their discharged workers, on occasion, to 'go and get a job from Kenyatta or Mboya . . .' Such people are not only untrue to Kenya, they do great harm to the Europeans who seriously wish to stay.

There is little I can add to all I've said before, in public here or in private discussions in London, about the festering sore of unemployment. I don't know whether some of you realise, even today, what unemployment means, in terms of loss of self-respect and human degradation, bitternesss, and the seeds of subversion. To meet this unemployment, in

[1] In a much-quoted phrase Mr. Mboya, when Chairman of the All African Peoples' Conference's first gathering in Accra, had in 1958 told the white man to "scram out of Africa." A glance at the text of that speech indicates that he was not referring to the Europeans as individuals, but to their colonial or racial rule.

a country with so much crying out to be done, calls for national outlook and dedication. We must transform the sense of our greatest peril into the sense that here is our greatest task.

Those who have decided to stay have got to create or discover human relationships, to bring into account things that you've hardly ever looked for: sensibilities and ambitions and loyalties and needs. You've got to understand that we all share human functions and frailties, and we're all in the same Kenya boat.

So often we talk of fears about personal security. The only way to dissolve fears is to remove their cause. Crime, of the kind that worries us, is rooted partly in economics, and partly in the psychology of this day and age, when the country has advanced so swiftly that sections of all communities could hardly keep in step. We need a fund of economic understanding and psychological resilience. Under both these headings it is up to each of us to give a lead.

We are all involved now in the business of building a nation. Your security fears will disappear when the people can see that you are working like everybody else, towards a goal that everybody wants to reach, for rewards that we all can share.

If you accept this, you are with us, not on sufferance but unaffectedly as colleagues and friends, important components of Kenya as a nation. Your Member, Mr. Welwood, told us in Legislative Council a fortnight ago, that many of you would feel unable to accept the consequences of independence, or some such phrase. Why should this be? There will be a Bill of Rights for all Kenya citizens which we—the political leaders—have designed and will defend. All who accept this will no longer be 'members of the immigrant community', but full members of a new community which will demand all our dedication, all our attachement to morality, all our strength.

Let me emphasise one thing, while

talking to you today. On the attainment of our independence all who were formerly 'non-Africans' must become full citizens of Kenya. As soon as you do so, any kind of discrimination in your status or your rights will disappear. Your interests will be as defensible in law, and of as great concern to the Government, as the interests of anybody else. But if you are not prepared to be citizens of Kenya, there will be no place for you here, except as aliens.

As a young nation Kenya cannot afford the luxury of squabbles with people who do not intend to stay. We have a tremendous economic and vocational struggle ahead. Either you are with us or you are not even on the field of play. We cannot let ourselves be weighted down by people who might cling to Kenya for a while, because they like 'the way of life', or because they're making money, or—so people often put it—'to see how things turn out'. We cannot give *carte blanche* to benefits, of these or other kinds, gained without national investment of dedication, sacrifice and strength.

I told you earlier about the first moment of truth. I tell you now that, in Kenya's history, this is the second and critical moment of truth.

With mutual trust, and a sharing of faith, and a pooling of all our talents and resources, we can meet together this challenge of building a nation, irrespective of background or creed. This is what we want. It is what Kenya needs: the dedicated contribution of every race, every tribe, every worker, every farmer, every civil servant, every businessman, every teacher, every doctor, every family.

People ask me then how I can talk about a nation amid all the surface differences between K.A.N.U. and K.A.D.U., amid the clamours for Somali seccession and *mwambao* and the claims of the Masai.[1] This is superficial thinking. Inevitably, the birth-pangs of a nation must be attended by different party outlook, different bargaining position, different viewpoint or approach. To date, our people have been dragged through history. Henceforth we will write our own history. And this is the point at which outlooks and loyalties will coalesce.

True, we have tribal differences and sensitivites. So often people point at the Congo and warn that Kenya is doomed to become another Congo. I do not share this view. We have passed the stage when this could have happened. We have passed through more trials than most African countries and I believe we have come to appreciate freedom to a point where we would be prepared to defend it with our lives. We do not intend to exchange British colonialism for either local dictatorship or Soviet and American economic colonialism.

Out of all the emergencies and instabilities, the economic recession of the past decade, the immediate challenge before us is that of recovery. And on this we must build. I've been frank with you throughout this speech. I've dealt with many of the bitter comments that got hurled at me and other African leaders. Let us forget the mistakes and the weaknesses of the past, on all and every side. Our duty now is to the future.

[1] At this time the minority party, Kenya African Democratic Union, tended to represent the conservative, pastoral Africans. The Somalis in the North East of the country were still pressing their claims for secession. Some elements at the coast wanted a separate existence *(mwambao)*. The Masai, divided by the Kenya-Tanganyika border, were unsure of their future position in the new states.

# 27 ALI DINAR
## THE LAST SULTAN OF DARFUR

*Darfur (Dār Fūr), land of the Fur, lies nearly a thousand miles southwest of Khartoum. It is a hot and harsh region dominated by the towering mass of Jabal Marra, with its more enervating climate, rising some 9,000 feet above the Sahil. The origins of the Fur are obscured in myth and legend; they speak their own Sudanic language, not Arabic, and although they are devout Muslims, practice customs not recognized by orthodox Islam. During the long history of the sultanate, spanning more than a thousand years, three dynasties prevailed—the Daju, the Tunjur, and the Kaira Fur. The history of Darfur is ancient and complex. Despite the defeat of Sultan Muhammad Fadl at Bara in 1821 by the advancing forces of Muhammad Ali, the Viceroy of Egypt (as an ancillary adventure to his determined efforts to conquer the central Sudan), the Fur maintained their independence until 1874. In that year, the Khedive of Egypt, Ismail Pasha, was finally able to incorporate the sultanate into his expanding empire by capitalizing upon the victory of the notorious slave-trader, Zubayr Rahma Mansur, over the Fur Sultan Ibrahim at the battle of al-Manawashi. Egyptian rule over Darfur, however, was transitory. All of the Sudan soon fell under the authority of Muhammad Ahmad, al-Mahdi, and his successor, the Khalifa Abd Allahi, upon their successful jihad (Holy War), which destroyed the Egyptian administration in the Sudan. The Mahdist State (1885–1898) in turn was overwhelmed by the Anglo-Egyptian imperial army led by General H. H. Kitchener in 1898. The British, however, were more concerned about the inviolability of the Nile waters and their security at Cairo and Suez than about Darfur, far to the west of the waters, despite its presence in the Nile basin. With limited financial and military resources, Kitchener and his successor, Sir Reginald Wingate, discreetly left the remote land of the Fur alone, to revive under the grandson of the former Sultan Muhammad al-Fadl (1779–1893)—Ali Dinar.*

*Ali Dinar Zakariya Muhammad al Fadl (1865–1916) was born at the village of Shuwaiya about eighty miles southwest of Nyala. He succeeded Abu Kairat as Sultan of Darfur in 1889 after the occupation of Darfur by the forces of the Mahdi. The Mahdist Amir of Darfur became increasingly suspicious of the loyalty of the Fur Sultan and exiled him to Omdurman, where the Khalifa Abd Allahi had succeeded the Mahdi upon the latter's death in June 1885. Upon the defeat of the Khalifa by the Anglo-Egyptian forces of Kitchener in 1898, Ali Dinar collected his followers and arms; he returned to al-Fashar, the capital of Darfur, and seized the throne. Here Ali Dinar reigned as Sultan, recognized by the Sudan Government, to whom he paid a modest tribute. He ruled Darfur with an efficiency marked by ruthlessness. At the outbreak of the First World War, his political sagacity deserted him, probably more through isolation than failure of intuition; he was persuaded by the Ottoman Turks and the intrigues of Sayyid Ahmad al-Sharif of Cyrenaica to declare a jihad on the British infidels in Khartoum. This venture precipitated the Anglo-Egyptian invasion of Darfur, the defeat of the Fur army at Birinjiya, and Ali Dinar's own death at Kulme, south of Zalingei, by a chance bullet. So ended the long history of the Sultanate of Darfur, the traditions of which remain vivid today in the memories of the Fur people. Ali Dinar's letters, and those of the British officers who marched against him, recount the dying days of the historic Sultanate of the Fur.*

From A. B. Theobald, *Ali Dinar: Last Sultan of Darfur, 1898–1916*, (Harlow, Essex: Longmans, Green and Co. Ltd., 1965), pp. 162–4, 167–9, 170–1, 179, 193–4, 203–4. Reprinted by permission of the author.

## Ali Dinar to Yusuf Muhammad al-Amin al-Hindi, January 11, 1916.[1]

I beg to inform you that Sultan Muḥammad Rashad al-Dīn[2] and Aulād al-Sanūsī,[3] after killing the Italians and all the Christians, and after winning a great victory over the enemies of Islām, have sent to us in the month of Ṣafar,[4] in charge of Ghais Abū Kurayem (Qais Abū Kuraim) and our men who were at Kufra, 2,500 Mauser rifles and 400 cases of ammunition. I send to you herewith samples of the ammunition, so that you may be able to see with your own eyes. Thanks be to God for all this. They have also sent us one hundred of their prisoners, all master armourers, of whom ninety died on the way from thirst, but ten arrived here all right and are now with us. The Sultan by his Firman has promised to send us sufficient arms and ammunition in charge of a big caravan. By God, this is all true, and when the hour comes, please God we shall fight with the spear and the *safāriq*.[5]

## Ali Dinar to Sayyid Ahmad al-Sharif ibn al-Sayyid al-Sharif Muhammad al-Sanusi, January 28, 1916.

We have been moved by religious zeal and fervent faith to rise by the power and might of God for the protection of the religion of God against the enemies of God, the infidels and opponents of Muslim laws, who are our neighbours in the Sudan. We shall shortly proclaim the *jihād* for the sake of God and you shall hear how the enemies of God will suffer hardship at our hands. . . . The Muslims in the eastern Sudan who are under British rule have all embraced Christianity and forsaken Islām. Their notables have written asking us to follow the Christian faith, intending to lead us astray, but we have not listened to them. Their letters and false articles published in the news-

[1] Yasuf Muhammad al-Amín al-Hindī (1865–1942) was a prominent Sudamese religious teacher and leader of the Hindīya sect of the Sammānīya religious order (tarīga).

papers, in which they praise the British Government, are sent herewith for you to read.

## Ali Dinar to Governor Kordofan and Inspector Nahud, February 7, 1916.

You Christians are infidels and dogs: your destination is hell, to which you will ultimately go. You have chosen to die. We also welcome death as martyrs in God's cause and to gain everlasting happiness, our final abode being paradise, where eternal peace reigns. We are Muslims, sons of Muslims, we believe in God, his angels, books, his Prophets and his word. Therefore, by God we shall fight you with the greatest zeal and by God's help you shall drink the bitter cup of death, and you shall taste utter destruction at our hands. Sorrow and annihilation shall befall you, and your souls shall be cast into fire and hell. Do not believe that we have any consideration for you, for your guns, rifles or machines. No, by God, we are not afraid of you, but will fight you with spears and *safariq*. . . . By God, if you move or remain still, I shall march upon you, by the will of God, wherever you may be. . . . The cause of my delay at present is lack of water on the road which is insufficient for the number of my troops, and if God wills, we shall meet as soon as rains fall. You should know that we have recently received a *firmān* from the Sultan of Islām, Muḥammed Rashed al-Dīn, in which he orders us to fight in God's cause and he has sent us sufficient ammunition and other materials of war.

## Ali Dinar to "The Governor of Hell in Kordofan and the Inspector of Flames in En Nahud," February 6, 1916.

You have used oppression and have abused your authority. You have become haughty and have pretended that you are invincible, so that your evil souls, which are at the disposal of God in this world, have induced you to pretend that you are proceeding to Umm Shanqa in our country. God be praised, what a wonderful miracle for a dead corpse to move under the hands of the washers. How can you reach Umm Shanqa? Is it by your intrigues and lies? . . . We belong to the party of God, and we shall be victorious. You are our enemies, and the enemies of God. By God, by God and by his Prophet, if you follow the advice of your father the devil (may be the curse of God be upon him and upon you) and come to Umm Shanqa, you will be utterly destroyed, and will be an example to other people like you. God is with those who are patient, and if he wishes, as soon as the rains fall, we ourselves shall march against you with innumerable Islamic armies who have devoted themselves to the *jihād* in the cause of God and his Prophet. . . . May God enable us to destroy you utterly, so that you will return defeated and disgraced. . . .

### Sir Reginald Wingate, Governor-General of the Sudan, to Sir Henry McMahon, British High Commissioner in Egypt, February 17, 1916.

Information has now been received that the Sultan [Ali Dinar] has considerably strengthened the garrison at Jebel Hilla, which is only eighteen miles from the Kordofan border and in Darfur. This place and Umm Shanga, some fifteen miles distant from it and also in Darfur, command the first permanent water supplies west of Nahud and are consequently of great strategic importance, as their occupation by strong enemy forces renders protection of Kordofan natives living between Nahud and the border—who at this time of year are entirely dependent on water stored in *tebeldi* trees and have no permanent wells—a matter of extreme difficulty. I have therefore been obliged to order the rapid concentration at Nahud of the remainder of the Darfur field force, a mixed force of about 2,000 men of all arms under the

command of Major P. V. Kelly, 3rd Hussars.

### Sir Reginald Wingate to General Sir John Maxwell, Commanding Officer, Egypt, February 18, 1916.

To my mind there is little or no doubt that Ali Dinar is acting on instructions and advice from the Senussi and his Turco-German advisers, and it might be necessary to deal him a blow before our enemies' propaganda and intentions have sufficient time to materialize; the main point, however, is to prevent trouble spreading into Kordofan and our own tribes becoming restive and unsettled owing to apparent inaction or pusillanimity on our part.

### Stewart Symes, Private Secretary to the Governor General, Sir Reginald Wingate, to Harold MacMichael, Liaison Officer, El Obeid, February 18, 1916.

Darfur remains the same, viz. to confine our action to the minimum necessary to uphold Government's prestige in Sudanese eyes and to protect local natives. Sultan's reported reinforcement of Jebel Hilla appeared to contribute a direct menace to latter, which it was represented could be only met by our military occupation of Jebel Hilla. Accordingly the army was instructed to assemble an adequate force for this purpose. Subsequent information showed the menace had been exaggerated, but in a military sense, it is still correct to say that the position of natives west of Nahud can best be secured by our occupation of Jebel Hilla.

The Sirdar[1] recognizes that our concentration of troops has aggravated the situation, but considers that time is still on our side. Once we enter Darfur territory, he thinks the psychological moment to push on to Fasher may arise. Consequently he wishes to postpone

[1] The Governor General, Sir Reginald Wingate.

crossing the frontier until we are in a military sense fully prepared to take immediate advantage of whatever opportunities offer, and are able to control a political situation, which, once the troops are actually engaged, may develop in a direction contrary to our present policy and intentions.

## Ali Dinar to Enver Pasha, Turkish Minister of War, March 13, 1916.

To fight a *jihād* is all that we desire, for Islam is lost and those accursed dogs, the English and the French, have made all the Muslims in the Sudan infidels, and have turned their hearts towards Christianity for the sake of worldly riches. . . . All have embraced Christianity, and have imitated the action of the Christians. Do not think there is any Islām left in the Sudan, for there is no real Islām except in Darfur, which God has protected through us, and screened its inhabitants against the evil teachings of the infidels. . . . Let us pray to God to protect Darfur against the intrigues of the infidels, because many of the people of Darfur have run away and joined those dogs, the English, who, being in urgent need for such, pay P.T. 50 reward to each who brings in a recruit. They are in extreme fear of you. As to ourselves, although we are short of arms and ammunition and have not so much as you have, we have plenty of horses and men, thank God. . . . Our arms are swords and spears and *safāriq*. These we have plentifully. . . . Nevertheless, our kingdom has become weak and poor, and all that we now own is faith in God and desire to promote his word, and to help His Majesty the Sultan, in order that we may please God Almighty. . . .

## Lt. Colonel P. V. Kelly to Sir Reginald Wingate, Governor-General, Sudan, June 17, 1916.

As you see, General, I had but little to do with the direction of the fight [the battle of Birinjiya], which was brought on prematurely. The result was a most happy one, and what more can one want? The Camel Corps got out of it with only four men slightly wounded. . . . Old Huddleston, I'll allow, blundered on without orders and there is no excuse for him, but still he has worked like a black for me, and I would not wish anything said to the old man for the world. . . . I hope, General, I have made it clear that I don't want it to go any further.[1]

## H.A. MacMichael to the Assistant Director of Education, June 27, 1916.

At our entry Fasher appeared almost deserted, but there were a good many people in the houses and much looting went on, especially at the palace, before guards could be put in. At the north end of the town two high scaffoldings had been erected by the Sultan as stations from which shots should be fired at the aeroplane next time it appeared. . . . The *suq* [that is, market] is a miserable series of narrow alleys with several high gallows by the side of it. On the lower gallows men were hung, on the higher ones they were spreadeagled and shot, in the Sultan's time.

The Sultan's palace is a perfect Sudanese Alhambra. The Khalifa's house in Omdurman is a hovel compared to it. There are small shady gardens and little fish ponds, arcades, colonnades, storerooms and every type of building. The floors are strewn with fine silver sand, the thatch on the roofs is the finest imaginable, and looks as if it has been clipped with scissors. The walls are beautifully plastered in red, and the interiors of the halls covered with great inscriptions from the Koran in handsome calligraphy or with chess board designs. Only the best *birsh* [straw matting] of bamboo has been used in the roofings. Trellis work in ebony is found in place of interior walls and the very flooring in the women's quarters, under the silvery sand, is impregnated with spices.

J.A. Gillan "Darfur 1916," *Sudan Notes and Records,* vol. XXII no. 1, 1939., p. 23.

This proved to be optimistic, partly due to the bad going and partly to the vagueness of our Fur guides, and it was close on 7.0 a.m. before some wisps of smoke in a valley warned us that we were almost on top of the quarry. The camp itself was invisible among the trees; not a sound of alarm could be heard, and there appeared to be no sentries on watch. The machine guns were quickly dismounted and a spray of bullets round the camp fires was the first announcement of our arrival. By the time we got down the slope and across a steep *khor,* the camp was empty and small parties could be seen bolting on horseback or foot in various directions.

Collecting a few men (our 'cavalry' were not all very clever at negotiating the *khor* and the friendlies were more interested in the camp loot than in battle) Huddleston dashed after what looked the best dressed party just disappearing round a hill. A few shots were exchanged from ridge to ridge, and after about the third rise we came on a thick-built form, with a strong and dignified face marred only by cruel, sensuous lips, with a bullet hole drilled through the centre of his forehead. It was Ali Dinar. Beside him lay his son Mohammed Fadl, wounded in the leg, while two other sons, Hussein and Seif El Din, and Hasan Sabil, the court chamberlain, stood by stoically awaiting what fate might bring.

## 28  SIR JOHN MAFFEY
## BRITISH RULE IN THE SUDAN

*In 1924 the White Flag League was founded by Ali Abd al-Latif for the purpose of driving the British from the Sudan and uniting Egypt and the Sudan under the Egyptian monarchy. In June the White Flag League demonstrated and Abd al-Latif was arrested. In August the cadets of the military school demonstrated in Khartoum. In November, after the assassination of Sir Lee Stack, Governor General of the Sudan, the Eleventh Sudanese Battalion mutinied in Cairo and was annihilated by British artillery. Although crushed, the Sudanese revolt brought a conservative reaction on the part of the British rulers. The overwhelming number of Sudanese tribesmen and leaders remained steadfastly loyal. The British repaid this devotion with confidence, but they viewed with alarm the new class of Western-educated Sudanese that had sympathized with the rebellion. To check the Sudanese élite, whose liberalism could not be reconciled with the authoritarianism of imperial rule, the British sought to enlist the traditional tribal authorities in the task of governing and isolating the élite. Such a policy coincided with the colonial policy of indirect rule, which was then being hailed as the key to stable advancement of dependent peoples. Sir John Maffey (1877–1969) served in the Indian civil service from 1899 to 1924 and was Governor General of the Sudan from 1926 until 1933, when he became Permanent Undersecretary of State for the Colonies. He was made first Baron of Rugby in 1947.*

From Sir John Maffey, *Minute by His Excellency the Governor General,* January 1, 1927 (Sudan Gov't Archives, Civil Secretary's Archives, January 9, 1933). Reprinted by permission of the Ministry of Interior.

The granting of powers to native magistrates and sheikhs is more in keeping with the prime principle [devolution of authority to tribal chiefs], but here again unless such machinery stands on a true native and traditional basis it is off the main drive. Advisory Councils cropped up as a possible means to our end but the proposal was not well received and I think there were good grounds for hesitation. Later on in certain intelligentsia areas, when we have made the Sudan safe for autocracy, such Councils may be innocuous or even desirable. Also Advisory Councils to Chiefs would be in keeping with the broad principle. Otherwise Advisory Councils contain the seeds of grave danger and eventually present a free platform for capture by a pushful intelligentsia.

If the encouragement of native authority in the true sense of the Milner formula is our accepted policy, before old traditions die we ought to get on with the extension and expansion in every direction, thereby sterilizing and localising the political germs which must spread from the lower Nile into Khartoum.

Under the impulse of new ideas and with the rise of a new generation, old traditions may pass away with astonishing rapidity. It is advisable to fortify them while the memories of Mahdism [revolt and control of the Sudan by the Mahdists, 1885–1898—ed.] and Omdurman are still vivid and while tribal sanctions are still a living force. The death of two or three veterans in a tribe may constitute a serious break with the past.

Such anxiety on my part may seem far-fetched to those who know the out-lying parts of the Sudan. Perhaps it is, for I realize the wide range of differing conditions. But I have watched an old generation give place to a new one in India and I have seen how easily vague political unrest swept over even backward peoples simply because we had allowed the old forms to crumble away. Yet the native states in India remain safe and secure in the hands of hereditary rulers, loyal to the King Emperor, showing what we might have done if we had followed a different course. We failed to put up a shield between the agitator and the bureaucracy.

Political considerations are still easy in the Sudan. But nothing stands still and in Khartoum we are already in touch with the outposts of new political forces. For a long time the British Administrative Officer in the Sudan has functioned as "Father of the People." In many places he will for a long time so continue. But this cannot last. The bureaucracy must yield either to an autocratic or to a democratic movement and the dice are loaded in favour of the latter. If we desire the former, the British Officer must realize that it is his duty to lay down the role of Father of the People. He must entrust it to the natural leaders of the people whom he must support and influence as occasion requires. In that manner the country will be parcelled out into nicely balanced compartments, protective glands against the septic germs which will inevitably be passed on from the Khartoum of the future.

Failing this armour we shall be involved in a losing fight throughout the length and breadth of the land. . . .

# 29  THE PROBLEM OF THE SOUTHERN SUDAN

## THE ADDIS ABABA AGREEMENT FEBRUARY 27, 1972

*One of the most intractable regional conflicts in Africa has been the civil war in the Sudan. Beginning in August 1955, the Equatorial Corps of the Sudan Army—troops who had been recruited from the local African ethnic groups—mutinied against the Sudan Government, which was dominated by Sudanese Muslims who regarded themselves as part of the Arab world. The mutineers were officially defeated, but many remained deep in the illimitable bush of the Southern Sudan. Lacking sophisticated leadership, the Southern Sudanese insurgents were regarded by their northern countrymen as bandits. The northerners failed to appreciate the many grievances of the Southern Sudanese people who, despite their own ethnic rivalries and political divisiveness, were united in seeking a greater determination in their own affairs. The first parliamentary regime (1956–1958) and the military regime of General Ibrahim Abboud (1958–1964) were not only determined to maintain the territorial integrity of the Sudan, but also to press Islam and Arabization upon the animist and Christian African Southern Sudanese.*

*With every passing year the Southern élite became increasingly more acute and articulate about their grievances, as they acquired education, often abroad, and grew militarily more formidable through the creation of an organized guerilla movement known as the Anya-Nya. Indeed, the "Southern Problem," as it came to be known, not only brought down the government of General Abboud, but also that of its democratically elected successor (1965–1969). When Colonel Jaafar Numayri seized power in 1969, he realized that an end to the civil war was essential both for the development of the Sudan and to broaden his own base of support. It was not, however, until he had subdued challenges to his regime from the Mahdists on the right and the Communists on the left that he sought peace with the Anya-Nya, the political and military leadership of which had been united under Colonel Joseph Lagu. Appointing Abel Alier, a respected Bor Dinka and lawyer as Minister for Southern Affairs, he initiated with Numayri's encouragement, secret meetings with southern leaders in exile. This led to the famous conference at Addis Ababa in February 1972. Here a negotiated peace was consummated, through the timely intervention of the Ethiopian Emperor Haile Selassie, between the Northern and the Southern Sudanese, granting to the Southerners regional autonomy. The Addis Ababa Agreement was hailed by both the East and West as an example to Africa and the world of how solutions to a protracted military conflict could be achieved through negotiation, compromise, and good will, rather than on the field of battle.*

*Draft Organic Law to Organize Regional Self-Government in the Southern Provinces of the Democratic Republic of the Sudan*

In accordance with the provisions of the Constitution of the Democratic Republic of the Sudan and in realization of the

From Mohamed Omer Beshir, *The Southern Sudan: From Conflict to Peace* (Khartoum: 1975), Appendix B, "The Addis Ababa Agreement on the Problem of the South Sudan: Draft Organic Law to Organize Regional Self-Government in the Provinces of the Democratic Republic of the Sudan," pp. 158–77. Reprinted by permission.

memorable May Revolution Declaration of June 9, 1969, granting the Southern Provinces of the Sudan Regional Self-Government within a united socialist Sudan, and in accordance with the principle of the May Revolution that the Sudanese people participate actively in and supervise the decentralized system of the government of their country, it is hereunder enacted:

*Article 1.* This law shall be called the law for Regional Self-Government in the Southern Provinces. It shall come into force on a date within a period not exceeding thirty days from the date of the Addis Ababa Agreement.

*Article 2.* This law shall be issued as an organic law which cannot be amended except by a three-quarters majority of the People's National Assembly and confirmed by a two-thirds majority in a referendum held in the three Southern Provinces of the Sudan.

## CHAPTER II: DEFINITIONS
*Article 3.*
  (i) 'Constitution' refers to the Republican Order No. 5 or any other basic law replacing or amending it.
  (ii) 'President' means the President of the Democratic Republic of the Sudan.
  (iii) 'Southern Provinces of the Sudan' means the Provinces of Bahr El Ghazal, Equatoria and Upper Nile in accordance with their boundaries as they stood on January 1, 1956, and any other areas that were culturally and geographically a part of the Southern Complex as may be decided by a referendum.
  (iv) 'People's Regional Assembly' refers to the legislative body for the Southern Region of the Sudan.
  (v) 'High Executive Council' refers to the Executive Council appointed by the President on the recommendation of the President of the High Executive Council and such body shall supervise the administration and direct public affairs in the Southern Region of the Sudan.
  (vi) 'President of the High Executive Council' refers to the person appointed by the President on the recommendation of the People's Regional Assembly to lead and supervise the executive organs responsible for the administration of the Southern Provinces.
  (vii) 'People's National Assembly' refers to the National Legislative Assembly representing the people of the Sudan in accordance with the constitution.
  (viii) 'Sudanese' refers to any Sudanese citizen as defined by the Sudanese Nationality Act 1957 and any amendments thereof.

## CHAPTER III
*Article 4.* The Provinces of Bahr El Ghazal, Equatoria and Upper Nile as defined in Article 3 (iii) shall constitute a self-governing Region within the Democratic Republic of the Sudan and shall be known as the Southern Region.

*Article 5.* The Southern Region shall have legislative and executive organs, the functions and powers of which are defined by this law.

*Article 6.* Arabic shall be the official language for the Sudan and English the principal language for the Southern Region without prejudice to the use of any other language or languages which may serve a practical necessity for the efficient and expeditious discharge of executive and administrative functions of the Region.

## CHAPTER IV
*Article 7.* Neither the People's Regional Assembly nor the High Executive Council shall legislate or exercise any powers on matters of national nature which are:
  (i) National Defence
  (ii) External Affairs
  (iii) Currency and Coinage
  (iv) Air and Inter-Regional River Transport
  (v) Communications and Telecommunications
  (vi) Customs and Foreign Trade except for border trade and certain

commodities which the Regional Government may specify with the approval of the Central Government.

(vii) Nationality and Immigration (Emigration)

(viii) Planning for Economic and Social Development

(ix) Educational Planning

(x) Public-Audit.

## CHAPTER V: LEGISLATURE

*Article 8.* Regional Legislation in the Southern Region is exercised by a People's Regional Assembly elected by Sudanese Citizens resident in the Southern Region. The constitution and conditions of membership of the Assembly shall be determined by law.

*Article 9.* Members of the People's Regional Assembly shall be elected by direct secret ballot.

*Article 10.*

(i) For the First Assembly the President may appoint additional members to the People's Regional Assembly where conditions for elections are not conducive to such elections as stipulated in Article 9, provided that such appointed members shall not exceed one-quarter of the Assembly.

(ii) The People's Regional Assembly shall regulate the conduct of its business in accordance with rules of procedures to be laid down by the said Assembly during its first sitting.

(iii) The People's Regional Assembly shall elect one of its members as a speaker, provided that the first sitting shall be presided over by the Interim President of the High Executive Council.

*Article 11.* The People's Regional Assem-

bly shall legislate for the preservation of public order, internal security, efficient administration and the development of the Southern Region in cultural, economic and social fields and in particular in the following:—

(i) Promotion and utilization of Regional financial resources for the development and administration of the Southern Region.

(ii) Organization of the machinery for Regional and Local Administration.

(iii) Legislation on traditional law and custom within the framework of National Law.

(iv) Establishment, maintenance and administration of prisons and reformatory institutions.

(v) Establishment, maintenance and administration of Public Schools at all levels in accordance with National Plans for education and economic and social development.

(vi) Promotion of local languages and cultures.

(vii) Town and village planning and the construction of roads in accordance with National Plans and programmes.

(viii) Promotion of trade; establishment of local industries and markets; issue of traders' licenses and formation of co-operative societies.

(ix) Establishment, maintenance and administration of public hospitals.

(x) Administration of environmental health services; maternity care; child welfare; supervision of markets; combat of epidemic diseases; training of medical assistants and rural midwives; establishment of health centres, dispensaries and dressing stations.

(xi) Promotion of animal health; control of epidemics and improvement of animal production and trade.

(xii) Promotion of tourism.

(xiii) Establishment of zoological gardens, museums, organizations of trade and cultural exhibitions.

(xiv) Mining and quarrying without prejudice to the right of the Central Government in the event of the discovery of natural gas and minerals.

(xv) Recruitment for, organization and administration of Police and Prison services in accordance with the national policy and standards.

(xvi) Land use in accordance with national laws and plans.

(xvii) Control and prevention of pests and plant diseases.

(xviii) Development, utilization, and protection of forests, crops and pastures in accordance with national laws.

(xix) Promotion and encouragement of self-help programmes.

(xx) All other matters delegated by the President or the People's National Assembly for legislation.

*Article 12.* The People's National Assembly may call for facts and information concerning the conduct of administration in the Southern Region.

*Article 13.*

(i) The People's Regional Assembly may, by a three-quarters majority and for specified reasons relating to public interest, request the President to relieve the President or any member of the High Executive Council from office. The President shall accede to such request.

(ii) In case of vacancy, relief or resignation of the President of the High Executive Council, the entire body shall be considered as having automatically resigned.

*Article 14.* The People's Regional Assembly may, by a two-thirds majority, request

the President to postpone the coming into force of any law which, in the view of the members, adversely affects the welfare and interests of the citizens of the Southern Region. The President may, if he thinks fit, accede to such request.

*Article 15.*

(i) The People's Regional Assembly may, by a majority of its members, request the President to withdraw any Bill presented to the People's National Assembly which in their view affects adversely the welfare, rights or interests of the citizens in the Southern Region, pending communication of the views of the People's Regional Assembly.

(ii) If the President accedes to such request, the People's Regional Assembly shall present its views within 15 days from the date of accession to the request.

(iii) The President shall communicate any such views to the People's National Assembly together with his own observations if he deems necessary.

*Article 16.* The People's National Assembly shall communicate all Bills and Acts to the People's Regional Assembly for their information. The People's Regional Assembly shall act similarly.

## CHAPTER VI: THE EXECUTIVE

*Article 17.* The Regional Executive Authority is vested in a High Executive Council which acts on behalf of the President.

*Article 18.* The High Executive Council shall specify the duties of the various departments in the Southern Region provided that on matters relating to Central Government Agencies it shall act with the approval of the President.

*Article 19.* The President of the High Executive Council shall be appointed and relieved of office by the President on the recommendation of the People's Regional Assembly.

*Article 20.* The High Executive Council shall be composed of members appointed and relieved of office by the President on the recommendation of the President of the High Executive Council.

*Article 21.* The President of the High Executive Council and its members are responsible to the President and to the People's Regional Assembly for efficient administration in the Southern Region. They shall take an oath of office before the President.

*Article 22.* The President and members of the High Executive Council may attend meetings of the People's Regional Assembly and participate in its deliberations without the right to vote, unless they are also members of the People's Regional Assembly.

## CHAPTER VII
*Article 23.* The President shall from time to time regulate the relationship between the High Executive Council and the central ministries.

*Article 24.* The High Executive Council may initiate laws for the creation of a Regional Public Service. These laws shall specify the terms and conditions of service for the Regional Public Service.

## CHAPTER VIII: FINANCE
*Article 25.* The People's Regional Assembly may levy Regional duties and taxes in addition to National and Local duties and taxes. It may issue legislation and orders to guarantee the collection of all public monies at different levels.

*(a)* The source of revenue of the Southern Region shall consist of the following:—
  (i) Direct and indirect regional taxes.
  (ii) Contributions from People's Local Government Councils.
  (iii) Revenue from commercial, industrial and agricultural projects in the Region in accordance with the National Plan.
  (iv) Funds from the National Treasury for established services.
  (v) Funds voted by the People's National Assembly in accordance with the requirements of the Region.
  (vi) The Special Development Budget for the South as presented by the People's Regional Assembly for the acceleration of economic and social advancement of the Southern Region as envisaged in the declaration of June 9, 1968.
  (vii) See Appendix B.
  (viii) Any other sources.

*(b)* The Regional Executive Council shall prepare a budget to meet the expenditure of regional services, security, administration, and development in accordance with national plans and programmes and shall submit it to the People's Regional Assembly for approval.

## CHAPTER IX: OTHER PROVISIONS
*Article 27.*
  (i) Citizens of the Southern Region shall constitute a sizeable proportion of the People's Armed Forces in such reasonable numbers as will correspond to the population of the region.
  (ii) The use of the People's Armed Forces within the Region and outside the framework of national defence shall be controlled by the President on the advice of the

President of the High Executive Council.

(iii) Temporary arrangements for the composition of units of the People's Armed Forces in the Southern Region are provided for in the Protocol on Interim Arrangements.

*Article 28.* The President may veto any Bill which he deems contrary to the Provisions of the National Constitution provided the People's Regional Assembly, after receiving the President's views, may reintroduce the Bill.

*Article 29.* The President and members of the High Executive Council may initiate laws in the People's Regional Assembly.

Article 30. Any member of the People's Regional Assembly may initiate any law provided that financial Bills shall not be presented without sufficient notice to the President of the High Executive Council.

*Article 31.* The People's Regional Assembly shall strive to consolidate the unity of the Sudan and respect the spirit of the National Constitution.

*Article 32.* All citizens are guaranteed freedom of movement in and out of the Southern Region, provided restriction or prohibition of movement may be imposed on a named citizen or citizens solely on grounds of public health and order.

*Article 33.*

(i) All citizens resident in the Southern Region are guaranteed equal opportunity of education, employment, commerce and the practice of any profession.

(ii) No law may adversely affect the rights of citizens enumerated in the previous item on the basis of race, tribal origin, religion, place of birth, or sex.

*Article 34.* Juba shall be the Capital of the Southern Region and the seat of the Regional Executive and Legislature.

## APPENDIX A: FUNDAMENTAL RIGHTS AND FREEDOMS

The following should be guaranteed by the Constitution of the Democratic Republic of the Sudan.

1. A citizen should not be deprived of his citizenship.
2. Equality of citizens.
   (i) All citizens, without distinction based on race, national origin, birth, language, sex, economic or social status, should have equal rights and duties before the law.
   (ii) All persons should be equal before the courts of law and should have the right to institute legal proceedings in order to remove any injustice or declare any right in an open court without delay prejudicing their interests.
3. Personal liberty.
   (i) Penal liability should be personal. Any kind of collective punishment should be prohibited.
   (ii) The accused should be presumed innocent until proved guilty.
   (iii) Retrospective penal legislation and punishment should be prohibited.
   (iv) The right of the accused to defend himself personally or through an agent should be guaranteed.
   (v) No person should be arrested, detained or imprisoned except in accordance with the due process of law, and no person should remain in custody or detention for more than twenty-four hours without judicial order.

(vi) No accused person should be subjected to inducement, intimidation or torture in order to extract evidence from him whether in his favour or against him or against any other person, and no humiliating punishment should be inflicted on any convicted person.

4. Freedom of Religion and Conscience.

(i) Every person should enjoy freedom of religious opinion and of conscience and the right to profess them publicly and privately and to establish religious institutions subject to reasonable limitations in favour of morality, health or public order as prescribed by law.

(ii) Parents and guardians should be guaranteed the right to educate their children and those under their care in accordance with the religion of their choice.

5. Protection of labour.

(i) Forced and compulsory labour of any kind should be prohibited except when ordered for military or civil necessity or pursuant to penal punishment prescribed by law.

(ii) The right to equal pay for equal work should be guaranteed.

6. Freedom of minority to use their languages and develop their culture should be guaranteed.

## APPENDIX B: DRAFT ORDINANCE ON ITEMS OF REVENUE AND GRANTS-IN-AID FOR THE SOUTHERN REGION

1. Profits accruing to the Central Government as a result of exporting products of the Southern Region.

2. Business Profit Tax of the Southern Region that are at present in the central list of the Ministry of Treasury.

3. Excise Duties on alcoholic beverages and spirits consumed in the Southern Region.

4. Profits on sugar consumed in the Southern Region.

5. Royalties on forest products of the Southern Region.

6. Royalties on leaf Tobacco and Cigarettes.

7. Taxation on property other than that provided in the Rates Ordinance.

8. Taxes and Rates on Central and Local Government Projects (5 per cent of net profits of factories, cooperative societies, agricultural enterprises and cinemas).

9. Revenue accruing from Central Government activities in the Southern Region provided the Region shall bear maintenance expenses e.g., Post Office revenue, land sales, sale of forms and documents, stamp duties and any other item to be specified from time to time.

10. Licences other than those provided for in the People's Local Government Act, 1971.

11. Special Development Tax to be paid by Residents in the Southern Region the rate of which should be decided by the People's Regional Assembly.

12. Income Tax collected from officials and employees serving in the Southern Region both in the local and national civil services as well as in the Army, Police and Prisons, Judiciary, and Political Establishment.

13. Corporation Tax on any factory and/or agricultural project established in the Region but not run by the Regional Government (5 per cent of the initial cost).

14. Contributions from the Central Government for the encouragement of construction and development; for every agricultural project, industrial project and trading enterprise (20 per cent of the initial cost as assessed by the Central Government).

15. New Social Service Projects to be

established by the Region or any of its Local Government units, and for which funds are allocated, shall receive grants from the National Treasury in the following manner:

Education institutions, 20 per cent of expenses

Trunk and through Roads and Bridges, 25 per cent of expenses

Relief and Social amenities, 15 per cent of expenses

Tourist attraction projects, 25 per cent of expenses

Security, 15 per cent of expenses

Grants for Post Secondary and University education within the Sudan, 20 per cent of grants, outside the Sudan 30 per cent of grants

Contribution for Research, Scientific Advancement, and Cultural Activities, 25 per cent of expenses.

## AGREEMENT ON THE CEASE-FIRE IN THE SOUTHERN REGION

*Article 1.* This Agreement shall come into force on the date and time specified for the ratification of the Addis Ababa Agreement.

*Article 2.* There will be an end to all military operations and to all armed actions in the Southern Region from the time of cease-fire.

*Article 3.* All combat forces shall remain in the area under their control at the time of the cease-fire.

*Article 4.* Both parties agree to forbid any individual or collective acts of violence.

Any underground activities contrary to public order shall cease.

*Article 5.* Movements of individual

members of both combat forces outside the areas under their control shall be allowed only if these individuals are unarmed and authorized by their respective authorities. The plans for stationing troops from the National Army shall be such as to avoid any contact between them and the Southern Sudan Liberation Movement combat forces.

*Article 6.* A Joint Commission is hereby created for the implementation of all questions related to the cease-fire including repatriation of refugees. The Joint Commission shall include members from all the countries bordering on the Southern Region as well as representatives of the International Committee of the Red Cross, World Council of Churches, All Africa Conference of Churches and United Nations High Commissioner for Refugees.

*Article 7.* The Joint Commission shall propose all measures to be undertaken by both parties in dealing with all incidents after a full inquiry on the spot.

*Article 8.* Each party shall be represented on the Joint Commission by one senior military officer and a maximum of five other members.

*Article 9.* The headquarters of the Joint Commission shall be located in Juba with provincial branches in Juba, Malakal and Wau.

*Article 10.* The Joint Commission shall appoint local commissions in various centres of the Southern Region composed of two members from each party.

## PROTOCOLS ON INTERIM ARRANGEMENTS

## CHAPTER I: INTERIM ADMINISTRATIVE ARRANGEMENTS
*(Political, Local Government and Civil Service)*

*Article 1.* The President of the Democratic Republic of the Sudan shall, in consultation with the Southern Sudan Liberation Movement (S.S.L.M.) and branches of the Sudanese Socialist Union in the Southern Region, appoint the President and members of an Interim High Executive Council.

*Article 2.* The Interim High Executive Council shall consist of the President and other members with portfolios in:

(a) Finance and Economic Planning.
(b) Education.
(c) Information, Culture and Tourism.
(d) Communication and Transport.
(e) Agriculture, Animal Production and Fisheries.
(f) Public Health.
(g) Regional Administration (Local Government, Legal Affairs, Police and Prisons).
(h) Housing, Public Works and Utilities.
(i) Natural Resources and Rural Development (Land Use, Rural Water Supply, Forestry and Cooperatives).
(j) Public Service and Labour.
(k) Minerals and Industry, Trade and Supply.

*Article 3.* The Interim High Executive Council shall, in accordance with national laws, establish a Regional Civil Service subject to ratification by the People's Regional Assembly.

*Article 4.* The President shall, in consultation with the Interim High Executive Council, determine the date for the election to the People's Regional Assembly, and the Interim High Executive Council shall make arrangements for the setting up of this Assembly.

*Article 5.* In order to facilitate the placement in and appointment to both central and regional institutions, the Southern Sudan Liberation Movement shall compile and communicate lists of citizens of the Southern Region outside the Sudan in accordance with details to be supplied by the Ministry of Public Service and Administrative Reform.

*Article 6.* The Interim High Executive Council and the Ministry of Public Service and Administrative Reform shall undertake to provide necessary financial allocations with effect from the 1972–73 Budget for such placements and appointments.

*Article 7.* The Mandate of the Interim High Executive Council shall not exceed a period of 18 months.

**CHAPTER II: TEMPORARY ARRANGEMENTS FOR THE COMPOSITION OF UNITS OF THE PEOPLE'S ARMED FORCES IN THE SOUTHERN REGION**

*Article 1.* These arrangements shall remain in force for a period of five years subject to revision by the President on the request of the President of the High Executive Council acting with the consent of the People's Regional Assembly.

*Article 2.* The People's Armed Forces in the Southern Region shall consist of a national force called the Southern Command composed of 12,000 officers and men of whom 6,000 shall be citizens from the Region and the other 6,000 from outside the Region.

*Article 3.* The recruitment and integration of citizens from the Southern Region within the aforementioned Forces shall be determined by a Joint Military Commission taking into account the need for initial separate deployment of troops with a view to achieve smooth integration in the national force. The Commission shall ensure that this deployment shall be such that an atmosphere of peace and confidence shall prevail in the Southern Region.

*Article 4.* The Joint Military Commission shall be composed of three senior military officers from each side. Decisions of the Joint Military Commission shall be taken unanimously. In case of disagreement such matters shall be referred to the respective authorities.

## CHAPTER III: AMNESTY AND JUDICIAL ARRANGEMENTS

*Article 1.* No action or other legal proceedings whatsoever, civil or criminal, shall be instituted against any person in any court of law for or on account of any act or matter done inside or outside the Sudan as from the 18th day of August 1955, if such act or matter was done in connection with mutiny, rebellion or sedition in the Southern Region.

*Article 2.* If a civil suit in relation to any acts or matters referred to in Article 1 is instituted before or after the date of ratification of the Addis Ababa Agreement such a suit shall be discharged and made null and void.

Article 3. All persons serving terms of imprisonment or held in detention in respect of offences herein before specified in Article 1 shall be discharged or released within 15 days from the date of ratification of the Addis Ababa Agreement.

*Article 4.* The Joint Cease-Fire Commission shall keep a register of all civilian returnees, which register shall serve to certify that the persons therein named are considered indemnified within the meaning of this Agreement provided that the Commission may delegate such power to the Diplomatic Missions of the Democratic Republic of the Sudan in the case of citizens from the Southern Region living abroad and to whom the provisions of this Agreement apply.

*Article 5.* In the case of armed returnees or those belonging to combat forces the Joint Military Commission shall keep a similar register of those persons who shall be treated in the same manner as provided for in Article 4.

*Article 6.* Notwithstanding the provisions of Articles 4 and 5 above a Special Tribunal with ad hoc judicial powers shall be established to examine and decide on those cases which in the estimation of the authorities do not meet the conditions for amnesty specified in Article 1 of this Agreement. The Special Tribunal shall be composed of a President appointed by the President of the Republic and not more than four members named by the Cease-Fire Commission.

*Article 7.* Cases referred to in Article 6 shall be brought to the attention of the Special Tribunal by request of the Minister of Justice.

*Article 8.* The Amnesty Provisions contained in this agreement as well as the powers of the Special Tribunal shall remain in force until such time as the President after consultation with the commissions referred to in this Agreement, decide that they have fulfilled their functions.

## CHAPTER IV: REPATRIATION AND RESETTLEMENT COMMISSION
### 1. *Repatriation*

*Article 1.* There shall be established a Special Commission inside and where required outside the Southern Region charged with the responsibility of taking all administrative and other measures as may be necessary in order to repatriate all citizens from the Southern Region who today are residing in other countries and especially in the neighbouring countries.

The headquarters of the Commission shall be in Juba.

*Article 2.* The Commission shall be composed of at least three members including one representative of the Central Government, one representative of the Southern Region and one representative of the U.N. High Commissioner for Refugees. For those commissions operating outside the Sudan, a representative of the host Government shall be included, plus the Central Government representative who shall be the Ambassador of the Sudan or his representative.

*Article 3.* The control of repatriation at the borders shall be assumed by the competent border authorities in co-operation with the representatives of the Resettlement Commission.

*Article 4.* The repatriation commission shall work very closely with the Commission for Relief and Resettlement to ensure that the operation and timing of the returning of refugees from across the borders is adequately co-ordinated.

## II. *Resettlement*

*Article 1.* There shall be established a Special Commission for Relief and Resettlement under the President of the Interim High Executive Council with headquarters in Juba and provincial branches in Juba, Malakal and Wau. The Commission, its branches and whatever units it may deem fit to create in other localities in order to facilitate its functions, shall be responsible for co-ordination and implementation of all relief services and planning related to Resettlement and Rehabilitation of all returnees, that is:

(a) Refugees from neighbouring countries;
(b) Displaced persons resident in the main centres of the Southern Region and other parts of the Sudan;
(c) Displaced persons including residual Anya Nya personnel and supporters in the bush;
(d) Handicapped and orphans.

*Article 2.* Although resettlement and rehabilitation of refugees and displaced persons is administratively the responsibility of the Regional Government the present conditions in the Southern Region dictate that efforts of the whole nation of the Sudan and International Organizations should be pooled to help and rehabilitate persons affected by the conflict. The Relief and Resettlement Commission shall co-ordinate activities and resources of the Organizations within the country.

*Article 3.* The first priority shall be the resettlement of displaced persons within the Sudan in the following order:
(a) Persons presently residing in overcrowded centres in the Southern Region, and persons desirous to return to their original areas and homes;
(b) Persons returning from the bush including Anya Nya Supporters;
(c) Handicapped persons and orphans.

*Article 4.* The second priority shall be given to returnees from the neighbouring and other countries according to an agreed plan. This plan shall provide for:
(a) Adequate reception centres with facilities for shelter, food supplies, medicine and medicaments;
(b) Transportation to permanent resettlement villages or places of origin;
(c) Materials and equipment.

*Article 5.* The Relief and Resettlement Commission shall:
(a) Appeal to international organizations and voluntary agencies to continue assistance for students already under their support particularly for students in secondary schools and higher institutions until appropriate arrangements are made for their repatriation;
(b) Compile adequate information on

students and persons in need of financial support from the Sudan Government.

*Article 6.* The Relief and Resettlement Commission shall arrange for the education of all returnees who were attending primary schools.

This Agreement is hereby concluded on this twenty-seventh day of the month of February in the year one thousand nine hundred and seventy-two, A.D., in this City, Addis Ababa, Ethiopia, between the Government of the Democratic Republic of the Sudan on the one hand and the Southern Sudan Liberation Movement on the other. It shall come into force on the date and hour fixed for its ratification by the President of the Democratic Republic of the Sudan and the Leader of the Southern Sudan Liberation Movement. It shall be ratified by the said two Leaders in person or through their respective authorised Representatives, in this City, Addis Ababa, Ethiopia, at the twelfth hour at noon, on the twelfth day of the month of March, in the year one thousand nine hundred and seventy-two, A.D.

In witness whereof, We the Representatives of the Government of the Democratic Republic of the Sudan and the Representatives of the Southern Sudan Liberation Movement hereby append our signatures in the presence of the Representative of His Imperial Majesty the Emperor of Ethiopia and the Representatives of the World Council of Churches, the All Africa Conference of Churches, and the Sudan Council of Churches.

FOR THE GOVERNMENT OF THE DEMOCRATIC REPUBLIC OF THE SUDAN

1. Abel Alier-Wal Kuai, *Vice-President and Minister of State for Southern Affairs*

2. Dr. Mansour Khalid, *Minister for Foreign Affairs*
3. Dr. Gaafar Mohamed Ali Bakheit, *Minister for Local Government*
4. Major-General Mohamed Al Baghir Ahmed, *Minister of Interior*
5. Abdel Rahman Abdalla, *Minister of Public Service and Administrative Reform*
6. Brigadier Mirghani Suleiman
7. Colonel Kamal Abashar.

FOR THE SOUTHERN SUDAN LIBERATION

MOVEMENT

1. Ezboni Mondiri Gwonza, *Leader of the Delegation*
2. Dr. Lawrence Wol Wol, *Secretary of the Delegation*
3. Mading de Garang, *Spokesman of the Delegation*
4. Colonel Frederick Brian Maggot, *Special Military Representative*
5. Oliver Batali Albino, *Member*
6. Angelo Voga Morjan, *Member*
7. Rev. Paul Puot, *Member*
8. Job Adier de Jok, *Member*

WITNESSES

1. Nabiyelul Kifle, *Representative of His Imperial Majesty, the Emperor of Ethiopia*
2. Leopoldo J. Niilus, *Representative of the World Council of Churches*
3. Kodwo E. Ankrah, *Representative of the World Council of Churches*
4. Burgess Carr, *General Secretary All Africa Conference of Churches*
5. Samuel Athi Bwogo, *Representative of Sudan Council of Churches*

ATTESTATION

I attest that these signatures are genuine and true

BURGESS CARR, *Moderator*

# 30   JOHN GARANG DE MABIOR
## THE GENESIS OF THE SUDAN PEOPLE'S
## LIBERATION MOVEMENT (SPLM), 1983

*On May 16, 1983, Colonel John Garang led the men of the 105th Battalion of the Sudan Army stationed at Bor into the bush of the Upper Nile Province, Southern Sudan, in rebellion against the government of President Numayri. Born in Wangkulei, north of Bor, on June 23, 1945, Garang received a high-school diploma from Magamba Secondary School in Tanzania in 1964, and a B.A. degree from Grinnell College in Iowa in 1969. He returned to the Sudan and served briefly with the Anya-Nya; after its integration with the Sudan Army following the signing of the Addis Ababa Agreement, Garang was commissioned as a captain. He attended the U.S. Infantry School at Fort Benning, Georgia, and, after a tour of duty in the Sudan, returned to the United States in November 1977 to take up his graduate studies at Iowa State University, from which he graduated with a Ph.D. degree in economics in December 1981.*

*Garang had many grievances against Numayri. They were widely shared, not only by his fellow Africans in the Southern Sudan, but by many Arabs in the North. Numayri had personally destroyed the Addis Ababa Agreement of 1972, which had granted regional autonomy to the South; unilaterally intervened to dissolve the Southern regional government; sought to redefine the boundaries of the Southern provinces to include oil discoveries in the Northern Sudan; ordered the transfer to the North of the Africans in the Sudan Army stationed in their Southern homelands; and finally, in September 1983, imposed the Sharia law of Islam upon the Sudan, to be binding on all citizens, whether Muslim, Christian, or animist. The last was the final chapter in a liturgy of discontent. In July 1983, Garang officially founded the Sudan People's Liberation Movement (SPLM) and the Sudan People's Liberation Army (SPLA), with the publication of the SPLM Manifesto defining its objectives. Garang's leadership did not go unchallenged, but by March 1984, he had emerged as the uncontested leader of the armed revolution. This revolt was not simply against the person of President Numayri, who was forced from power in March 1985 by a populist movement in Khartoum, but also against the whole system of government Numayri and his supporters represented, and which the notables of the great sectarian families inherited upon the President's fall from power.*

*When John Garang accepted the invitation to lead the mutineers, he was not an unknown junior officer, but a well-respected colonel attached to the headquarters of the Sudan Army at Khartoum. Nor was his dissaffection parochial or Southern. From the beginning he espoused a new democratic, federated governemnt for the whole Sudan, not just the South—a policy which he has consistently maintained to the present day.*

Nationalists, Patriots, Comrades, Fellow Countrymen,

The history of the Sudanese people from time immemorial has been the struggle of the masses of the people against internal and external oppression. The oppressor has time and again em-

From John Garang, *John Garang Speaks*, edited and introduced by Mansour Khalid, (London: KPI Ltd., 1987), pp. 19–25. Reprinted by permission.

ployed various policies and methods of destroying or weakening the just struggle of our people, including the most notorious policy of "divide and rule". To this end the oppressor has divided the Sudanese people into Northerners and Southerners; Westerners and Easterners, Halfawin and the so-called Awlad el Balad who have hitherto wielded political power in Khartoum; while in the South, people have been politicized along tribal lines resulting in such ridiculous slogans as "Dinka Unity", "Great Equatoria", "Bari Speakers", "Luo Unity" and so forth.

The oppressor has also divided us into Muslims and Christians, and into Arabs and Africans. Tomorrow when these divisions become outdated, the oppressor will contrive other ingenious schemes for keeping the Sudanese people and their just struggle divided and weak.

It was therefore natural that secessionist movements and chauvinistic tendencies developed in different periods in different areas of the Sudan thereby jeopardizing the unity of the people and prolonging their suffering and struggle. The Sudan People's Liberation Army (SPLA) has been founded to spearhead armed resistance against Nimeiri's one-man system dictatorship and to organize the whole Sudanese people under the Sudan People's Liberation Movement (SPLM), through revolutionary protracted armed struggle waged by the SPLA and political mass support.

The neo-colonial system that has developed in our country since 1956 and was represented by Nimeirism since 1969 is a regime in which a few people have amassed great wealth at the expense of the majority. This injustice has resulted in profound crises and distortions in our economy, politics, ethics and even religion which Nimeiri has perverted into an article of trade. A few of the system crisis problems include:

(a) The general fall in production and productivity especially of essential commodities such as dura, wheat and sugar

(b) The mounting rate of unemployment that has resulted in social instability and emigration

(c) Hy-per-inflation, currency problems and foreign indebtedness amounting to US10 billion dollars and

the consequent entrenchment of dependency relations

(d) An acute inadequacy and deterioration of social services in the whole country and particularly in rural areas

(e) The general social and moral bankruptcy that is reflected in the institutionalisation of corruption and bribery, the daily fear by any Sudanese of being apprehended by agents of the State Security Organization, and the absurd institution of "Kacha".[1]

These crises and many others have plunged the overwhelming majority of the people throughout the country into an abysmal ocean of poverty and suffering from which no land can be sighted unless and until this one-man system of Nimeiri that threatens to drown the nation is destroyed in its entirety.

The general exploitation, oppression and neglect of the Sudanese people by successive Khartoum clique regimes took peculiar forms in the Southern third of our country. Firstly, racial and religious segration was much more intensely meted out and felt in Southern Sudan than in other parts of the country. Secondly, development plans in the South such as the Melut and Mongalla sugar industries, Tonj Kengaf, Wau Brewery, Nzara and Mongalla textiles etc. remained on paper as development funds were embezzled in Khartoum while Southern Regional Governments watched on in impotence or participated in the looting. Development Schemes that were implemented in the South were those that did not benefit the local population, such as the extraction of oil from Bentiu via the Chevron projects

[1] Kacha is the forcible bundling of thousands of young men and women, mainly Southerners and Westerners, from the Khartoum market place and the shanty towns around it to be sent back to their ancestral homes in the distant regions, of the Southern Sudan, Kordofan, and Darfor.

and extraction of water via the Jonglei Canal. Socio-political neglect, economic backwardness and general under-development therefore became intensified and exacerbated in the South.

The burden and incidence of neglect and oppression by successive Khartoum clique regimes has traditionally fallen more on the South than on other parts of the country. Under these circumstances the marginal cost of rebellion in the South became very small, zero or negative; that is, in the South it pays to rebel. Nevertheless, your mad President Nimeiri and his habitually lying Vice-President Omer Mohammed al Tayeb have openly aggressed and agitated Southern Sudanese into rebellion and civil war. The following provocations precipitated the renewal of civil war in the Sudan:

(a) Nimeiri systematically started to dismantle his Addis Ababa Agreement. He singlehandedly and unconstitutionally dissolved Southern Assemblies and Governments one after the other in 1980, 1981 and 1983.

(b) He signed an unconstitutional Integration Treaty with Egypt to protect himself against insurrection in the South or any other parts of the Sudan.

(c) He unconstitutionally and unsuccessfully tried to change the boundaries of the Southern Region via his 1980 People's Regional Government Act. In this way he wanted to deprive the South of mineral rich or prime agricultural land such as Hofrat el Nahas, Kafia Kingi, Northern Upper Nile, Bentiu etc. *Natural resources, wherever they are found in the Sudan, belong to the whole Sudanese people.* The location of these resources in the South should not register any negative connotation and suspicions in the mind of a true Sudanese patriot and nationalist. But Nimeiri felt sufficiently agitated to the extent of at-

tempting to legislate the formal exclusion of these areas from the South. Such behaviour can only be explained by Nimeiri's halfhearted belief in Sudan unity, his belief in the hegemony of clique chauvinism and his mistrust of South Sudanese.

(d) Again, when Chevron Company discovered oil in 1978 Nimeiri started to talk about oil finds 450 miles southwest of Khartoum instead of telling the truth that the oil was in Bentiu in Southern Sudan and that it belongs to the whole Sudanese people. He continued to hatch more transparent tricks when he talked about carving out his so-called "Unity Province" to include Bentiu, Abyei and Kadugli with himself the "Oil Governor". When this failed he came up with another scheme to build the refinery in Kosti instead of Bentiu. Finally, he ended up deciding that all the oil was to be piped out of the country at Port Sudan against the interest of the Sudanese people whether in the South or the North.

(e) Nimeiri completed the abrogation of his Addis Ababa Agreement by agitating for the division of South Sudan into three mini-regions, consistent with his policy of divide and rule. In this way Nimeiri unilaterally proclaimed redivision of the South in June 1983 to the consternation of even his foreign sympathizers.

(f) In all these provocations there was an important catch for Nimeiri. As the old adage says, thieves and rogues end up outwitting themselves. In 1972 Nimeiri agreed to absorb 6000 Anyanya guerillas into his Army, to be stationed in the South. The absorbed Anyanya had opposed Nimeiri's policies since 1972 and they were increasingly becoming an obstacle to his schemes. He therefore decided to crush the absorbed Anyanya forces by summarily transferring them to the North where they would be neutralized. In this Nimeiri was an utter failure. He failed to deceive the South into abandoning armed resistance.

Nimeiri's provocations, recklessness and stupidities in the South resulted in the Akobo mutiny of 1975 which triggered off the Anyanya II Movement; in the Wau mutiny of 1976; in numerous grenade-throwing incidents in which lives were lost; in the Ariath incident of January 1983; the Bor, Pibor and Fashalla clashes of May 1983; in the Malual clash of the same month; the Ayod and Waat clashes of June and July 1983; in the Boma capture of hostages; in the guerilla warfare in Abyei and Bentiu and, finally, in the birth of the Sudan People's Liberation Army and the Sudan People's Liberation Movement as the most advanced forms of armed and political struggle in the Sudan.

From all that I have said, it is clear that a vanguard movement for the liberation of the whole Sudanese people had to have its origins in the South Sudan. Any armed struggle must have as its point of departure the immediate and genuine needs and demands of the masses of the people. This was the case in the South in 1955. At that time the armed struggle was led by reactionaries and it ended in a reactionary revolution in 1972. Again, such was the case in the South in 1975 and again it was led by reactionaries in the form of Anyanya II. Again, such was the case in the South in 1983, but this time the insurrection is led by revolutionaries fighting as the vanguard of the whole Sudanese people. Because of the oneness of the Sudanese people and the unity and integrity of Sudan, the armed struggle in the South must of necessity eventually engulf the whole Sudan.

The anarchy in production, the separatist tendencies in the various regions of

our beloved country, the moral decay and all the ills that I have enumerated *can only be solved within the context of a united Sudan under a socialist system that affords democratic and human rights to all nationalities and guarantees freedom to all religions, beliefs and outlooks.* A united and Socialist Sudan can be achieved only through protracted revolutionary armed struggle. Peaceful struggle has always been met with ruthless suppression and callous killing of our beloved people.

In pursuance of protracted revolutionary armed struggle the SPLA has been organised and has already achieved significant victories. In the first offensive after *16 May 1983*, it was the SPLA that captured and destroyed Malual Gahoth on 17 November 1983. At Malual Gahoth the enemy suffered 120 killed, 60 wounded and 1 helicopter shot down, while SPLA forces lost 12 killed and 30 wounded. Omer Mohammed Al Tayeb lied that the SPLA lost 480 killed. Any soldier would know that this could not be true; what, for example, could have been the size of the attacking force? Malual Gahoth is a small garrison where it is not possible to deploy even 200 men in an attack. Our attack force at Malual Gahoth was only 150 men. After Malual Gahoth, beginning from 12 December 1983, SPLA forces occupied for seven days the eastern half of Nasir, capital of the new Sobat Province. In Nasir the enemy suffered 267 killed, 173 wounded, 3 helicopters shot down, 3 river boats destroyed, 1 armoured personnel carrier and the Commander's Land Rover knocked out. The SPLA lost only 4 killed and 9 wounded in Nasir. Nimeiri and Omer hid these facts but they are true. The man in the street in Khartoum believes the SPLA from the funeral ceremonies of officers and soldiers held in the Three Towns. As Commander-in-Chief, I commanded and directed the battles of Malual Gahoth and Nasir. These important and successful battles heralded the victories of the Sudanese people that the SPLA was soon to achieve.

In its second offensive, beginning on 8 February 1984, and ending with the bombardment of Malakal on 22 February 1984, SPLA units under Lt. Col. Kerubino Kuanyin Bol, Lt. Col. William Nyuon Bany and Lt. Col. Kawae Makuei, attacked and overran all of Ayod, CCI Camp at Kilo 215 on the Jonglei Canal, CCI HQ at the Sobat Mouth and a Nile "Busta" Steamer at Wathkei. In its second offensive the SPLA inflicted untold and immeasurable havoc on Nimeiri's regime. In only two weeks Nimeiri's army suffered 1069 killed and 490 wounded to SPLA 30 killed and 59 wounded. The SPLA destroyed 9 T55 tanks, 8 APCs, 8 Magirus army trucks, 1 civilian CCI truck, 2 small Cesna planes, 2 bulldozers, 2 steamers, 2 fuel stations, 1 big winch, a large quantity of medicines and 2 long-range signal sets. The magnitude of these operations and the importance of Nimeiri's army forced CCI to stop digging the Jonglei Canal and Chevron Company to close down all its oil operations in the South. Hereafter, Nimeiri can no longer deceive the Sudanese people that prosperity, through exploitation of oil and water, is just around the corner. When the SPLA liberates our country under SPLM government, these two precious liquids shall be developed and used for the benefit of the whole Sudanese people.

The SPLA will continue to destroy Nimeirism or any other minority clique regime in Khartoum until genuine Sudanese unity is achieved and the SPLM transfuses the correct socialist blood into Nimeiri's Sudanese Socialist Union (SSU). Like he does with Islam, Nimeiri has also turned socialism into an article of trade. He correctly sees socialism as the genuine demand of the Sudanese people and uses the SSU to deceive the people that he is implement-

ing socialism while in reality he and his gang pillage and loot the country.

*We are aware that by declaring the SPLA/ SPLM as a socialist movement, Nimeiri will depict us as Communists.* This is only another cheap propaganda Nimeiri will use to beg sympathy, money and material assistance from the Western world. Nimeiri himself says he is a socialist by virtue of his membership and presidency of the Sudanese Socialist Union. Is he therefore a Communist?

The content of *our socialism cannot be determined mechanically and equated with Communism as Nimeiri would like the Western world to believe.* The conceptualization and particularization of socialism in the Sudan shall unfold as the armed struggle proceeds and as socio-economic development programmes are implemented during and after the war and *according to Sudanese local and objective conditions.*

It is not the first time that Nimeiri and other minority clique regimes in Khartoum have attempted to slander and blackmail a Sudanese movement in South Sudan. In the first civil war, the false propaganda and slander was that the Anyanya Movement was "imperialist inspired" and its leaders stooges of the Western world. This was because at that time Nimeiri's opportunism took him to Moscow. Today the accusation is that the SPLA/SPLM is "Communist inspired" and its leaders stooges of the Eastern world and/or Libya. This is because this time Nimeiri's opportunism has taken him to Washington. But in all this false propaganda, we want to underline the truth that Nimeiri and past clique regimes in Khartoum are directly responsible and accountable for all the civil wars in the Sudan.

We conclude by reiterating that the slogans of the SPLA are "National Unity", "Socialism", "*Autonomy*", *where and when necessary,* and "Religious Freedom". Our belief in and commitment to these slogans are irrevocable. *The SPLA welcomes and embraces all Sudanese nationalists, patriots and socialists;* in short, the movement belongs to the whole Sudanese people and will fight tirelessly for their unity, peace and progress.

## 31  HAILE SELASSIE
## AT THE LEAGUE OF NATIONS  JUNE 30, 1936

*Italy invaded Ethiopia in October 1935, and, despite heroic resistance by the Ethiopians, Italian troops marched relentlessly, behind clouds of poison gas and an intense air bombardment, to capture Addis Ababa, the capital, on May 5, 1936. The Emperor Haile Selassie (b. Tafari Makonnen, 1891–1975) fled into exile to plead for the collective security which was the cornerstone of the League of Nations—the very principle upon which the League had been founded—and to request that the members come to the aid of his beleaguered country. Although the League had voted overwhelmingly in October 1935 to condemn the Italian invasion, and even voted for limited sanctions against Italy, both Britain and France, in an humiliating effort to appease Benito Mussolini, lifted even these innocuous sanctions in July 1936. Undaunted by this impending capitulation to Italy, Haile Selassie was determined to argue the case for Ethiopia before the assembled members of the League in Geneva. As this diminutive man cloaked in black took the rostrum, from his seat in the fifth row of the Assembly Hall, he was greeted by obscenities shouted from the gallery by the Italian press corps. Unperturbed, he proceeded with calm determination before the embarrassed and humbled members to deliver the funeral oration of the League of Nations. He failed to move the League to act collectively as they had pledged to do upon signing the Covenant of the League, but he became overnight the conscience of a world over which the shadows of Nazi Germany and Fascist Italy were lengthening. His speech remains not only one of the most important political acts of the twentieth century, but a monument for all time.*

I, Haile Selassie I, emperor of Ethiopia, am here today to claim that justice which is due to my people, and the assistance promised to it eight months ago, when fifty nations asserted that aggression had been committed in violation of international treaties.

There is no precedent for a head of state himself speaking in this Assembly. But there is also no precedent for a people being victim of such injustice, and being at present threatened by abandonment to its aggressor. Also, there has never before been an example by any

From *Selected Speeches of His Imperial Majesty Haile Selassie I: 1918–1967*, (Addis Ababa: Ministry of Information, 1967), pp. 304–16.

government proceeding to the systematic extermination of a nation by barbarous means in violation of the most solemn promises made by the nations of the earth that there should not be used against innocent human beings the terrible poison of harmful gases. It is to defend a people struggling for its age-old independence that the head of the Ethiopian empire has come to Geneva to fulfill this supreme duty, after having himself fought at the head of his armies.

I pray to Almighty God that He may spare nations the terrible sufferings that have just been inflicted on my people and of which the chiefs who accompany me here have been the horrified witnesses. It is my duty to inform the governments assembled in Geneva, responsible as they are for the lives of millions of men, women, and children, of the deadly peril which threatens them, by describing to them the fate which has been suffered by Ethiopia.

It is not only upon warriors that the Italian government has made war. It has above all attacked populations far removed from hostilities, in order to terrorize and exterminate them.

At the beginning, towards the end of 1935, Italian aircraft hurled upon my armies bombs of tear-gas. Their effects were but slight. The soldiers learned to scatter, waiting until the wind had rapidly dispersed the poisonous gases. The Italian aircraft then resorted to mustard gas. Barrels of liquid were hurled upon armed groups. But this means also was not effective. The liquid affected only a few soldiers and barrels upon the ground were themselves a warning to troops and to the population of the danger.

It was at the time when the operations for the encircling of Makalle [in northern Ethiopia] were taking place that the Italian command, fearing a rout, followed the procedure which it is now my duty to denounce to the world. Special sprayers were installed on board aircraft so that they could vaporize, over vast areas of territory, a fine, death-dealing rain. Groups of 9, 15, 18 aircraft followed one another so that the fog issuing from them formed a continuous sheet. It was thus that, as from the end of January 1936, soldiers, women, children, cattle, rivers, lakes and pastures were drenched continually with this deadly rain. In order to kill off systematically all living creatures, in order the more surely to poison waters and pastures, the Italian command made its aircraft pass over and over again. That was its chief method of warfare.

The very refinement of barbarism consisted in carrying ravage and terror into the most densely populated parts of the territory, the points farthest removed from the scene of hostilities. The object was to scatter fear and death over a great part of the Ethiopian territory.

These fearful tactics succeeded. Men and animals succumbed. The deadly rain that fell from the aircraft made all those whom it touched fly shrieking with pain. All those who drank the poisoned water or ate the infected food also succumbed in dreadful suffering. In tens of thousands, the victims of the Italian mustard gas fell. It is in order to denounce to the civilized world the tortures inflicted upon the Ethiopian people that I resolved to come to Geneva.

None other than myself and my brave companions in arms could bring the League of Nations the undeniable proof. The appeals of my delegates addressed to the League of Nations had remained without any answer; my delegates had not been witnesses. That is why I decided to come myself to bear witness against the crime perpetrated against my people and give Europe a warning of the doom that awaits it, if it should bow before the accomplished fact.

Is it necessary to remind the Assembly of the various stages of the Ethiopian drama? For 20 years past either as heir apparent, regent of the empire, or as emperor, I have never ceased to use all my efforts to bring my country the benefits of civilization, and in particular to establish relations of good neighborliness with adjacent powers. In particular I succeeded in concluding with Italy the Treaty of Friendship of 1928, which absolutely prohibited the resort, under any pretext whatsoever, to force of arms, substituting for force and pressure the conciliation and arbitration on which civilized nations have based international order.

In its report of October 5, 1935, the Committee of 13 [of the League] recognized my effort and the results that I achieved. The governments thought that the entry of Ethiopia into the League, whilst giving that country a new guarantee for the maintenance of her territorial integrity and independence, would help her to reach a higher level of civilization. It does not seem that in Ethiopia today there is more disorder and insecurity than in 1923. On the contrary, the country is more united and the central power is better obeyed.

I should have procured still greater results for my people if obstacles of every kind had not been put in the way by the Italian government, the government which stirred up revolt and armed the rebels. Indeed the Rome government, as it has today openly proclaimed, has never ceased to prepare for the conquest of Ethiopia. The treaties of friendship it signed with me were not sincere; their only object was to hide its real intention from me. The Italian government asserts that for fourteen years it has been preparing for its present conquest. It therefore recognizes today that when it supported the admission of Ethiopia to the League of Nations in 1923, when it concluded the Treaty of Friendship in 1928, when it signed the pact of Paris outlawing war, it was deceiving the whole world.

The Ethiopian government was, in these solemn treaties, given additional guarantees of security which would enable it to achieve further progress along the pacific path of reform on which it had set its feet and to which it was devoting all its strength and all its heart.

The Walwal incident, in December 1934, came as a thunderbolt to me. The Italian provocation was obvious, and I did not hestitate to appeal to the League of Nations. I invoked the provisions of the treaty of 1928, the principles of the covenant [of the League]; I urged the procedure of conciliation and arbitration.

Unhappily for Ethiopia, this was the time when a certain government considered that the European situation made it imperative at all costs to obtain the friendship of Italy. The price paid was the abandonment of Ethiopian indepen-

dence to the greed of the Italian government. This secret agreement [of January 1935, between Britain and Italy, recognizing Italian influence over Ethiopia], contrary to the obligations of the covenant, has exerted a great influence over the course of events. Ethiopia and the whole world have suffered and are still suffering today its disastrous consequences.

This first violation of the covenant was followed by many others. Feeling itself encouraged in its policy against Ethiopia, the Rome government feverishly made war preparations thinking that the concerted pressure which was beginning to be exerted on the Ethiopian government might perhaps not overcome the resistance of my people to Italian domination.

The time had to come, thus all sorts of difficulties were placed in the way with a view to breaking up the procedure of conciliation and arbitration. All kinds of obstacles were placed in the way of that procedure. Governments tried to prevent the Ethiopian government from finding arbitrators amongst their nationals: when once the arbitral tribunal was set up, pressure was exercised so that an award favorable to Italy should be given. All this was in vain: the arbitrators—two of whom were Italian officials—were forced to recognize unanimously that in the Walwal incident, as in the subsequent incidents, no international responsibility was to be attributed to Ethiopia.

Following on this award, the Ethiopian government sincerely thought that an era of friendly relations might be opened with Italy. I loyally offered my hand to the Rome government.

The Assembly was informed by the report of the Committee of Thirteen, dated October 5, 1935, of the details of the events which occurred after the month of December 1934 and up to October 3, 1935. It will be sufficient if I quote a few of the conclusions of that report (Nos. 24, 25, and 26): The Italian memorandum (containing the complaints made by Italy) was laid on the Council table on September 4, 1935, whereas Ethiopia's first appeal to the Council had been made on December 14, 1934. In the interval between these two dates, the Italian government opposed the consideration of the question by the Council on the ground that the only appropriate procedure was that provided for in the Italo-Ethiopian Treaty of 1928. Throughout the whole of that period, moreover, the dispatch of Italian troops to East Africa was proceeding. These shipments of troops were represented to the Council by the Italian government as necessary for the defense of its colonies menaced by Ethiopia's preparations. Ethiopia, on the contrary, drew attention to the official pronouncements made in Italy which, in its opinion, left no doubt "as to the hostile intentions of the Italian government."

From the outset of the dispute, the Ethiopian government has sought a settlement by peaceful means. It has appealed to the procedures of the covenant. The Italian government desiring to keep strictly to the procedures of the Italo-Ethiopian Treaty of 1928, the Ethiopian government assented. It invariably stated that it would faithfully carry out the arbitral award even if the decision went against it. It agreed that the question of the ownership of Walwal should not be dealt with by the arbitrators, because the Italian government would not agree to such a course. It asked the Council to dispatch neutral observers and offered to lend itself to any inquiries upon which the Council might decide.

Once the Walwal dispute had been settled by arbitration, however, the Italian government submitted its detailed memorandum to the Council in support of its claim to liberty of action. It asserted that a case like that of Ethiopia cannot be settled by the means provided by the covenant. It stated that, "since this question affects vital interests and is of primary importance to Italian security and civilization," it "would be failing in its most elementary duty, did it not cease once and for all to place any confidence in Ethiopia reserving full liberty to adopt any measures that may become necessary to ensure the safety of its colonies and to safeguard its own interests."

Those are the terms of the report of the Committee of Thirteen. The Council and the Assembly unanimously adopted the conclusion that the Italian government had violated the covenant and was in a state of aggression.

I did not hesitate to declare that I did not wish for war, that it was imposed upon me, and I should struggle solely for the independence and integrity of my people, and that in that struggle I was the defender of the cause of all small states exposed to the greed of a powerful neighbor.

In October 1935, the fifty-two nations who are listening to me today gave me an assurance that the aggressor would not triumph, that the resources of the covenant would be employed in order to ensure the reign of right and the failure of violence. I ask the fifty-two nations not to forget today the policy upon which they embarked eight months ago, and on faith of which I directed the resistance of my people against the aggressor whom they had denounced to the world. Despite the inferiority of my weapons, the complete lack of aircraft, artillery, munitions, hospital services, my confidence in the League was absolute. I thought it to be impossible that fifty-two nations, including the most powerful in the world, should be successfully opposed by a single aggressor. Counting on the faith due to treaties, I had made no preparation for war, and that is the case with certain small countries in Europe.

When the danger became more urgent, being aware of my responsibilities towards my people, during the first six months of 1935 I tried to acquire armaments. Many governments proclaimed an embargo to prevent my doing so, whereas the Italian government, through the Suez Canal, was given all facilities for transporting, without cessation and without protest, troops, arms and munitions.

On October 3, 1935, the Italian troops invaded my territory. A few hours later only I decreed general mobilization. In my desire to maintain peace I had, following the example of a great country in Europe on the eve of the Great War, caused my troops to withdraw 30 kilometers so as to remove any pretext of provocation.

War then took place in the atrocious conditions which I have laid before the Assembly. In that unequal struggle between a government commanding more than 42 million inhabitants, having at its disposal financial, industrial and technical means which enabled it to create unlimited quantities of the most death-dealing weapons, and, on the other hand, a small people of 12 million inhabitants, without arms, without resources, having on its side only the justice of its own cause and the promise of the League of Nations, what real assistance was given to Ethioipia by the fifty-two nations who have declared the Rome government guilty of a breach of the covenant and had undertaken to prevent the triumph of the aggressor? Has each of the states members, as it was its duty to do in virtue of its signature appended to Article 15 of the covenant, considered the aggressor as having committed an act of war personally directed against itself? I had placed all my hopes in the execution of these undertakings. My confidence had been confirmed by the repeated declarations made in Council to the effect that aggression must not be rewarded, and that force would end by being compelled to bow before right.

In December 1935 the Council made it quite clear that its feelings were in harmony with those of hundreds of millions of people who, in all parts of the world, had protested against the proposals to dismember Ethiopia. It was constantly repeated that there was not merely a conflict between the Italian government and the League of Nations, and that is why I personally refused all proposals to my personal advantage made to me by the Italian government, if only I would betray my people and the covenant of the League of Nations. I was defending the cause of all small peoples who are threatened with aggression.

What have become of the promises made to me as long ago as October 1935? I noted with grief, but without surprise, that three powers considered their undertakings under the covenant as absolutely of no value. Their connections with Italy impelled them to refuse to take any measures whatsoever in order to stop Italian aggression. On the contrary, it was a profound disappointment to me to learn the attitude of a certain government which, whilst ever protesting its scrupulous attachment to the covenant, has tirelessly used all its efforts to prevent its observance. As soon as any measure which was likely to be rapidly effective was proposed, various pretexts were devised in order to postpone even consideration of the measure. Did the secret agreements of January 1935 provide for this tireless obstruction?

The Ethiopian government never expected other governments to shed their soldiers' blood to defend the covenant when their own immediately personal interests were not at stake. Ethiopian warriors asked only for means to defend themselves. On many occasions I have asked for financial assistance for the purchase of arms. That assistance has been constantly refused me. What, then, in practice, is the meaning of Article 16 of the covenant and of collective security?

The Ethiopian government's use of the railway from Djibouti to Addis Ababa was in practice hampered as regards transport of arms intended for the Ethiopian forces. At the present moment this is the chief, if not the only, means of supply of the Italian armies of occupation. The rules of neutrality should have prohibited transports intended for Italian forces, but there is not even neutrality since Article 16 lays upon every state member of the League the duty not to remain a neutral but to come to the aid not of the aggressor but of the victim of aggression. Has the covenant been respected? Is it today being respected?

Finally a statement has just been made in their parliaments by the governments of certain powers, amongst them the most influential members of the League of Nations, that since the aggressor has succeeded in occupying a large part of Ethiopian territory, they propose not to continue the application of any economic and financial measures that may have been decided upon against the Italian government.

These are the circumstances in which, at the request of the Argentine government, the Assembly of the League of Nations meets to consider the situation created by Italian aggression.

I assert that the problem submitted to the Assembly today is a much wider one. It is not merely a question of the settlement of Italian aggression. It is collective security: it is the very existence of the League of Nations. It is the confidence that each state is to place in international treaties. It is the value of promises made to small states that their integrity and their independence shall be respected and ensured. It is the principle of the equality of states on the one hand, or otherwise the obligation laid upon small powers to accept the bonds of vassalship. In a word, it is international morality that is at stake. Have the signatures appended to a treaty value only in so far as the signatory powers have a personal, direct and immediate interest involved?

No subtlety can change the problem or shift the grounds of the discussion. It is in all sincerity that I submit these considerations to the Assembly. At a time when my people are threatened with extermination, when the support of the League may ward off the final blow, may I be allowed to speak with complete frankness, without reticence, in all directness such as is demanded by the rule of equality as between all states members of the League?

Apart from the Kingdom of the Lord, there is not on this earth any nation that is superior to any other. Should it happen that a strong government finds it may with impunity destroy a weak people, then the hour strikes for that weak people to appeal to the League of Nations to give its judgment in all freedom. God and history will remember your judgment.

I have heard it asserted that the inadequate sanctions already applied have not achieved their object. At no time, and under no circumstances, could sanctions that were intentionally inadequate, intentionally badly applied, stop an aggressor. This is not a case of the impossibility of stopping an aggressor, but of the refusal to stop an aggressor. When Ethiopia requested and requests that she should be given financial assistance, was that a measure which it was impossible to apply whereas financial assistance of the League has been granted, even in times of peace, to two countries and exactly to two countries who have refused to apply sanctions against the aggressor?

Faced by numerous violations by the Italian government of all international treaties that prohibit resort to arms and the use of barbarous methods of warfare, it is my painful duty to note that the initiative has today been taken with a view to raising sanctions. Does this initiative not mean in practice the abandonment of Ethiopia to the aggressor? On the very eve of the day when I was about to attempt a supreme effort in the defense of my people before this Assembly, does not this initiative deprive Ethiopia of one of her last chances to succeed in obtaining the support and guarantee of states members? Is that the guidance the League of Nations and each of the states members are entitled to expect from the great powers when they assert their right and their duty to guide the action of the League?

Placed by the aggressor face to face with the accomplished fact, are states going to set up the terrible precedent of bowing before force?

Your Assembly will doubtless have laid before it proposals for the reform of the covenant and for rendering more effective the guarantee of collective security. Is it the covenant that needs reform? What undertakings can have any value if the will to keep them is lacking? Is it international morality which is at stake and not the articles of the covenant?

On behalf of the Ethiopian people, a member of the League of Nations, I request the Assembly to take all measures proper to ensure respect for the covenant. I renew my protest against the vio-

lations of treaties of which the Ethiopian people has been the victim. I declare in the face of the whole world that the emperor, the government, and the people of Ethiopia will not bow before force; that they maintain their claims that they will use all means in their power to ensure the triumph of right and the respect of the covenant.

I ask the fifty-two nations, who have given the Ethiopian people a promise to help them in their resistance to the aggressor, what are they willing to do for Ethiopia? And the great powers who have promised the guarantee of collective security to small states on whom weighs the threat that they may one day suffer the fate of Ethiopia, I ask what measures do you intend to take?

Representatives of the world, I have come to Geneva to discharge in your midst the most painful of the duties of the head of a state. What reply shall I have to take back to my people?

## 32   CHARTER OF THE ORGANIZATION OF AFRICAN UNITY

MAY 25, 1963

*After experiencing the exultation of international acclaim at the League of Nations in 1936, and a triumphal return as Emperor to Addis Ababa in 1941, Haile Selassie sought to achieve a dominant position as elder statesman among the new leaders of independent Africa. As Emperor of Ethiopia, he was particularly disturbed by the determination of Kwame Nkrumah completely to eliminate Western influence from the continent, since Ethiopia was dependent on the material and military assistance of the United States. Moreover, the emperor regarded himself as the living personification of independent Africa, the direct descendant of the millennia-old Solomonic tradition, and the leader of the oldest independent African state—which had, unlike colonial Africa, successfully defied the European imperialists. He regarded his prominent position in new Africa as a matter of right and reward. Consequently, he sought to claim the leadership for African unity in his address before the First Conference of Independent African States in Accra, Ghana in April 1958. He was challenged by Kwame Nkrumah and Sékou Touré, who argued for the political unification of Africa under a Marxist-oriented ruler instead of the mere economic cooperation advocated by the conservative emperor. The disagreements between African radicals and African moderates sharpened with the granting of independence to most of Europe's African colonies in 1960, when the more conservative states found themselves on the defensive against the dominating charismatic figure of Nkrumah in the ideological struggle for a definition of Pan-Africanism. To regain the initiative, Haile Selassie invited the leaders of Africa's independent states to Addis Ababa in 1963 to resolve the nature of African unity. The summit meeting opened on May 22, 1963, attended by thirty of the thirty-two independent African states. Adopting the role of mediator and conciliator, Haile Selassie dominated the proceedings. Following his appeal "that old wounds shall be healed and past scars forgotten," the members enthusiastically endorsed the establishment of the Organization of African Unity (OAU) to promote solidarity on the continent, to work for a better standard of living for the Africans, and to eradicate colonialism. Not surprisingly, the overwhelming choice for its new headquarters was Addis Ababa.*

We, the Heads of African and Malagasy States and Governments assembled in the city of Addis Ababa, Ethiopia;

Convinced that it is the inalienable right of all people to control their own destiny;

Conscious of the fact that freedom, equality, justice and dignity are essential objectives for the achievement of the legitimate aspirations of the African peoples;

Conscious of our responsibility to harness the natural and human resources of our continent for the total advancement of our peoples in spheres of human endeavour;

Inspired by a common determination to promote understanding and collaboration among our States in response to the aspirations of our peoples for brotherhood and solidarity, in a larger unity transcending ethnic and national differences;

Convinced that, in order to translate this determination into a dynamic force in the cause of human progress, conditions for peace and security must be established and maintained;

Determined to safeguard and consolidate the hard-won independence as well as the sovereignty and territorial integrity of our States, and to resist neo-colonialism in all its forms;

From *The Organization of African and Malagasy States* (Addis Ababa: May 25, 1963).

Dedicated to the general progress of Africa;

Persuaded that the Charter of the United Nations and the Universal Declaration of Human Rights, to the principles of which we reaffirm our adherence, provide a solid foundation for peaceful and positive cooperation among States;

Desirous that all African and Malagasy States should henceforth unite so that the welfare and well-being of their peoples can be assured;

Resolved to reinforce the links between our States by establishing and strengthening common institutions;

Have agreed to the present Charter.

## ESTABLISHMENT

### Article I

The High Contracting Parties do by the present Charter establish an Organization to be known as the "Organization of African and Malagasy States."

## PURPOSES

### Article II

1. The Organization shall have the following purposes:

   a. To promote the unity and solidarity of the African and Malagasy States.

   b. To co-ordinate and intensify their collaboration and efforts to achieve a better life for the peoples of Africa.

c. To defend their sovereignty, their territorial integrity and independence.

d. To eradicate all forms of colonialism from the continent of Africa; and

e. To promote international co-operation, having due regard to the Charter of the United Nations and the Universal Declaration of Human Rights.

2. To these ends, the Member States shall co-ordinate and harmonise their general policies, especially in the following fields:

a. Political and diplomatic co-operation.

b. Economic co-operation, including transport and communications.

c. Educational and cultural co-operation.

d. Health, sanitation and nutritional co-operation.

e. Scientific and technical co-operation.

f. Co-operation for defence and security.

## PRINCIPLES

### Article III
The Member States, in pursuit of the purposes stated in Article II, solemnly affirm, and declare their adherence to the following principles:

1. The sovereign equality of all African and Malagasy States.

2. Non-interference in the internal affairs of States.

3. Respect for the sovereignty and territorial integrity of each State and for its inalienable right to independent existence.

4. Peaceful settlement of disputes by negotiation, mediation, conciliation or arbitration.

5. Unreserved condemnation, in all its forms, of political assassination as well as subversive activities on the part of neighboring States or any other States.

6. Absolute dedication to the whole emancipation of the African territories which are still dependent.

7. Affirmation of a policy of non-alignment with regard to all blocs.

## MEMBERSHIP

### Article IV
Each independent sovereign African and Malagasy State shall be entitled to become a Member of the Organization.

## RIGHTS AND DUTIES OF MEMBER STATES

### Article V
All Member States shall enjoy equal rights and have equal duties.

### Article VI
The Member States pledge themselves to observe scrupulously the principles enumerated in Article III of the present Charter.

## INSTITUTIONS

### Article VII
The Organization shall accomplish its purposes through the following principal institutions:

1. The Assembly of Heads of State and Government.

2. The Council of Ministers.

3. The General Secretariat.

4. The Commission of Mediation, Conciliation and Arbitration.

## THE ASSEMBLY OF HEADS OF STATE AND GOVERNMENT

### Article VIII
The Assembly of Heads of State and Government shall be the supreme organ of the Organization. It shall, subject to the provisions of this Charter, discuss matters of common concern to all Member States with a view to co-ordinating and harmonising the general policy of

the Organization. It may in addition review the structure, functions and acts of all the organs and any specialized agencies which may be created in accordance with the present Charter.

### Article IX

The Assembly shall be composed of the Heads of State and Government or their duly accredited representatives and it shall meet at least once a year (every other year). At the request of any Member State, and approval by the majority of the Member States, the Assembly shall meet in extraordinary session.

### Article X

1. Each Member State shall have one vote.

2. All resolutions shall be determined by a two-thirds majority of those present and voting.

3. Questions of procedure shall require a simple majority. Whether or not a question is one of procedure shall be determined by a simple majority of all Member States present and voting.

4. Two-thirds of the total membership of the Organization shall form a quorum at any meeting of the Assembly.

### Article XI

The Assembly shall have the power to determine its own rules of procedure.

## THE COUNCIL OF MINISTERS

### Article XII

The Council of Ministers shall consist of Foreign Ministers or such other Ministers as are designated by the Governments of Member States.

The Council of Ministers shall meet at least twice a year. When .requested by any Member State and approved by two-thirds of all Member States, it shall meet in extraordinary session.

### Article XIII

The Council of Ministers shall be re-sponsible to the Assembly of Heads of State and Government. It shall be entrusted with the responsibility of preparing conferences of the Assembly.

It shall take cognisance of any matter referred to it by the Assembly. It shall be entrusted with the implementation of the decisions of the Assembly of Heads of State. It shall co-ordinate inter-African co-operation in accordance with the instructions of the Assembly and in conformity with Article II (2) of the present Charter.

### Article XIV

1. Each Member State shall have one vote.

2. All resolutions shall be determined by a two-thirds majority of those members present and voting.

3. Questions of procedure shall require a simple majority. Whether or not a question is one of procedure shall be determined by a simple majority of all Member States present and voting.

4. Two-thirds of the total membership of the Council shall form a quorum for any meeting of the Council.

### Article XV

The Council shall have the power to determine its own rules of procedure.

## GENERAL SECRETARIAT

### Article XVI

There shall be an Administrative Secretary-General of the Organization, who shall be appointed by the Assembly of Heads of State and Government, on the recommendation of the Council of Ministers. The Administrative Secretary-General shall direct the affairs of the Secretariat.

### Article XVII

There shall be one or more Assistant Secretaries-General of the Organization, who shall be appointed by the Council of Ministers.

## Article XVIII

The functions and conditions of services of the Secretary-General, of the Assistant Secretaries-General and other employees of the Secretariat shall be governed by the provisions of this Charter and the regulations approved by the Council of Ministers.

1. In the performance of their duties the Administrative Secretary-General and his staff shall not seek or receive instructions from any government or from any other authority external to the Organization. They shall refrain from any action which might reflect on their position as international officials responsible only to the Organization.

2. Each member of the Organization undertakes to respect the exclusive character of the responsibilities of the Administrative Secretary-General and the Staff and not seek to influence them in the discharge of their responsibilities.

## COMMISSION OF MEDIATION, CONCILIATION AND ARBITRATION

### Article XIX

Member States pledge to settle all disputes among themselves by peaceful means and, to this end, agree to conclude a separate treaty establishing a Commission of Mediation, Conciliation and Arbitration. Said treaty shall be regarded as forming an integral part of the present Charter [done July 21, 1964, in Cairo].

## SPECIALIZED COMMISSIONS

### Article XX

The Assembly shall establish such Specialized Commissions as it may deem necessary, including the following:

1. Economic and Social Commission.
2. Educational and Cultural Commission.
3. Health, Sanitation and Nutrition Commission.
4. Defence Commission.

5. Scientific, Technical and Research Commission.

### Article XXI

Each Specialized Commission referred to in Article XX shall be composed of the Ministers concerned or other Ministers or Plenipotentiaries designated by the Governments of the Member States.

### Article XXII

The functions of the Specialized Commissions shall be carried out in accordance with the provisions of the present Charter and of the regulations approved by the Council of Ministers.

## THE BUDGET

### Article XXIII

The budget of the Organization prepared by the Administrative Secretary-General shall be approved by the Council of Ministers. The budget shall be provided by contributions from Member States in accordance with the scale of assessment of the United Nations; provided, however, that no Member State shall be assessed an amount exceeding twenty per cent of the yearly regular budget of the Organization. The Member States agree to pay their respective contributions regularly.

## SIGNATURE AND RATIFICATION OF CHARTER

### Article XXIV

This Charter shall be open for signature to all independent sovereign African and Malagasy States and shall be ratified by the signatory States in accordance with their respective constitutional processes.

The original instrument, done in English and French, both texts being equally authentic, shall be deposited with the Government of Ethiopia which shall transmit certified copies thereof to all independent sovereign African and Malagasy States.

Instruments of ratification shall be deposited with the Government of Ethiopia, which shall notify all signatories of each such deposit.

## ENTRY INTO FORCE

### Article XXV

The Charter shall enter into force immediately upon receipt by the Government of Ethiopia of the instruments of ratification from two-thirds of the signatory States.

## REGISTRATION OF THE CHARTER

### Article XXVI

This Charter shall, after due ratification, be registered with the Secretariat of the United Nations through the Government of Ethiopia in conformity with Article 102 of the Charter of the United Nations.

## INTERPRETATION OF THE CHARTER

### Article XXVII

Any question which may arise concerning the interpretation of this Charter shall be decided by a vote of two-thirds of the Assembly of Heads of State and Government, present and voting.

## ADHESION AND ACCESSION

### Article XXVIII

1. Any independent sovereign African State may at any time notify the Administrative Secretary-General of its intention to adhere or accede to this Charter.

2. The Administrative Secretary-General shall, on receipt of such notification, communicate a copy of it to all the Member States. Admission shall be decided by a simple majority of the Member States. The decision of each Member State shall be transmitted to the Administrative Secretary-General, who shall, upon receipt of the required number of votes, communicate the decision to the State concerned.

## MISCELLANEOUS

### Article XXIX

The working languages of the Organization and all its institutions shall be English and French.

### Article XXX

The Administrative Secretary-General may accept on behalf of the Organization gifts, bequests and other donations made to the Organization, provided that this is approved by the Council of Ministers.

### Article XXXI

The Council of Ministers shall decide on the privileges and immunities to be accorded to the personnel of the Secretariat in the respective territories of the Member States.

## CESSATION OF MEMBERSHIP

### Article XXXII

Any State which desires to renounce its membership shall forward a written notification to the Administrative Secretary-General. At the end of one year from the date of such notification, the Charter shall cease to apply with respect to the renouncing State, which shall thereby cease to belong to the Organization.

## AMENDMENT TO THE CHARTER

### Article XXXIII

This Charter may be amended or revised if any Member State makes a written request to the Administrative Secretary-General to that effect; provided, however, that the proposed amendment is not submitted to the Assembly for consideration until all the Member States have been duly notified of it and a period of one year has elapsed. Such an amendment shall not be effective unless approved by at least two-thirds of all the Member States.

In faith whereof, We, the Heads of African and Malagasy States and Governments, have signed this Charter.

Done in the city of Addis Ababa, the 25th day of May, 1963.

Ahmed Ben Bella/Algeria, King Nwambudsa IV/Burundi, Ahmadou Ahidjo/Cameroun, David Dacko/Central African Republic, Francois Tombalbayne/Chad, Abbe Fulbert Youlou/Congo Brazzaville, Joseph Kasavubu/Congo Leopoldville, Hubert Maga/Dahomey, Haile Selassie/Ethiopia, Leon M'ba/Gabon, Kwame Nkrumah/Ghana, Sekou Toure/Guinea, Felix Houphouet-Boigny/Ivory Coast, William Tubman/Liberia, Hassan Mohammed Rida/Libya, Philibert Tsiranana/Madagascar, Modibo Keita/Mali, Mokhtar Ould Daddah/Mauritania, Hamani Diori/Niger, Abubakar Tafewa Balewa/Nigeria, Habemenshi/Rwanda, Leopold Senghor/Senegal, Milton Margai/Sierra Leone, Abdullah Osman/Somalia, Ibrahim Abboud/Sudan, Julius Nyerere/Tanganyika, Habib Bourguiba/Tunisia, Milton Obote/Uganda, Gamal Abdel Nasser/United Arab Republic, Maurice Yameogo/Upper Volta.

## 33.   THE DERG AND MENGISTU HAILE MARIAM

UNITY: FOUNDATION OF OUR INDEPENDENCE AND STRENGTH   MAY 1, 1988

*Despite the dominant role that Haile Selassie had played in the affairs of independent Africa—the establishment of the Organization of African Unity (OAU); mediation in the Algerian-Moroccan conflict in 1963; the Nigerian civil war of 1968–69; and the Sudanese Problem of the Southern Sudan which was momentarily resolved at Addis Ababa in 1972—the aging emperor could no longer command the unswerving loyalty of the Ethiopians. Grievances over spiraling inflation and pervasive corruption, as well as discontent among urban interest groups, erupted upon exposure of the government's concealment of the disastrous famine in the northern provinces of Walo and Tigray in 1973. On January 12, 1974, units of the Ethiopian Army mutineed in Nagelo in southern Ethiopia, protesting against poor food and plunging Ethiopia into six months of turmoil. From this revolt emerged the Coordinating Committee of the Armed Forces, Police, and Territorial Army, the* Derg *(an Amharic word for committee). The* Derg *was first established on June 28, 1974, and an obscure Major, Mengistu Haile Mariam, was elected chairman. With its motto of* Ethiopia Tikdem *(Ethiopia First), the objective of the* Derg *was to revolutionize the Ethiopian way of life. This included the abdication of the emperor on September 12th. On September 15th, the* Derg *adopted the more pretentious title of the Provisional Military Administrative Council (PMAC) with Mengistu as Chairman. By 1977, with the strong support of the Soviet Union, Mengistu had sufficiently consolidated his dominant position so that the PMAC virtually disappeared. All power reverted to him and to the council's rump Standing Committee, the Provisional Military Government of Socialist Ethiopia (PMGSE), which became the* de facto *central government of Ethiopia.*

*The* Derg *was officially established by its proclamation of September 12, 1974. Fourteen years later, on May 1, 1988, Mengistu Haile Mariam himself provided a self-assessment of his rule in the speech celebrating May Day. By this time, the Ethiopian Army had been defeated in Eritrea and Tigray, and Mengistu's policy of relocating northern Ethiopians on communal farms in the southern provinces was in disarray.*

## PROCLAMATION ON THE ESTABLISHMENT OF THE DERG SEPTEMBER 12, 1974.

Although the people of Ethiopia have looked, in good faith, upon the Crown as a symbol of their unity, Haile Selassie I, who has ruled the country for more than fifty years, ever since he assumed power as a Crown Prince, has abused the authority, dignity, and honor of office for the personal benefit and interest of himself, his immediate family, and retainers. As a consequence, he has led the country into its present inextricable situation. Moreover, as he has progressed in age, being eighty-two years old, he cannot shoulder the high responsibilities of his office.

The present parliamentary system is not democratic. The members of parliament have so far served not the nation but the ruling aristocratic class and themselves. Hence, the members of parliament have refrained from legislating on fundamental national matters such as land reform while legislating laws to promote their interests and that of their class, thereby adding to the misery of the people. The existence of this parliament is inimical to the philosophy and objectives of "Ethiopia Tikdem."

Likewise, the 1955 revised constitution was designed to give absolute power to the emperor while providing a democratic facade for the benefit of world public opinion. The constitution was not conceived to safeguard the rights of the people. In fact, the constitution abrogates the natural rights of man by decreeing that these rights were granted to the

From Bereket Habte Selassie, *Conflict and Intervention in the Horn of Africa*, (New York: 1980), Appendix 2, "Proclamation on the Establishment of the Dergue," pp. 179–81. Reprinted by permission.

people by the emperor. As such, the 1955 constitution diametrically opposes the present popular movement for economic, political, and social reforms.

The feudal system of government has mismanaged the affairs of the country, leading it into the present economic, social, and political quagmire. Therefore, the following proclamation has been promulgated to establish a provisional administrative machinery for the transitional period and for the progress of the country and the security of the people.

1. This proclamation may be cited as the Provisional Military Government of Ethiopia Proclamation, No. 1/1967.

2. Haile Selassie I has been deposed as of today, Meskerem 2, 1967 (September 12, 1974).

3. a. The Crown Prince, His Highness Merid Azmatch Asfa Wossen, will become King of Ethiopia.

   b. The coronation ceremony will be held as soon as the Crown Prince returns to his country.

   c. The King will be head of state with no power in the country's administrative and political affairs.

4. Until the people elect their genuine representatives in truly democratic elections, Parliament (the Senate and Chamber of Deputies) has been closed down forthwith.

5. a. The revised constitution of 1955 is suspended.

   b. The new draft constitution, the promulgation of which has been demanded by the Armed Forces Committee as a matter of urgency, shall be put into effect after necessary improvements are made to include provisions reflecting the social,

economic, and political philosophy of the new Ethiopia
and to safeguard the civil rights
of the people.

6. The Armed Forces Committee
has assumed full government power until
a legally constituted people's assembly
approves a new constitution and a government is duly established.

7. All courts of law throughout the
country shall continue their normal functions.

8. It is hereby prohibited, for the du-
ration of this proclamation, to oppose the
aims of the philosophy, "Ethiopia
Tikdem," to engage in any strike, hold
unauthorized demonstrations or public
meetings, or to engage in any act that
may disturb public peace and security.

9. A special military tribunal shall be
established to try those who contravene
the orders enunciated in No. 8 of this
proclamation and also to try former and
present government officials who may be
charged with corruption and abuse of
power. Judgments handed down by the
special military tribunal are not subject
to appeal.

10. All existing laws that do not contravene the provisions of this proclamation and those of future orders shall
remain in effect.

11. This proclamation shall be in
force as of Meskerem 2, 1967 (September 12, 1974).

The Committee of the Armed Forces,
Police, and Territorial Army
Addis Ababa, September 12, 1974

*   *   *

## MENGISTU HAILE MARIAM

### Unity: Foundation of Our Indepen-
### dence and Strength    May 1, 1988

Dear Workers, Peasants and Members of
the Revolutionary Armed Forces!

From Ministry of Information Press Depart-
ment (Addis Ababa: May 1, 1988).

Patriotic Citizens deployed in all fields of
endeavor and all heroic Ethiopian People!

Members of the Diplomatic Corps and
Esteemed Guests!

On this historic day which commemo-
rates the universal call for unity and co-
operation among the workers of the
world who are the makers and the moving force of civilization and social progress, the peoples of the world speak
effusively about peace and justice,
equality and prosperity.

They view with hope the fruits of their
sacrifice and the goals they aspire to attain. Our own struggle and aspiration,
too, constitute an inseparable and integral element of this same vision.

We, moreover, feel proud of the reality that we are active and vanguard participants in this historic process.

We, therefore, devote special attention to International Workers' Day (May
Day)—a day of solidarity and of op-
timism.

I thus feel greatly honoured in ex-
pressing best wishes to the entire working people of Ethiopia on the occasion of
this year's historic observance of the
event.

The working people in pre-revolution
Ethiopia, gripped by the gloomy order of
feudalism and isolated from their class
allies, i.e. from the working people of
the world, were denied not only of the
opportunity of openly observing International Workers' Day but were kept ignorant of its historic significance.

Among the numerous radical popular
measures taken immediately following
the upsurge of our revolution, was the
decision which made the commemora-
tion of May Day statutory.

It is to be recalled, however, that major obstacles were put in the way of the
first observance of this historic event,
particularly in our capital and at this
square.

It is to be recalled, too, that the enemies of our revolution, then at the initial stage of mounting their obstructionist campaign, attempted to create terror by the use of force everywhere including at this very spot.

Besides hatching clandestine operation, the enemies of the Ethiopian people made numerous other attempts to achieve their aims by creating chaos and confusion everywhere including in urban centres.

The machination was, however, foiled by the masses of the people who valiantly faced the enemies chanting, "who is afraid of death?".

They also launched cross-border aggression by co-ordinating their strategy from within the country and abroad.

Once again, the masses nipped the enemy plots in the bud by mobilizing from one corner of the country to the other under the historic rallying cry of "Revolutionary Motherland or Death!".

The victories thus attained through bitter sacrifice made it possible to devise wide-ranging strategy for progress and lay significant foundations for development.

A whole network of basic but commendable development infrastructure was spread to change the face of the rural areas, which had long remained in a medieval state, by organizing and agitating the peasantry, launching literacy campaign in diverse nationality languages and increasing the level of formal education by more than three-fold.

Side by side with these efforts and the measures taken to improve the quality of life in the urban areas, we unfolded far-reaching plans for gradually reducing and ultimately eradicating major social problems in the foreseable future.

As our enemies never desisted from putting our country to trial by arming and deploying their agents of destruction through the traditional corridors in the north and as we were forced to marshall considerable part of our resources to thwart such aggression, we have, however, been unable to fully attain our development objectives.

As I pointed out in my last report to the Eighth Regular Plenum of the CC of the WPE, the extent of the sacrifice paid by the sons and daughters of the people who fell martyrs defending the Motherland and the Revolution against the mercenary war of paid traitors in the north had best be assessed by every family and household.

Apart from the lives sacrificed and the blood spilt, if the financial and material resources wasted in containing this protracted mercenary war during a single year alone were invested in constructive work, it would have enabled us to build at least four major factories, four hospitals, and four universities or build a railway network connecting one corner of our country to the other. I am saying this not to exaggerate the gravity of the situation but to underline the enormity of the destruction and waste being sustained.

Nevertheless, we have strained hard to create conditions favourable for basic development in diverse areas of endeavour. Our efforts have borne fruit and we have now reached a new and decisive stage where we are to make a dramatic leap forward.

It has been said time and again and practically demonstrated that the main purpose of the intensified destructive campaign of the enemies is to obstruct our development programmes. What is it that makes the current situation really different? What has prompted the northern secessionist and terrorist forces in particular into resorting to the ultimate anti-people policy of "suicide mission?" What exactly do they mean by "a suicide mission?" For how long should we stand by when Ethiopia's beloved sons and daughters are being sacrificed and the nation's resources wasted in this manner in northern Ethiopia?.

Unlike so many peoples in the developing world, the Ethiopian people had never been subjected by colonialism nor accepted sham freedom under neo-colonialism to fail to acquire a vision of their destiny.

They are a people who, in the tradition of their unbending spirit and heroic past, have demonstrated that they are the sole masters of their destiny.

More significantly still, they have shaped a constitution through their own direct participation and without any outside interference under which they expressed their free will and have established a people's democratic republic to exercise their right to self-administration.

The Republic covers not only central bodies created following the general election but also regional state organs and institutions to be established on various levels through the democratic and direct participation of the people to exercise regional self-administration in accordance with objective conditions prevailing in the various parts of the country.

The fact that the Ethiopian people have thus assumed direct political power and are now unambiguously the sole masters of their own destiny has not been welcomed by states thriving on a relation of dependence which they impose on others or latter day neo-colonialists and their collaborators.

The efforts of recent years in the economic sector, supplemented by the co-operation of their allies, have concretely confirmed to the Ethiopian people that their country is endowed with a variety of mineral resources.

As I have on various occasions tried to point out in my reports of gains in the economic field, sizeable deposits of prime gold, tantalum, iron-ore, limestone, marble, silicon, potash, phosphate, natural gas, coal, geo-thermal sources, platinum and uranium (of yet undetermined quality and quantity) have been discovered.

Having past the exploration stage,

most of the minerals are now favourably poised for a full fledged development and we expect the commissioning of some of them as of 1989.

Energy is the necessary precondition for the proper or adequate development of these mineral resources and the eventual broadening of the country's industrial base and it is fortunate that Ethiopia happens to be one of those countries richly endowed with water resource applicable both for hydro-power and agriculture.

The recently commissioned 150–160 Megawatt Melka-Wakena Hydro Electric Power Station alone, built by Ethio-Soviet-Czechoslovak cooperation, has raised by 50% our country's energy production.

In addition, the 300 Megawatt Gilgel Gibe Hydro-Electric Power Project which is in the process of implementation will inevitably further boost our energy output.

It is established that without even reckoning natural gas and geo-thermal based energy, the power that can be generated from our numerous rivers is enough to meet our energy needs and those of our neighbours.

The Progress we have made in the industrial sector too is exemplary. However, some time will inevitably have to pass before we can fully reap the fruits of the industrial plants we have already set up or are under construction or at the planning stage, but there is no doubt that the effort underway will have a significant impact on our bid for industrial self-reliance.

Contrary to the attempts made by some circles to exaggerate the gravity of the situation, we have enough capability to attain self-sufficiency in food.

If we make special all-round attempt to overcome the vicissitudes of nature and achieve the desired results, if we make appropriate use of our innumerable rivers and place hitherto idle land under cultivation, and if we develop and exploit our livestock resources, we are certain of speedily overcoming famine which is one of the causes of our travail and the object of unhealthy comments directed at us.

Although for several reasons, which are familiar to all of us, drought in the northern parts of our country is no longer a recurrent incident but a permanent phenomenon and that the toil of the peasantry has been of little avail, the poor soil and the consequent crisis we are facing is not really typical of Ethiopia from the view point of productivity. It is the result of ecological imbalance.

The implementation of the strategy we have mapped out to combat drought and boost agricultural productivity will no doubt render the present problem a mere temporary feature.

Ethiopia is endowed with agricultural potentials, various mineral and vast energy resources, which many developing countries lack, and in particular, united people that fully realise their history-making role and jealously guard their independence.

The revolution has created favourable conditions for us to acquire a greater awareness of our identity and we are now firmly on the road to freeing ourselves from backwardness and on the path to prosperity in equality while safeguarding our independence. That is precisely the reason behind the hullabaloo and the aggressive stance of our enemies. The realization that the wishful thinking they had indulged in during the PMAC period, that things would change for the better for them and that they could even win us over to their thinking is now completely shattered by the establishment of the PDRE, may very well be the cause for the present stepped up destructive activity. They had to give up hope because, contrary to their conspiracy and aspiration, the popular democratic power, envisaged by the revolution at the outset has become a reality. Thus, a vigorous misinformation campaign, frenzy effort to undermine our international relation with a view to plunging us into an economic crisis, and the fielding of their paid agents—separatists and terrorists—for scaled-up havoc, has become their timely and urgent task.

They try to present themselves as advocates of truth. But if they had stood for truth—or even a grain of truth—they would not have been so much painfully agrieved by our freedom and by our choice of achieving self-determination.

Contrary to the disinformation of our enemies, our call is for equality and mutual respect. We are ready on this basis to promote mutually advantageous relation of cooperation with all states or parties. The scope for such cooperation is very wide. In fact, we have already developed principled cooperation with many states. Any conscious person would note that the action of our enemies is a futile exercise in rumour-mongering and baseless propaganda.

Dear Compatriots!

As I have attempted to explain earlier, unlike the assertion of our enemies, the people of Ethiopia have laid a reliable foundation for a lasting development. We are certain, henceforth, that by a united and accelerated forward march, we shall achieve our desired objectives. It is actually this certainty that has prompted our enemies into acts of destruction.

Development and not war is the interest and aspiration of this people which never in the past had been known to have compromised on the issue of defending national unity from assailants. True to this tradition, our people have once again risen rallying around the motto, "Everything to the War Front" to crush the enemies which declared war on us from the northern part of our country.

This historic and decisive stand of our people has scared the paid agents, much as it has evoked pride even among non-Ethiopians who know and respect the true identity of our people. It has also caused panic among those who aid and abet the hirelings.

From the very day on which the national call was made to them, our people, having risen with indignation befitting their sense of patriotism, have reaffirmed Ethiopia's longstanding and historic sensitivity to encroachment on her national unity.

The people not only emerged chanting, "I defy for my country" in response to the national call to defend the Motherland but also held discussions in their villages and places of work, thereby grasping more than ever before the nature of the conspiracy of expansionists and neocolonialists.

They have thus realized during the discussion that the paid agents' reckless destruction of socio-economic infrastructure built by the sweat and meagre resources of the people is sheer vandalism designed to frustrate the popular struggle against poverty and dependence and for a speedy emancipation from a life of pauperism.

Expenditure amounting to billions of Birr are channelled to withstand the war of annihilation unleashed by the hirelings, who receive arms and other forms of support from Ethiopia's enemies. Had this money been used for development purposes and the collossal destruction perpetrated by the bandits been averted, we would have achieved rapid progress and alleviated substantially our social problems. Awareness that our development has thus been frustrated has caused indignation to our people.

The incalculable destruction wrought by the secessionists in the northern part of our country is an act directed against the very existence of the Ethiopian people and their property. It is a destruction affecting directly or indirectly the life and household of each and every Ethiopian. In short, it is a destruction perpetrated to imperil the life of all Ethiopians and that of Mother Ethiopia.

Never in the long history of this country was there any instance in which we Ethiopians took enemy assault with equanimity nor bowed down to the enemy with submission. Likewise, the determination to defend ourselves of the war just declared on us has become a matter about which there will be no question whatsoever. For us, there can be nothing more overriding than our freedom and unity for whose defence all of us—whatever our age, sex, or religion are at one to rise in arms. This is precisely the message the Ethiopian people wish to get across to the world at this moment.

Our country has never been wanting in heroes. Sons and daughters she had, whose valour and exploits had made them immortal heroes not only of their national history but also of the history of anti-colonial struggle of peoples, sons and daughters she has now, too, who would quickly react against any negative reference to their country, to say nothing of assault against her. In quick response to the mobilization call, the reserves of the first and second rounds of the National Military Service reported to duty and joined the ranks of fighters at the front. Similarly, members of the People's Militia and those of the Revolutionary Defence Squad from every corner of the country mobilized with courage and confidence, thereby proving once again our people's unquestionable commitment—a commitment which we had never doubted.

In this regard, I am extremely proud that I am an Ethiopian. I believe that all Ethiopians are also sincerely proud of their country and fellow citizens. I am confident that in this spirit Ethiopians will, until final victory, intensify their effort with greater determination and live up to the obligation and responsibility they are called upon to shoulder in their respective fields of areas of assignment.

Dear genuine sons and daughters of Ethiopia!

There has not been a moment when parties inimical to the unity and efforts of the independent development of our people refrained from trying to hoodwink world public opinion of Ethiopia's genuine stand and honest efforts.

The deafening propaganda mounted by the mentors of the secessionist bandits and the bravado sounded in an attempt to glorify the adventurous acts of their agents in the village of Afabet in north-eastern Eritrea a few weeks ago was most surprising. By this very action, they have openly demonstrated their hostile stance towards us and their apprehension of our resoluteness to ensure respect for our national unity. [Afabet was the site of a disastrous defeat of the Ethiopian army by the Eritreans.]

On the contrary, we have at present started a movement to thwart with popular force the attack directed against the unity of our country and the well-being of our people. It is at this juncture that they have embarked on a different sort of propaganda campaign. Hence, harmonizing their propaganda in tune with that of their agents, they are spreading baseless rumours that, "Ethiopia is to use chemical weapon in the war zone for massive destruction and that relief supplies to victims of drought will be discontinued". As a matter of fact, it is the Ethiopian people themselves and not anybody else who will have to determine the kind of weapon or strategy to be employed to repel the attack against the unity of the Motherland. The crux of the matter is not in the way in which the war is to be conducted, but how the root cause of the war triggered off by the colonialists is to be eliminated.

It is characteristic of our enemies to try to give distorted interpretation of our legitimate and popular effort. It is to be recalled that in the wake of the revolution, they felt so encouraged by the attacks of counter-revolutionary forces as to foretell that: "Ethiopia is disintegrating and its revolution being reversed." But when we mustered our strength and our revolutionary army brought the enemy which was rejoicing over momentary victory down to its knees, the outcry this time was that "Ethiopia is arming herself beyond her needs," "She will disrupt peace in the Horn of Africa," "She will invade her neighbours." No wonder then that the malicious disinformation campaign should focus on a different theme now when we, stiffened by our valiant people who readily responded to the national call, hardly threw a punch to crush the terrorists and effectively respond to their challenge.

It is no secret that the Ethiopian people have risen with determination to safeguard their country's unity and sovereignty. An official call has been made, and the people are responding officially and actively to this call. They cannot live in a state of war forever. They cannot hand down a legacy of the burden of war and tribulation to the future generation. They have made intensive effort to resolve the problem through peaceful means. But the people's patience has been interpreted by the terrorists as weakness. An effort is underway to respond immediately to the terroristic challenge and to translate into action self-administration which the people have embarked upon thanks to the favourable conditions created by the founding of the Republic. This effort cannot be deterred by the machination of the terrorists.

The nature of the plot being woven against us is to create an obstacle to the aspiration of our people, especially by using, as of late, the drought relief aid as a pretext should be clearly understood.

Incidentally, how many non-governmental foreign relief organizations are operating in our country to supplement our massive endeavour to overcome the effects of drought? To what extent, in particular, is their participation in distributing emergency relief supplies? It has become imperative to explain the truth based on accurate information so that there could be a clear understanding of this issue.

In addition to various Ethiopian relief aid organizations, the number of non-governmental organizations operating in the country is 47.

Seven of these are deployed in Eritrea and Tigray regions, while only four of these agencies are participating directly in day-to-day relief supply operations. Fifty-eight foreign personnel are engaged in relief work in the two regions, of which 31 are deployed in day-to-day relief supply operation. On the other hand, 1,893 Ethiopians are taking part in the relief work.

Of the amount of food aid distributed in the two regions during the month of January 1988, the share of each organization is as follows:

| | |
|---|---|
| The International Committee of the Red Cross About . . . . . . . . . | 18% |
| The International Organization Against Famine. . . . . . . . . . . . . | 0.1% |
| The Organization known as 'Kaleheywot'. . . . . . . . . . . . . . . . . | 1.8% |
| Ethiopian Religious Organizations. . . . . . . . . . . . . . . . . . . . . . | 33% |
| The Relief and Rehabilitation Commission which is the main relief aid outlet of our government . . . . . . . . . . . . . . . . . . . . | 47% |

Foreign relief organizations maintained a staff of 31 expatriates and 372 Ethiopians in the two regions, while Ethiopian organizations alone had mobilized 1,521 Ethiopians.

Hence, 80% of the work of distribut-ing day-to-day emergency relief supply was handled by Ethiopian organizations and 99% of the personnel working in all the organizations were Ethiopians. A few foreign relief workers have been moved from the north to other areas at present, owing to the serious security situation created by terrorists in the area. Using this to confuse world public opinion and to maintain that the absence of foreign aid workers would deprive relief to about two million people, is clearly baseless to any observer.

Unlike the previous feudal government and its collaborators, we did not hide the recurrent natural calamity that had affected us. We reported it to our people and to the world at large.

It was we ourselves who appealed to governmental and nongovernmental organizations that were willing to supplement our national efforts to help people affected by the natural calamity which was beyond our control. Not a single organization has been sent to Ethiopia by the order, compulsion or initiative of Mr. Reagan.

We are not only free people committed to the defence of our independence but also have a government under which law and order prevail. Therefore, organizations which come to carry out relief or other activities have to be guided by the wishes and interests of this government. They will not be allowed to become bandits acting outside the interest of the people and the law of the land.

Accordingly, various governmental and non-governmental welfare organizations whose numbers have been mentioned above have, for a long time, made substantial humanitarian contributions for which we have expressed our gratitude and indebtedness on various occasions.

What is saddening more than anything else is the claim by many, including personalities of the stature of the President of the United States, that the departure of a small number of relief workers from northern Ethiopia would result in depriving two million people from receiving relief aid. Naturally, the claim is aimed at misleading world public opinion about the current situation in Ethiopia. It is difficult to assume that those who make such claims are not aware of the relief distribution methods. It is also obvious that these claims were made without taking into consideration the objective reality prevailing in northern Ethiopia at present. It is evident that these claims are no more than expressions of deep hatred to us.

The recent speech made by the President of the United States is not different from the many hostile and anti-Ethiopia remarks voiced on several occasions by high-ranking officials of his administration. It is both surprising and saddening to note that the leader of a great power making unfounded and damaging pronouncements with claims that emergency relief distribution had completely stopped in northern Ethiopia. The purpose of such claims is solely to mislead world public opinion.

The fundamental fact that should be borne in mind here is that there cannot be any external body or individual that can become more concerned than the Ethiopian people themselves for their well-being and prosperity. Any idea contrary to this fact cannot be accepted by Ethiopia, and I say on this occasion that it is appropriate and useful that Mr. Reagan and the like should take note of this.

The claim by the United States Administration and some of its accomplices that Ethiopians are incapable of handling relief distribution without help from expatriates is based on an old, unscientific, colonial and racist views about Africans. Therefore, the attempt to promote political hegemony under the guise of relief aid has no acceptance whatsoever.

Although it is known that Ethiopia's relation with her friends is based on equality and mutual respect, our enemies still try to distort this fact and ascribe to it wrong interpretation so as to turn it into an instrument for their destructive propaganda.

While it is possible to talk with us directly through normal diplomatic channels on any matter that concerns us, trying to use or pester certain friends of ours to serve as go-betweens is not only valueless but a mere exercise in futility.

In addition, they try to present Ethiopia as one that does not want peace. Ethiopia, of course, wants peace and wants it for the attainment of her wide-ranging development objectives and programmes. It is also well known that peace has been the main guiding principle of her external relations which she has consistently followed for years.

We need not go far to prove this point. Recently a commendable step has been taken by Ethiopia and Somalia to make peace prevail in the region, strengthen bilateral relations on the basis of mutual benefit and concern for each other and put an end to the feeling of hostility that was responsible for the loss of many lives and damage to property for a long time. Now hostility is being replaced by a policy of good neighbourliness based on norms of international law. This commendable step is a living and timely proof of Ethiopia's good intention. As a result of the agreement reached in Mogadishu recently between the two neighbouring countries, the mutual withdrawal of troops to agreed distance from common boundary is being implemented. In addition, it is hoped that other matters covered by the agreement will be implemented step by step.

It is also to be recalled that the Ethio-Sudan Joint Ministerial Committee recently met in Djibouti and exchanged views on certain basic points. Accordingly, it met again in Addis Ababa and made strenuous efforts to translate into deeds the responsibility entrusted to it.

Since the outcome of the Committee's effort has been made public through a joint communique, its fruit will be realized or determined with contacts at heads of state level in the future.

It is ironic, however, that while we continue to work hard to maintain the unity and independence of our country, accelerate its economic growth, improve the standard of living of our people and make our part of the world a zone of peace, hostile propaganda campaign, aimed at distorting our identity and trying to destroy our endeavours should be waged against us. All those who stand for truth should take note of this fact.

Dear Compatriots!

I have outlined the objective reality presently prevailing in the country. Even now we have to be vigilant. Hostile propaganda campaigns are being waged against us on many fronts. Our enemies are bent on endangering the very existence of our country. They are doing all they can to undermine under the cover of humanitarian relief aid our efforts to withstand the effects of natural calamities. They are also working hard to frustrate our efforts to remove the name of our country from the list of relief aid recipients thereby obstructing our development schemes. At the same time, imperialist-paid agents continue to impede our economic progress, destroy public property, hamper the implementation of our economic development programmes and complicate social problems. Unless these agents cease their destructive activities, our enemies who are using them and proding them from behind will not hesitate to push our Motherland to even more dangerous situation. At the moment they are encouraging the terrorists in their last bid to endanger the unity and survival of our Motherland, through their lavish propaganda, information, material and arms provisions.

In view of this, the Eritrean secessionist group has set up its counterpart in Tigray region to further its anti-Ethiopia mission. In accordance with the order given to them by their patrons recently, the mercenaries in Tigray have announced publicly that their superiors have taken over the task of coordinating the action of the two terrorist groups into a unified "suicide mission."

What is this collaboration or front of "suicide mission"? Is it class solidarity? Ethnic solidarity? What is it? As is known, the Eritrea merecenaries used to hoodwink revolutionaries by claiming to be opposed to the backward feudal order which existed in pre-revolution Ethiopia and to have an anti-imperialist stance. When their true identity was unmasked by the Ethiopian Revolution, it was a well-known fact that they resorted to devising means for auctioning the country by claiming that "the relation between the people of Ethiopia and Eritrea is colonial" and "that Eritrea is an Arab country." This treacherous plot has lasted for about 25 to 30 years, subjecting the Eritrean people to death and starvation, to seek refuge elsewhere or live as subservients. The people know this very clearly and that is why they are siding with our Revolutionary Army in the fight against these mercenaries.

How do the people of Tigray view this? Would the Tigray mercenary group say that the relation between the people of Tigray and Ethiopia is a colonial one? Has Tigray also become Arab? What kind of relation and front is this?

What will the Tigray people benefit if Eritrea seceded from Ethiopia? Do the Ethiopian people have interests other than those of the people of Tigray and Eritrea? What wrong did the Ethiopian masses of the people do to the people of these two regions? Is this for or against the people of these regions? What wrong did this Government do against these people? What wrong did this Party do to these people?

Do they want the people of Tigray to be subjected to the misery and sad plight that the Eritrean people had faced during the last 25 years? Is this in the interest of the people? It cannot be. It is in the interest of the mercenaries. The people of the two regions have been subjected to hunger, misery, disease and war due to various historical and geographical encounters and situations.

It is well-known that since Eritrea and Tigray had been stepping stones for enemy attacks over the years, they had been scenes of battles. Moreover, the people had been subjected to numerous difficulties because of the power rivalry that prevailed among the ruling aristocrats. No less grave were the difficulties they had faced and the attacks they had suffered from time which were caused by bandits and narrow nationalists.

Moreover, we all know that the people of the two regions are exposed to the misery of hunger and famine because of the problem caused by ecological deterioration and land degradation. This, in part, was among the typical causes for the upsurge of the Ethiopian Revolution. On this historic day and at this historic forum, I would like to recall the question raised by a Tigray peasants' representative, when we held a seminar at the Addis Ababa University in connection with the historic Rural Land Proclamation in March, 1975.

The purpose of the seminar was to explain to Ethiopian peasants the Proclamation's value and significance and the ways in which it was to be implemented. It was at this historic seminar that the Tigray peasants' representative put the following question: "We, the peasants of Tigray region, consider this Rural Land Proclamation as a popular victory; it is like a dream come true. And we will die and make sacrifices for its realization. But what we would like to explain to this forum is that the problem of peasants in Tigray region is different from others. Not only are we short of farmlands, but also we face the problem of lack of rain. The soil, too, is not fertile; so we are constantly exposed to hunger and suffering. "Would our Great Revolution give

us land in the other parts of Ethiopia?". Unhesitatingly, I answered, "Yes." We have struggled immensely to keep our pledge and fulfil this promise. This was, in fact, one of the reasons that made us promote the objectives of the resettlement programme. Unfortunately, the peasants of Tigray region even now have not made full use of this opportunity due to the obstacles put by the mercenaries.

Fellow citizens, do you think Ethiopians of the 10th century, let alone those of the 20th century, who may be influenced by reactionary thought, would form a solidarity and a front of "suicide mission" of this kind under the spell of plot and insurrection?.

This is not only saddening but a shameful act. What should be remembered is that Ethiopia was the pride of the black people and served as an example for unity and independence. How then could this be possible? As is correctly known, it is not Ethiopians but mercenaries who are the perpetrators of the act which is not in the interest of the Ethiopian people.

This solidarity and front of "suicide mission" is a gross blunder which history and the people will never forgive under any circumstances. That is why the mercenaries, not the Ethiopian people, Party and Government, that are responsible for every pain caused in the two regions.

Since the nature of the conspiracies hatched against our Motherland and the coordinated war declared on us is clear to all, we have to move without delay and with force realizing that there will be no respite until we take the struggle to its final conclusion.

It seems that our genuine effort to develop our country independently and to build a society wherein equality and prosperity shall prevail, has frightened all the anti-Ethiopia forces. We must realize that we can spare our country the consequences of open aggression not by abandoning our objectives but by defending them. We can do best by implementing those objectives which frighten our enemies and continue with our development endeavours so that equality and prosperity will prevail in this land of ours.

Our peaceful policy and our desire for peace alone are not enough to defend us against enemy aggression. We have, therefore, to press ahead with the slogan "every thing to the war front". There is no other alternative to this correct, determined and popular stand which we have taken, in order to bring the mass movement to its ultimate conclusion.

Our enemies want to see our country weakened and bring her entirely under their control. If not, they want to see her divided and fragmented to the extent that she could be subjected to the whims of others. Since the aim of our enemies is to degrade and humiliate our people by destroying our unity, which has been the secret of our strength for ages, all genuine Ethiopians have to rise up and mobilize themselves in unison more than ever before.

To safeguard the trust of the present and past generations and to be spared from the blame of the future generations, we have to wage a relentless struggle, undaunted by petty and transient interests and without loosing faith and confidence on the vast economic and human resources of our country, we will be able to attain within a short period of time the progress and aspiration we have set for ourselves.

Let us work hard! Let us struggle! Victory will be ours!

Everything to the War Front
Our Motherland Never Lacked Heroes!
We Shall Reliably Defend Her Unity!!

# 34  OGINGA A. ODINGA
## NOT YET UHURU   OCTOBER 25, 1969

*Oginga A. Odinga (1911– ) was educated at the Alliance High School and Makerere College in Uganda. A flamboyant leader among the Luo people of western Kenya, he was a teacher before becoming a successful commercial entrepreneur and politician. In 1952, Odinga was converted to Kenya nationalism by Jomo Kenyatta, the Kikuyu leader, and he remained loyal to Kenyatta during the latter's detention at Lokitaung, and later during the campaign for self-government and independence, in which Odinga's leadership of the Luo was crucial. On December 12, 1963, Kenya became independent, and Oginga Odinga became Vice-President of the republic. He was, however, overshadowed by the dominant personality of Jomo Kenyatta, the President and Mwalimu (teacher), and alienated by the patronage passed on to the Kikuyu élite, who acquired the crucial posts and profits in the new government. Odinga's loyalty to Kenyatta and the Kenya African National Union (KANU) was steadily eroded until he broke with both, politically and philosophically, in 1966.*

*Despite his earlier years as a consummate businessman, Odinga had become increasingly influenced by the ideology of African socialism which held that the independence of Africa would not be complete until political independence was complemented by economic independence, and that this could only be achieved by the application of socialist principles. His advocacy of African socialism brought him succor and support from the Soviet Union—much to the distress of the more conservative Kikuyu who were enjoying the privileges and profits of government offices.*

*Odinga's desertion of KANU to form the Kenya Peoples Union (KPU) presented potential political problems for Kenyatta. Odinga not only commanded the allegiance of the Luo, but, in an alliance with other Kenyan ethnic groups and disgruntled Kikuyu, he threatened to bring down the Kenyatta government. The Kikuyu and the Luo, however, rallied to their own ethnic loyalties, culminating in the confrontation at Kisumu, the major town in Luo land, on October 25, 1969. After he presided over the opening of a hospital, Kenyatta's departing car was stoned by an angry Luo crowd, into which the President's bodyguards fired, killing and wounding an unknown number of Odinga supporters. Kenyatta retaliated swiftly. Odinga was arrested, and the KPU banned. Although he was released in 1977, Odinga stayed under house arrest until 1983. His vision of African socialism and development remained undiminished by the machinations of the Kikuyu ruling clique that had come to enjoy their privileged position in the government of Kenyatta's Kenya.*

When we hang out the national flag for *uhuru* meetings and rallies we don't want the cries of *wapi uhuru (where is uhuru?)* to drown the cheers. Our independence struggle was not meant to enrich a minority. It was to cast off the yoke of colonialism and of poverty. It is not a question of individuals enriching themselves but of achieving national effort to fight poverty in the country as a whole.

Kenyatta's cry to Kaggia before a vast crowd at a public meeting

'What have *you* done for yourself?' is a sign of the depths to which our spirit of national sacrifice for *uhuru* has sunk. Is there no need for national sacrifice? Has *uhuru* given the people what they need? The landless don't think so, nor do the unemployed. There are fewer people in jobs today than there were in 1960. Between now and 1970 400,000 new jobs will be required for school-leavers—this apart from the existing population of unemployed. We have come to understand that *uhuru* is a matter of dealing with poverty.

Government's policy guidelines are contained in the Sessional Paper on African Socialism and the Development Plans for 1964–70. The Sessional paper outlined an economic policy wherein a private sector, cooperatives and a state-owned sector are supposed to comple-

From Oginga Odinga, *Not Yet Uhuru* (London: Heinemann Educational Books Ltd., 1968), pp. 310–15. Reprinted by permission.

ment one another. The only industry nationalized by the Government since *uhuru* has been the Kenya Broadcasting Corporation (now the Voice of Kenya), and this by Achieng Oneko when he was Minister of Information and in the face of strong opposition by some members of the Cabinet. A critic of the Sessional Paper on African Socialism wrote in Tanzania's *Nationalist* that it sounded as if it had been drafted by neither an African nor a socialist. Its drafter turned out to be an American professor-adviser. Before it could be properly debated, the paper was pushed through Parliament; the very few worthwhile clauses it contains have been overshadowed by economic planning and direction firmly founded in capitalist control.

The role of the public sector is visualized only in a very minor sense (as one of KANU's critics said 'the State sector of ownership is still in the mouth).[1] Many

[1] From time to time and with a flourish of trumpets, the government announces the formation of companies in which the country has a share. One such was the Development Finance Corporation of Kenya. But the corporation was launched with a third British government capital and a third West German, while the U.S. Government held the remaining third. The impression is given that the Government is enlarging the state sector of ownership, but in reality this is not so. The Agricultural Development Corporation is heavily financed by Britain, West Germany, and to some extent by the United States. Britain made her participation conditional on the employment of British officers to run the Corporation. The Kenya Government might

pages are taken up in a valueless argument about the respective merits of capitalism and so-called socialism. Throughout the confused talk about African Socialism for Kenya there is the basically false assumption that there can be a harmony of interests between private capital, including private foreign capital, and Government as the representative of the public interest in Kenya. The cooperative movement is dismissed in one paragraph in the Sessional Paper. Nothing is said of the force cooperatives can become in breaking the circle of poverty on the land by helping the farmers, organized collectively to improve production, enjoy better yields, and thus provide not only domestic savings for economic expansion, but also national enthusiasm for development and mass participation without which no building of socialism is possible.

The targets for Kenya's Economic Development Plan for 1964–70 (both the original Plan and the revised) are modest, taking into account Kenya's potential economic resources. There is major emphasis on the agricultural sector, whereas what any underdeveloped country needs is an industrial base, and a meagre allocation to industry under the public capital expenditure programme, meaning that the Government as such is evading responsibility for the development of this sector. Private ownership was the vital force in the past; under these plans it will continue to be so under *uhuru*.

Relying so heavily on agriculture has grave dangers for the economically dependent country. The prices of raw materials have fallen steadily in the world market and the prices of manufactured

have money invested in the corporation, but, subscribed by loans with strings attached, she is not an independent agent. When the National Assurance Company of Kenya was established, Parliament was given the impression that it is a state-owned company. But Kenya holds under 10 per cent of the shares and the balance is held by overseas British insurance companies, all of which are also active as private companies in the insurance market in Kenya.

goods have risen. The imperialist countries, as under colonialism, have the whip hand over our economies. There is much talk in the Sessional Paper about 'economic growth' but nothing about the forces of imperialism which inhibit the economic growth of all African countries, and how only our independence of external forces will remove the restraints on real planning for socialism and hence on our economic growth.

\* \* \*

We have frequent examples of our continued dependence on external forces and the inability or unwillingness of Kenya's government to assert our independence. The power of outside pressures and aid constantly influence our foreign policy. The most tragic recent example is Kenya's appeasement of Britain on the Rhodesian crisis.

Imperialist tactics in southern, central and east Africa are clear. They are to hold back the assault on the southern strongholds of colonialism and White domination for as long as possible; to protect and preserve strategic and economic interests in the Congo; and in East Africa, using Kenya as a base, to keep careful watch on and if necessary to isolate and undermine the new state of Tanzania which is making rapid progress in building socialism and is the cutting edge of the revolutionary forces of Pan-Africanism for the total liberation of our southern half of the continent.

Yet when Kenya was represented at the Accra OAU Conference, her policy at that crucial juncture was influenced not by the needs of strong anti-colonial policies in Africa but by her nervousness to hold on the the £18 million loan being negotiated with Britain for the purchase of settler farms in the latest scheme of the Agricultural Development Corporation.

Kenya's instructions to her representatives at the OAU conference at Accra were not to support a call for the use of force by Britain to bring down the illegal

Smith regime—but not to state this explicity lest Kenya and Kenyatta's stock fall in the Pan-African world. Murumbi who represented Kenya had been a member of the OAU meeting which was advocating the use of force by Britain. When the time came for the Lagos Commonwealth Prime Ministers' Conference, Murumbi was replaced by Gichuru who led the Kenya Delegation of behalf of the President. It looked very much as though it was Britain's pressure on Kenya that resulted in the replacement of Murumbi by Gichuru as leader of the delegation. Gichuru in Lagos appeared to fulfil the fondest hopes of the British Government when, in an interview on television, he is alleged to have said, when asked whether he thought that Rhodesia was ready for immediate majority rule:

It would be very stupid if we were to ask for an immediate takeover. The Africans in Rhodesia are not as well organized as they are here in West Africa or in East Africa, if I might claim that much.[1]

Gichuru denied in the debate referred to that he had made this remark; Parliament, however, rose in protest at this policy.

At the OAU Addis Ababa Conference, Kenya broke the front of Pan-African unity on the question of severing relations with Britain in protest against Britain's Rhodesia policy and her action was largely responsible for the subsequent inability of the OAU to act decisively on Rhodesia.

Kenya's stock has therefore fallen in Africa. It will fall even lower if these policies and this dependence on external forces are not reversed.

Inside Kenya the struggle before us will be stern and exacting. We are struggling to prevent Kenyans in black skins with vested interests from ruling as successors to the administrators of colonial days.

What form will the struggle in Kenya

[1] House of Representatives Official Report, February 1966, cols. 875–879.

take? Is our country to see government and high office riddled with corruption and men in power using force and manoeuvre to block the expression of the popular will? But in the long run, the wishes of the people must prevail.

Kenya's problems in the age of *uhuru* are formidable. We have to deal with landlessness, combat unemployment, give the children more schools and the people more hospitals, push up living standards of the poor in a world where the gap between the rich countries and the poor is daily growing wider.

A Kenya government backed by popular enthusiasm and national mobilization would have a chance of finding a way to solve these problems. A government that is isolated from the people, because government and wealth are in the hands of an elite that is taking power to itself, will plunge our country into pain and tragedy.

Every year that passes swells the throng of those who will not put up with the policies of our government as they are now operated. School-leavers become the unemployed and the unemployed become the bitter men of the streets. The jobless, the frustrated, the peasants starving on the land, will endure much hardship, but how much more and for how long?

I do not imagine for a single moment that these formidable problems are easily solved; but to begin to solve them, one must recognize that these *are* the key problems—and the Kenya Government turns its eyes away from these questions to examine private bank balances and the lists of vacant company directorships.

I do not delude myself that now that I have broken with the government in power and launched a party that will seek for a really just solution for the people of our country, that it will be an easy struggle and that we will not face great difficulties. But it will not be the end of what I stand for if I do not score immediate victories. For our cause is the cause of the people of Kenya and so must triumph, however long and hard the struggle.

## 35.  JULIUS K. NYERERE
# THE ARUSHA DECLARATION  JANUARY 29, 1967

*Julius Kambarage Nyerere (1922?–) was born in Butiama in the British Mandate of Tan-
ganyika and later qualified as a teacher at Makerere College in Uganda. He then took degrees in
history and economics at Edinburgh University before returning to Tanganyika, where in 1954
he reorganized the incipient nationalist movement into the Tanganyika African National Union
(TANU). As the undisputed leader of TANU, he not only successfully negotiated the independence
of Tanganyika (Uhuru) on December 9, 1961, but committed the country to evolution with the
guidance of socialist ideology. He upheld this commitment both before and after the union with
Zanzibar in 1963, which created the Republic of Tanzania.*

*"Yet it gradually became clear that the absence of a generally accepted and easily understood
statement of philosophy and policy was causing problems, and some Government and Party
actions were having the effect of encouraging the growth of non-socialist institutions, values, and
attitudes."[1] Nyerere reacted by emphasizing the importance of hard and rational work. Self-help
became a cornerstone of Nyerere's concept of freedom. This was first expressed in the motto Uhuru
na Kazi (Freedom and Work), with particular regard to farming, the very manifestation of
traditional African life—as symbolized by the popular Swahili proverb: Mgeni siku mbili;
siku ya tatu mpa jembe (Treat your guest as a guest for two days; on the third day give him a
hoe).*

*The goal of socialism through hard work, combined with President Nyerere's growing concern that
the commitment to socialism was not fully understood by the people of Tanzania, resulted in a
meeting of the leaders of TANU called by the President at Arusha in January 1967. There, on
January 29th, the National Executive Committee of TANU committed themselves to the Arusha
Declaration, which was published in Swahili on February 5th. The original draft was written
and submitted to the TANU leadership by President Nyerere himself, but a number of his
recommendations were amended during the proceedings. The document emphasizes frugality and
self-denial. Everyone, whatever his position in the state, was to be considered a worker, while the
means of production—from banks to industry to agriculture—would be nationalized for the
people. The Arusha Declaration marked not only a public commitment to socialism, but a
dramatic decision about the future course of Tanzania's development. Although Nyerere had been
determined to build a socialist society since independence, the First Five Year Development Plan,
in fact, had acknowledged the role of private enterprise in the economy.*

*The Arusha Declaration made explicit not only the sweeping nationalization of all commercial
enterprises and the reduction of the inequity of income between wage earners—particularly civil
servants—and peasant farmers, but a reorientation towards development in the rural areas.
Development would be concentrated around what became known as the Ujamaa (socialist)
villages, in which "a group of families will live together in a village and will work together on a
common farm for their common benefit. . . . For the land will be 'our land' to all the members of
the village; the crops will be 'our crops,' the common herd of animals will be 'our herd.' "[2]*

**PART ONE**

**The TANU "Creed"**
THE POLICY OF TANU IS TO

BUILD A SOCIALIST STATE. THE
PRINCIPLES OF SOCIALISM ARE
LAID DOWN IN THE TANU CON-
STITUTION, AND THEY ARE AS
FOLLOWS:—

[1] Julius K. Nyerere, *Freedom and Socialism:
Uhuru na Ujamaa* (London: 1968), p. 1.
[2] *Ibid.*, pp. 405–06.

Whereas, TANU believes:—

(a) That all human beings are equal;

(b) That every individual has a right to dignity and respect;

(c) That every citizen is an integral part of the Nation and has the right to take an equal part in Government at local, regional and national level;

(d) That every citizen has the right to freedom of expression, of movement, of religious belief and of association within the context of the law;

(e) That every individual has the right to receive from society protection of his life and of property held according to law;

(f) That every individual has the right to receive a just return for his labour;

(g) That all citizens together possess all the natural resources of the country in trust for their descendants;

(h) That in order to ensure economic justice the State must have effective control over the principal means of production; and

(i) That it is the responsibility of the State to intervene actively in the economic life of the Nation so as to ensure the well-being of all citizens and so as to prevent the exploitation of one person by another or one group by another, and so as to prevent the accumulation of wealth to an extent which is inconsistent with the existence of a classless society.

Now, therefore, the principal aims and objects of TANU shall be as follows:—

(a) To consolidate and maintain the independence of this country and the freedom of its people;

(b) To safeguard the inherent dignity of the individual in accordance with the Universal Declaration of Human Rights;

(c) To ensure that this country shall be governed by a democratic socialist government of the people;

(d) To co-operate with all political parties in Africa engaged in the liberation of all Africa;

(e) To see that the Government mobilizes all the resources of this country towards the elimination of poverty, ignorance and disease;

(f) To see that the Government actively assists in the formation and maintenance of co-operative organizations;

(g) To see that wherever possible the Government itself directly participates in the economic development of this country;

(h) To see that the Government gives equal opportunity to all men and women irrespective of race, religion or status;

(i) To see that the Government eradicates all types of exploitation, intimidation, discrimination, bribery and corruption;

(j) To see that the Government exercises effective control over the principal means of production and pursues policies which facilitate the way to collective ownership of the resources of this country;

(k) To see the Government co-operates with other States in Africa in bringing about African Unity;

(l) To see that the Government works tirelessly towards world peace and security through the United Nations Organization.

## PART TWO

### The Policy of Socialism

(a) *Absense of Exploitation:*

A true Socialist State is one in which all people are workers and in which neither Capitalism nor Feudalism exist. It does not have two classes of people: a lower class consisting of people who work for their living, and an upper class consisting of those who live on other people's labour. In a true Socialist State no person exploits another, but everybody who is able to work does so and gets a fair income for his labour, and incomes do not differ substantially.

In a true Socialist State it is only the following categories of people who can live on other people's labour: children, the aged, cripples and those for whom the State at any one time cannot provide with employment.

Tanzania is a state of Peasants and Workers, but it is not yet a Socialist State. It still has elements of Capitalism and Feudalism and their temptations. These elements could expand and entrench themselves.

(b) *Major Means of Production to be under the Control of Peasants and Workers:*

The way to build and maintain socialism is to ensure that the major means of production are under the control and ownership of the Peasants and the Workers themselves through their Government and their Co-operatives. It is also necessary to ensure that the ruling party is a Party of Peasants and Workers.

These major means of production are: the land; forests; mineral resources; water; oil and electricity, communications; transport; banks; insurance; import and export trade; wholesale business; the steel, machine-tool, arms, motor-car cement, and fertilizer factories; the textile industry; and any other big industry upon which a large section of the population depend for their living, or which provides essential components for other industries; large plantations, especially those which produce essential raw materials.

Some of these instruments of production are already under the control and ownership of the people's Government.

(c) *Democracy:*

A state is not socialist simply because all, or all the major, means of production are controlled and owned by the Government. It is necessary for the Government to be elected and led by Peasants and

Workers. If the racist Governments of Rhodesia and South Africa were to bring the major means of production in these countries under their control and direction, this would entrench Exploitation. It would not bring about Socialism. There cannot be true Socialism without Democracy.

(d) *Socialism is an Ideology:*

Socialism is an Ideology. It can only be implemented by people who firmly believe in its principles and are prepared to put them into practice. A true member of TANU is a socialist, and his compatriots, that is his fellow believers in this political and economic faith, are all those in Africa or elsewhere in the world who fight for the rights of the peasants and workers. The first duty of a TANU member, and especially of a TANU leader, is to live by these principles in his day-to-day life. In particular a TANU Leader should never live on another's labour, neither should he have capitalist or feudalist tendencies.

The realization of these socialist objectives depends a great deal on the leadership, for as stated above, Socialism is an ideology, and it is difficult for leaders to implement it if they do not believe in it.

## PART THREE

### The Policy of Self-Reliance

*We are at War:*

TANU is involved in a war against poverty and oppression in our country; this struggle is aimed at moving the people of Tanzania (and the people of Africa as a whole) from a state of poverty to a state of prosperity.

We have been oppressed a great deal, we have been exploited a great deal and we have been disregarded a great deal. It is our weakness that has led to our being oppressed, exploited and disregarded. We now intend to bring about a revolution which will ensure that we are never again victims of these things.

*A poor Man does not use Money as a Weapon:*

But it is obvious that in the past we have chosen the wrong weapon for our struggle, because we chose money as our weapon. We are trying to overcome our economic weakness by using the weapons of the economically strong—weapons which in fact we do not possess. By our thoughts, words and actions it appears as if we have come to the conclusion that without money we cannot bring about the revolution we are aiming at. It is as if we have said, "Money is the basis of development. Without money there can be no development".

This is what we believe at present. TANU leaders, and Government leaders and officials, all put great emphasis and dependence on money. The people's leaders, and the people themselves, in TANU, NUTA, Parliament, UWT, the Co-operatives, TAPA and in other national institutions think, hope and pray for MONEY. It is as if we had all agreed to speak with one voice, saying: "If we get money we shall develop, without money we cannot develop".

In brief, our Five-Year Development Plan aims at more food, more education and better health; but the weapon we have put emphasis upon is money. It is as if we said: "In the next five years we want to have more food, more education and better health and in order to achieve these things we shall spend £250,000,000". We think and speak as if the most important thing to depend upon is MONEY and anything else we intend to use in our struggle is of minor importance.

When a Member of Parliament says that there is a shortage of water in his constituency and he asks the Government how it intends to deal with the problem, he expects the Government to reply that it is planning to remove the shortage of water in his constituency—WITH MONEY.

When another Member of Parliament asks what the Government is doing about the shortage of roads, schools or hospitals in his constituency, he also expects the Government to tell him that it has specific plans to build roads, schools and hospitals in his constituency—with MONEY.

When a NUTA official asks the Government about its plans to deal with the low wages and poor housing of the workers, he expects the Government to inform him that the minimum wage will be increased and that better houses will be provided for the workers—with MONEY.

When a TAPA official asks the Government what plans it has to give assistance to the many TAPA schools which do not get Government aid, he expects the Government to state that it is ready the following morning to give the required assistance—of MONEY.

When an official of the Co-operative Movement mentions any problem facing the farmer, he expects to hear that the Government will solve the farmer's problems—with MONEY. In short, for every problem facing our Nation, the solution that is in everybody's mind is MONEY.

Each year, each Ministry of Government makes its estimates of expenditure, i.e., the amount of money it will require in the coming year to meet recurrent and development expenses. Only one Minister and his Ministry make estimates of revenue. This is the Minister for Finance. Every Ministry puts forward very good development plans. When the Ministry presents its estimates, it believes that the money is there for the asking but that the Minister for Finance and his Ministry are being obstructive. And regularly each year the Minister for Finance has to tell his fellow Ministers that there is no money. And each year the Ministries complain about the Ministry of Finance when it trims down their estimates.

Similarly, when Members of Parliament and other leaders demand that the

Government should carry out a certain development, they believe that there is a lot of money to spend on such projects, but that the Government is the stumbling block. Yet such belief on the part of Ministries, Members of Parliament and other leaders does not alter the stark truth, which is that Government has not money.

When it is said that Government has no money, what does this mean? It means that people of Tanzania have insufficient money. The people pay taxes out of the very little wealth they have; it is from these taxes that the Government meets its recurrent and development expenditure. When we call on the Government to spend more money on development projects, we are asking the Government to use more money. And if the Government does not have any more, the only way it can do this is to increase its revenue through extra taxation.

If one calls on the Government to spend more, one is in effect calling on the Government to increase taxes. Calling on the Government to spend more without raising taxes is like demanding that the Government should perform miracles; it is equivalent to asking for more milk from a cow while insisting that the cow should not be milked again. But our refusal to admit that calling on the Government to spend more is the same as calling on the Government to raise taxes shows that we fully realize the difficulties of increasing taxes. We realize that the cow has no more milk—that is, that the people find it difficult to pay more taxes. We know that the cow would like to have more milk herself, so that her calves could drink it, or that it would like more milk which could be sold to provide more comfort for itself or its calves. But knowing all the things which could be done with more milk does not alter the fact that the cow has no more milk!

*What of External Aid?*

One way we employ to try to escape the need for increased taxation for development purposes is to put emphasis on money coming from outside Tanzania. This money from outside falls into three categories:—

(a) *Grants:* This means that another Government gives our Government a sum of money as a free gift for a given development scheme. Sometimes it may be that an Institution in another country gives our Government or an Institution in our country financial help for development programmes.

(b) *Loans:* The greater portion of financial help we expect to get from outside is not in the form of gifts or charity, but in the form of loans. A foreign Government or a foreign institution, such as a Bank, lends our Government money for the purposes of development. Such a loan has repayment conditions attached to it, covering such factors as the time period for which it is available and the rate of interest.

(c) *Private Investment:* The third category of financial help is also greater than the first. This takes the form of investment in our country by individuals or companies from outside. The important condition which such private investors have in mind is that the enterprise into which they put their money should bring them profit and that our Government should permit them to repatriate these profits. They also prefer to invest in a country whose policies they agree with and which will safeguard their economic interests.

These three are the main categories of external finance. There is a great deal of talk on this question of getting money from external sources. Our Government and our leaders and other people keep on thinking about ways of getting money from outside. And when we get the money, or even the promise of it, our newspapers, our radio, and our leaders announce the news so that everybody may know that salvation has been obtained or is on the way. When we get a gift we make an announcement; when we get a loan or a new industry we make an announcement. In the same way, when we are given the promise of a gift, a loan or a new industry, we make an announcement of this promise. Even when we have merely started discussions with a foreign Government or institution for a gift, a loan, or a new industry, we make an announcement—even though we do not know the outcome of the discussions. Why do we do all this? Because we want people to know that we have started discussions which will bring prosperity.

## Do Not let Us Depend upon Money for Development

It is stupid to rely on money as the major instrument of development when we know only too well that our country is poor. It is equally stupid, indeed it is even more stupid, for us to imagine that we shall rid ourselves of our poverty through foreign financial assistance rather than our own financial resources. It is stupid for two reasons.

Firstly, we shall not get the money. It is true that there are countries which can, and which would like to help us. But there is no country in the world which is prepared to give us gifts or loans, or establish industries, to the extent that we would be able to achieve all our development targets. There are many needy countries in the world. And even if all the prosperous nations were willing to help the needy countries, the assistance would still not suffice. But prosperous nations are not willing to give all they could. Even in these prosperous nations, the rich do not willingly give money to the Government to relieve want.

Money can only be extracted from the rich through taxation. Even then tax revenue is not enough. However heavily we taxed the citizens of Tanzania and aliens living here, the resulting revenue would not be enough to meet the costs of our development programme. Neither is there any Government in the world which can tax the prosperous or rich nations in order to help the poor nations. Even if there was such a government, the revenue would not be enough to do all that is needed. But in fact there is no world Government. Such money as the rich nations offer to poor nations is given voluntarily, either through their goodness or for their own benefit. For all these reasons it is impossible for us to get enough money for development from overseas.

## Gifts and Loans will Endanger our Independence

Secondly, even if it were possible for us to get enough money for our needs from external sources, is this what we really want? Independence means self-reliance. Independence cannot be real if a Nation depends upon gifts and loans from another for its development. Even if there was a Nation, or Nations, prepared to give us all the money we need for our development, it would be improper for us to accept such assistance without asking ourselves how this would affect our independence and our very survival as a nation. Gifts which start off or stimulate our own efforts are useful gifts. But gifts which weaken our own efforts should not be accepted without asking ourselves a number of questions.

The same applies to loans. It is true that loans are better than "free" gifts. A loan is intended to increase our efforts or make those efforts more fruitful. One condition of a loan is that you show how you are going to repay it. This means you have to show that you intend to use the loan profitably and will therefore be able to repay it.

But even loans have their limitations. You have to give consideration to the ability to repay. When we borrow money from other countries it is the Tanzanian who pays it back. And as we have already stated, Tanzanians are poor people. To burden the people with big loans, the repayment of which will be beyond their means, is not to help them but to make them suffer. It is even worse when the loans they are asked to repay have not benefited the majority of the people but have only benefited a small minority.

How about the enterprises of foreign investors? It is true we need these enterprises. We have even passed an Act of Parliament protecting foreign investments in this country. Our aim is to make foreign investors feel that Tanzania is a good place in which to invest because investments would be safe and profitable, and the profits can be taken out of the country without difficulty. We expect to get money through this method. But we cannot get enough. And even if we were able to convince foreign investors and foreign firms to undertake all the projects and programmes of economic development that we need, is that what we actually want to happen?

Had we been able to attract investors from America and Europe to come and start all the industries and all the projects of economic development that we need in this country, could we have done so without questioning ourselves? Would we have agreed to leave the economy of our country in the hands of foreigners who would take the profits back to their countries? Supposing they did not insist on taking their profits away, but decided to reinvest them in Tanzania. Would we accept this situation without asking ourselves what disadvantages it would have for our Nation? How can we build the Socialism we are talking about under such circumstances?

How can we depend upon gifts, loans and investments from foreign countries and foreign companies without endangering our independence? The English people have a proverb which says: "He

who pays the piper calls the tune". How can we depend upon foreign Governments and Companies for the major part of our development without giving to those Government and countries a great part of our freedom to act as we please? The truth is that we cannot.

Let us therefore always remember the following. We have made a mistake to choose money, something which we do not have, to be our major instrument of development. We are mistaken when we imagine that we shall get money from foreign countries, firstly, because to say the truth we cannot get enough money for our development and, secondly, because even if we could get it such complete dependence on outside help would have endangered our independence and the other policies of our country.

## We Have Put too Much Emphasis on Industries

Because of our emphasis on money, we have made another big mistake. We have put too much emphasis in industries. Just as we have said "Without Money there can be no development", we also seem to say "Industries are the basis of development, without industries there is no development". This is true. The day when we have lots of money we shall be able to say we are a developed country. We shall be able to say: "When we began our development plans we did not have enough money and this situation made it difficult for us to develop as fast as we wanted. Today we are developed and we have enough money". That is to say, our money has been brought by development. Similarly, the day we become industrialized, we shall be able to say we are developed. Development would have enabled us to have industries. The mistake we are making is to think that development begins with industries. It is a mistake because we do not have the means to establish many modern industries in our country. We do not have either the necessary finances or the technical know-how. It is not enough to say that we shall borrow the finances and the technicians from other countries to come and start the industries. The answer to this is the same one we gave earlier, that we cannot get enough money and borrow enough technicians to start all the industries we need. And even if we could get the necessary assistance, dependence on it could interfere with our policy on Socialism. The policy of inviting a chain of capitalists to come and establish industries in our country might succeed in giving us all the industries we need, but it would also succeed in preventing the establishment of socialism unless we believe that without first building capitalism, we cannot build Socialism.

## Let Us be Concerned about the Peasant Farmer

Our emphasis on money and industries has made us concentrate on urban development. We recognize that we do not have enough money to bring the kind of development to each village which would benefit everybody. We also know that we cannot establish an industry in each village and through this means effect a rise in the real incomes of the people. For these reasons we spend most of our money in the urban areas and our industries are established in the towns.

Yet the greater part of this money that we spend in the towns comes from loans. Whether it is used to build schools, hospitals, houses or factories, etc., it still has to be repaid. But it is obvious that it cannot be repaid just out of money obtained from urban and industrial development. To repay the loans we have to use foreign currency which is obtained from the sale of our exports. But we do not now sell our industrial products in foreign markets, and indeed it is likely to be a long time before our industries produce for export. The main aim of our new industries is "import substitution"—that is, to produce things which up to now we have had to import from foreign countries.

It is therefore obvious that the foreign currency we shall use to pay back the loans used in the development of the urban areas will not come from the towns or the industries. Where then shall we get it from? We shall get it from the villages and from agriculture. What does this mean? It means that the people who benefit directly from development which is brought about by borrowed money are not the ones who will repay the loans. The largest proportion of the loans will be spent in, or for, the urban areas, but the largest proportion of the repayment will be made through the efforts of the farmers.

This fact should always be borne in mind, for there are various forms of exploitation. We must not forget that people who live in towns can possibly become the exploiters of those who live in the rural areas. All our big hospitals are in towns and they benefit only a small section of the people of Tanzania. Yet if we have built them with loans from outside Tanzania, it is the overseas sale of the peasants' produce which provides the foreign exchange for repayment. Those who do not get the benefit of the hospitals thus carry the major responsibility for paying for them. Tarmac roads, too, are mostly found in towns and are of especial value to the motor-car owners. Yet if we have built those roads with loans, it is again the farmer who produces the goods which will pay for them. What is more, the foreign exchange with which the car was bought also came from the sale of the farmer's produce. Again, electric lights, water pipes, hotels and other aspects of modern development are mostly found in towns. Most of them have been built with loans, and most of them do not benefit the farmer directly, although they will be paid for by the foreign exchange earned by the sale of his produce. We should always bear this in mind.

Although when we talk of exploitation we usually think of capitalists, we should not forget that there are many fish in the sea. They eat each other. The large ones eat the small ones, and the small ones eat those who are even smaller. There are two possible ways of dividing the people in our country. We can put the capitalists and feudalists on one side, and the peasants and workers on the other. But we can also divide the people into urban dwellers on one side, and those who live in the rural areas on the other. If we are not careful we might get to the position where the real exploitation in Tanzania is that of the town dwellers exploiting the peasants.

## The People and Agriculture

The development of a country is brought about by people, not by money. Money, and the wealth it represents, is the result and not the basis of development. The four prerequisites of development are different; they are (i) People; (ii) Land; (iii) Good Policies; (iv) Good Leadership. Our country has more than ten million people and its area is more than 362,000 square miles.

## Agriculture is the Basis of Development

A great part of Tanzania's land is fertile and gets sufficient rains. Our country can produce various crops for home consumption and for export.

We can produce food crops (which can be exported if we produce in large quantities) such as maize, rice, wheat, beans, groundnuts, etc. And we can produce such cash crops as sisal, cotton, coffee, tobacco, pyrethrum, tea, etc. Our land is also good for grazing cattle, goats, sheep, and for raising chickens, etc.; we can get plenty of fish from our rivers, lakes, and from the sea. All of our farmers are in areas which can produce two or three or even more of the food and cash crops

enumerated above and each farmer could increase his production so as to get more food or more money. And because the main aim of development is to get more food, and more money for our other needs, our purpose must be to increase production of these agricultural crops. This is the fact the only road through which we can develop our country—in other words, only by increasing our production of these things can we get more food and more money for every Tanzanian.

## The Conditions of Development
(a) *Hard Work:*

Everybody wants development; but not everybody understands and accepts the basic requirements for development. The biggest requirement is hard work. Let us go to the villages and talk to our people and see whether or not it is possible for them to work harder.

In towns, for example, the average paid worker works seven-and-a-half or eight hours a day for six or six-and-a-half days a week. This is about 45 hours a week, excluding two or three weeks' leave every year. This means that an urban worker works for 45 hours a week in 48 to 50 weeks a year.

For a country like ours these are really quite short working hours. In other countries, even those which are more developed than we are, people work for more than 45 hours a week. It is not normal for a young country to start with such a short working week. The normal thing is to begin with long working hours and decrease them as the country becomes more and more prosperous. By starting with such short working hours and asking for even shorter hours, we are in fact imitating the more developed countries. And we shall regret this imitation. Nevertheless, wage-earners do work for 45 hours per week and their annual vacation does not exceed four weeks.

It would be appropriate to ask our

farmers, especially the men, how many hours a week and how many weeks a year they work. Many do not even work for half as many hours as the wage-earner does. The truth is that in the villages the women work very hard. At times they work for 12 or 14 hours a day. They even work on Sundays and public holidays. Women who live in the villages work harder than anybody else in Tanzania. But the men who live in villages (and some of the women in towns) are on leave for half of their life. The energies of the millions of men in the villages and thousands of women in the towns which are at present wasted in gossip, dancing and drinking, are a great treasure which could contribute more towards the development of our country than anything we could get from rich nations.

We would be doing something very beneficial to our country if we went to the villages and told our people that they hold this treasure and that it is up to them to use it for their own benefit and the benefit of our whole Nation.

(b) *Intelligence:*

The second condition of development is the use of INTELLIGENCE. Unintelligent hard work would not bring the same good results as the two combined. Using a big hoe instead of a small one; using a plough pulled by oxen instead of an ordinary hoe; the use of fertilizers; the use of insecticides; knowing the right crop for a particular season or soil; choosing good seeds for planting; knowing the right time for planting, weeding, etc.; all these things show the use of knowledge and intelligence. And all of them combined with hard work to produce more and better results.

The money and time we spend on passing on this knowledge to the peasants are better spent and bring more benefits to our country than the money and the great amount of time we spend on other things which we call development.

These facts are well-known to all of us. The parts of our Five-Year Development Plan which are on target, or where the target has been exceeded, are those parts which depend solely upon the people's own hard work. The production of cotton, coffee, cashewnuts, tobacco and pyrethrum has increased tremendously for the past three years. But these are things which are produced by hard work and the good leadership of the people, not by the use of great amounts of money.

Furthermore the people, through their own hard work and with a little help and leadership, have finished many development projects in the villages. They have built schools, dispensaries, community centres, and roads; they have dug wells, water-channels, animal dips, small dams, and completed various other development projects. Had they waited for money, they would not now have the use of these things.

## Hard Work is the Root of Development

Some Plan projects which depend on money are going on well, but there are many which have stopped and others which might never be fulfilled because of lack of money. Yet still we talk about money and our search for money increases and takes nearly all our energies. We should not lessen our efforts to get the money we really need, but it would be more appropriate for us to spend time in the villages showing the people how to bring about development through their own efforts, rather than going on so many long and expensive journeys abroad in search of development money. This is the real way to bring development to everybody in the country.

None of this means that from now on we will not need money or that we will not start industries or embark upon development projects which require money. Furthermore, we are not saying that we will not accept, or even that we shall not look for, money from other countries for our development. This is

NOT what we are saying. We will continue to use money; and each year we will use more money for the various development projects than we used the previous year because this will be one of the signs of our development.

What we are saying, however, is that from now on we shall know what is the foundation and what is the fruit of development. Between MONEY and PEOPLE it is obvious that the people and their HARD WORK are the foundation of development, and money is one of the fruits of that hard work.

From now on we shall stand upright and walk forward on our feet rather than look at this problem upside down. Industries will come and money will come but their foundation is THE PEOPLE and their HARD WORK, especially in AGRICULTURE. This is the meaning of self-reliance. Our emphasis should therefore be on:—

    (a) The Land and Agriculture,

    (b) The People,

    (c) The Policy of Socialism and Self-Reliance, and

    (d) Good Leadership.

(a) *The Land:*

Because of the economy of Tanzania depends and will continue to depend on agriculture and animal husbandry, Tanzanians can live well without depending on help from outside if they use their land properly. Land is the basis of human life and all Tanzanians should use it as a valuable investment for future development. Because the land belongs to the Nation, the Government has to see to it that it is used for the benefit of the whole nation and not for the benefit of one individual or just a few people.

It is the responsibility of TANU to see that the country produces enough food, enough cash crops for export. It is the responsibility of the Government and the Cooperative Societies to see to it that our people get the necessary tools, training and leadership in modern methods of agriculture.

(b) *The People:*

In order properly to implement the policy of self-reliance, the people have to be taught the meaning of self-reliance and its practice. They must become self-sufficient in food, serviceable clothes and good housing.

In our country work should be something to be proud of, and laziness, drunkenness and idleness should be things to be ashamed of. And for the defence of our Nation, it is necessary for us to be on guard against internal stooges who could be used by external enemies who aim to destroy us. The people should always be ready to defend their Nation when they are called upon to do so.

(c) *Good Policies:*

The principles of our policy of self-reliance go hand in hand with our policy on Socialism. In order to prevent exploitation it is necessary for everybody to work and to live on his own labour. And in order to distribute the national wealth fairly, it is necessary for everybody to work to the maximum of his ability. Nobody should go and stay for a long time with his relative, doing no work, because in doing so he will be exploiting his relative. Likewise, nobody should be allowed to loiter in towns or villages without doing work which would enable him to be self-reliant without exploiting his relatives.

TANU believes that everybody who loves his Nation has a duty to serve it by co-operating with his fellows in building the country for the benefit of all the people of Tanzania. In order to maintain our independence and our people's freedom we ought to be self-reliant in every possible way and avoid depending upon other countries for assistance. If every individual is self-reliant the ten-house cell will be self-reliant; if all the cells are self-reliant the whole ward will be self-reliant; and if the wards are self-reliant the District will be self-reliant. If the Districts are self-reliant, then the Region is self-reliant, and if the Regions are self-reliant, then the whole Nation is self-reliant and this is our aim.

(d) *Good Leadership:*

TANU realizes the importance of good leadership. The problem is that we have not prepared proper plans for the training of leaders. The Party Headquarters is now called upon to prepare specific plans for the training of leaders from the national level down to the leaders of the ten-house cells, so that all may understand our political and economic policies. Leaders must be a good example to the rest of the people through their actions and in their own lives.

## PART FOUR

### Tanu Membership

Since the founding of the Party greater emphasis has been put on having as large a membership as possible. This was justified during the struggle for independence. Now, however, the National Executive Committee feels that the time has come for emphasis to shift away from more size of membership on to the quality of the membership. Greater consideration must be given to a member's commitment to the beliefs and objectives of the Party, and its policy of Socialism.

The Membership Clause in the TANU Constitution must be closely observed. Where it is thought unlikely that an applicant really accepts the beliefs, aims and objects of the Party, he should be denied membership. Above all it should always be remembered that TANU is a Party of Peasants and Workers.

## PART FIVE

### The Arusha Resolution

Therefore, the National Executive Committee, meeting in the Community Centre at Arusha from 26.1.67 to 29.1.67, resolves:—

### A. THE LEADERSHIP

1. Every TANU and Government leader must be either a Peasant or a Worker, and should in no way be associated with the practices of Capitalism or Feudalism.

2. No TANU or Government leader should hold shares in any Company.

3. No TANU or Government leader should hold Directorships in any privately-owned enterprises.

4. No TANU or Government leader should receive two or more salaries.

5. No TANU or Government leader should own houses which he rents to others.

6. For the purposes of this Resolution the term "leader" should comprise the following: Members of the TANU National Executive Committee; Ministers, Members of Parliament, Senior Officials of Organizations affiliated to TANU, Senior Officials of Para-Statal Organizations, all those appointed or elected under any clause of the TANU Constitution, Councillors, and Civil Servants in high and middle cadres. (In this context "leader" means a man, or a man and his wife; a woman, or a woman and her husband).

### B. THE GOVERNMENT AND OTHER INSTITUTIONS

1. Congratulates the Government for the steps it has taken so far in the implementation of the policy of Socialism.

2. Calls upon the Government to take further steps in the implementation of our policy of Socialism as described in Part Two of this document without waiting for a Presidential Commission on Socialism.

3. Calls upon the Government to put emphasis, when preparing its development plans, on the ability of this country to implement the plans rather than depending on foreign loans and grants as has been done in the current

Five-Year Development Plan. The National Executive Committee also resolves that the Plan should be amended so as to make it fit in with the policy of self-reliance.

4. Calls upon the Government to take action designed to ensure that the incomes of workers in the private sector are not very different from the incomes of workers in the public sector.

5. Calls upon the Government to put great emphasis on actions which will raise the standard of living of the peasants, and the rural community.

6. Calls upon NUTA, the Co-operatives, TAPA, UWT, TYL, and other Government institutions to take steps to implement the policy of Socialism and Self-reliance.

### C. MEMBERSHIP

Members should get thorough teaching on Party ideology so that they may understand it, and they should always be reminded of the importance of living up to its principles.

## 36. APOLLO MILTON OBOTE

## THE COMMON MAN'S CHARTER: FIRST STEPS FOR UGANDA TO MOVE TO THE LEFT DECEMBER 18, 1969.

*The publication of "The Common Man's Charter" on December 19, 1969, marked the conviction by President Obote and his supporters in the Uganda People's Congress that national consolidation, ideological cohesion, and economic development could only be achieved with an organizational structure that would generate popular support from the people of Uganda. Since 1966, Obote had ruled Uganda more by manipulation than by ideology. In 1969 he sought to bring definition to his regime by advocating a pattern of economic development to appeal to "the common man"—the overwhelming majority of Ugandans who lived by their own labor—as distinct from the minority who "exploited" the labor of others. The aim of the Charter was to commit all Ugandans to live by their own work and receive in return an appropriate share of the wealth of their respective societies. This goal, Obote argued, could only be achieved by organizing Ugandan society on socialist principles whereby collective ownership through parastatal bodies and co-operatives was to be implemented. The "Move to the Left," however, proved to be riddled with ambiguities, and compromised by ethnic rivalries and the power of nationalism.*

1. We the members of the Annual Delegates' Conference of the Uganda People's Congress, assembled on this Eighteenth Day of December, 1969, in an Emergency Meeting in Kampala, being the body charged under the Constitution of the Uganda People's Congress with the responsibility "to lay down the broad basic policy of the Party" and being conscious of our responsibility and of the fact that the Government of the Republic of Uganda, District Administrations and Urban Authorities are currently run by our Party and on policies and programmes adopted by our Party, and recognising our responsibility to the people of Uganda as a whole and to the association of Uganda, Tanzania and

From Dr. A. Milton Obote, "The Common Man's Charter" (Entebbe: The Government Printer, 1969).

Kenya in the East African Community and to Uganda's membership of the Organisation of African Unity, do hereby adopt this Charter for the realisation of the real meaning of Independence, namely, that the resources of the country, material and human, be exploited for the benefit of all the people of Uganda in accordance with the principles of Socialism.

2. We hereby commit ourselves to create in Uganda conditions of full security, justice, equality, liberty and welfare for all sons and daughters of the Republic of Uganda, and for the realisation of those goals we have adopted the Move to the Left Strategy herein laid as initial steps.

3. We subscribe fully to Uganda always being a Republic and have adopted this Charter so that the implementation of this Strategy prevents effectively any one person or group of persons from being masters of all or a section of the people of Uganda, and ensures that all citizens of Uganda become truly masters of their own destiny.

4. We reject, both in theory and in practice, that Uganda as a whole or any part of it should be the domain of any person, of feudalism, of capitalism, of vested interests of one kind or another, of foreign influence or of foreigners. We further reject exploitation of material and human resources for the benefit of a few.

5. We reject, both in theory and in practice, isolationism in regard to one part of Uganda towards another, or in regard to Uganda as a whole to the East African Community in particular, and Africa in general.

6. Recognising that the roots of the U.P.C. have always been in the people right from its formation, and realising that the Party has always commanded us that whatever is done in Uganda must be done for the benefit of all, we hereby reaffirm our acceptance of the aims and objectives of the U.P.C. which we set out below in full:—

"(i) To build the Republic of Uganda as one country with one people, one Parliament and one Government.

(ii) To defend the Independence and Sovereignty of Uganda and maintain peace and tranquillity, and to preserve the Republican Constitution of Uganda.

(iii) To organise the Party to enable the people to participate in framing the destiny of our country.

(iv) To fight relentlessly against Poverty, Ignorance, Disease, Colonialism, Neo-Colonialism, Imperialism and Apartheid.

(v) To plan Uganda's Economic Development in such a way that the Government, through Parastatal Bodies, the Co-operative Movements, Private Companies, Individuals in Industry, Commerce and Agriculture, will effectively contribute to increased production to raise the standard of living in the country.

(vi) To protect without discrimination based on race, colour, sex or religion, every person lawfully living in Uganda and enable him to enjoy the fundamental rights and freedom of the individual, that is to say,

*(a)* Life, Liberty, Security of the person and Protection of the Law.

*(b)* Freedom of conscience, of expression and association.

*(c)* Protection of Privacy of his home, property and from deprivation of property without compensation.

(vii) To ensure that no citizen of Uganda will enjoy any special privilege, status or title by virtue of birth, descent or heredity.

(viii) To ensure that in the enjoyment of the rights and freedoms, no person shall be allowed to prejudice the rights and freedoms of others and the interests of the State.

(ix) To support organisations, whether international or otherwise, whose aims, objects and aspirations are consistent with those of the Party.

(x) To do such other things that are necessary for the achievement of the aims, objects and aspirations of the Party".

7. Republicanism in Uganda, just like the political Independence of Uganda, is now a reality, but the demand and struggle for Uhuru has no end. This is part of life and part of the inalienable right of man. It is also the cornerstone of progress and of the liberty of the individual, the basis of his prosperity and the hallmark of his full and effective participation in the affairs of his country. October 9th, 1962, therefore, was the beginning of a much greater struggle of many dimensions along the road to the goal of full Uhuru. During the last seven years the U.P.C., by action and exhortation, has shown to the people of Uganda that it is wrong and deceitful to treat and regard the 9th October, 1962, as the end of the road; or the day on which the people of Uganda as a whole reached a stage in their development when all that remained was to divide the spoils on the principle of the survival of the fittest; or that the well-to-do, the educated and the feudal lords must and should be allowed to keep what they have, and get more if they can, without let or hindrance.

8. The Party has always made it clear to the people that the only acceptable and practical meaning of October 9th, 1962, is that the people of Uganda must move away from the ways and mental attitudes of the colonial past, move away from the hold of tribal and other forms of factionalism and the power of vested interests, and accept that the problems of poverty, development and nation-building can and must be tackled on the basis of one Country and one People. The Strategy laid down in this Charter aims at strengthening the fundamental objective of the Party. We do not believe that any citizen of Uganda, once free of the mental attitudes of the colonial past, freed of the hold of tribal and other forms of factionalism, and free of the power of vested interests, will find himself or herself at a disadvantage. On the contrary, it is our firm belief that such a citizen will gain that part of his/her freedom which has so far been in the hands of others, and which enabled those others to exploit for their own benefits not only the wealth of the country, but also the energy of our people, thereby arresting the mental development of our people.

9. Less than ten years ago the most prominent and explosive political issues which faced the people of Uganda had in reality, and in practical terms, nothing to do with the people as such. The issues were "The form of government suitable for an independent Uganda" and "Who was to be the Head of State on the achievement of Independence?" These issues were made to appear as of national importance, not because when solutions were found they would advance the lot of the common man, but because the feudalists, on account of their hold on the people, saw Independence as a threat to their then privileged positions and sought to make these positions synonymous with the interests of the common man. It cannot be denied that the then privileged positions of the feudalists were a barrier to the full and effective participation of the common man in the Government of Independent Uganda. The feudalists wanted to continue to rule as they used to before the coming of the British and they did not want the common man to have a say in the shaping of the destiny of an independent Uganda. That situation, however, is no longer with us. Uganda is now a Republic. We hold it as the inalienable

right of the people that they must be masters of their own destiny and not servants of this or that man; that they must, as citizens of an Independent Republic, express their views as freely as possible within the laws of their country, made, not in separate Parliaments, but in one Parliament in which the people as a whole have an equal say through their representatives.

10. The Republican status, therefore, has taken Uganda further towards the goal of full Uhuru. It must not be accepted, however, that our new status by itself is sufficient, or that it has removed exploitation and has brought full Uhuru. We realise that it is, by itself, an advance towards the goal of full Uhuru, but because we are also convinced that more has yet to be done, this Charter has been adopted, and its Strategy is, in our view, a logical development from the fact that we have been moving away from the hold of feudal power since 1966. For so long as that feudal power was a factor in the politics and the economy of Uganda, it could not be disregarded. Thus the reason for this Charter. It must also be noted that in a society in which feudalism is an important and major political and economic factor, that society cannot escape being Rightist in its internal and external policies. With the removal of the feudal factor from our political and economic life, we need to do two things. First, we must not allow the previous position of the feudalists to be filled by neo-feudalists. Secondly, we must move away from circumstances which may give birth to neo-feudalism or generate feudalistic mentality.

11. The Move to the Left is the creation of a new political culture and a new way of life, whereby the people of Uganda as a whole—their welfare and their voice in the National Government and in other local authorities—are para-

mount. It is, therefore, both anti-feudalism and anti-capitalism.

12. In 1968, the U.P.C. Delegates' Conference passed the following resolution on the important matter of nation-building:—

"NOTE with deep satisfaction the liquidation of anti-national and feudal forces, and the introduction of the Republican Constitution.

THANK the leaders of the Party and the Government on initiating the revolution for economic, social and political justice.

RECOGNISE that the most important task confronting the Party and the Government today is that of nation-building.

RESOLVE that its entire human and material resources be committed in that task of nation-building.

DIRECT that the National Council of the Party do examine ways and means for active involvement of all institutions, State and private, in joint endeavour with the Party to achieve and serve a nation united and one".

13. We have no doubt whatsoever about the high priority which must be given to nation-building, and we are fully aware that there may be many people in this country who are either uninformed or misguided, who have not yet come to appreciate the importance of nation-building. We, therefore, consider it our responsibility to inform the uninformed, and to guide the misguided. It is also our responsibility to enlighten the people about the necessity of all the institutions in this country and the people as a whole being actively involved in the joint endeavour to serve the Nation.

14. When the U.P.C. proposes a policy or programme on behalf and for the benefit of the people of Uganda, the meaning of the phrase "people of Uganda" is always clear and definite. It

is, One People under One Government in One Country. Accordingly, over the seven years of Independence the Party has indicated more than sufficiently that to belong to a clan, a tribe, a linguistic group, a region or a religion, is neither an advantage nor a disadvantage to any citizen of Uganda. The fact of being a citizen of Uganda, however, is a decided advantage which gives him fundamental rights and freedoms, and affords him full opportunity to exercise his social duties and obligations to his clan, tribe, region or religion, save as forbidden by laws passed by Parliament. These laws, as it is clearly stated in Principle 6 of the U.P.C. Aims and Objects, and in the Republican Constitution, are desirable so as to enable all citizens to enjoy their fundamental rights and freedoms without infringing upon the rights and freedoms of any other citizens to do the same.

15. In seven years of Independence we have experienced that the mass of our people are law-abiding citizens, who believe in the security of their families, stable conditions around their homes and throughout Uganda; who appreciate the need for expanding economic and social services, and who are desirous to work hard to improve their conditions of living and participate fully in the political control of governmental institutions. This experience is in contrast to another, namely, the desire of foreign powers and institutions to choose leaders for us, to influence the policies of the Government of Uganda to the benefit of foreign interests, and to use the sons and daughters of Uganda to advance these interests. In our experience we have not found a single instance where foreign interests have sought to use the masses of the people to serve the interests of foreigners. We have, however, had abundant instances where the well-to-do, the educated and the feudal elements have been bought to serve the interests of foreigners. This kind of corruption of the intentions and

frustration of the wishes of the people may be tolerated in countries where nationhood has been firmly established, illiteracy is almost unknown and other factional issues do not play any important part in elections or in formulation of Government policies. Uganda has not yet reached that stage of development; but even when we eventually reach that stage we will not tolerate, on principle, the corruption of the intentions and the frustration of the wishes of the people.

16. One of the most important considerations facing the people of Uganda, in the view of the U.P.C., is the future of the youth. We have only to look at the figures of all the young men and women in the Universities, in the Secondary Schools, in other institutes of learning and in the Primary Schools, to speak nothing of those who are at home, to realise that these are citizens of Uganda who are being prepared to shoulder responsibilities of consolidating further the political independence we now have, and to open more and more avenues which will lead the people of Uganda to real, economic and social independence.

17. If, here in Uganda, we adopt the policy of developing our country and preparing our youth within the confines of tribal governments, tribal parliaments and traditions, and as tools of sectionalism and factionalism of any kind, we would neither be making a contribution to the African Revolution, nor would we be giving these young people what is within our power to give them—that is, the broadening of their horizon to look at the whole of Uganda and not just a part of it as the centre and platform of their operations. It is our duty and responsibility to accept these young people irrespective of the corner of Uganda which may be their birthplace. The whole of Uganda is their inheritance and we must not deny either all of them or a majority of them or even a minority of them, that

heritage. They are growing in a different world—a world very different from the world in which those who faced the British when they first imposed colonial rule in Uganda lived. Young people are growing in a world which is becoming smaller and smaller, and for us to make that world even smaller by inducing them, directly or indirectly, to become the exponents of tribal Herrenvolk principles, religious bigotry and fanaticism and feudalistic selfishness, and capitalistic rapacities would be to do a disservice that Africa will never forget, and a disservice that will certainly reduce the mental capacities of our young men and women. Uganda cannot afford to be so heartless to her youth.

18. It is not only the youth whom we must think about. Those who are grown up are equally important. Even the old and the infirm are important. The tribal confines and security are no longer strong enough to give them the requirements of modern times, or to protect their lives and property or to give that important recognition of human dignity and citizenship of a sovereign State.

19. We reiterate the fact that the struggle for Independence was not a one-tribe struggle, nor was it a struggle confined to people professing one religion. The colonial power heard voices from all corners of Uganda. The struggle, however, was not that different parts of Uganda should return to the days of tribal quarrels, disunity and wars, but to move to the new era wherein all people of Uganda are one and the country is one, and to regain our dignity as human beings.

20. We recognise that ours is a society in transition. We want to bring out our considered assessment of the present situation as the starting point for our adoption of the Move to the Left Strategy set out in this Charter. Uganda is a country which is already independent politically.

It is that status that makes it the responsibility of the people of Uganda to shape their destiny. Before the 9th of October, 1962, the people of Uganda did not have that responsibility or power, The sixty-nine years of colonial rule, during which an alien way of life was not only planted but also took root, resulted in the phenomenon of developing our human and material resources to bear the imprint of this factor in our society. What was planted in Uganda during the era of British protectorate appeared in the eyes and minds of our people as the final word in perfection regarding the development of our material resources and human relationship. Consequently, both before and after Independence, our people have been living in a society in which an alien way of life has been embedded. The result has been that most of our people do not look in to the country for ideas to make life better in Uganda, but always look elsewhere to import ideas which may be perfectly suitable in some other society but certainly unfitting in a society like ours. The more we pursue that course, the more we artificially organise our society, our material resources and human relationship, and the more we perpetuate a foreign way of life in our country.

21. We cannot afford to build two nations within the territorial boundaries of Uganda: one rich, educated, African in appearance but mentally foreign, and the other, which constitutes the majority of the population, poor and illiterate. We do not consider that all aspects of the African traditional life are acceptable as socialistic. We do not, for instance, accept that belonging to a tribe should make a citizen a tool to be exploited by and used for the benefit of tribal leaders. Similary, we do not accept that feudalism, though not inherently something peculiar to Africa or to Uganda, is a way of life which must not be disturbed because it has been in practice for cen-

turies. With this background, we are convinced that Uganda has to choose between two alternatives. We either perpetuate what we inherited, in which case we will build on a most irrational system of production and distribution of wealth based on alien methods, or we adopt a programme of action based on the realities of our country. The choice adopted in this Charter is the latter. We must move away from the ways of the past to the avenues of reality, and reject travelling along a road where the signpost reads: "Right of admittance is belief in the survival of the fittest". To us, every citizen of Uganda must survive and we are convinced that Uganda has to move to the Left as a unit. Conditions must be created to enable the fruits of Independence to reach each and every citizen without some citizens enjoying privileged positions or living on the sweat of their fellow citizens.

22. The emergence and growth of a privileged group in our society, together with the open possibilities of the group assuming the powers of the feudal elements, are not matters of theory and cannot be disregarded with a wave of the hand. Nor should the same be looked at from a doctrinaire approach. It is for this reason that in this Charter we do not intend to play with words, even if those words have meanings, such as "capitalism" or "Communism". We are convinced that from the standpoint of our history, not only our educational system inherited from pre-Independence days, but also the attitudes to modern commerce and industry and the position of a person in authority, in or outside Government, are creating a gap between the well-to-do on the one hand and the mass of the people on the other. As the years go by, this gap will become wider and wider. The Move to the Left Strategy of this Charter aims at bridging the gap and arresting this development.

23. We identify two circumstances in which the emergence of a privileged class can find comfort and growth. First, there is our education system which aims at producing citizens whose attitude to the uneducated and to their way of life leads them to think of themselves as the masters and the uneducated as their servants. Secondly, the opportunities for self-employment in modern commerce and industry and to gain employment in Government and in other sectors of the economy are mainly open to the educated few; but instead of these educated few doing everything possible within their powers for the less educated, a tendency is developing where whoever is in business or in Government looks to his immediate family and not to the country as a whole in opening these opportunities. The existence of these circumstances could lead to actual situations of corruption, nepotism and abuse of responsibility. It is unrealistic for anyone to believe that the answer to such situations lies in the strict application of the laws. Much as the laws might assist in preventing such crimes being committed against the nation, it is our view that the answer lies in tackling the roots of the problem, namely, to generate a new attitude to life and to wealth, and new attitudes in exercising responsibilities. Our country is fortunate in that these problems have not taken deep roots and the crimes which they generate are universally condemned by the society. If we do not take initial effective measures to change the course of events at this stage of our history, it may be too late to avoid violence in future years. It is because we are convinced that this is the right moment to reorientate our course that we have adopted the measures set out in the Move to the Left Strategy of this Charter.

24. The ordinary citizen of Uganda associates economic development of this

country with a rise in his own private real income. This income may accrue to him from self-employment, *i.e.*, farming, fishing, cattle-keeping, or paid employment. What is of crucial importance to the ordinary citizen is that Government should provide him with certain social services free and that his income should rise faster than the cost of living, so that he can afford more goods and services for his own use. But there are also three other major dimensions of economic development which must concern our Government. These are: the distribution of the national income, the structure of the economy and the creation of institutions conducive to further development and consistent with the Socialist Strategy outlined in this Charter.

25. Let us begin with the examination of the distribution of income in our country. It is obvious that for development to take place, there should be a rise in the average income per head (*per capita* income). This can only occur if the rate of growth of national income exceeds the rate of population growth. For this reason our Government must always place great emphasis on the fast rate of growth of the economy and the national income. Indeed, increased production and wealth is one of the three major goals of the current Plan ("Work for Progress") 1966–71. We are fully convinced that this emphasis is not misplaced, since raising the standard of living of the Common Man in Uganda must be the major aim of our Government. It is possible, however, for the overall rate of growth to rise without affecting large masses of the population. This is a danger that we must guard against. We must not, either because of inertia, corruption, or academic love for the principle of the theory of free enterprise, fail to take bold corrective measures against this danger.

26. There is also the danger that eco-

nomic development could be unevenly distributed as between regions of the country. The fact is that there is no automatic mechanism within our economic system to ensure an equitable distribution of the national income among persons, groups of persons or regions. We need only to stretch our eyes not to the distant future but to the years immediately ahead of us, taking into account the fact of our present expanding economy, to recognise that if no new strategy is adopted now, inequalities in the distribution of income will change dramatically the status of millions of our people, and might result in our having two nations—one fabulously rich and living on the sweat of the other, and the other living in abject poverty—both living in one country. In such a situation, political power will be in the hands of the rich and the maximum the Government will do for the poor will be paternalism, where the lot of the masses will be not only to serve the well-to-do, but to be thankful on their knees when opportunity arises to eat the crumbs from the high table.

27. The nature of our economy today is such that the resources are not allocated by a central authority. The reality of the situation is that allocation of resources in Uganda today is directly proportionate to the distribution of income. The practical fact which emerges from this can be illustrated in this way. If 5 per cent of the population receive, say, 50 per cent of the national income among them, this small minority possesses the power to command at least half of the productive resources of the country. With so much wealth at their disposal, their consumption habits will affect the whole economy. As it happens, these habits will be characterised by the consumption of luxurious goods not produced in the country but imported from outside, or produced in the country at extremely high cost. If the goods have to be imported, then the bulk of the popu-

lation must produce for export in order to pay for the import of such luxurious goods. Our argument for a change to make it impossible for such a situation to develop as a feature of Uganda is that the consumption habits of the very rich not only impinge directly on the disposal of one of the very important resources of the country, namely, foreign exchange, but also constitute a negation of the real meaning of our Independence. The crucial point here is that inequitable distribution of income leads directly to nondevelopment of resources which could cater for the consumption needs of the poor, since the masses cannot afford to pay for the goods which would be produced, and instead the economy becomes dependent on exports of primary commodities in order to pay for imports of luxurious goods for the rich. The end result is a constant problem of unfavourable balance of payments and external debts, and a neglect of the welfare of the Common Man.

28. We must examine the argument in another way. A redistribution of income which puts more purchasing power in the hands of the Common Man, who constitutes the greatest proportion of the population, would give an impetus to the development of local industries. This is because the needs of the masses are unlikely to be of the luxurious type. As the mass of the people of Uganda begin to acquire higher and higher incomes, they would in all probability acquire more and more of the goods produced in their country; but to open the door only to the rich to buy at high prices any quantity of imported goods and locally produced goods at high costs, which put them beyond the means of the Common Man, is to disregard the existence of the mass of the population or to acknowledge their servitude to the rich.

29. The heart of the Move to the Left can be simply stated. It is both political and economic. It is the basic belief of the Uganda People's Congress that political power must be vested in the majority of the people and not the minority. It is also the fundamental belief of the Uganda People's Congress that economic power should be vested in the majority and not in the minority, as is the case at present. It is, therefore, our firm resolution that political and economic power must be vested in the majority.

30. The structure of Uganda's economy is characterised by: an excessive dependence on agriculture as a source of income, employment and foreign exchange; a heavy dependence on exports based on two major export crops; heavy dependence on imports, particularly of manufactured products; and the limited participation of Ugandans in the modern industrial and commercial sectors of the economy. It has therefore been the policy of the Party to diversify the economy to make it less dependent on foreign trade, to promote the participation of citizens in all sectors of the economy, and the Move to the Left is intended to intensify these efforts through collective ownership, viz. Cooperatives and State enterprises.

31. Economic development demands, among other things, capital (money). We recognise that a country cannot depend upon capital from outside because this, apart from being unpredictable, is subject to variation by various factors and has always got strings attached to it. We are convinced from experience that this country is capable of generating sufficient capital out of the savings of all the citizens. We therefore propose that a suitable scheme where savings of the citizens can be effectively tapped and correctly channelled into further economic development should be introduced.

32. To this effect we propose that the system be based on the present basis of

calculation upon which wage-earners pay contributions of a fraction of their earnings into the Social Security Fund. The basis of the calculation of that part of the income of the wage-earners that goes into contributions to the National Social Security Scheme should apply proportionately to the income earned by all other persons, either by way of salary or other method of determinable income. With the exception of the wage-earner who is already required by law to make contribution to the National Social Security Scheme, all other persons will either pay direct or have it deducted and paid into an approved scheme.

33. The present banking institutions cater mainly for the needs of commerce and industry. It is not possible for the peasants, who constitute the majority of our population, to advance their lot through financial assistance in the form of loans from these commercial banks. Even if they were to do so, they would spend a substantial part of, if not, their entire income, in paying back these loans. It is, therefore, imperative that a new banking system, to be known as the Co-operative Bank, be established to cater solely for the peasants who are members of the Co-operative Unions. The policy of such a Bank should include a provision to the effect that the Co-operative Union of the person applying for a loan from the Bank gives a guarantee and takes over administration of the repayment of the loan, and that the loan in the majority of cases should be given in relation to what the applicant is already doing.

34. We reiterate the fact that there can be no investment unless somebody first makes a corresponding saving. This applies equally to local and overseas investment.

35. With regard to local investment, we have now proposed a scheme for compulsory saving in a number of schemes, and the establishment of Co-operative Banks.

36. With regard to foreign investment, we fully realise that foreign investors want guarantees, and we consider that the Foreign Investment (Protection) Act covers this adequately and generously. Much as we appreciate the need to attract foreign investment, we are fully convinced that the economic future of this country depends on local capital formation and local savings and investment.

37. In future we would wish to see foreign investments coming into Uganda under the Foreign Investment (Protection) Act engaging in priority projects and not projects decided solely on the basis of profitability. Similarly, local investments should be controlled in such a way that they are made in priority projects determined by the needs of the economic development of the country.

38. In our Move to the Left Strategy, we affirm that the guiding economic principle will be that the means of production and distribution must be in the hands of the people as a whole. The fulfilment of this principle may involve nationalisation of the enterprises privately owned.

39. The issue of nationalisation has already been determined and therefore it is a settled matter. It was in the 1962 Constitution, as it is in the Republican Constitution of 1967. Therefore no citizen or person in private enterprise should entertain the idea that the Government of Uganda cannot, whenever it is desirable in the interests of the people, nationalise any or all privately-owned enterprises, mailo and freehold land and all productive assets or property, at any time, for the benefit of the people. The Party, therefore, directs the Government to work along these lines.

40. In this Charter, we lay emphasis first on the people being given massive education in operating and establishing institutions controlled, not by individuals, but by the people collectively. This massive education should aim at reorientating the attitudes of the people towards co-operation in the management of economic institutions, and away from individual and private enrichment. We therefore direct the Government to give education to the people to acquire new attitudes in the management of our economy where collective exploitation of our resources to the benefit of all will take the place of individual and private enterprise aimed at enriching a few.

41. We must move in accordance with the principles of democracy. That is the way that brings human progress. Ideas must be generated and sifted, and citizens—educated or not—must be able to think for themselves, learn to work together, and to participate in the processes of governing themselves.

42. The Move to the Left involves government by discussion. This Charter and the principles enunciated herein should be widely disseminated through mass media of communication, and discussed by study groups and individuals all over the country.

43. Principles are a good thing but they are no substitute for hard work. The success of the Charter demands full commitment of leaders to its realisation, acceptance by the mass of the population, and hard work by all.

44. The adoption of the Charter provides an opportunity to the Common Man for the realisation of the full fruits of his labour and of social justice.